OP cloth 7⁵⁰

bb - 17⁹⁹

REBEL HEARTS

Kevin Toolis

REBEL HEARTS

Journeys within the IRA's Soul

St. Martin's Press ☙ New York

A THOMAS DUNNE BOOK.
An imprint of St. Martin's Press

REBEL HEARTS: JOURNEYS WITHIN THE IRA'S SOUL.
Copyright © 1995 by Kevin Toolis. All rights reserved.
Printed in the United States of America. No part of this
book may be used or reproduced in any manner
whatsoever without written permission except in the case
of brief quotations embodied in critical articles or reviews.
For information, address St. Martin's Press,
175 Fifth Avenue, New York, N.Y. 10010.

ISBN 0-312-14478-4

First published in Great Britain by Picador, an imprint of
Macmillan General Books

First U.S. Edition: April 1996

10 9 8 7 6 5 4 3 2 1

For Storme

Contents

Preface

The London Underground is not a place associated with the political future of Ireland. But amongst bomb warnings, the adverts for shampoo and college courses I once saw a poem by Sheenagh Pugh called 'Sometimes'. 'Sometimes', the poet wrote, 'the muscadel grape outlasts the blast of frost, sometimes a field of hard-frozen sorrow thaws and a people sometimes step back from war.'

The convoluted political history of Ireland, thus far, is not the history of provident 'sometimes' but the triumph of hatred over tolerance, murder over mutual agreement, and embittered division. It is a land where, in the words of one of the interviewees in this book, so much blood has flowed under the bridge for so long that almost everyone has forgotten where the stream of blood began and for what reasons. *Rebel Hearts* is a timely reminder of the human history and human sorrow behind yesterday's Troubles' headlines.

But this book is not just another history of Ireland's Troubles; Ireland has too much history and no account of the past will save the Irish, Ulster Protestant or Ulster Catholic, from a destructive future of their own creation. *Rebel Hearts* is a guidebook to the Republican Soul and the world of those men and women in the IRA, killers, brothers, informers, chieftains and martyrs, who suffered and who inflicted sorrow in Ireland's Troubles. I hope this account will allow the reader to cut their way through the propaganda fog of the last twenty-five years and achieve a clearer understanding of the principal protagonists, the rebels, the Provisional IRA.

The 'Irish Question' has dogged English politics for four hundred years and will continue to measure out its irresolution in blood and human lives until there is peace in Ireland. And there will only be peace in Ireland through compromise, negotiations, complex political deals and a transfer of power away from the British Crown.

The IRA ceasefire and the ongoing peace talks have brought Ireland to a rare 'sometimes' point in its history. There is a greater chance now than ever before to turn back from the road that leads to hedgerow assassination, masked men, cold revenge, betrayal and murderous indifference. There is a chance not to glorify but to bury the bloodstained past. There is a chance for a historic accommodation, a covenant of peace not a covenant of blood between Protestant and Catholic, Unionist and Republican. 'Sometimes,' the poet on the Underground said, 'a people step back from war.' Sometimes, as in South Africa, they do. May it happen in Ireland too.

London, 1995

Acknowledgements

A lot of news editors have wittingly or unwittingly aided the researching of *Rebel Hearts*. I would like to thank Biff Grimes of the *New York Times*, Paul Vallely of the lost *Sunday Correspondent*, Kim Fletcher of the *Sunday Telegraph*, and Angus MacKinnon of *GQ* for their belief in my reporting skills.

In Northern Ireland many journalistic colleagues shared their insights into the IRA but I would particularly like to record the contributions of Anne Maguire and Domnhall McDermott. Sadly the finest flowers often blossom unseen by the wider world and their premature deaths were a great loss.

Seamus Kelters was full of insight and a databank of hard facts, Kathleen Bell at the *Irish News* library was a mine of information.

I would also like to thank the many individuals, Unionist or Republican, over the years, who agreed to be interviewed and share their time and thoughts with me, including Rita, the Doris family, the Finucanes, the Flood family, the MacManuses and the people of Achill Island, especially Thomas and Mikey.

In the world of publishing, David Godwin first commissioned the book and then acted as 'uncle' in his new role as agent. David Chalfant laboured on my behalf in New York and won me time and cash to complete the project.

And finally there is Dea, the love of my life and fire of . . .

List of Abbreviations, Organizations and Terms

Active service Term used by the IRA to describe when its members were on an IRA operation.

British Army The troops of the British Government who serve tours of duty in Northern Ireland.

Catholic Adherent to the Catholic Church; Catholics comprise forty-three per cent of the Northern Irish population and total 645,000 people. Although they are the biggest single religious denomination, Catholics are in a minority in the state. Across the disputed border, Catholics compose the overwhelming majority of the Irish Republic's four million population.

Celtic A Catholic identified Scottish football team.

Crown A term used to denote the British Government and all the forces, like the British Army, and institutions that compose the British State – whose constitutional head is the Queen.

Fenian A term, usually pejorative, for a Catholic that implies he or she is a Republican. The original Fenians were an Irish-American revolutionary group in the 1860s.

Fianna Fail A socially conservative political party in the Irish Republic with republican leanings.

Fine Gael A conservative political party in the Irish Republic who are strongly opposed to the IRA and whose historical forbears fought on the pro-Treaty side against the IRA in the 1922 Irish Civil War.

IRA   Irish Republican Army. The IRA's aim is to force the British Government to leave Ireland either by political violence or negotiation.

Loyalist   A Protestant strongly, often violently, opposed to a United Ireland.

MI5   The British domestic intelligence service that has overall control of the British Government's battle against the IRA.

MI6   Britain's overseas intelligence services. MI6 once fought against MI5 for control of spying operations in the Irish Republic and has in the past run its own agents in Dublin.

Nationalist   A member of the Catholic population who aspires to a reunited Ireland by non-violent means.

OC   Officer Commanding.

Official IRA   Republican paramilitary faction. The Officials split from the Provisional IRA in 1969. They declared a ceasefire in 1972 and have since played an extremely limited role in the conflict in Northern Ireland.

Oglaigh na hEireann   Gaelic term for the Irish Republican Army.

Protestant   Adherent to any of the different non-Catholic Christian denominations in Northern Ireland. The Protestant population stands at 855,000 and comprises fifty-seven per cent of the total population of Northern Ireland.

Provisionals   Another name for the modern-day IRA, which split in 1969 at the outbreak of the Troubles into two factions, the Official IRA and the Provisional IRA. The Provisionals soon eclipsed their Official rivals and the term Provisional is now virtually synonymous with the IRA.

Provos Shortened term for members or supporters of the Provisional IRA.

Republican A supporter of a United Ireland. The term in Northern Ireland is usually synonymous with a supporter of the Provisonal IRA.

Republican Movement A term used to cover both Sinn Fein, the legal political wing of the IRA, and the IRA, the illegal military wing, of the republican organization.

RIR Royal Irish Regiment. See UDR.

RUC Royal Ulster Constabulary, the heavily armed police force of Northern Ireland.

SAS Special Air Service, a small but elite unit of the British Army that specialized in the ambush and assassination of IRA men on active service.

SDLP Social Democratic Labour Party, the main constitutional Catholic nationalist party.

Sinn Fein The legal political wing of the IRA.

SOCO Scene of Crimes Officers, who forensically examine murder scenes.

Special Branch The RUC's powerful intelligence division which recruits and runs most of Northern Ireland's informers.

Stiff To murder.

Stormont The seat of government in Northern Ireland.

Taig A term, usually pejorative, used by Loyalists to describe Catholics.

Volunteer Term used by the IRA to describe its members, in counterpoint to the salaried professionals of the RUC and the British Army.

UDA Ulster Defence Association, the once legal but now banned Protestant paramilitary group which in the early Troubles was the biggest paramilitary group in Ulster.

UDR Ulster Defence Regiment, a regiment of the British Army that is almost exclusively recruited from Ulster's Protestant population. UDR soldiers have borne the brunt of the IRA's assassination campaign and over two hundred individual UDR soldiers have been killed. A considerable number of UDR members have been convicted of involvement in sectarian killings of Catholics. Nationalist politicians have accused the regiment of being a sectarian force with secret links with illegal Protestant paramilitaries. In 1992 the regiment was merged with the Royal Irish Rangers to form the Royal Irish Regiment.

UFF Ulster Freedom Fighters, an illegal Protestant paramilitary group whose main activities involve the sectarian killing of Catholics and the assassination of Republicans. The UFF is a cover name for the UDA.

UVF Ulster Volunteer Force, an illegal Protestant paramilitary organization involved in the sectarian murders of Catholics and the assassination of Republicans associated with the IRA.

Unionist A Protestant who believes in maintaining Northern Ireland's political union with Great Britain.

Whack A verb meaning to murder.

1

ARCHIVES

It was an overcast Sunday morning in January and the Irish Republican Army was waiting at the end of the lane. The victim, a man in his fifties, left noon Mass a few minutes early to avoid the crowd of fellow church-goers blocking the narrow road outside St Brigid's. He walked over to his car with the old lady to whom he had offered a lift, helped her into the passenger seat, walked round to the driver's door, got in and was turning the key in the ignition when two young men in duffel coats, with hoods up, walked over to the Mercedes. One drew a gun and fired five bullets through the driver's window. The first round hit High Court Judge William Doyle in the face, the others in the head, the last in the chest; seventy-two-year-old Mrs Convery was hit by a ricochet in the leg. Women in the emerging congregation, hearing shots and seeing murder, began to scream. The two killers turned, running through the church-goers towards their getaway car parked down the avenue. Two doctors in the crowd, one of them the Judge's brother Dennis, ran to the car and vainly tried to resuscitate the Judge, but it was over, he was dead. Canon Patrick McAlister, who had just celebrated the Holy Sacrament of Mass, administered the Last Rites on the roadway outside his church.

I arrived about half an hour after the Judge had been murdered. The green Mercedes was still by the kerb, just opposite the entrance to St Brigid's, in a tree-lined street off Belfast's prosperous Malone Road. Already, the car was isolated by the white plastic police tape. The Mercedes had ceased to be a car and had become an exhibit of death. A few stragglers gaped but the majority of the congregation had gone, leaving flak-jacketed policemen, armed with M1 carbines, shifting their weight from foot to foot to keep the circulation going, guarding this evidence of Sunday morning murder.

Soon the SOCO men, Scene of Crimes Officers, would arrive to paw their way through the Mercedes' ashtray, the side compartments, the detritus of another's life, and bureaucratically record the last forensic moments of someone else in Northern Ireland. They would dust for the fingerprints that everyone knew would not be there – the gunmen were wearing gloves – and record photographically the exact position of the car and its contents for the file of evidence at the trial of Doyle's killers, who everyone knew would never be caught and whose trial would never happen.

Glass fragments littered the seat and the ground outside the driver's window, and the tan leather seats were covered in drying blood. Aside from the stains, the upholstery on the driver's seat was unmarked – all of the IRA's bullets were still inside Judge Doyle, the body already declared 'dead on arrival' at the Royal Victoria Hospital a couple of miles away. High Court Judge William Doyle was already on the conveyor belt for a post-mortem that would slit him open and extract the bullets that might just match those of other bullets extracted from other IRA victims now or in killings to come. Next week Royal Ulster Constabulary (RUC) men would come to noon Mass at St Brigid's with clipboards to interview members of the congregation in search of the eyewitnesses they knew they would never find and who everyone knew had seen nothing. At the far side of the tape, down the avenue of trees and out on the main road, the light Sunday afternoon traffic circulated unmolested by the immediacy of this death.

I peered in through the shattered driver's window: supposedly a reporter but really a voyeur. On the shelf at the back lay the Sunday tabloid papers. I knew in that moment that I had reached the right place at the right hour. I was in Belfast for this: for death and killing and violent republicanism.

Doyle was a servant and officer of the British Crown, the British Government, in Ireland. He sat in judgement on IRA suspects. He had power and wielded authority. He was a living symbol of the Crown and therefore an enemy of the rebels, the IRA, and they killed him for it. For in Northern Ireland power, authority and legitimacy were in murderous dispute.

Judge Doyle was also the enemy within. He was a Catholic on a Protestant/Unionist judicial bench which asserted the authority of the British Government. He blurred the lines of an ancient struggle but made himself an easy 'stiff' (murder victim) by his regular attendance at Mass at St Brigid's. During the week the Judge was escorted everywhere by armed RUC bodyguards and was invulnerable. But at weekends, perhaps tired of the oppressive security, he shed his judge's robes, dismissed his guards and reverted to domestic routine amidst the Victorian mansions of the Malone Road. He must have thought he was safe; he must have thought the Malone Road with neat gardens, Mercedes cars and money was immune from the Troubles. He was wrong. Someone in the congregation at St Brigid's had recognized him and told the IRA, and they came on the right Sunday to kill him.

There was an awful Irish intimacy about his death, murdered at Mass in front of the congregation, fingered by someone who was part of that Catholic congregation. The IRA did not need to travel to kill Doyle. Their supporters were already there in St Brigid's, also dressed in suits and Sunday best on the Malone Road, hidden amongst the smiling schoolgirl choir or walking back down the aisle slyly staring after Holy Communion. I wondered what were the passions that allowed, perhaps compelled, someone to kill in that way in that place.

Judge Doyle's killing was somewhere in the middle of what was known as Ireland's Troubles. For twenty-five years a little sniping war has been fought in the north-western corner of Europe; Doyle was victim two thousand and something. The exact number does not matter; there was a lot of killing before and a lot of killing after. And there is still some, a little, killing to come. The death toll is three thousand and something now.

It was called the Troubles because the exact nature of the conflict was difficult to define. It was not a war in any conventional sense. There was no artillery, no tanks or fighter planes, the electricity worked and so did the telephones. There were no set-battles, no definitive front-lines, no victories and no total defeats. Ninety-nine per cent of the time the land was at peace. You could have lived and worked in Ulster and never have seen a soldier, never heard a word spoken in anger. You could have had a holiday in Northern Ireland. A tourist driving round in a hired car would have seen small sleepy villages, lush green fields, the prosperous Victorian-built city of Belfast and the impressively preserved medieval walls of Derry. The good people of Ulster, inured to sectarian slaughter and terrorist bombing, would have been shocked and appalled if a visitor was mugged. Crime levels in Ulster were ridiculously low. The Troubles were not general anarchy, mayhem or chaos. It was rare for the innocent, the unaligned, or the uninvolved to get killed in the crossfire. All the killing was directed, pinpointed, reserved for special occasions and special places. You had to seek out the Troubles; you had to know where the strata of conflict erupted into public view.

The word itself, 'Troubles', vague and ill-defined, was a euphemism, but it suited the vague and ill-defined nature of the war in Ireland. It has many sub-definitions: a thing that causes distress; an occasion of affliction; a misfortune; a calamity; public disturbance, disorder or confusion. The Troubles disturbed life – they did not destroy it. Most of the time, for most of the people, nothing untoward happened. The pursuit of capitalism, the rearing of children, the growing of crops, the manufacture of industry, were unaffected. At other times, usually in certain specific places, there were riots, disturbances, threats, beatings, car hijackings, men in masks, fear, and murder. The Troubles, and this is important to remember, were acts of rebellion rather than revolution. No one had a plan to proclaim a 'liberated' Northern Ireland a Marxist state.

The euphemism of the Troubles was useful because it was hard to classify these events, these troubles; the grounds and nature of the conflict mutated even within the small confines of Northern Ireland, which is just over five thousand square miles and has a population of one and a half million people. In Belfast, the capital of Britain's Irish 'province', the urban Catholic unemployed in the IRA plotted murder from their British-taxpayer-built council houses, ambushing British soldiers, firing rockets at police jeeps and 'stiffing' vulnerable targets, like Judge Doyle, whilst their Protestant adversaries hijacked cars, drove into Catholic districts and shot 'taigs' (Catholics) at random. In Derry, seventy miles away, the IRA had no such opponents but the organization had long been substantially penetrated by the British security forces. Both sides waged an intelligence war against each other that revealed itself in the dead bodies of IRA informers found in plastic bags along the border with the Irish Republic if the IRA succeeded, and the dead bodies of blown-up soldiers if the British security forces failed. In the countryside of Tyrone and Fermanagh, the IRA's soldiers, known as Volunteers, fought a more traditional guerrilla-style campaign, sniping at armed soldiers, blowing up barracks and crossing from the immunity of farmhouses in the neighbouring Irish Republic to assassinate lone members of a British Army militia, the Royal Irish Rangers (RIR). In the 'Provisional Republic of South Armagh', just sixty miles south of Belfast, the IRA controlled the ground and the British Army were safe only in their concrete bunkers or high up in the sky protected by circling Vietnam-style helicopter gunships.

The Troubles were spasmodic. Their public history was a roll-call of the high points of atrocity and outrage: fifteen killed by a Loyalist bomb in McGurk's Bar in Belfast in 1971; thirteen civil rights marchers killed by British soldiers on Bloody Sunday

in Derry in 1972; nine civilians dismembered by IRA car bombs
on Bloody Friday in Belfast in 1972; twenty-one disco-goers
blown up by the IRA in Birmingham in 1974; thirty-three
shoppers blown up by Loyalist car bombs in Dublin and
Monaghan in 1974; twelve diners burned to death by an IRA
fire-bomb in La Mon restaurant in 1977; ten IRA hunger-
strikers dead in prison in 1981; eight IRA Volunteers killed by
the SAS at Loughgall in 1987; eleven civilians blown up by the
IRA at a Remembrance Day ceremony in Enniskillen in 1987;
five civilians shot dead in a bookie's shop by Loyalists in Belfast
in 1991; and two children killed by an IRA bomb in Warrington in 1992, and on and on and on. The gaps between
significant acts of collective murder were filled by a steady
drumbeat of individual whackings (murders) or stiffings.

People often tried to explain the Troubles in terms of other
conflicts, but this was not Cuba, nor Algeria, nor South Africa
nor Vietnam. It was Ireland and the tenacity of the struggle
between the rebels and the Crown was older than all the 'isms'
of the twentieth century. The Troubles were an endless series
of small military skirmishes. The objective was to go on killing
the enemy wherever you could find him, and thereby wear out
his will to fight on. The ultimate goal was fairly clear. Ireland
was and is divided; six of the nine historic counties of the
province of Ulster are under British rule, the other twenty-six
counties constitute the Republic of Ireland. The IRA were
fighting to remove the British Crown from what they regarded
as Irish soil and reunite Ireland. The British Government were
fighting to defend the Northern Irish state and the desire of the
850,000 strong Northern-Irish-born Protestant population to
remain separate from the rest of Ireland. It is the longest war
the world has ever known.

I was still standing next to the Mercedes when it began to rain,
soft flicks of water sat on the skin of the Judge's car, a breeze
got up, and it grew colder. I walked back through the empty

streets of the Malone Road district to my rented room. I sat down next to the gas fire, drank some tea and tried to write down what I had seen and what I had felt. I tried to remember a clear point, a moment of origin, that would explain why I was in Belfast, why I was fascinated by the IRA and their violent struggle, why I too was a Republican, but I could not. There never is a discrete, documentable moment of beginning in any story of this nature; there are just moments of departure.

I was ten years old when Ireland's Troubles broke out again in 1969. I was born the sixth of seven children to Irish emigrant parents who had settled in Scotland. In Edinburgh my parents, the seven children and the lodger who attached herself as a permanent addition to the family lived packed into a large stone tenement apartment on the fringes of the half-demolished Irish quarter, the Pleasance. When the sixties civil rights marches in Northern Ireland erupted in violence on our newly acquired colour television set we believed that our fellow Catholics in Ulster were standing up for their rights. We admired people who 'stood up for themselves' and refused to be cowed, even if we were not really sure what they were standing up for. We disliked the occasional marches of sectarian Protestant Orangemen through the streets of the Pleasance.

My first school was St Patrick's Roman Catholic Primary in the heart of the Pleasance. Our most famous old boy was James Connolly, the Edinburgh-born Irish Republican leader executed by the British for leading the 1916 Easter Rising. This fact was never mentioned by the teachers – perhaps they were not even aware of it themselves. As Catholics we were different from the majority Protestant population; we could not take part in what we were told was the heresy of worshipping the Queen of England as the head of our faith. St Patrick's did not play the National Anthem 'God Save the Queen' and we never prayed for her longevity.

But I never thought of myself in Scotland as Catholic with a capital 'C'. If, as teenagers, we had allegiances it was an allegiance to pop groups, the Who or Genesis or Led Zeppelin.

I changed schools to Holy Cross Primary, the junior offshoot of a prestigious grammar school from which the aspirant Catholic middle classes launched themselves. I did not know it, but I was changing class. Saving up to buy an Afghan coat and sleeping, or attempting to sleep, with the daughters of Edinburgh's more prosperous burghers soon occupied far more of my energies than concern for the civil rights of Catholics in Ulster or the re-emergence of violent Irish republicanism. I stopped going to confession when I was twelve after I discovered girls and masturbation and was too embarrassed to tell the priest. At fourteen I stopped even going to Mass and sneaked off to the movies instead. At fifteen I was more inclined to Communism, being a hippy, smoking marijuana and losing my virginity. The Troubles in Ireland were news from a distant country.

Neither of my parents was Republican. My father, Patrick Toolis, worked as a building foreman and never voted for anyone other than the British Labour Party all his life. He was one of the most gentle men you could ever meet and he loved to sing for his exhausting brood of children. His songs were always love ballads; only rarely would he sing rebel songs that commemorated the glories of a lost republic. My mother, Mary Gallagher, was more animated; her fiery personality ruled our household, but she too had little time for a country in which she had only known poverty and hardship. Ireland was her past and Edinburgh, where she worked as a nurse, raised her children and prospered, was her daily life.

But we had another place, another identity in the world. Every summer my father would borrow his firm's noisy diesel workmen's van, pack it with a dozen children and aunties, and drive the four hundred miles to our real 'home' in Achill Island, County Mayo, on the extreme west coast of Ireland. Every year in the sixties and seventies as Northern Ireland was engulfed in communal violence we drove the same route from Edinburgh to the Stranraer ferry on Scotland's west coast, past the farms where my mother worked picking potatoes as a thirteen-year-old girl, and sailed across the Irish Sea. As the ferry docked at Larne we grew anxious and drew into ourselves. We believed that the North was populated by hate-filled Orangemen who would foam at the mouth at the sight of our Catholic flesh. We were as convinced as anyone that the whole of Northern Ireland was a war zone. We had no real understanding of what was taking place there and no desire to tarry and find out.

As the van hurtled through the North, I would look out of the windows at the blue- white- and red-painted kerbstones and the Union Jacks on flagpoles in private gardens that told us this was Protestant territory and a hostile land. During the early days of the Troubles we drove through Belfast and saw the soldiers, barricades and rolls of barbed wire of a city at war. It looked too much like the television reports for comfort. Father found a new route and for the next twenty years we skirted around the far side of Lough Neagh to avoid Belfast and any potential contact with the hostile natives.

In all those years we were rarely stopped and never once searched by the British security forces. Once the British soldiers saw our British-registered number plate and heard my mother's carefully enhanced Scottish accent, they relaxed – this vanload of Scottish children was not the enemy. At one of these infrequent roadblocks, my mother once gave a couple of Scottish soldiers some tins of beer as we waved and pretended we liked 'our boys' while secretly believing them to be oppressors of Catholics like us. The few security checks that did occur made us tense, and I have had a lifelong aversion to customs posts and immigration officials ever since. At the border we all breathed exaggerated sighs of relief as we drove into the 'real' Ireland, which we called the South. My aunties, safely out of earshot of the last custom post, complained about the apparent lack of security and declared that we could have smuggled tons of bombs underneath the already luggage-crammed seats. The IRA smuggled bomb material into the North and we were driving in the opposite direction but everyone nodded in rigorous agreement, happy to be clear of dangerous territory.

In reality every adult, and probably every child, in that van would have been aghast at the thought of risking themselves to help the IRA.

In the South the roads quickly decayed into potholes as we drove deeper into a world that was ten or fifteen years behind the material wealth of urban Scotland. Cows and men on bicycles were masters of the road. Unkempt vegetation burst out from the hedgerows; there were always makeshift road-works, old oil drums and loose chips, crooked bends and juddering ramps. Our lumbering vehicle slowed to a crawl as we negotiated the choked main streets of middle Ireland, past the shops whose outsides were festooned with big yellow gas bottles and compressed turf briquettes. There were shrines to the Virgin Mary by the roadside and strange sweets and bottles of apple-flavoured Cidona, shaped like artillery shells, with teeth-breaking bakelite stoppers. This was also another country.

As the long journey neared its end we stopped for some last-minute shopping in the small town of Newport in County Mayo, buying a huge slab of freshly slaughtered cow or lamb from the local butcher who stayed open to ten in the evening. If we were lucky we would catch the first peaty smoke of turf fires – indelibly imprinted on my mind as the smell of 'home'. We plunged on into the West. In the van, the squabbling children, finally exhausted, gradually fell asleep, leaving the adults to contemplate the last twenty miles in peace.

At last we crossed over on to the island. The moment I grew to savour was when we drove into the driveway of my grandfather's house. My father turned off the noisy van engine and we tumbled out into the darkness. Above us the stars shone like a great silver reef and our ears were filled with the dull thunder of the surf pounding on the three-mile-long beach just yards away that marked the very fringes of the European Continent.

Home was the tiny depopulated village of Dookinella, a hamlet of four households perched on the rim of the ocean, bound on one side by the Atlantic that stretched to America and on the other by two two-thousand-foot mountains, Minuan and Slievemore. Home was an elemental place of soaring cliffs, lashing rain, incredible storms, thatched cottages, tiny fields, drystone walls, brilliant sunshine, and relentless struggle. Home was our place in the world, the place from where all the Toolises had come, the place where we had land, where we were burrowed so deep into the earth that our name was written into it: the ancient townland title for the area is Dookinella Thulis. There had once been thirty households in Dookinella and the clan of Toolis big enough for my great-uncle's mother and father, both Toolises but only distantly related, to marry. Now the drystone houses had collapsed and the descendants of their inhabitants were scattered across America and Australia. We were the last Toolises in Dookinella. It was an end of the earth, our end of the earth, a place where passing traffic was so unfamiliar that the dogs of the villagers continued to attack and drive off cars as if expelling a foreign enemy.

In my childhood the village was dying, as poverty drove the remaining families on to the boat for England, but my aunts and grandparents still clung to the land. To us children, their toy farms, with the three or four cows they owned, seemed like ranches. My maternal grandfather, Patrick Gallagher, had one pig and four cows and a horse called Dolly, who kept escaping from the field and whose mane and tail hair he sold to the tinkers who passed through the island from time to time.

Home was also a place of tight family bonds, neighbours, kinship and community; I was related in some fashion to everyone in the village and in the village beyond and the village beyond that. Regardless of the fact that I had not been born in Achill, I was always greeted by Sean, the aged farmer who lived across the road, and welcomed 'home'. Great-uncle Edward, a few houses along, born in Manhattan but whose family re-emigrated back to the island, told stories of hardships on the docks in New York during the Great Depression. Brendan, a shepherd with jet-black Spanish hair and beautiful blue-eyed sheepdogs, was always buying me 'minerals' – fizzy drinks – in the local bars, discussing sheep, the state of the North and the world beyond our island.

Home was also a place where from the age of nine I was conscripted as another pair of hands. I learned all about the boredom and relentless labour of peasant farming. The summer months were dedicated to saving hay for winter fodder for the cows. There were no machines, only human bodies. The fields of grass were cut by my grandfather with a scythe. Each individual swathe of grass in the four or five acres of fields was then turned by hand, using long wooden rakes to aid the drying of the wet green underside. After a couple of days of good weather the yellowing grasses were shaken with hand pitch-forks and again left to dry. Only then could the hay be gathered into haystacks or tramcocks, and if it rained you had to start all over again. If the weather held, the tramcocks were taken by donkey cart to the farmyard and made into a reek – a hay house with a thatch roof to protect it from rain.

'Bringing in the reek' was a great day. The labour was long and arduous, all the neighbours came to help, but by evening the hay was saved and the adults, particularly my grandfather, were happy. As a boy I was set different tasks; sometimes I would be sent through the still heat of the summer's day down the beach-pebble road to the dank bar of the Crossroads Inn, a mile away, to order bottles of beer or Guinness for the men; sometimes I was a donkey cart driver, holding the donkey still by the halter as the hay was loaded into the cart or driving the full cart back to the farmhouse; and sometimes I was a tramper – jumping up and down in the hay as it was being built into a reek to compress it. At the end of the day everyone sat around the kitchen table and ate huge mounds of potatoes boiled in their skins with hunks of roasted lamb. Grandfather Gallagher had a special way of peeling the skins off the potatoes by spearing the potato with his fork and stripping off the skin with his knife. He then dipped the edge of the blade into the salt dish and tapped the salt over his food. Even in his early seventies he was a physically powerful man, over six foot tall, who could heave huge weights of hay above his head and pile them on to a cart. He had different coloured eyes, one blue and one blue-grey.

I was taken to my first wake when I was nine after a distant relative of my father succumbed to one of the cancers that seemed to ravage the island. The corpse was dressed in the man's best brown suit and laid out in an open coffin placed in the cramped front sitting room of the wake house. The islanders believed that the prayers of the sexually innocent, children, went 'straight up to heaven', so I was encouraged to sit and pray at a small makeshift altar next to the wooden casket. Groups of adults were sitting chatting; plates of snuff and cigarettes, taken out of their packets and arranged in a circle, were being passed around; other guests were being fed in the kitchen and the men offered bottles of beer. I knelt down and looked at the waxy figure, the mouth wedged shut and the bloodless hands knotted together with rosary beads. At the urging of my mother, I kissed its forehead; I was disgusted and revulsed but also shocked – the coldness of this dead thing was far from human life.

My grandfather Patrick Toolis, born in 1885, had like my father spent most of his life in working exile. He had been a ganger, an overseer, on the potato squads that had been conscripted every summer for generations from the island to harvest potatoes for the farms of the west coast of Scotland, returning to the island in the winter. Grandfather had a reputation as a hard man, frugal and tight with money. He had ruled his tattie squad with an iron rod – he had given my mother a job at thirteen when she first visited Scotland as a 'tattie-hawker' in 1940 – and acquired the taste for Scots whisky and two twenty-packets of cigarettes a day that he harboured into his eighties.

Grandfather Gallagher, also Patrick, had also spent most of his working life on the farms and building sites of Scotland and England as an itinerant labourer, moving with the work from job to job and returning to the island in late summer when the harvest needed to be saved, or in March, around St Patrick's Day, to cut the turf. Leaving and coming 'home' with hard-earned wages was life.

On the other side of the bay from Dookinella, just beneath Slievemore Mountain, lay the graveyard where all the Toolises were buried. We buried Grandfather Toolis there in November 1979 and returned in the spring to bury Grandfather Gallagher on a storm-lashed day when the only colour on the mountain was the women's headscarves. Hours before, in the company of my sister-in-law, I had buried the ashes of one of my brothers, Bernard, as was his wish, on top of Minaun Mountain, which overlooks Dookinella. A decade later we would all return to bury my father Patrick Toolis, as one day they will gather to bury me.

Grandfather Toolis's father, Padraig na Páidrin – Pat the Rosary – also Patrick Toolis, who died in 1929, was buried there too, but his grave, the simple inscription hand-hewn, was lost to us, obliterated by lichen and storms. Sean, our neighbour, remembered his wake and told stories of how Pat the Rosary was known as a devout man who could lead the prayers of the local people at funerals and other rituals involving the dead; he was a kind of holy man, a semi-official priest. But there was also a hidden meaning in his nickname: Padraig na Páidrin, after 1844, on the eve of the Great Famine, was the first man amongst the villagers of Dookinella to read. He had been educated by Protestant missionaries from the Achill Mission established in the 1830s on the island. The missionaries had built a school in Dookinella as a means of winning converts. No trace of the school remains, and no one remembers those who turned their faith, but Padraig na Páidrin was infamous long after amongst the villagers for his love of the written word, often abandoning the vital tasks of haymaking at the approach of a newspaper.

Beyond Padraig na Páidrin lay great-great-grandfather Martin Toolis, whose grave site was utterly lost but who was probably born some time in the early 1800s. We, my family, my community, had been living in Dookinella for generations. We were there in the summer of 1838, six years before Pat the Rosary's birth, when His Majesty's Royal Engineers Captain Stotherd and Lieutenant Chaytor undertook the first ordnance survey of the island and named Dookinella Thulis after us, the people who lived on the land. We had been living in this place of Dookinella, between the ocean and the mountains, far beyond the limits of human memory.

Like my ancestors I grew to love the land, love the lost place-names. I braved the dangers of *carraig na leim*, the terrifying 'rock where you jump' which stood as a lone pinnacle in the ocean and required the hardy and the foolish to jump on to its slippery surface before jumping again to safety on nearby fishing rocks. It was a test of manhood and I took several attempts before I managed it. I climbed high up on the side of the mountain to *grua na geapall*, the 'green on the top', a strange marshy tract on Minuan. I spent hours in the treacherous coves beyond the slippy rock, where the Atlantic roared and where it was possible to walk for two or three miles on headlands cut off by the powerful turning tides. This was our place, my place, my home.

In truth we were a defeated people. Dookinella had become our haven and our home as the last refuge in the long war of dispossession waged by the Crown in Ireland in the sixteenth and seventeenth centuries. How my family came to arrive in Achill from their native Ulster is unknown. According to the epic seventeenth-century Irish poem *The Annals of Four Masters*, a section of the O *Tuathalain* (ancient Gaelic version of Toolis), a clan of the powerful O'Donnel family, had fled to Achill in 1602 in the aftermath of the Battle of Kinsale in 1601 when the power of the last great Gaelic chieftains was destroyed by the forces of the Crown.

Another branch of the sept, or clan, stayed behind in Ulster, but were dispossessed of their lands in the 1640s as the Irish natives futilely rose against the English colonizers and the hated Plantation. The natives slaughtered Crown loyalists but whatever savagery the Irish inflicted upon their masters, His Highness the Lord Protector Oliver Cromwell repaid the debt of blood in full many times over in his savage 1650s campaign of conquest which crushed all Irish opposition to English rule. According to the Cromwellian Army's Physician-General, Dr William Petty, half a million natives out of a total Irish population estimated at one and a half million perished by the sword, plague, famine, hardships and banishment between 1641 and 1652.[1]

Under the 1652 Act of Settlement the entire Irish nation was deemed guilty of rebellion and their lands subject to forfeiture. After all possible military opposition was removed, the Government of the Commonwealth of England turned to plunder, and confiscated Irish lands, parcelling out native estates to those soldiers and financiers who had supported the army of conquest. The native Irish were expelled and transported to what amounted to designated reservations in the recesses of Ireland's most barren province, Connaught, in an early example of what later centuries would know as 'ethnic cleansing'. The orders for removal and transportation of a nation were recorded by Cromwell's Commissioners in fifty-six bound volumes known as *The Books of the Commonwealth*.[2] On 2 July 1653 Matthew Thomlinson, President of the Council of State in Whitehall, issued instructions to the new English ruler in Ireland, Commander-in-Chief Charles Fleetwood:

It is thought fit and resolved that all and every of the persons aforesaid [natives of various designated categories] shall before the Ist day of May, which shall be in the year 1654, remove and transplant themselves into the Province of Connaught . . . and that whatsoever person or persons aforesaid shall after the said first day of May 1654 be found inhabiting or remaining in any part of the Provinces of Leinster, Munster or Ulster without a pass from you shall be reputed as spies and enemies and shall for the same offence suffer death.[3]

Commissioners were appointed to oversee the administration of the edict, taking care to disperse and break up historic septs or clans to prevent them forming new alliances in exile. The great work of transportation proved tedious and lengthy. A committee of Commonwealth Army colonels met in Dublin on 12 February 1655 to finally assign the transported native populations of specific counties into designated ancient baronies in Connaught: 'The inhabitants of the Province of Ulster (except Down and Antrim) to be transplanted into the Baronies of Muckmullen . . . and into the Baronies of Moyrisk, Burrishoole and the half Barony of Erris.'[4]

Achill Island is in the ancient barony of Burrishoole. Somewhere in those annals of Plantation my ancestors met their dispossession and were cast out. There was nothing passed down, no family heirlooms, no bible, no glorious past remembered; we were the victims of history not its protagonists. We were driven west into the poorest fringes of Ireland's most barren, depressed county, Mayo, in its most depressed province, Connaught. We were driven until there was no place further west to go.

We did not even own the land to which we were exiled. We were tenants, the last peasants of Northern Europe, of the various landowners who over the following centuries bought and sold the land my forefathers came to cherish.

The Toolises were but one strand on the island. Grandfather Gallagher's family also came from Ulster, maybe at the same time, and many of the island's surnames show that they too suffered the same fate. Grandfather Gallagher was heartbreakingly proud of his horse Dolly and his few green fields, but his land was only fit for hardy mountain sheep; his 'fields' were mere paddocks carved out from stony earth and barren bogland. For centuries the land on Achill had been unable to sustain its population for more than four or five months of the year. The accounts of eighteenth- and nineteenth-century travellers testify to Achill as a place of famine and penury, where disease-ridden islanders lived crammed into drystone houses that were little more than hovels. At the time of the Great Famine, Padraig na Páidrin was just one amongst the thousand island schoolchildren who were saved from starvation by the proselytizing charity of Protestant missionaries. In this century, in 1921, my father was born in a drystone thatched cottage whose design had not changed in hundreds of years, in a village devoid of every basic necessity. When my brother was born on the island in 1949 it was in a house that, like every other house on the island, had neither electricity nor running water; Grandfather Gallagher did not receive a mains water supply until the 1970s.

The only thing that Achill produced in quantity was people. Each and every generation for the last 150 years has learned to bear the same lesson, to shed its sons and daughters to the wider world. It was normal for husbands to leave their wives and children for six, nine or twenty-four months at a time, work in England, live in squalid digs and only ever return home for short holidays. Men and women might marry, beget and rear a handful of children, and yet never live together for more than two weeks a year. Even today the island is still a reservation of generational unemployment, thwarted lives and despair. This was home. Hell or Connaught was the slogan of Oliver Cromwell when he drove the Irish rebels from their lands. The elemental wastes of Achill were as close to hell as Connaught could provide.

On the edge of Dookinella, close to the foreshore, stands a small monument. Surrounded by low stone walls, a twenty-foot-high upright stone pillar commemorates a son of the village. I often remember seeing the monument as I walked to the pub with the order for beer or went beachcombing along the wild strand at the back of the houses, but I cannot recall when I first started asking about the *sagart a run* (beloved priest) hanged by the British as a rebel. There were stories told of the priest's flight from his pursuers after the last rebel stronghold at Killala was retaken in late September 1798. With his brother-in-law James Toolis, on the flight from Killala to Achill, the priest is purported to have seen a dead fish on the strand and to have warned his companion: '*Iompuigh abhaile, a Sheumais, beidh mise gabhtha*' (Return home, James, I shall be captured). Or it was related how the priest, hidden in the thatch of a house in a nearby village, was discovered by chance after a yeoman fired a musket round in frustration through the roof and an old woman was heard to cry out in Gaelic: 'The priest is dead.' His name was Father Manus Sweeney and he was hanged in Newport on 9 June 1799 for 'being concerned in rebellion and levying money for the French' in the 1798 rebellion against the Crown.

The monument had been erected after Irish Independence on the spot old villagers insisted was the priest's birthplace. The priest was still a hero to the people of Dookinella. He had resisted, stood up to the Crown, joined the rebels, fought for Irish freedom against the English. Father Sweeney had been executed but the seeds of resistance had been scattered further with his death. Those seeds lived on in the fireside stories and on, too, in the hearts of those who applauded or committed themselves to resistance. Rebellion and republicanism were in the blood of this defeated people. Perhaps it was there one night as I sat by the turf fire listening to old Sean, with the wind howling a gale, or to Brendan, who had worked in the North and after Bobby Sands died in 1981 was never seen in public without his Sinn Fein badge of the hunger-striker on his lapel, that my journey to Belfast and the taped-off street, the bloody seat and the dead judge had begun. I had come back to find out about this thing, this resistance, to explore my own rebel heart.

*

Judge Doyle was buried two days after his murder. The Requiem Mass was held in St Brigid's and a few of the then powerful men in Northern Irish politics, the deputy British Secretary of State Lord Gowrie, the British Lord Chancellor Lord Hailsham and the Northern Ireland Lord Chief Justice Sir Robert Lowry attended the funeral as if to mark the burial as an occasion of state. There were wreaths from the British Secretary of State for Northern Ireland James Prior, the Lord Mayor of Belfast and the Circuit Judges of England and Wales. In his sermon Dr Cahal Daly, Bishop of Down and Connor and later Primate of Ireland, brought all the force of his rhetoric down on his fellow Catholic perpetrators of this 'unspeakable evil'. 'For we suffer at what is being done to our society and by members of our own community; for having come from us, they are not of us. By their words of hate and their policies of murder, they cut themselves away from the community of love which is the Christian Church.'

The church was packed, the occasion solemn, but in the end hollow. The Bishop's words would soon be overtaken by other sermons and fresher deaths. Judge Doyle's assassination did not shift the balance of power towards the British or the IRA. It was not a milestone, just a marker on a long road. Judge Doyle was just another stiff amongst the numerous, more anonymous casualties on a road that stretched back into the bowels of Irish history and forward into the same repetitious landscape of kerbside murder.

Doyle was not the first nor the last British judicial figure to die in Ireland. One of his predecessors, Resident Magistrate Alan Bell, met much the same fate on a Dublin tramcar. Bell was sitting reading a newspaper when two young men tapped him on the shoulder: 'Come on Mr Bell, your time has come.' His assassins pulled him off the tram and killed the Magistrate like a squealing pig in the road. The date was March 1920. Like Doyle's killing it was just another encounter in the endless war between Irish rebels and the Crown.

Bell's killing and that of Doyle were conducted in accordance with the Troubles' contradictory but rigid rules of engagement. The principal protagonists were the IRA and the British Government. The loyalist Protestant groups, like the Ulster Volunteer Force (UVF) or the Ulster Freedom Fighters (UFF), were little more than murder gangs and came a poor third. Each of the protagonists were constrained to work and fight within a quasi-civil framework. The IRA could bomb, shoot and murder but there were strong political restraints against the use of indiscriminate terror and the killing of large numbers of civilians. The British could have gunned down the IRA leadership in one afternoon on the streets of Belfast, Derry and Dublin, but did not do so for fear of widening political support for the republican struggle in the adjacent Republic.

Because it was not a big war, the British Government said it was not a war at all but a battle against a criminal terrorist conspiracy. To sustain that belief, one had to ignore the thirty thousand combat troops in Ulster, the squadrons of helicopter gunships and the extensive network of military bases along the three hundred-mile border with the Irish Republic designed to withstand hundred-pound flying bombs. The IRA said it was a real war and their soldiers, their Volunteers, were fighting against a colonial regime. But that did not stop Republicans complaining about human rights abuses perpetrated by British soldiers, or attempting to sue, often successfully, the British Army in the British Northern Irish courts for compensation for wrongful imprisonment. Nor did it stop the IRA's Volunteers and their families from claiming British welfare state benefits every week. Ulster's Protestants constantly proclaimed their loyalty to the British Crown and their desire to be treated as any other British subject, but when it came to accepting the democratic will of the British people in ways perceived to be contrary to their interest they had no hesitation in pulling out guns, hijacking cars and killing people.

If you had walked through the streets of IRA strongholds in West Belfast and Derry you would have seen, amidst the mothers wheeling baby buggies, fifteen-strong patrols of British

Army soldiers in combat gear armed with assault rifles and general purpose machine-guns. But those khaki patrols were just walking targets; this 'Green Army' hardly ever shot anyone. The real armies of the Troubles had no uniform apart from a gun and remained indistinguishable from the civilian population until they materialized at the killing zone. The two men who killed Judge Doyle were, a moment before, just faces in a crowd, a moment after, a couple of duffel coats fleeing through a congregation. Minutes later they abandoned their hijacked vehicle and disappeared into the streets of Belfast. The soldiers who killed for the British were members of their special forces unit, the SAS, and their most common camouflage was denim jeans and trainers.

The IRA talked up the Troubles and described them in the terminology of military warfare, labelling their convicted Volunteers as 'prisoners of war'. In contrast, the British Government talked the Troubles down and constrained itself to appear to act within a civil framework so that every action by the State's security forces had the protection of a legal statute. The British therefore amended the Northern Irish legal system to enable the State to use criminal law statutes as their principal instrument of repression. IRA members were arrested, tried and found guilty of criminal offences under a judicial system which had few of the constitutional standards prevailing in other Western countries. But as in their past dealings in Ireland, the Crown also operated a small secret state that utilized a vast electronic surveillance network, hundreds of paid informers and small groups of SAS assassins to track and in certain circumstances kill individual IRA opponents.

Clausewitz said that war is politics pursued by other means. In Ireland, murder was politics pursued by other means. The IRA, a clandestine grouping within the nationalist Catholic community, did not have the firepower, forces or money to openly defy the British State. But the IRA did have enough resources to find and murder the Crown's messengers on their days off. Shooting Doyle was a denial of British authority and an assertion of the power of the IRA and its political aspiration for the removal of the British presence. It was an act of physical militant defiance, an act of rebellion against what was perceived to be an illegitimate state.

The Troubles are almost as old as Irish history itself. They wax and wane with different historical epochs but they have never ceased in eight hundred years. In Tudor times the Catholic Gaelic *tadagh* (natives) resisted the Anglo-Norman conqueror. In the seventeenth century the Protestant Planters fought the dispossessed Catholic kernes (rebels). In the eighteenth century the Protestant Peep O'Day Boys attacked at dawn, murdering the enemy in their beds, whilst the Catholic Defenders came upon the enemy on the road and smashed their heads into the dust. It was colonialist Protestant Planter against Catholic Irish native. It was Prod against Papist. It was Protestant Royal Ulster Constabulary policeman against Catholic Irish Republican Army guerrilla. It was the British Crown versus the Irish. It was a creeping war of submerged hatreds that ran back into history and was explosively fuelled by contemporary political events. The objective was always the same — to remove the British Crown presence from Irish soil.

The key protagonists of the Troubles were the rebels, for without their unflagging commitment to fight on against overwhelming odds the conflict would have withered. The current rebels, known as the Provisional IRA, were drawn principally from the ranks of Ulster's working-class Catholic communities. Most IRA members were poorly educated and only a handful of the Movement had a university degree. The Provisionals' 'army' was estimated to be six hundred active IRA Volunteers with an annual budget of between three and five million pounds. These IRA soldiers were poorly trained and poorly equipped, with a limited ill-assortment of smuggled weapons. Each Volunteer was outnumbered sixty to one by the better armed, better trained and professionally salaried forty-thousand-strong security forces of the Crown, whose annual budget was estimated to be in excess of one billion pounds. Nearly four hundred IRA Volunteers have been killed and countless others injured, often in their own premature explosions. Almost every IRA Volunteer has been arrested and at some stage imprisoned, often for decades, by Northern Ireland's emergency power courts. Hundreds of IRA prisoners are still serving record life-terms in Northern Ireland's Maze Prison, hundreds of others have already left decades of their lives there. There was no monetary reward in joining the IRA and, by necessity of its clandestine nature, limited social status in membership. But despite the odds the IRA were never short of Volunteers.

The IRA are a minority political force within the 640,000-strong Catholic community, but not an insignificant one. The IRA and their political party, Sinn Fein, command about thirteen per cent of the total electoral vote in Northern Ireland or about forty per cent of the Catholic/Nationalist vote. Thirteen per cent or 83,000 votes is a substantial figure when one considers that Sinn Fein's electoral platform endorsed blowing up cities, shooting policemen in the head and punishing local criminals by dropping concrete blocks on their legs.

As a philosophy, Irish Republicanism is the unqualified belief that a United Ireland is an intrinsic good, and the demand for Irish national self-determination so pressing, so overwhelming, that this goal must be pursued at all costs but principally and immediately by force of arms. Ireland must be reunited and the illegitimate British Crown Government forced to leave that portion of the country, Northern Ireland, over which it rules and claims jurisdiction. All other political questions and struggles in Ireland are secondary and inferior to the resolution of the 'national question'.

But what is unchallengeable doctrine for Republicans is not so self-evidently true for the mass of the Irish people. The 850,000 Protestant population of Ulster, the majority within the Northern Irish state, are utterly opposed to a United Ireland. More importantly, the mass of the southern Irish population, who constitute four million out of the total Irish population of five and a half million, although paying lip service to the concept of a United Ireland, express little urgency about their desire to see an all-Ireland state established. The burning urgency of the Irish electorate's demand for Irish reunification, as measured by votes for Sinn Fein in the Irish Republic, is felt by less than two per cent of the population.

Economically there is no merit in any of the republican arguments for the reunification of the island. Northern Ireland is a poor country beset with decaying, unprofitable industries and sustained by massive subsidies from the British taxpayer. The total annual net cost of maintaining the Crown's Irish province is £3.4 billion, £2,200 per annum for each and every one of Her Majesty's Irish subjects. The Irish Republic is poorer still and it is beyond the economic means of any foreseeable Dublin Government to sustain such a level of public investment. If Britain is a colonial oppressor, then it is a peculiarly benign and indulgent overlord.

Outside their Ulster strongholds, the IRA were universally reviled as a terrorist organization guilty of some of the bloodiest acts in recent political history. In the British, Irish and American media, the IRA's leadership were frequently portrayed as a 'criminal godfather conspiracy' in charge of a membership of bloodthirsty fanatics.

But far from weakening the Republican cause, these obstacles merely make it all the more formidable and more profound. It is a faith shared by a band of brothers against impossible odds. No other Western political movement is so tenuously grounded in political reality, so consciously espouses a doctrine of self-sacrifice, promises so much pain and death for its followers and offers so little in return.

After the collapse of Soviet Communism, political language lost use of the notions of sacrifice, martyrdom, millenarian generational conflict and historical destiny. But the Volunteers of the IRA did not. In an obscure rain-sodden corner of north-western Europe there was still a small group of believers who were prepared to lay down their lives for a cause. All the troops, the barracks, the fortifications, the billions of pounds spent on security, the informers, the intelligence networks of Special Branch, Scotland Yard's Anti-Terrorist Branch, Britain's domestic intelligence service, MI5, and the world's best equipped anti-terrorist police force, the Royal Ulster Constabulary, failed to destroy the IRA or mitigate its ambition of forcibly bringing into being a United Ireland. The Republican credo has exhausted the will, the bribes, the threats and the retributions of countless Crown rulers. It has endured the twenty-five years of military occupation by British soldiers, the never ending procession of its own black-bereted coffins, the cruelties inflicted by its own Volunteers, the hundreds and thousands of lost prison years of its sons and daughters, the stalemates, the setbacks, the grinding poverty. It cannot be bargained with, bought, sold, traded, appeased, cajoled, repressed, diverted, destroyed or rationalized away by economic argument. It is ultimately an ideal, a religion, and its supporters will not stop until they achieve that goal. In a world of broken ideologies Irish Republicanism is the last great political passion in Europe.

In the winter of 1982 I was home for Christmas. Christmas Day was clear and mild, and I left grandfather's house alone and walked back along the shore towards the monument of the *sagart a run*. The memorial plaque carved in granite shows in bas-relief the side view of a handsome man and an inscription in Gaelic. I could not read it, I have never learned the language of my forefathers, but I understood that it declared the priest to be a 'noble and patriotic' man who had died for Ireland. I could not read Gaelic but I could feel the language of resistance. It asserted itself in his act of will in striking rebellion and in the simple and profound belief of my neighbours that resistance to tyranny had not ended just because of defeat. It asserted that the human spirit could not this side of death be entirely quenched and that even if an individual was lost there would always be someone, somewhere, amongst the apparently cowed people who was prepared to carry on the struggle. I was determined to undertake a journey to find the priest, to find myself, to find the rebel heart that beats somewhere in part of every human breast. A few days later I left home for Belfast.

There should be a word of warning at this point of departure. This is not a history book or a chronological account. The last thing Ireland or the Irish or English need is another history book to explain the past. Ireland already suffers from too much history; in that country history is a disease, a canker from the past that poisons the present. History is a weapon, a poker you keep in your pocket to beat the present senseless and so reorder its alignment to the past and justify present murder. Nor have I sought here to order, arrange, direct or sanitize my journeys in Ulster or my encounters with Republicans. When I went to Ulster I was not seeking history but a sense of my self. If anything this book is a haphazard travel guide to the Republican Soul, to the rebel heart.

NOTES

1. Quoted in Peter Berresford Ellis, *Hell or Connaught!, The Cromwellian Colonisation of Ireland 1652–1660*, Blackstaff Press, Belfast, 1988, p. 9.

2. The originals were destroyed in 1922 in the opening moments of the Irish Civil War when Free State forces opened fire on republican positions in Dublin's Four Courts, which then contained the Public Records Office.

3. Transcribed from the original manuscripts and contained in R. Dunlop, *Ireland Under the Commonwealth*, Manchester University Press, Manchester, 1913, p. 357.

4. Dunlop, ibid., p. 765.

2

DEFENDERS

On Monday, 3 June 1991, at 7.30 am, three IRA Volunteers from the East Tyrone Brigade drove a hijacked car into the Protestant village of Coagh close to the shores of Northern Ireland's biggest lake, Lough Neagh, to kill an off-duty member of the UDR. The IRA plan was to shoot their target, a local building worker and part-time soldier who lived in the village, as he stood waiting for his employer's early morning work's van. But as their car neared the pick-up point, the IRA men drove into an SAS ambush; eight members of Britain's special forces unit opened up at close range, directing over two hundred rounds of high-velocity rifle fire into the vehicle. The IRA driver, twenty-two-year-old Tony Doris, from Coalisland ten miles away, was hit and the car smashed into two parked cars on the kerbside. The two other IRA men, thirty-seven-year-old Pete Ryan and thirty-eight-year-old Lawrence McNally, were shot as they attempted to flee. A huge fireball engulfed the crashed cars and the intense heat incinerated the three IRA men – identification was only possible through dental records and molten personal jewellery.

Four days after the Coagh ambush Republicans came to Tony Doris's home town to bury their fallen comrade. Coalisland was once a prosperous mining and mill town but by the 1990s its industries had decayed and the town's shops and civic buildings were scarred by neglect. Coalisland had become a rural backwater of unemployment and state benefit poverty.

On the morning of Doris's funeral, all approaches to the small Catholic town were sealed off by RUC roadblocks, and the identities and car boots of anyone attempting to enter the security cordon checked. Coalisland's centre, already dominated by an obtrusive blank-concrete-walled police/military fortress, was invaded by a phalanx of thirty grey RUC armoured jeeps. Squads of the RUC's elite units, armed with rapid-fire Heckler and Koch sub-machine-guns, stood on the street corners; platoons of British Army soldiers were dug into the surrounding fields. Over two hundred riot-gear-clad RUC men, some fingering their plastic bullet guns and batons, filled the narrow lane surrounding the Doris home in the drab Meenagh Park council house estate on the outskirts of town; other RUC men squatted in the Doris garden, stood by the family's back door or wedged themselves between mourners gathering outside the garden gate. A massive security operation was under way to prevent an IRA guard of honour of balaclavaed gunmen firing shots over Doris's coffin, the traditional republican salute to a dead Volunteer.

None of the Republican mourners should have been surprised at the police numbers. Since the late eighties the RUC's policy towards republican funerals had been to police with paramilitary strength. The RUC's presence had, along with the black flags draping every lamp post along the funeral route, become just another part of the republican funeral ritual, spawning its own peculiar protocols. When the hour of the funeral approached the all too familiar litany of ultimatums, demands and counter-demands began, with each side playing out their own well-rehearsed steps.

The Doris family refused to allow the coffin to leave their home until the police pulled back from the gates of their small front garden. The helmeted RUC commanders, strutting around like nineteenth-century squires with leather riding crops under their arms, stood firm; and then – possibly with an eye on police overtime costs – relented. When Tony Doris's coffin eventually emerged from the family home it was draped in the

Irish tricolour and his jersey from the local Gaelic Amateur
Athletic Association. On top lay a black beret and a pair of
black leather gloves – symbols of his membership of Oglaigh
na hEireann, the IRA. There were the traditional scuffles,
arguments, a few sparring blows between the police and some
of the more hefty male mourners, before the proceedings settled
into a steady rhythm of symbolic confrontation.

The funeral cortège wound its way through the shuttered
streets of the town, closed for the morning out of respect for its
fallen son, preceded by two hundred policemen, all dressed in
body armour, carrying truncheons and bearing small riot
shields. Groups of mourners, including Tony's mother Kate and
his sisters, Ann, Joan and teenage Donna, took turns in
shouldering the coffin as the slow cavalcade made its way
to the republican plot in the graveyard, high on a hill overlooking the decayed Victorian mills and the fortress from where
Doris's living enemies co-ordinated their part in his death
pageant.

In the graveyard a thousand mourners massed round the tall
Celtic cross that marked the republican grave; the local schools
had closed for the day and the crowd was a sea of freckled
faces, young girls, weary mothers, old and young men. Behind
them, just twenty yards from the brown, chalky wound in the
green earth, stood yet another squad of RUC officers, armed
with riot guns.

There were the usual Catholic obsequies, the prayers for the
dead man's soul and his living relatives. And then there were
the republican rites: the solemn folding, military-style, of the
tricolour and the passing, stiffly, of the beret and gloves to his
mother; and the laying of wreaths. A local priest, brother of
one of the 1981 hunger-strikers, then led the mourners in a
decade of the rosary in Gaelic. His voice sang out in the ancient
language; the crowd, united as one, returned the chant as if
speaking a rune, as if being gathered there on an Irish hillside
to bury an Irish hero was nothing new or remarkable but just
another familiar saga, repeated and repeated.

Surprisingly, Doris was only the second young man from

Coalisland to die in the IRA's struggle and the first to be buried in the town's republican plot. The Celtic cross was inscribed with only one predecessor, Colm McGirr, who had been ambushed and killed in December 1983 by the SAS as he sought to retrieve weapons from an IRA arms dump. But although McGirr's name was listed on the republican memorial, the McGirr family had preferred to bury their son in the family grave amongst the maze of grey and black headstones higher up the hill.

I stood in the midst of the crowd just behind Belfast Sinn Fein councillor Mairtin O Muilleoir as he gave the funeral oration. A British Army helicopter whirled above us and across the opaque sky another helicopter hovered half a mile away. The surrounding green fields were filled with British Army snipers, soldiers and RUC riot squads.

'There is something dreadfully wrong and shameful,' declared O Muilleoir, 'in a country where a young man like Tony has to go out to give up his life for his liberty.' He continued:

> And it is no consolation that it has been happening in these fields and these byways for hundreds of years . . . We ask why a young man, in the prime of his youth, who had so much to give a New Ireland, a free Ireland, had to die. We do not blame Tony for his wish to be free, we blame first of all those politicians in Dublin, who, by deserting us, to the bigots all around us, won their freedom, or bought their freedom on our backs . . . we warn them that we will not be going away and that it is the death of our Volunteers, Tony, Pete [Ryan] and Lawrence [McNally], which will ensure that we will not be interned and wiped out, that we will not be killed and cleared off the political scene and that we will not forget what we have gone through.

O Muilleoir, in his early thirties, was wearing a cheap suit, a seventeen-year-old's first suit. The material had degraded in the wash and tiny nylon bobbles were stuck to the blue pinstripe and there was an unhealthy scattering of dandruff on the collar. But none of that seemed to matter; the shabby suit, the harsh flat Belfast vowels, the sullenness of the crowd, the dull wash of the rotor blades and the humid sky threatening rain only made the menace and bitterness of his words more poignant.

And we blame also the people who rule the roost in this dirty little state, we saw their representatives on our television screens, they gloated over our deaths, they defiled our characters, they rejoiced in delaying these funerals, and they whooped with joy today to see us gathered burying our dead. Their representatives the RUC are gathered round here today to intimidate us and to prevent us from showing our respect. They won't intimidate us and they won't stop us. . . . We will show our dignity today in gathering here and laying Tony to rest and we warn them that we will not be your punch-bag any more, the days of Stormont are gone, you will not with impunity kill us, intern us, harry us and harass us any more because we are a risen people.

The crowd, physically and psychologically confined by the RUC riot squad and the clattering helicopter, strained and seethed like an animal in a net.

Those people too have a hard lesson to learn. They have been killing people in Tyrone for hundreds of years, they have been killing Irish people in these fields for over a thousand years, but we will teach them the lesson that no matter how many people they kill, how many of our number they kill – and it is always open season on nationalists, they can kill us in our beds, they can kill us in the streets, they can kill us in the fields, they can come in the dark of night, we have no protection – we will teach them a lesson that no matter how many of our number they do to death we will continue on. The British may be slow learners but we are very, very patient teachers. And no matter how often they cut us down, others will pick up and follow on.

O Muilleoir had no need to illustrate his message; the proof was all around us in the skies above, in our ears from the incessant droning wash, and in the green fields. From that graveside there could be no doubt that this huge security operation was designed to contain and corral a people rising up against the forces that sought to subdue them.

In the afternoon the same funeral congregation and more gathered in the townland of Ardboe, just on the outskirts of Coagh village, to bury Peter Ryan in a twelfth-century grave-yard on the shores of the Lough. Like his IRA comrade Lawrence McNally, Ryan was a very experienced Volunteer with an extensive paramilitary record that stretched back into the early seventies. Both men had been wanted by the British authorities in connection with a number of killings in the Tyrone area and both men had been on the run, living across the border in County Monaghan in the Irish Republic. For Ryan's funeral, the fields again were burdened with police and soldiers, the waters of Lough Neagh patrolled by Royal Marines and the sky filled with huge troop-transporting Chinook helicopters. The unusually dry weather turned the earth into a soft white-grey dust that rose in the air under the massed but muted thudding of the mourners' feet and clung to their clothes and hair as they trod their way down to the Lough shore led by a lone bleating piper. Nothing could dampen the dust, and the mourners took on the chalk-like hue of penitents and this interminable funeral, delayed and harassed, the aura of a pilgrimage. At the graveside another passionate, threatening and bonding oration was read out, declaring that 'the path of freedom' would not be abandoned just because Volunteers had been killed and warning the British and the massed ranks of the riot-clad policemen that 'like Pete we are not afraid of you'.

Within another hour it was over; the mourners went home,

leaving tyre tracks in the fields of Ardboe; the Chinook helicopters filled their bellies with troops and took off north across the Lough; the RUC's armoured jeeps pulled out of Coalisland and headed back to Protestant Belfast; the town's shops and pubs sparked again into life; the security cordon dissolved away. Every move had been programmed to a relentless choreography and we were all, mourners, soldiers, policemen, reporters, acting out our given roles in another macabre Irish passion play. All that was left behind us were the entombed blackened bodies of the IRA men and the public declaration of Doris's secret life. His name would soon be inscribed on Coalisland's Republican Celtic cross. The world could now know what most of Tony's family and friends knew anyway, that he was, in their long vowels, an I-R-A M-A-A-N.

Coagh is a tiny village of 650 people; a couple of pubs, a garage, a post office and a few shops all set around an oblong square. The houses are an unmemorable mixture of neat pebble-dash bungalows, older stone cottages and a couple of brick council house estates set against a lush landscape of green fields, meandering empty country lanes and fertile hedgerows. There is something of an American mid-West feel about the village; it is an empty waystation on the road to nowhere in particular. By the time I visited, the thick oily stain on the roadway from the burnt cars and IRA bodies was already fading and outwardly Coagh had reverted to being an obscure backwater off the main road network. The only clue to another identity lay in the painted kerbside stones, red, white and blue, the colours of Protestant Ulster, and the Union Jacks flying from the mast poles, marking out the boundaries of a tribal compound. Hidden away in the back streets I found murals of gun-toting balaclavaed gunmen that glorified the UVF, who claimed responsibility for killing Republicans in the district. But beyond these symbols there was nothing in Coagh to give a clue to Tony's spectacularly violent death. None of the villagers wanted to talk about the SAS operation and none of them wanted to be seen talking to a reporter. Ulster's Protestant culture, like Afrikanerdom in the apartheid era, is a siege mentality that breeds suspicion and a fear of strangers; in the small public house in the centre of the village the barman politely told me to stop asking questions, otherwise I risked being shot.

The Coagh villagers did have a justifiable reason for not wanting to talk or be identified. Doris's death was a marker in a bitter vendetta between the gunmen of the IRA and the gunmen of the UVF. Coagh and the adjacent district of Ardboe, whose combined population was just over a thousand people, had been at the centre of a wave of assassination and retaliation which within the space of three years in the late eighties and early nineties had cost the lives of thirty men. In September 1988 the IRA had bombed and destroyed Coagh police station; the station had long been abandoned by the RUC as a security risk and the only fatality was a police Alsatian guard dog, Max. But the blast injured ten villagers, tore the roofs off scores of homes and ripped down power-lines, plunging the village into darkness. When the houses were rebuilt, an unconsciously ironic sign was attached to the abandoned police station's door: 'In an emergency phone 999.' The nearest manned police station was twenty minutes' drive away over potential IRA-controlled country roads. The Protestants of Coagh believed, as their Planter forefathers believed, that they were besieged.

The Coagh–Ardboe killings, with their particular twists and personalities, were the freshest cycle of a blood feud that stretched back across the centuries to the Plantation of Ulster in the summer of 1610, when the native Gaelic Catholic population of Tyrone were forcibly dispossessed and their land resettled by Scottish Presbyterians or Planters. Those natives who remained were pushed into swampy enclaves on the shores of Lough Neagh, the site of the current villages of Coagh and Ardboe. In other countries and in other lands, history happens and then dies; the conquistadores seize the Inca and destroy his empire for ever; the native Americans are dispossessed and the US Cavalry and the white man win; the Aborigines are hunted off their land and a new country of white settlers is born. The slate is wiped clean. But in Ireland history does not die. The natives did not disappear or forget, and never ceased to resist. The Planters maintained their conquest by force of arms.

Writing to London in May 1615, the newly appointed land agent, George Canning, complained that native 'woodkerne' – the sons of the dispossessed Catholic landowners – were waging guerrilla warfare against the Plantation.

> The newes here is nothing but the contynuall troubles in theis partes, both by sea and land. There were never sithence I came hither soe many kernes out in the woodes as nowe; they are in five or six severall Companies, soe that men can travel no way, neare anie woodes, without great danger, except they goea good Companie together, and well provided ... divers robbeires and some murders have been committed neare us sithence that tyme, and they are nowe grown soe bould that, on tuisdaye last, being the 7th of the month, a companie of rebels, about 6 of the clock in the afternoone, entered into an Englishman's home, six miles on the side of Derry, upon the highway ... they wounded the man verie sorre, soe that he wil verie hardlie skape with life, and took seven and eight pound in money and all the rest of the goods that were worth carrying ... These mischeifes and miseries causeth us to stand continuallie upon our guard, and when we travell we take good strength with us; wherefore might it please you, when you send those materialls I wrote for in my last, alsoe to send over some more armes, as musketts, callivers powder, and bullets (the last calliver' bullets you sent were all too big).[1]

Tyrone was continually wracked by futile republican uprisings and bitter sectarian strife. In the 1780s, a decade before Manus Sweeney's revolt, a clandestine Catholic militia, the Defenders, was formed in nearby Armagh to defend its coreligionists from attacks by Protestant Peep O'Day Boy vigilantes, who were killing and expelling Catholics from the county in a protracted struggle for domination of the linen trade. Defenders militantly asserted the rights of the oppressed Catholic majority by attacking their Protestant rivals, raiding the homes of Protestants for arms, destroying the property of landlords, mutilating cattle, burning farms and planning a mythic Rising where the Plantation would be reversed and all Protestants put to death.

Violent death was a frequent visitor to the green fields of Tyrone: he came at night in the guise of men rapping on the door of an isolated farmhouse; he hid behind the hedge of a road too frequently travelled; he waited in the dark lane for the man of the house to return home; and he lurked in the hearts of other Tyrone men. Over the centuries the names changed but the strata of conflict remained inviolate, and the methods of resistance immutable.

Defenderism was earthed in the grievances of its local adherents and was never more than a loose association of Catholic militants wreaking immediate revenge on their hated over-masters. In Armagh and Tyrone sectarian rivalry climaxed at the Battle of the Diamond in Armagh in 1795, when twenty Defenders were killed in a clash with the Peep O'Day Boys — who renamed themselves the Orange Order in honour of their victory. But by then the confused doctrines of Defenderism had already spread across Ireland and much of the real fighting in the 1798 Rebellion was instigated by rebellious Defenders rather than revolutionary United Irishmen.

The latest Troubles only reignited the fuse of history; three centuries after their conquest the natives of Tyrone were again in rebellion, and the Planters and Orangemen of Coagh forced still to maintain their lands by power of arms. Like a

vampire, the crime of the dispossession of the Plantation rose
from the grave to prey upon the living and demand revenge for
the dead.

I drove the ten miles of back country roads to the place from
where Tony had set out that morning to kill, his home town of
Coalisland. Outwardly, Tony's short life was unremarkable.
He was born and brought up on the fifty-house Meenagh Park
council estate on the outskirts of Coalisland. It was the poor
end of a poor town and had a reputation as a republican
stronghold; five men from the estate had been killed by the
British security forces. On the edge of the estate, close to
the Doris home, a cracked memorial stone marks the spot
where one of the victims was shot dead as he took a short-cut
through a hedge. The inscription reads: 'Martin McShane,
Aged 16, Murdered by British security forces on December
14th 1971.'

Tony was the second youngest in a family of five, three girls
and two boys. Tony's father Pat was unemployed for long
periods in a town where many men were unemployed for
long periods and the family's standard of living was poor.
Tony went to the local Catholic primary school and then on
to St Joseph's High School; he was a bright but uninterested
pupil and left without any academic qualifications. He played
Gaelic football for the Coalisland Gaelic Amateur Athletic
Association and liked powerful cars. He was proud of his
driving skills, though he lost his licence for six months, and in
another time and another place would probably have become a
mechanic. His girlfriend Brigid was nineteen and they had
a three-month-old daughter, Roisin. Like most of the other
young men on the Meenagh Park Estate, he was unemployed.
Tony's lifestyle was typical of thousands of young working-
class men brought up anywhere in the poorer parts of Northern
Europe and like many of these young men, Tony too had a
grandfather who had been involved in armed conflict in the

twentieth century. In Tony's case it was in Ireland, where his grandfather Johnny Doris had fought for the old IRA in Derry in 1916.

Joining the IRA was not difficult in Meenagh Park – it was the obvious career move for a young man with time on his hands. But it was not Tony Doris's only choice. His brother Martin passed his A-Levels and went on to study medicine, defying the stereotype of Republicans as nihilistic unemployed bombers. Tony stayed behind, turning down offers of employment in America, his family claim, and joined Oglaigh na hEireann. To his family Tony stood out from the other defeated young men of Meenagh Park. 'Tony joined the IRA because of the constant harassment that the people in the town got. Tony had to do something about it. The rest of them would just sit there and do nothing but Tony didn't,' said his sister Joan. Tony was a rebel.

Soon after Tony's death, I went round to see his family. I sat for hours with Tony's sisters around their kitchen table as they shared cigarettes, ran loads of clothes in the tumble-drier, made cups of tea, alternately shouted at or comforted Ann's two-year-old child and swore at the newspapers for the way they reported Tony's death. Around the table there was a warm, close feeling which stirred up memories of my own Irish Catholic childhood. After a time the sisters began to call me by my first name, Kevin, in a soft familiar tone that only Irish women or those who have been surrounded by Kevins all their lives can.

Joan, the middle sister, who had returned from America for her brother's funeral, led the discussion and answered most of my questions. Tony's death had heightened her sense of embitterment. She was the first to bring up the red heart-shaped mock St Valentine's Day card dropped into the front garden by soldiers from the nearby barracks a week after Tony's death. The card read: 'Tony loves the SAS. From Her Majesty's Forces. May you rot in hell Tony. Ha, Ha, Ha!' The family had interpreted the card as a mark of the fear and respect Tony had commanded amongst the soldiers whilst he was alive, but the crude attempt to inflict pain had hurt. The sisters had been pointed out in the street to British soldiers by RUC policemen and barred from entering Crown buildings by security men in a local town.

The personal abuse seemed to have only increased their sense of outrage and defiance. As I sat sweating in the heat of their kitchen all of Tony's relatives constantly defined themselves as an I-R-A M-A-A-N's family. When I heard them say it, I-R-A M-A-A-N, I felt it meant something to them that was lost in translation to the outside world. Later, when I asked Joan out on a date, one of the first questions she asked me was what was I doing in a car with an I-R-A M-A-A-N's sister. Like the rest of her family, Joan had become an adjunct to her brother's identity.

At the kitchen table, I sat asking the same question over and over again — why had Tony joined the IRA? The logic of the question was unintelligible to the Doris family. In their minds the mere description of life in Coalisland was sufficient to explain why Tony had joined the IRA. My naive question shook this natural assumption. They searched for ways to explain something that was so obvious it was inexplicable.

'You couldn't blame Tony for rearing up. He had a lot of threats from them,' said his sister Joan.

'He seen what was happening to other lads too, and we believe in a free Ireland,' said his sister Ann.

'I can understand why anyone would pick up a gun and shoot them. The people in the UDR are only in it for one thing — they are bigots,' said his sister Donna.

'He did not like anyone being killed but the only answer he saw was a British withdrawal. The only answer he seen was to become an IRA Volunteer. He had seen the SDLP doing nothing, just sitting there. He wanted to get something done to build up a strong war to force the British out of this country,' said his schoolfriend Daniel McShane, brother of the murdered Martin.

'He saw the Hunger Strikes and he joined the IRA,' said Donna.

'They put the Catholics in beside the Lough on bad land. Protestants had all the good land,' said his father Pat.

'We were sitting back and they were treating us like slaves,' said McShane.

'I suppose it was just Coalisland where he was reared up. He had no choice, when he was on his way to school his bags were searched,' said Joan.

'We are not fighting for Dublin, Meath or Monaghan, we are fighting for Tyrone. What have they got to do with us? It's our country, not theirs [Protestants]. Across the water there is less discrimination and more education,' said Donna.

'Protestants own most of the business and the best land. You can see it in the land, right green land compared to weedy land near the Lough,' said Tony's uncle, Jimmy.

'I want equality, we have the right to own our own land. The Protestants have taken the land away. It's not their fault that they have it ... The only way to change it is to wage war against the British Government. In a new Ireland everything would be equally shared. Everyone would have the right to own the land. One man would not have a big lump of cake and the other a wee pinch,' said McShane.

Their answers ran in circles; Tony joined the IRA because of the harassment he received for being a well-known member of the IRA. No one could point to a single event or incident that provoked his commitment but everyone, his father, his mother, his sisters and his friends, returned again and again to the harassment by soldiers that Tony encountered on the street. Tony did not like being stopped and searched by 'them', members of the British security forces who patrolled the nationalist town. 'He was angry about it. He always stood up to them when he met them on the road. He was arrested when he was sixteen, when he was still at school. They lifted him up and bent him over the back of a chair, they kicked him and spat on him. He had not done anything at that stage,' said his mother Kate.

According to Coalisland's mild-mannered, academic Sinn Fein councillor Francie Molloy, the principal inflictors of harassment were the locally recruited Protestant members of the UDR:

The UDR from Coagh came into Coalisland, which is a ninety-nine per cent nationalist town, and patrolled around the town. They would stop schoolchildren on their way to school, get them to turn out their school bags, or stop cars. Anyone who had a republican connection or had given them a bit of mouth became a target. They would search and read anything, letters, private documents from your solicitor, even if it was obvious that there was no security force connection. The UDR man could read every one of those documents, he could even count the money in your pocket, even though he was your next-door neighbour. The only qualification he needed was that he was a member of the UDR. It led to great tension. You could cut the air with a knife. It was not fear but total hatred whenever you saw them. It made people feel low and it engendered total hostility towards the Loyalist community and gave the impression that this is a Catholic versus Protestant war. But it had nothing to do with religion; it was the simple arming of one section of the community against the other whilst you deprive that other section of any means of defending themselves.

A day later I had a brief taste of what that harassment was like when I visited Tony's grave in the company of his uncle. We were standing at the grave site overlooking the town when a British Army foot patrol appeared, making its way towards a railway track, 150 yards below us. As I looked across at the railway line, the last soldier pointed his rifle at me by peering down the weapon's telescopic sight, as if he was preparing to shoot. My heart raced and I felt the need to freeze so that no gesture on my part could be misinterpreted as a sniper's movements. I tried hard to assure myself that this was an everyday event in Coalisland and the soldier was well trained. But all I could really think was that this green uniform could kill me by squeezing on his trigger finger; if his aim was good the round would blow my chest apart. The soldier had the gun, the British Army and the RUC press office behind him to deliver and vindicate his version of my suspicious movements, the imaginary rifle in my hands, and the confused gun battle that would result in my death; I was just another suspect Fenian in a suspect Fenian sort of place. I felt powerless and afraid, and then the soldier lifted his weapon up towards the sky and disappeared down the railway embankment.

The same night I phoned the Doris home and asked Joan Doris out on a date. I was not really sure why I wanted to do it; perhaps it was because I wanted her, perhaps it was because I wanted to be with this special sexual prize, an I-R-A M-A-A-N's sister, and perhaps I wanted to identify myself as an I-R-A M-A-A-N's sister's boyfriend. I picked Joan up from Meenagh Park at around ten on a Saturday evening after finishing an interview with a building contractor who worked for the security forces – whom her brother had almost certainly conspired to murder. Joan got in the car and suddenly I was the interrogee. Phoning her had caused consternation in the Doris household; Coalisland men never phoned anyone to make a date but moved in slowly, presumably after years of getting to know you at a school. Joan had been questioned and teased for hours about what she had done to provoke my attention. A drumbeat of questions as to my suitability as a male companion for a nice Irish Catholic girl commenced.

'What age are you? Are you married?'

'No.'

'Do ya have a girlfriend?'

'Yes.'

'Why did you ask me out then? Why are you so forward? If you're expecting some tittle-tattle about Tony then you're sorely mistaken.'

I fended off her questions as best as I was able and suggested we go somewhere close, in Coalisland, for a drink.

'Are you mad?' For Joan, being with this reporter and stranger was just as compromising as being with an I-R-A M-A-A-N's sister. Tony's life had been brought to an end by an informer; Joan's world, as the sister of the dead Tony, was filled with mistrust. We could never be an innocent couple; if we had been seen together in Coalisland Joan might have been asked what we had talked about, what kind of questions I had asked.

We drove around the outskirts of Coalisland searching for a neutral venue, when we suddenly saw the swinging amber stopping light of a British Army mobile patrol.

'Now we're for it. They're stopping,' declared Joan.

My heart sank and in my nervousness I slammed on the brakes too early in my fear of overshooting the patrol. As I lowered the window my mind raced, imagining what would happen when the soldiers recognized Joan after running her identity details through the vast Army computer databanks that hold information on the entire Catholic population of Northern Ireland. To the left and to the right there were more armed soldiers. I passed my driver's licence to the soldier.

'Where are you going to, sir?' asked the soldier as he scrutinized my English licence and passed it to his companion to radio the details through to the Army's computer centre. I rhymed off the name of the nearest big town.

'Dungannon.'

The soldier on the left was staring hard at Joan in the passenger seat. She looked straight ahead ignoring him.

'And where are you coming from?'

'Coalisland.'

I looked across at the soldier on the left. He seemed to be

signalling something to one of his mates on the opposite side of the road. We waited, as if for a credit card authorization, for the computer's verdict. I passed.

'No probs,' the soldier said and passed me my licence. I wound the window up and we drove on.

'If you'd said Meenagh Park he would have had you out of here like a shot. It would be Charlie-Charlie Ten and out you get.'

'What would be the point in that?' I asked.

'Just to stand up to them.'

Her reply shocked me. It seemed as if she was willing her own harassment. I did not understand. Part of what had attracted me to her was that impression of personal enterprise she had projected. Joan had not been defeated by Coalisland, by the poverty and the hopelessness, she had found an escape route.

'So when are you going back to the States?'

'I don't know.'

'Didn't you have a job there?'

'Yeh, but I like it here, close to home and my family.'

'Everything has a price, sometimes you have to leave home to get a job.'

'No, I would not want them to know that they had put me out.'

'Who are the "them"?'

'The Protestants, the so-called security forces.'

I had been mistaken; now it seemed that Joan cleaved to her tribe, to the narrow world of Meenagh Park, to lifetime unemployment, to family relationships and to a future as determined as the route of Tony's funeral procession. Soon she would marry someone from Meenagh Park.

The barrage of her suspicion could not be overcome.

'How do I know you're not an SAS man? How do I know you are not going to take me somewhere and tie me up against a tree?'

There was no defence I could proffer apart from appealing

to the obvious. But what was the obvious? Because of the earlier interview that evening I was dressed in a blazer and tie. Maybe the people of Coalisland thought that blazers and ties were off-duty SAS gear. I was a complete stranger who said he was a journalist; my name might be fake. I could not bridge the gap between us. The bickering was also wearing away at my patience and we still had not found a place to drink – we were running out of time.

Finally, Joan suggested we drive to 'Protestant Cookstown', twenty minutes away. It was already a quarter to eleven. By the time we arrived it would have been too late for the bars, which closed at eleven o'clock. And I was now worried about being seen with Joan. Something had got into me, fear or cowardice, something of the suspicion of Tyrone; I equivocated, I did not want to end up in the wrong bar at the wrong time.

And then out of nowhere Joan spoke. 'If I asked you, would you take me to Coagh? I have never seen the place that Tony died.'

Coagh was just ten miles away, but it was a mark of its real distance that Joan, who had flown back from Texas for her brother's funeral, had never travelled those last few miles. 'And stop there?' I asked vainly, hoping she would say something like: 'No, no, just drive through at eighty miles an hour.'

'Yes.'

If this was the test, then I was failing. Coagh was the last, worst place on earth to go with Joan Doris. In my mind I envisioned her kneeling to say a decade of the rosary at the spot of her brother's incineration, whilst battalions of masked UVF men emerged from the side streets to seize hold of me and kick me to death. If I went with Joan I could never go back to Coagh and, as I tried to assure myself, I did still want to interview some of the families living there. After a long pause I said, 'No, I don't think I could do that.'

I cannot remember her next blur of words but they ended with: 'Why not?'

'Because you are identified with one side and I am not.'

And that was the end of our evening out. I turned the car around and dropped Joan back at her parents' house. Afterwards I knew I had been fooling myself. My attempt to be identified with the Republican cause through Joan was just a pretence; I could pull out of my disguise, through fear, cowardice or professional calculation, whenever I wanted to. I was not a part of this struggle; I lived in another land and I had another life. But Tony – and Joan, an I-R-A M-A-A-N's sister – never had that option; their enemies, armed and empowered, would always be all around them, patrolling in their home town streets, waiting at the bottom of the lane, pointing them out to their soldier companions. The Dorises would always be Roman Catholics, always subversives, always rebels, always guilty. They would always be the kerne, the Defender, the terrorist, who had to be suppressed. Joan Doris's only defence was to provoke those enemies by embracing their judgement of her.

I turned the car and drove back towards Belfast. I met no one on the road; the Army patrols had gone and I was glad for the silence of my own thoughts. I was weary of the loyalties and identities that dominated and controlled life in Northern Ireland.

'Standing up to them' started Tony Doris on the road to joining the IRA and inevitably further harassment as the UDR's interest in him increased. In the small Coalisland community, the total population is ten thousand; his involvement in the Republican Movement was a poorly guarded secret. Tony drove the bus that took the wives and children of convicted IRA men to visit their relatives in prison; he travelled and took part in republican marches across Ireland; he sold the IRA paper *Republican News*; he was an active election worker for Sinn Fein and, supposedly in secret, an IRA Volunteer. He was frequently arrested and interrogated under the Prevention of Terrorism Act. The police raided his family home at six in the morning, smashing the front door, leaving his terrified teenage sister Donna, in the midst of her school exams, shaking for three days. 'I suspected Tony was in the IRA,' said his old school-friend and fellow Meenagh Parker, Daniel McShane. 'You do not like asking anyone questions along them lines like, no matter how close you are. Even your ma and father would not ask that. It's a secretive way, you must be under command of whoever. But I knew and believed what he was doing was right and that he was doing his best.'

Two days after his death RUC Headquarters issued a statement outlining their version of Tony's life as an IRA terrorist:

> Tony Doris was believed to have been an active member of the Provisional IRA in the Coalisland area for a number of years. He had been arrested on several occasions and inter-viewed about terrorist activity, including murder, but was released due to lack of evidence. In 1990 he was charged with possession of explosives but the charges were later withdrawn. Until the time of his death he was still suspected of continuing involvement in terrorist activity.

Tony's official obituary in *Republican News* was more detailed about his career as a Volunteer:

> While Tony Doris was still just a young man he was already an experienced and leading IRA Volunteer. He had joined Oglaigh na hEireann in 1987, having begun working with the Republican Movement from the age of sixteen . . . Like so many of his fellow nationalists he was unemployed and in common with most young nationalists in Tyrone, he was the target of unceasing harassment from British forces as he tried to live a normal daily life. He had received many death threats over a number of years and recently members of the Crown forces had repeated these threats on his life to others who knew him. Tony was arrested and detained in

Gough Barracks[2] on eight separate occasions ... He was
attached to the Coalisland unit of the East Tyrone Brigade
from 1987 onwards and was made OC of that unit from
early 1991.

Tony was a killer; forensic tests on two rifles recovered from
the burnt-out car proved they had been used in the murder of
three Protestant Coagh villagers two years before. Two of the
dead were old age pensioners and the triple killing, part of the
Coagh–Ardboe vendetta, had been denounced at the time as a
sectarian attack. In all probability Tony had been involved as
well in the murder of another Protestant civilian killed by the
same gun. There were probably more murders and many other
murder attempts. No one disputed that Tony and the others
were on their way to kill someone else when they were
ambushed by the SAS. In the immediate aftermath of Tony's
death, the British authorities claimed that the IRA men intended
to wipe out a group of Protestant workmen. The IRA denied
the charge but admitted they wanted to hit a 'military target' –
a notorious part-time member of the UDR.

Tony was judged to be a republican terrorist, a gunman
intent on sectarian massacre. But to his friends, family and
community in Meenagh Park Tony was not an aggressor, not a
terrorist killer, but their defender. 'We are proud of the lads
because they are standing up to them. Them fellas [in the
IRA] have some guts to pick up a weapon and go out, because
they are surrounded. They have no way out, they are surrounded by one of the best elite units in the world – the SAS –
but they are taking them on and they are succeeding at it,' said
McShane.

There was little sympathy for the man Tony intended to kill.
McShane related:

If a Protestant man is shot, if he is a part-time member of the
so-called security forces then there is a big uproar about it –
this man was a holy man and he was a good hard-working

man – but they never say he bate [sic] people at night and was up to all kinds of badness. The UDR are the ones giving all the information to the ones that are carrying out all these killings. There is no arms finds against them. No one is charged with the killings of Catholics. They haven't even found the weapons. There was two wee girls killed in Lurgan [a nearby town] by the UVF and no one has been charged. Then the Army is in the next day laughing, saying: 'Look what the UVF did for us, great men.'

'They never raid UVF strongholds, they never raid their houses,' said Kate, Tony's mother. 'When they are shot they never claim the bodies, they do not have a military funeral, they do not say they were in the UVF, they say they were not in it.'

'The IRA are a guerrilla army, the UVF are terrorists, they [the UVF] go out to intentionally shoot innocent people. The IRA intentionally go out to pick on the British Government. Good enough, there are casualties in all wars but the IRA do not mean to have innocent casualties. If the IRA were like the UVF they would just go out and riddle your man there and say he was in the UVF, just say he was UVF,' said McShane.

'They say they let psychopathic Loyalist killers like Michael Stone out of prison to carry out these attacks,' said Donna.[3]

Tony was just one of nearly thirty IRA Volunteers who had been ambushed and shot dead in SAS undercover operations or by Protestant paramilitaries in the county between 1985 and 1993, two-thirds of all IRA casualties in that period.

In the war between the British Army and the IRA, Tyrone had become the inner frontier and been turned into a vast armed camp. The British Army had built and rebuilt their garrisons using thousands of tons of concrete and legions of

Protestant workmen to turn their barracks into impregnable fortresses. Hillsides bristled with watchtowers and microwave communications dishes, and the sky, both day and night, was alive with the clatter of helicopters picking up and dropping off twenty-strong foot patrols. In the nature of guerrilla warfare, Tony's comrades could never openly oppose the British Army. But the real battle was over who controlled the ground when the uniformed troops of the 'Green Army' passed by. To the west in County Fermanagh and towards the south in County Armagh, where the population balance shifted towards a nationalist majority, the British Army had ceded day-to-day control of the ground to the Provisionals. Parts of Tyrone were already overrun by Republicans, making it dangerous for locally recruited members of the Ulster Defence Regiment to live, work or even travel unarmed in certain districts.

The county had become Protestant Ulster's last stand. If the IRA had won control in Tyrone they could have tactically cut Northern Ireland in half along the line of the River Bann, the traditional boundary between the Protestant-dominated East and the Catholic-dominated West. The British Army would still have been able to control the skies but Oglaigh na hEireann would be the real lords of the fields. To the indigenous, mutually antagonistic communities, Protestant and Catholic, living cheek by jowl next to each other's homes, fields and districts, Tyrone was the final battleground that must be held at all costs; every field was a Catholic field or a Protestant field; every tree, every hedge, was a potential boundary point between two hostile communities.

To understand Tony it was necessary to understand what kind of war the East Tyrone Brigade were fighting, what they were fighting for and what they, and Tony, believed in.

This point of departure begins in 1985 when Tony was just sixteen and the British Army, reacting to an increased threat from the Provisionals, decided to upgrade its fortifications along the border with the Irish Republic and establish an interlocking network of observation-towers in the republican stronghold of South Armagh, which lies to the south of Tyrone. The roads had long before been abandoned to the IRA and all troop movement, from strongpoint to strongpoint, was by military helicopter.

The new threat from the Provisionals was quite simple: the IRA were building bigger and better bombs, up to two thousand pounds, which were capable of destroying the existing fortifications and killing anyone inside them – the car bomb had given way to the lorry bomb. IRA engineers had also perfected a new weapon, a home-made vertical mortar constructed from oxygen cylinders that was capable of firing a fifty-pound high-explosive warhead three hundred yards, thus foiling the existing perimeter defences. The IRA used their mortar weapon for the first time in an attack on Newry Police Station, on the border of County Armagh, in February 1985. The mortar soared over the thirty-foot-high perimeter defences and landed on the flimsy wooden roof of a makeshift canteen packed with policemen and women; nine of them were killed. Overnight a new industry was born – the security force contractor trade – as every major barracks and police station in Northern Ireland was reassessed in the light of this new threat. A huge rebuilding programme, employing hundreds of civilian workers, was initiated.

Just outside the northern Tyrone county border in the staunchly Protestant town of Magherafelt, two brothers, Jim and Harry Henry, with decades of experience in the building trade between them, decided in 1985 to set up their own construction company to service the security force trade. Henry Brothers was a lucrative business. Constant work was guaranteed and the value of each contract was two hundred to three hundred per cent above the normal civil price for similar work. The work itself was bread-and-butter construction fare, apart from the walls and concrete foundations being feet, rather than inches, thick. The British Ministry of Defence was a profitable paymaster and in Northern Ireland's depressed economy there was no shortage of workers. The average labourer was paid six hundred pounds a week whilst skilled men were earning eight hundred pounds, a relative fortune by Ulster's standards. Henry Brothers quickly prospered; the company even exported and installed its bomb-proof windows in London's Palace of Westminster, and both founders were soon wealthy men.

The IRA, with the East Tyrone Brigade to the forefront, immediately launched a major offensive against border bases and barracks to thwart the rebuilding strategy. In the course of the next five years the IRA attacked over a hundred bases across Northern Ireland, demolishing thirty-three and severely damaging many of the rest. It was a devastating onslaught; the vast majority of the bases were located in civilian areas, surrounded by schools, houses, churches. The IRA just blitzed them anyway, using huge thousand-pound bombs that destroyed the bases but also made hundreds of civilians temporarily homeless and caused tens of millions of pounds' worth of damage to adjacent property. The IRA were unrepentant; under its legal commitments, the British Government was forced to pay compensation for this damage, thus adding to the economic burden of supporting the Northern Irish state.

But as fast as the IRA attacked the bases, the security forces and their civilian employees rebuilt them, making them even stronger. In August 1985 the IRA Army Council, which controlled all IRA operations, declared that anyone who provided services or materials to the security forces, from the supplier of fresh vegetables to the Royal Ulster Constabulary Headquarters in Belfast to the rural garage owner who sold petrol to off-duty policemen, was a 'legitimate target'. But the real anger was directed at the building contractors. 'We are of the opinion that the contractors involved are assisting the British in reinforcing their illegal and immoral presence . . . we view their activities as mercenary – making money at the expense of the oppressed nationalist people . . . They are building fortresses and interrogation centres which are being used to oppress our people and subject them to continuing undemocratic rule.' A week later a Catholic contractor, Seamus McAvoy from Coalisland, became 'the first of those engaged in assisting the British war machine' to be 'executed' for supplying the RUC with mobile offices. Nearly thirty others were soon to pay the same price for defying the IRA's threat.

It may sound absurd – 'the British war machine' – but on the ground it was easier to understand. The reinforced Coalisland security base that Mr McAvoy died trying to rebuild rises like a medieval fortress in the centre of the Catholic town. From behind its forty-foot-high walls a huge 120-foot communications tower, dotted with spy cameras and electronic eavesdropping equipment, dominates the area. On one of the days I visited the town, six civilian workers, guarded by British troops, were attaching cables high up on the tower in preparation for the installation of more spying equipment. I sat just across the street in a bar filled with the local unemployed. The men in the bar looked out at the workers on the tower, looked out at the cameras that would soon be spying on them, looked out at the six hundred pounds a week they could never earn, looked out at jobs the IRA would shoot them for doing, and then, with a look of quiet hopeless rage on their faces, returned to their pints. It was not hard to figure out who was their enemy.

Magherafelt is on the border of County Derry and County Tyrone and from the beginning of the IRA campaign Henry Brothers' defiant stance enraged both the South Derry and East Tyrone IRA Brigades. Both Brigades were united in a common purpose – to murder Henry Brothers' founders. The IRA first tried to kill Jim Henry on the afternoon of 25 October 1986 as his car was parked on a piece of waste ground in Magherafelt. A motorcycle drew alongside and an IRA gunman fired half a magazine through the window into the driver's head at point-blank range. But the driver was not Jim Henry; the dead man was the company's twenty-five-year-old shop manager Kenneth Johnston, who had had the misfortune to borrow the car from his boss half an hour earlier for a business meeting.

There were no mistakes the second time around. The IRA came for Harry Henry at his home on 21 April 1987. The family was watching television at eleven in the evening when the doorbell rang. Harry Henry went to the door and was confronted by an IRA man, one of five, who demanded the keys to his car. Henry refused, so the raider pulled out a gun, pushed his way into the house and smashed the telephone. Again the gunman demanded the car keys and told Henry to go out the back and start the car. Henry told them he wanted to put his slippers on. The raider replied: 'You'll not need them where you are going.' They took Henry outside and shot him four times in the head before stealing the car. The murder was to be the catalyst for the wave of assassinations that would soon engulf Coagh and Ardboe.

Killing those viewed as collaborators was not a new stratagem. Writing to London in May 1615 the land agent George Canning recorded the murder of a Catholic convert:

> The dangers of these troubles have hindered the setting of land much ... There are yet divers out in rebellion in the woodes, and somes tymes light uppon passengers and robb them and sometymes light into houses and doe manie villanyes; the last weeke they toke an Irishman as he was keeping cattell in the woodes uppon the mercer's proportion, and hanged him with a withe in a tree, and tis thought for no other cause but that he had conformed himself and gone to our church.[4]

The tactic was repeated again and again throughout the Troubles, by the Defenders, the Land Leaguers of the nineteenth century and by the IRA in the War of Independence in the 1920s. The rebels' aim was to isolate the Crown's military forces by forcing Army commanders to divert troops away from military duties, harass their supply lines and exact revenge. The Provisional IRA's campaign was effective; the costs of maintaining, never mind rebuilding, British garrisons after 1985 soared as every nail and every toilet roll had to be supplied directly through the military command structure and flown in by helicopter. The embattled British Army garrison in the IRA stronghold of Crossmaglen even had to fly out its garbage. The biggest surprise of the whole campaign was that the IRA had not tried it before 1985.

His brother's murder failed to deter Jim Henry from working for the security forces, although his lifestyle changed irrevocably. Like his security force clients, Jim Henry was forced to live in a fortress, his own heavily protected works compound just outside Magherafelt. Huge fences surround the yard and spy cameras monitor all traffic in the area. Discreetly armed guards search all persons and vehicles entering the compound. The main buildings are built to withstand mortar attack and there are hot lines to the nearest security force bases. Henry Brothers' yard became in all but name a security force base itself and its workforce a civilian arm of the British Army.

There was a good reason for the elaborate defences; on 13 December 1988 the IRA extended their barracks-bombing campaign to include Henry Brothers and mortar-bombed the compound. Like the twenty-four-hour guards who patrolled his works' perimeter, Jim Henry was never off duty from the IRA death threat. 'The IRA targeted our firm because we work for the security forces,' said Jim Henry. 'We have worked for the security forces and kept working for them, and intend to go on working for them. The IRA are murderers. You could not call them anything else. It took five of them to take my brother Harry out and blow the head off him. You do not forget these things.'

The bombing of barracks and the assassination campaign against the Henry Brothers' collaborators were just two of the three interlinked strands of the East Tyrone Brigade's war. The final strand, which culminated in the Coagh ambush, began with the killing of a more specific human target, a member of the UDR from Coagh.

At 11.45 am on 26 April 1988 in the village of Ardboe, two masked men carrying rifles stopped local farmer Peter Devlin as he was checking cattle in a field close to his home. The men said they were from the Irish Republican Army and demanded the keys to Devlin's bungalow. When Devlin refused, the men at first threatened to shoot him but then ignored him and jumped over a wire fence leading to the back of his house and disappeared. Five minutes later the local Cookstown Council bin lorry arrived on its weekly run to collect Devlin's household rubbish. One of the workmen, twenty-three-year-old Edward 'Ned' Gibson, was just about to empty the bin when the masked IRA men emerged from the back of the house. They had come for him.

One gunman shot the unarmed council worker where he stood and then moved in on the stricken victim as he lay dying on the roadway. At point-blank range, the IRA gunman pumped two rounds into Gibson's head; nine other rounds were recovered from his body. The IRA men then escaped in a hijacked car, abandoning the vehicle two miles down the road, close to the cross of Ardboe graveyard where Pete Ryan was buried three years later. The killers were long gone before the security forces arrived.

Edward Gibson's death did not make headlines. He was not important enough to matter to the outside world. He was murdered because he was a member, part-time, of the UDR; he wore a Crown uniform and, like Judge Doyle, the IRA killed him for it. Nor was Ned Gibson the first member of his family to die at the hands of his republican enemies. His wife's uncle, a reserve policeman, and another close relative, again a part-time UDR man, had also been shot dead by the IRA in the recent past. Over two hundred UDR men have been killed since the Troubles were renewed and each year saw a steady drip of isolated killings as individual UDR men were targeted and assassinated on their farms, in their homes or at their work-places by IRA Volunteers.

Officially the UDR, renamed the Royal Irish Regiment in 1992, was a part of the British Army. In reality the UDR was a locally recruited militia drawn exclusively from the Protestant community, whose first loyalty lay not with a distant parlia-ment across the water or the never ending stream of bewildered English soldiers and haughty government ministers who consti-tuted its authority in Ulster, but with their own Protestant community in a Protestant land besieged by enemies. Unlike their British overlords, the UDR did not go back to Aldershot or Dortmund after a quick six-month tour. The UDR were Ulstermen and sons of the Protestant community; the Troubles were their war against the historic enemy, Ulster Catholics; their battlefield was their own village, their own district; and their war would never stop at the end of an operational tour. When they were on duty, backed by the helicoptered might of the British Army, they were lords of the fields. They had the power to carry arms openly and penetrate deep into republican territory in Ardboe or the back lanes of Meenagh Park and stop, question and detain that enemy. The wider Catholic population, not just Republicans, regularly complained that they were harassed, abused and threatened at UDR roadblocks; Catholic politicians and priests constantly recited a long litany of sectarian murders, anti-Catholic attacks and crimes that members of the UDR had been convicted of in the Northern Irish courts.

But at the end of their armed patrols, UDR men had to go home to ordinary houses in ordinary country lanes. They were part-time soldiers and part-time civilians; they shopped, they drank, they had children and routines, they were seen, they could not carry a gun all of the time. They were easier to stiff.

Like his assassinated relatives, Ned Gibson was at his most vulnerable when he was off duty, separated from his armed

UDR patrol companions, and swimming as a lone Protestant fish in the republican sea that surrounds Coagh. Without his gun, Private Gibson was not empowered; he was just an ordinary bin-man and his uniform in the cupboard at home in the Protestant bastion of Coagh could not protect him from the IRA's East Tyrone Brigade.

'Ned Gibson walked the roads of Ardboe with an SLR, a self-loading rifle. The magazine was not there for shooting pigeons. He accepted when he joined the UDR that he was trying to quell the Republican Movement. It is obvious that if he was caught he was going to be shot. I know that because as a Sinn Fein councillor I am a legitimate target to loyalists,' said Francie McNally, the brother of Lawrence McNally killed by the SAS in Coagh.

In a bid to shield him from the IRA, Private Gibson's employers, Cookstown District Council, had frequently switched him between jobs. On the morning of his murder Gibson, who had been in the UDR for less than a month, was only assigned to that particular bin lorry minutes before it left the depot, yet the IRA were waiting. Their intelligence was remarkable; someone, probably several people, had built up a superb little dossier on Private Gibson. In a place like Tyrone, where each community had to cross through the enemy's territory on a daily basis, and every hedgerow had eyes and ears, it did not take long to find out enough to kill a man. Private Gibson must have been spotted in his UDR uniform, either on patrol or at home in Coagh; someone else must have identified him as a council worker; the bin lorry route would have been checked; enough information, from outwardly ordinary members of the nationalist community, would have been collated to arrange the hit; the IRA leadership sent their gunmen in to stiff Ned.

The IRA did not fight a sectarian war. It did not, as Francie McNally pointed out, kill Ned Gibson just because he was a Protestant; they killed him because he was a member of the UDR. But since every member of the UDR was a Protestant, the distinction was understandably lost on their relatives and friends. To these people, Ned was not an anonymous statistical digit in some endless struggle; Ned was part of their small community, a brother, a nephew, a colleague and a comrade in their war against the IRA. It was inevitable that Tyrone's Protestant community saw the IRA campaign as sectarian warfare against them. In revenge for Gibson's killing a Protestant mob in Coagh attacked the homes of the remaining few Catholic families in the village, later forcing them to abandon their houses. It would have been foolish to believe that Loyalist paramilitaries in Tyrone needed much of an excuse to kill Republicans, but after Ned Gibson's killing it was clear that some of them positively decided to strike back. A UVF death squad was formed.

Francie McNally, already the focus of Protestant rage as the sole Sinn Fein councillor in the Coagh area, went straight to the top of the UVF target list. 'After Gibson was shot, whenever I was stopped by the UDR on the road they started to call me Ned, because I was a Cookstown District councillor and the intelligence on Gibson was fucking top-class. They thought I was the only one that had that intelligence available to me. They haven't changed their mind about that yet.'

Death threats forced Francie McNally to abandon his isolated bungalow home in favour of a barricaded council house in the middle of an Ardboe housing estate. Standing in his kitchen, he pointed out through the window, past the twelve-foot-high sharpened metal stakes that surrounded his back garden. 'Do you see that house, two hundred yards away? That is where it begins – that is hostile territory. Those people want to kill me. I suppose they really do hate me.' And then, incongruously, he burst out laughing.

Behind Francie, his twelve-year-old son was wearing an IRA T-shirt depicting a row of masked IRA men firing a volley of shots over a coffin next to a famous republican slogan: 'Life springs from death and from the graves of the patriot dead spring living nations.' Hanging on the wall beside them, next to the kitchen window, was a kitschy embroidered plaque: 'Peace be to this House'.

To the UDR, Francie was the public face of IRA terrorism and his enemies wanted to see him dead. He must have had more death threats than hot breakfasts but Francie still laughed a lot and it was hard not to like him. He was a bulky man with the physique of a body-builder and close-cropped hair. Nicknamed 'the Bull', he was a raw, unsophisticated survivor with enough peasant cunning to outwit his enemies. He lived under siege but his eyes sparkled and he was, in a word, relaxed. 'Until I was elected in 1985 they have never had someone to directly point to. But after that, if the IRA did anything, the Loyalists would say: "That cunt." That was the mentality. No matter who was stopped at checkpoints by the UDR my name kept coming up again and again. They even wrote my name on the roadside, a'graw. "Councillor McNally is next."'

Francie tried not to take chances; two other local Sinn Fein councillors in neighbouring districts had been assassinated as part of the Coagh–Ardboe feud and he had no wish to join them. Francie's home was a small fortress; the doors were armoured, the windows barred; there were numerous devices to prevent intruders from breaking into the house late at night with sledge-hammers and guns and murdering Francie in his bed. Francie also moved around a lot and he never, ever, went out after dark. 'It's a Mexican stand-off. It's a case of you owe them two lives or three or they owe you two or three. It is who kills who now. They [the Loyalists] think they still owe us [the Republicans] one. That is how I think they would be thinking. It could be me.'

Five months after Ned Gibson was killed, the UVF came for Francie at his bungalow at 10.20 pm on 24 November 1988. Francie's brother Phelim, twenty-eight, an amateur musician not directly involved in politics, was playing 'Dawning of the Day' on the accordion in Francie's kitchen when there was a light knock on the door. Francie asked: 'Who's there?', but there was no reply. When a man stalked past the kitchen window Francie reached up and switched off the light and ran to a front bedroom window to check the car in the driveway – the man in the driver's seat was wearing a balaclava. 'Then I knew it was a murder bid. But there was no time to think. I heard two bursts of sustained automatic gunfire. I knew what I was going to find when I went back because Phelim had stayed in the kitchen. I went to the kitchen door and heard his last sigh. He was dead.' Four hours later Phelim's wife gave birth to their sixth child.

Phelim was guilty of being Francie's brother and their enemies rejoiced in his death. Another McNally brother, Peter, was stopped at a UDR roadblock three months later and had a gun jammed in his mouth. The soldiers threatened to 'splatter his brains all over a field' and told him, 'We didn't get the right one but it was all right so long as it was a pig from the same sow.'

On the wall of Francie's sitting room there was another handwritten plaque: 'In memory of my dear brother Phelim. Murdered on the 24-11-88.' The photograph was fading and out of focus but the memory of Phelim's killer was not. Francie was certain that he could identify him; he had seen his face and spoken to him at a UDR roadblock where the man boasted of the deed to come. 'If the police put up every man they had on their list in the local UDR on 21 November 1988 [three days before Phelim's death] I told them that I could pick out the man. They said that would be totally out of the question but I could just walk up and pick him out.'

Tyrone is a tiny world of a few market towns, rural villages and farms. I asked Francie if he had ever had a casual ordinary conversation with his enemy, his neighbour. He shrugged his broad building-worker shoulders and shook his head in the direction of the stakes in the back garden and the houses two hundred yards away. 'No, I have never spoken to them. You bump into them in Cookstown on Saturday if you are out shopping with the wife and kids. You can rub shoulders with them. They could be standing next to you in a supermarket queue. I have been that close to them but they would not say anything. You look at them and they look at you.'

In the corner of the sitting room his wife Annie sat chain-smoking. The years of waiting for the front door to crash down had been hard and Annie was far more obviously afraid than Francie. The strain had aged her prematurely and her conversation readily turned to the multiplicity of routes, borrowed cars, taxis and disguises Francie employed to stay one step ahead of the other side. She tried to keep her fear under control for the sake of the kids, and for Francie. 'One night we were on our way to a corpse house after Martin McCaughey was killed by the SAS and we got stopped. We rolled the window down just enough to slip the driving licence through. The UDR were so angry I was sure they were going to kill Francie. We just sat there waiting for a policeman to come. My heart was in my mouth,' she said.

In other parts of Northern Ireland Sinn Fein has evolved into a political party with a social agenda; some Sinn Fein councillors talk about drains and social security payments with dull sincerity. But with Francie, I felt such political niceties were a waste of time. Francie did not get elected to Cookstown District Council to run the refuse department more efficiently but to overthrow British rule in Ireland. His candidacy was an act of near suicidal bravery that drew Loyalist gunmen to him like moths to a flame; his attendance at council meetings was defiance in the face of his enemies, who saw him as nothing more than an IRA murderer. Nor did Francie flinch from open support of the IRA's assassination campaign.

I have no qualms about the IRA killing a UDR man or an RUC man. But these Coagh–Ardboe killings are different; I would go as far as to say that these killings stand out on their own, separate from all operations in Northern Ireland. It seems to be the two sides against each other. I do not support the killing of Protestants. If the IRA went to Coagh and put an eight-hundred-pound bomb in the middle of it and killed all round them, I would not clap my hands and say that was great. Killing women and children is achieving nothing. It would be better killing one of the right men doing the killing, than killing two dozen that were not involved.

I asked one more question. What was it like to kill your neighbour? Francie looked up and shrugged: his face was for the first time weary.

It's a sorry thing when you have to set up a man to get shot. It's a sad state of affairs. You have men in Ardboe trying to set up a man in Coagh to kill him. And you would have men there trying to set up someone here to kill him. It is sad but if you look at it, it's easy to see the reason for that. The IRA are defenders and any man who says he is a Republican would not say anything else. I would always have described them as defenders even before all these shootings started.

On 14 February 1989 the UVF struck again, assassinating local Sinn Fein councillor John Davey from the nearby district of Magherafelt, ten miles from Coagh, as he drove home from a council meeting. Davey was a high-profile Sinn Feiner with a paramilitary record that stretched back to the 1950s. He was widely viewed, in the Protestant community, as being an 'IRA godfather' and a key IRA organizer. Davey's murder was to be the key link between the Coagh–Ardboe cycle and the IRA's war against the Henry Brothers.

It soon emerged through the courts that Harry Henry's son Robert was involved in (and was later charged with) conspiring to murder Davey. According to his own court testimony soon after his father's murder, Robert Henry was given photographs by a UDR soldier of the men whom Army intelligence officers believed to be responsible for his father's murder. Three of the men, who included two senior Tyrone Brigade commanders,

Jim Lynagh and Patrick McKearney, were killed on 8 May 1987, two weeks after his father's murder, in a major SAS ambush during an abortive barrack-bombing of Loughgall Police Station in the neighbouring county of Armagh. RUC ballistic tests proved that the IRA men's weapons had been used to murder Harry Henry and Kenneth Johnston. Robert Henry testified that his mind became filled with hatred and revenge, and he became involved in an abortive UVF bid to import one million pounds' worth of arms. More importantly, Robert Henry became involved in the plot to kill Davey and transported the guns, two AK47 rifles, to a hiding place in Tobermore from where they were picked up by the UVF shooters and used to kill the councillor. The rifles were recovered by the police but the conspiracy to murder charges were later dropped and Robert Henry was convicted of possession of firearms and sentenced to twelve years. But Robert Henry's involvement convinced the East Tyrone Brigade that the UVF assassins either worked for or were closely associated with the Magherafelt construction firm. Due to the nature of their work, the IRA threat and the security clearances required, the overwhelming majority of Henry Brothers' personnel were Protestant. A relatively high number of the workers were also local part-time members of the UDR, whom the IRA believed passed on intelligence to the UVF death squad. The IRA's determination to hit Henry Brothers and the alleged UVF cell amongst its workforce intensified.

There was no direct evidence to support this IRA claim and their allegations are bitterly denied by the firm's director Jim Henry. But in the paranoid world of mid-Ulster, suspicion alone was enough to condemn a man to death. 'I just cannot understand why anyone would cite the company for that. The company has always taken a stand that we will work within the law. You cannot be responsible for a person who has had his father killed and who has seen other people killed as well. We are not responsible for what people do in their own time,' said Jim Henry.

The first IRA counter-strike came a month after Davey's

death, on 7 March 1989, in the village of Coagh. An IRA hit team, believed to have included Tony Doris, Lawrence McNally and Peter Ryan, drove into the village's garage and at point-blank range fired forty-six rounds at the owner, Leslie Dallas, and two old age pensioners, seventy-one-year-old Ernie Rankin and sixty-eight-year-old Austin Nelson. Forensic tests later proved that the guns used in this attack were the same weapons recovered from Tony's hijacked car at the SAS ambush two years later. As the gunmen drove off, some eyewitnesses claimed they whooped with triumph and fired celebratory rounds in the air.

The attack was universally condemned as pure 'sectarian murder', obscuring the real nature of the operation. At first the IRA claimed all three dead were UVF members but they soon admitted that Nelson and Rankin had been shot in error. The primary target of the attack was Leslie Dallas, the man the IRA were convinced was the UVF's Commanding Officer in East Tyrone and the main organizer behind the Davey killing. Dallas's family denied the IRA claim but Dallas did have a history of Loyalist paramilitary involvement dating back to the 1970s and Ulster was an unforgiving place. The pensioners had been mistaken for two paramilitary associates of Dallas, who the IRA claimed were in the garage minutes before their attack.

The blood cycle was now full and turning. On 29 November 1989, six months later, the UVF retaliated in kind by murdering the East Tyrone Brigade's Officer Commanding, Liam Ryan, at the bar which he owned on the shores of Lough Neagh in Ardboe. The gunmen struck late at night just after closing hours by knocking on the door of the Battery Bar. When Ryan opened the door, a man, holding a handgun in a classic military two-handed grip, shot him in the head and killed customer Michael Devlin; another customer was shot three times in the legs but survived. A second gunman then sprayed the bar with automatic rifle fire.

When news of the attack was broadcast Republicans say

that Robert Henry was heard to shout out from his prison cell in Belfast's Crumlin Road Jail: 'That only leaves one left to get!'

'Whatever he had heard about Liam, he tied him into the killing of his father,' said Francie McNally.

Liam Ryan, a US citizen, had appeared in court in the United States in 1984 on IRA arms trafficking charges. At the time of his trial in New York, the IRA's American fund-raising arm, Noraid, posted $750,000 bail for Mr Ryan after he was charged with buying arms for the IRA under a false name. The rifles were seized along with a huge cache of other weapons aboard the *Marita Ann* trawler in 1984 and traced back to him. He was later given a suspended sentence, and returned to Ardboe and bought the Battery Bar from his cousin Pete Ryan's family. After his death, the local IRA admitted that Liam Ryan was a Volunteer and he was given a paramilitary funeral.

In their statement claiming responsibility for the killings, the UVF said the bar was used as an IRA base 'to launch attacks against the Protestant community', including the murders of Leslie Dallas and the old age pensioners earlier that year. Forensic tests proved that the guns used in the Battery Bar killings were also used in the killing of Phelim McNally – indicating that the same gang, if not the same killers, had carried out the attack. Local Republicans believed the killers escaped by boat across the lake, although a getaway car was found burnt out less than a mile away. This car and its alleged role was to play a key part in the targeting of a subsequent IRA retaliatory strike.

The Battery Bar was a highly professional hit indicating that the gunman had probably received extensive military training. Like the Dallas killing, the Battery Bar attack had sectarian overtones, but beneath the surface the logic and targets were driven by a directed intelligence. In Tyrone, the UVF and the IRA, like their Peep O'Day Boys and Defenders forerunners, were mirror images of each other. Both were small

semi-secret organizations whose leaders would be well known
to both the Crown security forces and their enemies from their
previous convictions for terrorist offences. The rank and file
members were hard men in their twenties and thirties, whilst
the leaders, cunning and intelligent, were a bit older. The
paramilitaries were physically brave, aggressive, violent; tough
guys whom you would not want to cross in the wrong bar.
They were the local thugs turned community warriors. Neither
of their respective communities would wholly endorse their
actions but most ordinary citizens protected them by shutting
their eyes and ears. No one, Catholic or Protestant, would have
informed on their respective paramilitaries out of communal
solidarity and for one other very good reason: if the paramilitaries found out they would have shot the informant in the
head.

The IRA by its clandestine nature could only gather its
intelligence by surreptitious surveillance, but the UVF almost
certainly had access to sensitive material gathered by the UDR
in the course of their legitimate duties. Through its unofficial
links with sympathetic members of the British security forces,
the UVF would have little difficulty identifying their IRA
enemies; the names and photographs of known IRA members
were widely circulated on photomontages within the Ulster
security forces, which included members of the UDR based in
Coagh. 'I would say that the UVF does get some of their
information from the security forces. Some people have been
charged with getting information from the security forces, so
it's obvious it goes on,' admitted Coagh unionist councillor
Victor McGahie, himself a former member of the security
forces.

In Northern Ireland this issue of 'collusion', of covert
links between the security forces and illegal Protestant paramilitaries, was explosive. In Tyrone, Republicans claimed that
there was evidence of cross-membership between the legitimate
UDR and the outlawed UVF. Those claims were strenuously
but not very convincingly denied by British Government minis-

ters. Hard evidence of collusion was extremely difficult to obtain but in the tight-knit Protestant communities of Tyrone it would be surprising if material had not flowed from the UDR or RUC into paramilitary hands. In 1990 an outside police inquiry into collusion, led by Cambridgeshire Deputy Chief Constable John Stevens, virtually imprisoned the entire leadership of the biggest Loyalist paramilitary group, the Ulster Defence Association, for receiving intelligence documents. Mr Stevens' team failed to press charges against any serving member of the Crown security forces for handing over the documents.

The East Tyrone Brigade IRA leadership had a hit-list of fifteen men who they believed constituted the main core of the UVF in Coagh and in nearby Portadown. The IRA would have known individual names and their occupations, and would have tried to build up more information, second- or third-hand, about each target. Some of the intelligence would be hazy; the IRA were unlikely to know who the shooters were or who carried out a particular killing or where the arms came from. But there was no need for such detailed information; for the IRA, and the UVF, it was sufficient to know that the target was associating with a known prominent activist or had a past criminal record for terrorist offences to confirm their guilt. To kill them, the IRA would have needed to know something about the target's routines, the type of car they drove, the time of their arrival at work or the layout of their house. Much of this type of information was gleaned from casual but regular observation.

The local IRA Brigade had twenty to thirty active members whose identities, like Tony Doris's, was often an open secret within their community. Information on IRA members was widely available to their Protestant enemies through security force leaks, and individual IRA men were inevitably more vulnerable. 'That was the overwhelming advantage they had over people in Ardboe,' said Francie McNally. 'If people here was fit to go into Coagh and stand there taking down all the details, who is who and what is what, who runs with who, and then someone else gave you information about what they were involved in, and then the CID gave you information about this and that, they would not have stood a chance. You would wipe them out in two weeks.'

In their next attack the Provisionals renewed their offensive against Henry Brothers. One of the firm's lorry drivers, forty-year-old Thomas Jameson, a part-time member of the UDR, was ambushed on 8 March 1990 as he returned from delivering concrete supplies to a UDR base. He died in a hail of rifle fire as the mixer lorry he drove had to slow at a sharp corner along an isolated Tyrone road. Jameson's killing was a classic illustration of the power of a small armed group to control vast tracts of territory. The police and the Army might hold their strongpoints in the towns but every worker, every supplier, had to travel through the IRA's potential hunting ground, the isolated hinterlands of Tyrone, to get there. No army can patrol all of the roads all of the time and no military machine can fly concrete-mixer lorries in by helicopter. There were only so many roads to travel on and it was well within the IRA's capacity to watch them all.

Republicans in Tyrone did not have a monopoly on grief. Jameson's funeral was also an occasion for the expression of a community's rage and sorrow. Two thousand mourners followed the cortège through the streets of Magherafelt. The coffin was draped in the Union Jack and an honour guard of Jameson's UDR comrades presented arms. Democratic Unionist MP Reverend William McCrea gave the sermon:

The murderers of Tommy Jameson must feel proud of their dastardly deed. They brutally murdered a hard-working, honest and decent Ulsterman. A man who loved his family and worked tirelessly to provide for their needs. A man who was totally inoffensive, yet loyal to his Queen and country. He was no coward like the yellow cowards that took away his life. These bloodthirsty vermin excused their vile deed by stating that Tommy worked for a building firm allegedly involved in security work. Indeed they saw an honest hard-working man driving a cement lorry as a threat to achieving their goal of a blood-soaked united Ireland. These Roman Catholic terrorists in the IRA are liars. They needed no excuse to murder Tommy Jameson. He was a Protestant and that was enough, just as they have done to the Protestant community along the border ... I say to the government today, we are sick of promises. We have the right to demand firm resolute military action to crush this uprising in this part of Her Majesty's domain.

The undercover war between the SAS and the IRA ran in parallel with the attacks on the barracks and the murder of collaborators. On 9 October 1990 an SAS squad ambushed and killed two leading East Tyrone Brigade members, Dessie Grew, thirty-seven, and a former Sinn Fein councillor Martin McCaughey, twenty-three, as they sought to retrieve rifles from an arms dump near Loughgall. The exact details of the incident were never revealed but Republicans claimed that both Grew and McCaughey had bullet wounds to the temple, suggesting they had been finished off at close range by the traditional SAS execution method. Grew was a leading IRA figure in Armagh and had a list of terrorist convictions that stretched back to the early seventies. At the time of his death he was wanted in Germany for the October 1989 murder of Royal Air Force Corporal Maheshkumar and his six-month-old baby, and in Holland for the May 1990 killing of two Australian tourists, mistaken for off-duty British soldiers.

In the aftermath of the October 1990 SAS ambush it emerged that McCaughey had been wounded in a disputed shoot-out between undercover soldiers and the IRA in the republican stronghold of Cappagh in the Tyrone hinterlands seven months earlier. Republicans claimed that two soldiers had been killed after a high-speed shoot-out through the village and eyewitnesses reported seeing corpses hanging from the undercover soldiers' vehicle. The RUC denied there were fatalities but there was no doubt that a major confrontation had taken place.

On 3 March 1991 the UVF renewed their offensive by striking in Cappagh again with an attack on a republican bar. Four men were shot dead in what Republicans at first claimed was a random sectarian attack. Three of the men were ambushed as they drove into the car park. One of the UVF gunmen then poked a muzzle through a toilet window and fired blind into the interior, killing the fourth victim, Thomas Armstrong. Thirteen months later the IRA acknowledged that the three men in the car, John Quinn, Malcolm Nugent and Dwayne O'Donnell, were all members of the Tyrone Brigade.

For the East Tyrone Brigade leadership, Cappagh was the turning point. Although the IRA maintained the fiction that the attack was a random assault, the UVF had assassinated three Volunteers right in the midst of Tyrone's republican heartland. The UVF were simply stating the truth when they claimed the shootings were a direct hit on the 'IRA's command structure' and the greatest single blow the Loyalists had ever inflicted on their republican adversaries. The IRA did not believe the Loyalists could have carried out the attack without the help of the security forces. The IRA's reasoning ran as follows: Cappagh is a physically remote village in the Tyrone hinterlands and the only way in or out is through seven miles of unmarked and unlit country lanes; the area is normally subjected to intensive patrolling by the security forces and locals claimed that in the week prior to the killings security force activity had actually been stepped up; the IRA men's car was a recent acquisition and would not have been immediately identifiable as belonging to the driver John Quinn. And yet the UVF squad were waiting in the car park of Boyle's Bar for that exact car to pull up. The UVF's intelligence was highly accurate. In order to make the hit and escape, the IRA leadership believed the UVF shooters had to be assured of a clear 'run-back' or escape route from the security forces.

The IRA's revenge was not long in coming. On 9 April 1991 a ten-man unit, in an elaborate operation, murdered Derek Ferguson, a cousin of the local hardline Unionist MP Reverend William McCrea. The IRA claimed that Mr Ferguson, a close friend of Leslie Dallas, was a member of the local UVF, although the claim was denied by his family. According to republican sources, Mr Ferguson was allegedly seen in the car used in the Battery Bar attack, and later found burnt out. Such evidence was enough in the IRA's eyes to seal Mr Ferguson's death warrant.

On the last day of May 1991 the IRA launched their biggest assault ever on an Army installation by rolling a lorry packed with two thousand pounds of explosives into the perimeter wall of Glenanne UDR Barracks in nearby County Armagh. The huge bomb, one of the largest ever constructed in Northern Ireland, destroyed the base and killed three UDR men.

The next operation of the IRA's war in Tyrone was shattered by the SAS ambush in Coagh. The IRA's plan had been to kill the part-time UDR soldier, notoriously hated and feared by the local nationalist community because of his threats to Catholics at road checkpoints. His assassination had a three-fold purpose: to kill another UDR soldier; to hit the security force contractors by killing one of their employees; and to strike at the UVF by demonstrating the power of the IRA to kill their alleged associate right in the heart of their stronghold. All three strands of the war would have come together in one operation.

But the IRA's 'flying column' was betrayed, almost certainly by an informer within their own ranks. The UDR man's presence at the pick-up point had been a bait to lure Ryan and McNally across the border and into an ambush. Tony Doris and his IRA companions drove into a carefully prepared SAS trap. As the IRA car passed a pre-determined spot in Coagh's main square, an SAS soldier fired the first of two hundred high-velocity rounds into the target. Tony Doris died in the hail of gunfire.

Tony's ten-mile journey that began in republican Meenagh Park ended in Protestant Coagh, but the patient lessons to the British and the Protestants continued. Other Volunteers soon picked up from where he had left off. Two months later, on 6 August 1991, near Cappagh, the IRA murdered another alleged leader of the UVF in mid-Ulster, ex-UDR man Eric Boyd, as he drove home from work. The IRA's claim was again denied by the victim's family. The Loyalists in turn then struck back by assassinating another local Sinn Fein councillor, Bernard O'Hagan, as he arrived for work as a lecturer in Magherafelt on 16 September 1991. In January 1992 the IRA used a landmine to blow up what they believed was a Henry Brothers' work's van, full of construction workers returning home from a job on an Army base. The van belonged to a different security force construction firm but eight workers were killed. In February four IRA Volunteers were ambushed and killed by the SAS after fruitlessly launching a heavy machine-gun assault against the strongly reinforced walls of Coalisland's military base. The UVF killed a couple more Catholics . . . the IRA killed some more UDR men and attempted to kill a couple of UVF men . . . the familiar pattern of the Troubles' way of death kept churning on.

The East Tyrone Brigade's campaign appeared chaotic; it sprawled over hundreds of square miles of Northern Ireland, including parts of the two adjacent counties. The targets shifted haphazardly, from the killing of UDR men to the bombing of British Army barracks, from the murder of building contractors or workers to the assassination of Loyalist paramilitaries. To try to understand the IRA's rationale I asked a Sinn Fein contact to arrange a meeting with the leaders of the Tyrone Brigade. He put me in touch with an intermediary and we drove to a small village in the Tyrone hills where a meeting of the National Graves Association, the republican organization that looks after IRA Volunteers' graves, was taking place. Outside the small community hall my intermediary chatted to a young man I shall call Fergus. Fergus was in his twenties and he was tall and lean, and dressed in poor farmworker's clothes with steel-capped boots; he looked as if he had just stepped down from a tractor. He was nervous and fidgety, and as my intermediary introduced me, Fergus cut across the conversation, ignoring me, saying he had spotted a UDR man driving a concrete lorry near a local village that morning. The information itself was innocuous, in another country it could have been village gossip, but Fergus's intensity gave it a sense of menace; the intelligence groundwork for another murder was being initiated. My intermediary reintroduced me and the conversation faltered as Fergus became aware that I was an outsider.

After a few minutes I was led into an Irish sitting room with an oilcloth-covered table and a line of chairs around the walls to wait as my intermediary arranged the meeting. There was, as there always is in these kinds of things, much toing and froing; strange men appeared at the door, looked at me as if I was an exotic animal, then disappeared, and there were whispered conversations and then silence. I passed the time chatting to two young men who were waiting for the National Graves Association meeting to begin. The UDR, they told me, were bigoted, black-hearted Protestants who just two days before had abused Martin McCaughey's mother and refused to call an ambulance when she had collapsed at a roadblock. They named individual UDR men who had threatened to kill them after stopping them at roadblocks near the village. It seemed that every act against the villagers, the Republicans, was absorbed into a predetermined framework of perceived oppression and remembered litany of the other side's atrocities: how no one did anything about the killing of innocent Catholics; how their oppressors were immune from the law; how their oppressors were the so-called law. One of the young men solemnly produced a brown paper bag containing a small cracked ceramic plate showing the face of a man and held it out to me as if to symbolize the depths of their oppression. The plaque was from the headstone of Eugene Kelly, a twenty-six-year-old IRA Volunteer killed by the SAS in the 1987 Loughgall ambush, and as the young men explained, it was the second time it had been smashed by patrolling British soldiers in an act of spite. Any awareness of the repercussions from the murders carried out by Eugene Kelly or the IRA did not exist in that room. But there was something in the atmosphere of the village, the unlit streets and the cloistered talk of conspirators, that I had only ever encountered once before, in the depths of the anarchy of Afghanistan: a sense that, outside, enemies were lurking and the night was hostile. As we talked I had taken notes and the young men had given me their names, but as I was later leaving one of them ran up to me and begged me not to identify him. He was genuinely afraid.

Fergus came into the room and picked up a chair. In my nervousness I stood up, in an exaggerated gesture of politeness, to help him but he waved me aside, sheepishly mumbling a token of thanks, and left without looking at me. My intermediary returned and I was asked to go to a room upstairs; it was a small shabby bedroom with blankets and a cheap quilt on the bed. I was instructed to sit on a chair facing the ugly wallpapered wall with my back to the door. Behind, from outside the door, I could hear the sounds of other doors closing and the noise of footsteps on the stairs. After a minute the room door opened and two men entered. From the corner of my eye I could see that one of them had a pillowcase over his head. On the instructions of the other voice, who asked me to stand up, the pillowcase man patted me down for weapons and then, embarrassed at this unfamiliar physical intrusion on a stranger, apologized. I recognized his voice – it was Fergus. The older voice did the introductions.

'We are the leaders of the East Tyrone Brigade of the Provisional IRA,' he said flatly.

I never saw his face. It was less of an interview and more of a lecture. The older man, who did most of the talking, was hard, unrelenting, full of command; the voice was intelligent, direct, confident, dismissive of theoretics – the voice of a self-educated sergeant. It was a voice to be afraid of, a voice that I thought had not hesitated, and would not hesitate, to order the death of its enemies.

Fergus's voice was softer, more unsure and more dangerous; it was a voice that needed constantly to prove itself, assert itself amongst harder men. It was the voice of a younger executive who wanted, regardless of the costs to others, to get ahead. Like lots of men in his position, Fergus seemed to lack imagination; his vision was narrowly focused on the rigid certainties of his time and his place.

I sat in the chair listening as they sometimes coldly, sometimes passionately, described a world of IRA bombings, murder campaigns, SAS ambushes, landmine attacks, Loyalist assassins, military occupation and the Henry Brothers. Like their Defender predecessors they came from a small world. They were Tyrone men fighting to free *this* piece of green earth from alien English domination; Belfast was forty-two miles away and was another country. Tyrone had always been a 'fighting county' they said, and always would be until the Brits left. When they spoke of 'the Brits' it was as if they were describing some monstrous alien virus, a virus that had no feeling but whose tentacles, MI5, the RUC, the SAS, the Army, had to be attacked and its constituent cells, British Army soldiers/collaborators, killed.

The older man was angry and a torrent of complaint about how the IRA was misrepresented as cowards for refusing to fight the British Army in the open or how Republicans were labelled sectarian killers poured out of him.

'We have our aim. Our aim is to get the British out of Ireland

and we will not be deflected into a war with Protestants,' he said.

'If we wanted to shoot Protestants, sure there are thousands of them,' countered Fergus.

'Ideally we want to hit the British Army. Hitting them is better. But they are harder to hit now because they rarely leave their barracks so we have to settle for RUC or UDR men . . . It's all the same in end.'

'But religion has got nothing to do with it,' said Fergus. 'If they were Catholics we would still be shooting them.' He paused as if waiting confirmation on some point. 'We've shot Catholic RUC men before.'

The other voice grunted assent.

I tried to ask questions about Tony's career as an IRA Volunteer but was quickly rebuffed.

'We never talk about things like that. Let's just say all three of them were dedicated Volunteers. A lot of people owe their lives to them three boys, they were a flying column,' said the older man.

'Some of the Coagh villagers say that the men who killed Dallas fired rounds into the air to celebrate and whooped with triumph as they left the village,' I ventured. The claim made him angrier still.

'They don't know what they are fucking talking about. We are not a sectarian force. The boys fired two shots to clear the weapons and the so-called whoop was just one of them shouting: "Drive on to fuck." It was just the adrenalin. This talk is just done to blacken the name of the IRA.

'We have no problems with Protestants. They are a very easy people to talk to, although many of them have a false sense of security because they are propped up by the British. There are now even unemployed Protestants.'

Fergus was more unsure. 'The Protestants have all the best jobs in Cookstown. They get to work inside . . . in the factories,' his voice betraying a heightened sense of grievance.

After the SAS Coagh ambush the IRA had abducted a

Catholic man from Coagh and interrogated him as a suspected informer. The man survived and was released after convincing the Brigade's interrogators he was innocent. I asked if the abducted man had been questioned as part of the IRA investigation into Tony's death.

Again the older man replied. 'We can say that it was a military target, that's enough. The other man was arrested for a different matter,' he added, lying thinly.

'What about Henry Brothers?'

'Let's get one thing straight. No British soldier is going to come here, beat the shit out of our people and then trot back at night to a nice warm barracks for a pint and a game of darts. We will beat the shit out of them by blowing up those barracks. Now it can take us months, sometimes years, for us to blow them up, so we are not going to allow the Brits to rebuild them overnight.'

Whenever the IRA leaders spoke of Henry Brothers it was with hatred; it filled the dingy room. It was so cold and ancient it could have filled the universe.

'Henry Brothers are collaborating in the oppression of the nationalist people by taking part in that work, just as the British Crown is forcing those workers to prostitute themselves because of the huge money involved. They are corrupting the people. They have been warned countless times to stop.'

Suddenly Fergus broke in. 'These people have been warned and they know the risks but they will not stop. If you shoot them, they will stop, just like UDR sergeant Mr Jameson.'

Fergus's voice gloated over the surface of the words 'Mr Jameson' and in that second I knew he was the UDR man's killer. The voice took pleasure from the memory and in the opportunity to remind his superior of his past deed.

'We are constantly misrepresented,' the older man continued. 'Every time we attack a police station we are accused of endangering the lives of civilians. But if the British Army did not build their bases next to chapels and schools, that would not happen. They say we are scared to fight them in the open but if they build their bases in the open we'll see who'll fight in the open then.'

Throughout the interview the older man's tone had been overbearing; now it turned threatening. 'Right, we've answered enough of your questions, now you'll answer some of ours. Have you met the UVF in Coagh?'

'I haven't had a chance to speak to them yet,' I answered through a dry throat.

'What about the RUC?'

'They only talk to their pet journalists.'

'So what have you heard about our Volunteer's death?'

'Nothing much . . . just some talk about the fourth member of the team.'

His voice grew urgent. 'The fourth man!'

'The gossip is the SAS watched them dig up the weapons.'

There was a long pause.

'Did they say who this man was?'

'They mentioned a name, Malloy . . . Malone . . .'

'Malone!'

'Maybe that's right,' I volunteered.

Without realizing it, I had uttered the name of a notorious local IRA men whom Tyrone Protestants believed was the major IRA player in their midst. Maybe the information was accurate; I had no way of knowing. I was just repeating blindly a name mentioned to me. But my two IRA interrogators seemed dumbstruck by the revelation. By now I was wanting out of the room and wanting these questions to end. But I did not feel it was in my power to leave.

There was another long silence which I broke. 'I don't know any more.'

'This meeting is over. Give us a few minutes to clear the area.'

They left abruptly and once again I heard through the walls the sounds of people moving in other rooms. I waited for my intermediary to rescue me. When no one came I got up and walked down the stairs. I found him in the downstairs room and greeted him like a long-lost childhood friend. I was anxious to leave; I had briefly been the subject of a hostile interrogation by the East Tyrone Brigade and it had been a frightening experience.

There was little said in the interview that I did not already know. What was different was the feeling: beneath the words was a tightly wound rage. It was a rage against the British and their Protestant Planters that reached back across the centuries; it was a rage that believed Protestants still held the best jobs, the best land and the best houses; it was a rage that would never end until the balance of political power in Northern Ireland fundamentally shifted from the Protestant community or the British withdrew.

For the protagonists, like Tony and Fergus, the IRA's war was a rolling campaign against powerful and dangerous enemies. Ambush at the hands of unseen assassins lurked around every corner; no one was safe and no group entirely in control. Each death carried its own chain of reaction and counter-reaction; the UVF's pinpoint hit in Cappagh convinced the IRA that British Intelligence was directing the Loyalist paramilitary campaign; by killing Gibson the IRA closed off a whole sector of council jobs for part-time UDR men and drove home the message that no off-duty UDR man was safe anywhere in a republican area; by bombing the workers' coach the IRA frightened anyone who sold petrol to an off-duty policeman; by hitting Tony Doris in a pre-arranged ambush, British Intelligence provoked a paranoid hunt for an informer within the IRA's ranks.

The East Tyrone Brigade were not an army but a band, a company of latter-day woodkernes, of ordinary farmworkers, mechanics, tractor drivers, the unemployed, the odd school-teacher, inheritors of the dispossession, who gathered together to kill particular known enemies like Edward Gibson, Thomas

Jameson and Harry Henry. The IRA were not waging war but a sporadic assassination campaign in the tiny rural communities of Tyrone to attack the enemy within their midst. There was no grand strategy, no master plan, just an endless going-on, a limitless petty attrition. The East Tyrone Brigade set only parts of the agenda; they too were subjected to the forces of the British Crown and the human frailty of the informers within their own ranks. The interplay of these disparate forces did not change the underlying realities; in their hearts the IRA's Volunteers saw themselves as defenders. It did not matter that there could never be a military victory. 'Standing up to the British', standing up to the Protestants by bombing and killing, served its own purpose by maintaining the spirit, the very possibility, of resistance in the face of an overwhelming enemy.

Before I left Tyrone, I drove down to the twelfth-century cross of Ardboe on the Lough, where Ned Gibson's killers abandoned their getaway car and where Pete Ryan is now buried in the graveyard. It is the site of an ancient monastery and the Christian monks had carved biblical parables, the Sacrifice of Isaac and Daniel amongst the Lions, into the cross's face. The water laps the shoreline and far off across the Lough you can just make out the lights of Belfast. It is a wild and haunting place.

On the other side of the graveyard, across the mound of plastic flowers that marks Pete Ryan's grave, is a wishing tree. It is the local custom to take a coin, hammer it into the trunk and make a wish. The wishing tree of the Cross of Ardboe is now studded with hundreds, thousands, of coins – the wishers have killed the tree. In the midst of the wild fecundity of Tyrone's green fields, its branches are bare and sterile. Its limbs have been blackened by the poisonous metal that has pierced its flesh in a thousand mutilating incisions, just as the soil of Tyrone has poisoned the hearts of men.

NOTES

1. Letters of 11 May 1615 from Derry. George Canning, as quoted in *An Historical Account of the Plantation of Ulster* by Rev George Hill, M'Caw, Stevenson & Orr, Belfast, 1877, p. 36.

2. The main RUC interrogation centre in Northern Ireland where republican suspects were held and interrogated under the Prevention of Terrorism Act.

3. Michael Stone was a notorious Loyalist gunman who attacked three thousand republican mourners at a Belfast funeral. See Chapter 3.

4. Letter of 16 May 1615, from Derry. George Canning as quoted in Hill, ibid., p. 40.

3

BROTHERS

At 7.25 pm on 12 February 1989 a masked gunman of the Ulster Freedom Fighters (UFF) smashed through the front door of Northern Irish defence lawyer Patrick Finucane's home and murdered him in front of his wife and three children. The family, including nine-year-old John and teenagers Catherine and Michael, were sitting down for their Sunday evening meal when they heard the crash of breaking glass from their hallway. Finucane and his wife Geraldine jumped up from the kitchen table and opened the glass door which separated the kitchen from the hallway. Halfway down the hall they saw a gunman, dressed in black and wearing a camouflage jacket, striding towards them with a gun in his hand. Finucane threw himself against the glass door in an abortive attempt to keep the gunman out. At the same moment the gunman opened fire, shattering the glass and hitting Finucane in the chest and stomach. Pat Finucane fell back on to the kitchen floor, lying face up. The killer then entered the kitchen and finished off his target at close range, firing twelve rounds into Finucane's head and neck as Geraldine and Catherine began screaming and the youngest child John looked on in bewildered silence. 'He was very cold, cool, methodical. I definitely got the impression that this was not the first time he had done this,' said Geraldine, who was hit in the ankle by a ricocheting bullet. The gunman left and drove off in a hijacked taxi later found abandoned near the loyalist Shankill Road district.

'At about 7.30 I got the phone call from Geraldine. She was hysterical, crying,' said Seamus, Patrick Finucane's younger brother.

I'm not too sure if she knew at that stage he was dead, I think she did. I dropped everything. When we got there the street was sealed off but I just ran up through. I ended up nearly fighting with the RUC at the door, they were not going to let me in. They were using the family phone for communications and they had their radios in their hands. There was us, Pat's family, wanting to make phone calls and us waiting on phone calls and the cops are using the phone. I told them to stop using it. Once they had the SOCO team in, I went in and identified the body. I knew there and then that whoever had shot Pat had done it before. Pat had one [bullet] in the forehead. He was hit fourteen times altogether, five times in the head. It looked very professional and clinical.

Patrick Finucane was not a typical victim of the Troubles. He lived in a prosperous area of Belfast and had a lucrative career as a founder-partner of the successful legal firm, Madden and Finucane, which specialized in criminal law. He was a graduate of Ireland's most prestigious university, Trinity College, Dublin, and had an international reputation. He had two legal test cases against the British Government before the European Commission on Human Rights in Strasbourg at the time of his death and had spoken at legal rights conferences in America and Europe. He was not, like Judge Doyle, an official of the Crown in Ireland, nor was he active in a paramilitary organization, nor was he a random Catholic victim of Protestant paramilitaries. He was the first defence lawyer to be killed in Northern Ireland.

Three weeks before Finucane's murder the Parliamentary Under-Secretary of State for the British Home Office, Douglas Hogg MP, told the House of Commons: 'There are in Northern

Ireland a number of solicitors who are unduly sympathetic to the cause of the IRA.' Hogg did not name these 'sympathetic' solicitors but in the tiny world of the Northern Irish criminal courts it was obvious at whom Hogg's threats were directed – Patrick Finucane. Geraldine said:

> I was frightened of Hogg's comments and so was Pat. He was visibly upset. We had not taken the threats so seriously before but now they took on a whole new meaning. We had security around the house but it was security against burglars not assassins. We thought about applying for firearms but that was a big step. There was only three weeks between Hogg's statement and Pat being shot. When you are living a busy life and you are both at work and the kids, three weeks is just a flash.

Hogg's statement and Finucane's subsequent murder produced a host of conspiracy theories linking Britain's domestic intelligence service, MI5, with the killing. Later, at the trial of a Crown agent in the Northern Irish courts, it was revealed that British Military Intelligence did have a high-level spy at the heart of the UFF and was manipulating the organization's targets. Outside the courtroom it was further alleged that the spy, Brian Nelson, had supplied the head of the UFF's active service unit with intelligence material on the lawyer and had allegedly driven the assassin on a dummy run to reconnoitre the Finucane household. The plan had been to kill both Finucane brothers – 'the Provo with qualifications' (Pat) and the 'Provo bomber' (Seamus) – as they met for their regular Sunday night dinner. No warning of the impending attack was ever passed on to the Finucane brothers and it appears that members of Britain's intelligence forces played a role in Finucane's killing. But Nelson's testimony only revealed the mechanics of assassination, not the rationale for the murder of Pat Finucane.

The group who killed him, the UFF – a cover name for the

then legal Ulster Defence Association – claimed Finucane was 'an officer in the IRA' who was murdered as part of their 'inevitable retaliation' for attacks by the IRA on Loyalists 'and those members of the security forces who share their lunch with them'. The UFF allegation was strenuously denied by Finucane's close legal partner and friend Peter Madden and greeted with scepticism by journalists and lawyers in Belfast. Said Peter Madden:

> Pat expressed his disapproval of the system by challenging it in a court of law. He was concerned that the criminal justice system was being used as a weapon in a battle to classify a violent political uprising as a criminal conspiracy. But he wasn't someone who would go out and make political statements. He wasn't a member of Sinn Fein. He was very professional about the way he voiced his disapproval of the Diplock system [special juryless courts that tried IRA suspects] and would only have done so at legal conferences and the like.

The UFF did not provide any evidence to substantiate their allegation, but then they did not need to; the only justification necessary in the Troubles was the sanction of your own community. In loyalist eyes, Patrick Finucane was guilty: guilty of being the brother of two well-known IRA Volunteers, Seamus and Dermot, and guilty of being the brother of a dead IRA Volunteer, John; guilty of defending too many IRA Volunteers successfully in the courts; guilty of having too high a profile; and guilty of being a smart Fenian.

Finucane's murder was investigated and condemned by a number of international civil rights organizations. There were reports from the New York-based Lawyer's Committee for Human Rights, from Amnesty International and from the London-based civil rights pressure group, Liberty. The investigators found that Finucane was not the only defence lawyer to complain that the security forces had told clients during police interrogations that 'their lawyer was a Provo bastard who they were going to get'. All the reports concluded that RUC interrogators systematically threatened the lives of defence lawyers appointed to represent paramilitary suspects.[1]

The reports merely confirmed the obvious: that the legal system in Northern Ireland was deeply compromised by the Troubles, and its investigative and court procedures distorted in favour of the Crown. Dissent in Ulster has always been viewed as a threat to the state, and Finucane's work in continually challenging legal statutes, seeking judicial reviews of inquest procedures or representing IRA clients in prominent trials was perceived as an act of rebellion. Finucane's killers and his many enemies in the police and the British Army did not recognize any division between his professional conduct and his private beliefs and personal relationships. They saw no difference between being an IRA man's brother, defending IRA men and being an IRA man. 'Even I have got to admit that Pat's killing was a good hit,' says Seamus.

I knew Pat Finucane. He was a good person who led a frenetic life trying to help people, either innocent or guilty, who were being overwhelmed by a very powerful prosecution machine. He was a tall, lanky man who held his own counsel; if you asked a question he would pause a little before replying, as if debating precisely how much he should tell you or what sort of angle he should take. Like a good lawyer his face never betrayed his thoughts, a trait I was later to discover he shared with his youngest IRA Volunteer brother Dermot.

In 1979 Pat Finucane and Peter Madden formed the legal partnership, Madden and Finucane. Pat's background and his family's reputation in republican circles were instrumental in attracting a steady stream of republican clients accused of paramilitary offences, but the firm also had Loyalist clients and did not discriminate by religion or politics as a basis for representation. The firm specialized in what were known in

Northern Ireland as Scheduled Offences under the emergency power legislation of the Troubles and it quickly gained a reputation for pioneering a variety of legal devices to win compensation for or defend its clients' interests against the authorities. The compensation claims were almost always directed at the security forces, particularly the RUC, on the grounds of alleged mistreatment whilst in police custody or for false imprisonment, and the total compensation figure ran to many hundreds of thousands of pounds.

'Pat revolutionized the whole detention system, the whole prison system. He took habeas corpus actions in the courts and won them and forced the police to produce prisoners in court who were being beaten up in police custody. He was successful in a whole range of cases that were embarrassing for the British Government but were unknown outside legal circles,' said Peter Madden as we sat in his law offices.

Pat first became publicly known in 1981 when he represented the dying Bobby Sands during his hunger strike and was repeatedly interviewed on television about his client. He also represented clients in a string of high-profile cases involving alleged shoot-to-kill tactics by the authorities, where IRA suspects were killed by members of the security forces in disputed circumstances. Sinn Fein hired him to represent one of their councillors in a test case in 1988 to challenge the legality of the British Home Secretary's decision to ban interviews with Sinn Fein members from television and radio.

Pat never hid himself away behind secretaries or answering machines; his home phone number and address were listed in the Belfast telephone book. The family's evenings were often interrupted by desperate calls from suspects in police custody requesting Pat's attendance at the interrogation centre. To cope with the calls, Geraldine Finucane bought an ansaphone but her husband frequently turned it off; Pat liked the calls and liked to be needed.

Geraldine had first met Pat at Trinity College when they were students together in 1968. It was a middle-class Belfast

Protestant girl meets working-class Belfast Catholic football
player type of romance that resulted in what is still known in
Ulster as a 'mixed marriage'. The couple met at a sports fixture
where Pat, a keen and almost professionally skilled soccer
player, was representing one of the University teams. Pat, his
wife says, never forgot the sacrifices his family made to send
him to what was still in the 1960s the cultural citadel of
Ireland's Protestant Ascendancy, but his charm and sporting
abilities made him a popular student. The couple married in
1970 and after toying with the idea of emigrating to the States
or London, returned to live in Belfast. At first Pat had been
unsure what career to undertake; he had studied philosophy
and English, and it was some time before he chose law, but he
quickly established that it was his métier. 'Pat wanted to make
his mark. He enjoyed the law. In Pat's view the law was there
for everyone to use,' said Geraldine.

Pat Finucane was not a saint. His legal career in later years
was both personally and financially rewarding by the modest
standards of the Northern Irish Bar. He enjoyed the trappings
of wealth and success; he chose to live in the comfortable but
dangerous leafy lanes of middle-class North Belfast away from
the squalor and safety of his clients' communities. In the early
years of his marriage as he studied for his legal articles, the
couple had been forced to live in the grim republican Lenadoon
district and endure the barricades and foot patrols of military
occupation. 'Pat once told me that he "didn't want to walk
around with empty pockets". He remembered that from his
childhood, walking around with empty pockets. So when we
had money he enjoyed it, he enjoyed the space in the house,
meals out and holidays, even though it would take him a week
to wind down,' recalled Geraldine.

I first met Pat in the early eighties when the Northern Irish
legal authorities were staging large trials against paramilitary
defendants on the uncorroborated statements of turned paramilitaries known as supergrasses, who were given immunity
from prosecution and a new identity overseas in return for

testifying against their former comrades. The trials were held in Belfast's high-security Crumlin Road Courthouse with its anti-rocket wire fences, armed guards, metal detectors, body searches and identification procedures that required all visitors to give their names and addresses to two separate squads of RUC men. In the vast high-ceilinged courtroom, green-uniformed RUC men sat at the end of each bench in the public gallery at the back of the court and filled all the front rows. The dock of the court, which often contained forty defendants, was surrounded by a human wall of blue-uniformed prison officers, whilst in front of them rows and rows of black-gowned bewigged barristers fiddled with their papers; the redundant jury box was packed with the sun-tanned faces of Ulster's well-paid secret policemen from RUC Special Branch. The top of the court was dominated by the vivid scarlet splodge of the judge's robes and the wigged man within them, who under the juryless Northern Irish Diplock court system was the sole arbiter of guilt and innocence. These forbidding show trials were largely ignored by the British media and the only outsiders who regularly attended court were a few local journalists and the prisoners' relatives, hemmed in by the green uniforms of the RUC men.

The term 'supergrass trial' was a misnomer because what was taking place was not one but many separate trials of different defendants on totally unrelated charges compressed into one set of judicial proceedings. In one case some defendants were jointly charged with conspiring to murder members of the security forces but also faced separate charges of conspiring to murder each other as part of an alleged dispute within their paramilitary organization. Some supergrass charges were trivial – such as failing to disclose information about an act of terrorism, which normally carried a maximum six-month sentence. But others were deadly serious – murder, attempted murder, causing explosions – all of which could carry life sentences. In Britain, such serious charges would have necessitated a separate trial over many days for each individual defendant. Yet within one morning I listened to a supergrass relate to the court the material evidence for a murder charge – it took twenty minutes. The only common element in the proceedings was the evidence of the supergrass and the two armed Special Branch men who flanked the witness box whenever the informer testified. Many of the defendants, both Loyalist and Republican paramilitaries, were probably guilty of something but it was impossible to distinguish truth from falsehood in the mouth of a coached witness whose main concern was pleasing his RUC masters by convicting as many of his former comrades as possible.

Pat fought the supergrass trials both as a lawyer and as a legal expert in the media. He was generous to journalists with his hard-pressed time and was always ready to explain an abstruse legal point. His cool and detached manner never entirely concealed the depth of his opposition and dismay at the abuse of legal procedure by the authorities. Many of the supergrasses had dubious criminal records and a proven propensity to lie about the seriousness of their own involvement in the crimes they accused their former comrades of participating in. A number of Finucane's clients were indicted on charges so vague and all-encompassing they were impossible to refute. It was not uncommon for a defendant to be accused of conspiring with persons unknown to murder persons unknown between the dates of 1 January 1977 and 31 December 1977. 'The standard of evidence the cops are using,' Pat told me as we sat in a Belfast solicitors' club one evening, 'is akin to me and you having this conversation and then in the morning the police breaking your door down at 5 am and charging you with conspiracy to murder the Lord Chief Justice on the basis that I said you did that. It's all verbal. There is no material evidence, no proof, to back up these claims. But that doesn't seem to stop the cops arresting dozens of people.' Eventually the Northern Ireland Court of Appeal agreed with Pat Finucane, overturning all convictions based on the sole evidence of supergrasses.

Pat always came across as someone who genuinely cared

about his clients. Some of the supergrass defendants were imprisoned for up to four years as they awaited trial on charges that were continually chopped and altered as different informers added to or retracted from their statements. This judicial delay was also bitterly criticized by Pat as a form of internment on remand. In our many conversations together I became convinced that if I ever got into legal trouble in Northern Ireland, Pat was the best lawyer I could hope for.

When word of his death came on the Monday morning news, I was filled with the futile anger that all the Troubles' deaths brought. I was angry at his killers, angry at Douglas Hogg for his arrogance and apparently casual licence with someone else's life, and angry at the police and intelligence services who set Pat up and who must have welcomed his death.

Pat Finucane had touched a lot of lives and my own grief was a pale shadow of that felt by his family and friends. Four years after his killing, I went to interview his partner in Madden and Finucane in the same suites of offices from where Pat had worked. The shabby office seemed even more run-down than it was in Pat's time. Old files tied up with fading pink ribbon littered desks and filing cabinets. It's hard to judge these things, but there was a mood of defeat and resignation in the air. Pat's killing had hit Peter Madden hard; the spirit of what once had been Northern Ireland's most creative and crusading legal firm had been savaged. Pat had been the star, the fighter, Peter had been the accountant, the office manager, the solid bottom in the firm; they had made a good team.

Peter Madden is a clever, dependable man, a lawyer not given to fanciful construction, but it is his firm belief that his partner was murdered on the orders of the British Government. When I asked Peter Madden to talk about Pat's assassination, he stopped and told me: 'I don't like to talk about it.' And then this moderate man began to cry at his desk in memory of Patrick Finucane.

*

Seamus Finucane was right: killing Pat was a good hit because Pat was a far greater danger to the Crown than any individual IRA man. Pat Finucane was a living symbol of what it was possible for someone from the underclass in Northern Ireland to become. His parents were working class, his brothers were in the IRA, but he was a lawyer, a man with standing and position, someone who could not easily be pushed around, someone who could challenge and humble the judges and policemen in the courts, someone whom his community could turn to for help and someone who had not turned his back on the Republican cause. Pat Finucane was a rebel in a courtroom and his weapons were the Crown's own laws. Killing him drew a new, more circumscribed, limit around the nature of acceptable legal opposition in Northern Ireland; after Pat, defence lawyers were also 'legitimate targets'.

Pat Finucane's life and death, like his brothers' lives in the IRA, was a creation of the Troubles. His story is not the story of an individual but a tale of brothers, of a family, caught up in catastrophe and living or dying in its aftermath.

Belfast is a small city. It was three miles from the place on the loyalist Shankill Road where Finucane's assassins hijacked the taxi to his home at Fortwilliam Drive where he was shot. The killers' route would have taken them along the Shankill past a small road, Percy Street, and its abandoned lots, that runs towards the neighbouring Catholic district of the Falls. The rationale for the UFF's journey of murder on that winter's evening in 1989 started here twenty years before on the very night Ulster's Troubles began again.

In August 1969 the Northern Irish state, founded in 1922 with the partition of Ireland, collapsed in the flames of communal riots. The initial flashpoint was Derry, where a Protestant march near a Catholic area provoked the two-day riot that became known as the Battle of the Bogside. Northern Ireland's security forces were driven to the point of collapse, the Stormont Government lost control and British Army troops had to be called in to restore order. But by then it was too late to preserve Ulster's Unionist state; the rioting spread to Belfast where the majority Protestant working-class population vented their rage on the far smaller Catholic community. Whole streets were burnt out and thousands of Catholic families made homeless as Protestant mobs, with the support of an ill-trained B-Special police reserve, rampaged unchecked through the streets, redrawing territorial divisions and expelling the traditional enemy.[2]

For one family, the Finucanes of Percy Street, on the wrong side of the unofficial boundary between the Protestants of the Shankill and the Catholics of the Falls Road, the night of 14 August 1969 would for ever change their lives as their home and the homes of Catholic neighbours were attacked and fire-bombed. The family were forced to become refugees in their own city. Percy Street was the fountainhead from which the family's future sprang, a future that inflicted injury and death upon the Finucane family and inflicted death and injury upon the family's enemies. As they grew to manhood, John, Seamus and Dermot were each in turn to join a revived IRA and forge a place close to the most dramatic and violent events of the next twenty years. That day of 14 August 1969 was the beginning of a cycle of violence that would leave two of the brothers dead and result in two other brothers spending decades in prison. Soldiers and policemen would be shot, some would be killed, and civilians would be injured as the Finucane brothers struck back again and again at the Crown in Ulster.

In the spring of 1968 forty-eight-year-old Patrick Finucane (senior), his wife Kathleen and their eight children had moved into No. 78 Percy Street. It was a large five-bedroomed house, a mansion by the grim standards of Catholic West Belfast, which had some of the poorest social housing in Western Europe. The family of seven boys, Pat, John, Liam, Gerard, Seamus, Martin and Dermot, and one girl, Rosaleen, quickly settled into what was a religiously mixed neighbourhood on the boundaries of Shankill Road. 'We moved from Sevastopol Street off the Falls Road,' said the second youngest brother, Martin Finucane, who was nine in 1968.

> Sevastopol Street was damp and cramped, there were four or five kids to a bed, but in Percy Street, Dermot, Seamus and I had our own room, we even had our own beds for instance. It was great. Percy Street had a parlour, its own living-room, a kitchen and then upstairs two rooms on the first floor, three or four rooms on the second floor and then there was two attics. My mother was a housewife and my father worked in Andrew's Flour Mill, which was opposite the house. We inherited the house from my father's sister, who died, and when we moved in the neighbours were great. But being so young I did not realize that the neighbours that were helping us were Catholic. All the people to the right of us going towards the Shankill were all Protestant.

The Finucanes were not Republicans. The family's father, Patrick, was a devout Catholic who was not interested in politics. 'My father was a daily communicant. He went to Mass before he went to work and every Sunday we were bathed, washed and frogmarched off to church. Every night we would sit down and do the rosary. If anyone knocked on the door no one answered until the rosary was finished. We were not allowed to go out and play. My Da always used to say, "The family that says the rosary together, stays together."'

The higher Catholic birth rate and the pressure on West Belfast's limited housing stock made it inevitable that Catholic families in the relatively peaceful sixties would encroach on former Protestant territory. Percy Street was part of the new front-line and exposed the Finucane children to hitherto unknown dangers. 'We were playing hurley [an Irish ball game] with sticks and a ball in the street in Percy Street and these big boys came along and the next minute they got leathered into us. They started to kick the shit out of us. We were kids,

Dermot was eight and I was ten, Seamus was eleven. They started calling us "Fenian bastards". We did not have a clue what Fenians were and then when they were going away they shouted down to us "Fuck the Pope". We looked at one another and said, "Who is the Pope and what has he got to do with it?"' recalled Martin.

In August 1969 the simmering religious tension broke out into open sectarian warfare outside the Finucanes' front door. Said Seamus:

I was twelve at the time. On the opposite side of the road was a shop where the local Orange band used to practise and that was our first big clue that something big was happening. Up until then there had been the odd bit of trouble; you could not wear a Celtic scarf or play hurley and one weekend a crowd of drunken louts tried to break into the priest's house on the corner. But the difference in religion would not have been a big thing, I had Protestant friends.

A couple of people in the Orange band lived at the back of the shop and so when we saw them putting their shutters up during the day of August 14 we knew that there was going to be big trouble that night, things were going to be intensified. And then we noticed that the B-Specials were out on the corners patrolling and that they were getting tea and sandwiches. Naively, we also thought that it was just going to blow over in a couple of days. We had only lived in Percy Street for a year and my family had put a lot of money and effort into that house. We did not understand the danger we were in and so when it started we were petrified. My mother and father watched everything from their bedroom window and we sat on the stairs with hammers, hatchets and pokers, waiting on them coming in.

What the Finucane parents were watching as their children waited on the stairs was a mob rampaging down Percy Street looting and burning Catholic homes as they went. The Finucanes were trapped in their own home and cut off from the safety of the Falls Road by barricades designed to seal the Catholic district off from marauding Protestant rioters. Their oldest sons, Pat, eighteen, and John, sixteen, were unable to reach the house because of the mobs, the riots and the barricades. Outside, the enraged crowd screamed and chanted and attempted to smash their way through the shutters hastily erected by Mr Finucane. His parents' fear etched itself on nine-year-old Dermot's memory:

> I was just a kid watching the adults talk about life and death saying: 'The Loyalists have broken into such-and-such an area and they are burning everyone's homes out.' And you would be sitting there terrified, not making a sound; you were like a mouse, just listening. I had these visions that the Loyalists were going to overcome the barricades and I knew from the way that the adults were talking that we did not have enough to defend ourselves. I didn't really have a sense of who 'they' were. I just thought of them as crazy people, angry people, who would just come up and stab you to death, shoot you.

The Protestants first attacked the home of a local Republican. 'He had some sort of republican tie and the mob were doing their damnedest to break into his house and burn him out,' recalled Martin.

> Obviously some people in the street, some of our Protestant neighbours, knew of his connections. It was the same with us. They tried to smash the front door down to get in but my father's barricade prevented them. When that failed the windows were smashed and they tried to get in through them but the boards held. My father would go up the stairs to get a higher view of things to see what the crack was and that was when I was first aware that there were B-Specials outside and they were lined up on the opposite side of the road just watching what was going on.

By daylight the rioting had burnt itself out. Said Dermot:

Our whole street was engulfed in flames. In the morning I remember going out and seeing that the bottom half of Percy Street and all of neighbouring Divis Street was gutted, the houses burnt to shells. It looked as if two armies had been fighting each other. There was smoke from the remains of a double-decker bus and the street was full of smashed glass and bottles. I remember going out and seeing the Loyalists shooting down into the Falls area.

Martin recalled:

My brother John arrived back. He had been working in the Flour Mill on the night shift but had had to flee after he was shot at by a Loyalist sniper. He spent most of his night getting people out of nearby Beverley Street, he was helping them to flee. Our Pat was out too, probably rioting, but neither he nor John could not get anywhere near our house because that was where most of the Protestants were congregating.

The next morning we all got together to see what damage had been done and my parents were standing at the door and they came down and said: 'If youse ain't out tonight youse are getting burned out the night.' They were our neighbours, just neighbours. John then left and came back with a Land-Rover from the Flour Mill and took some of our stuff, but mostly it was just our bodies. Overnight we were refugees. The Falls Road was still blocked off by barricades so the only way out was through the Shankill. The troops were on the streets then and we had a British Army escort all the way.

Being the youngest, Dermot's memories are vaguer:

My mother and father told me that they tried to burn us out that night and some Protestant man was shouting: 'Don't burn it, it's too good a house. We'll keep it for one of our own.' The next morning we were out at four or five and all the houses were smouldering in the street and shops were burnt out and these women came over to us and said: 'Youse are next ya Fenian bastards. Get out tonight or else youse are next.' And we just went in, packed suitcases, and left, leaving furniture and everything else. Later on the house fell into the hands of the UDA. I remember seeing it in a UDA magazine. It was their headquarters for a bit, 78 Percy Street. The thing I most clearly remember is that the adults were terrified and as a child you picked that up. I can remember thinking we were going to be killed soon, our area would be overrun by hostile Indians.

Said Seamus:

We had our holidays booked for Butlins for the Saturday. It would have been the Friday morning we moved out, so we all decided to go there anyway as we did not get that many holidays. My aunt got transport and went over to the house to rescue our possessions. When she arrived she found our neighbours brazenly walking out of the house with the spin-drier and clothes. She grabbed our things back. At the same time my father had to give up his job in the mill because of the threats alleging that he was a member of the IRA, which was laughable if you knew my father.

Martin recalled a slightly different version of the flight from Percy Street:

My mother went back to get our stuff and found the neighbours inside our house lifting whatever they could get. My mother went in and screamed her mouth off but they did not take any notice of her but slowly left in their own time. My father only had a small Land-Rover, there was no way he could have got the beds, the wardrobes. We lost every-thing; my mother lost all her wedding rings, her jewellery rings, all her valuables. Seventeen years of hard work, buying settees, carpets, beds, everything, the house itself, was just gone. We had to start from scratch. If 1969 had not happened we would have been a very, very well-off family. Pat would have been a lawyer, John's wages were just starting to come into the house, my dad had two jobs. Me, Seamus, Liam and Dermot would have probably ended up in college, but 1969 just blew everything away. John lost his job; he was threatened with death at the mill and he did not go back. My father had to give up his job at the mill as well and we lost our home.

The Finucanes were not alone. One thousand five hundred Catholic families and three hundred Protestant families were burnt out or lost their homes. Along with the rest of the displaced, the Finucanes fell back on their community in the Catholic heartland of West Belfast. At first they stayed with relatives and then squatted in a two-bedroom flat; the family's brief taste of private home ownership and separate bedrooms was over. As the Finucane family's economic fortunes plunged, Belfast descended into an urban battleground, where sectarian riots, shootings and bombings were a daily occurrence.

British troops were first deployed in Belfast on 15 August as peacekeepers. The troops were hailed as saviours and a local priest was quoted in the following day's Catholic nationalist paper, the *Irish News*: 'People rejoiced when British troops arrived.' Seventeen months later, on 5 February 1971, the Provisional IRA shot and killed the first serving British Army soldier in the recent Troubles; Gunner Robert Curtis died within a mile of Percy Street. By then the British Army were no longer viewed by Catholics as peacekeepers but as oppressors and assassins. Even if they had wanted to, it is unlikely that the Armed Forces of the Crown in Ireland could ever escape the burden of their historical actions. Called in to protect the

Catholic population, the troops were soon imposing the Protestant-dominated Crown's version of civil order on Catholic
streets and shoring up the old sectarian Stormont regime. It
was impossible to be neutral. The RUC and Stormont Government ministers, seeing everything through the prism of the
past, were convinced they were dealing with another insurrection by the IRA and ignored the role of the B-Specials in
burning and looting Catholic homes. Any action undertaken by
Catholics to defend themselves was automatically interpreted
as offence.

The Catholics viewed the Army's actions from their own
sectarian standpoint. The British Army's attempts to restore
peace in Belfast without a fundamental shift in the balance of
power meant restoring a Protestant peace and leaving the
Catholic population once again at the mercy of the better-
armed Protestant population. Every seizure of illicit arms
was an attempt to deprive Catholics of the means to defend
themselves, every arrest of a Republican, the loss of one of
the community's sons. Through a series of heavy-handed
security operations, culminating in the June 1970 three-day
curfew of the Falls Road district and the indiscriminate firing
of tear-gas into the crowded residential district, the Catholic
population grew to see the troops as an army of occupation.
The Provisional IRA were reborn from the ashes of August
1969.

The Provisionals' campaign sprang spontaneously from the
despair and anger of the Catholic population. It was a defensive
rage that desperately sought out an ideology to explain its
actions and that of its enemies. Catholic alienation might have
confined itself to futile resentment towards British troops had it
not been for a score of old IRA men in the North and the
Republic who had nurtured the dream of a United Ireland
across decades of public indifference and failure, and who,
more importantly, had access to a limited supply of weapons.
These die-hard Republicans pulled out the old ideological cloak
of Irish republicanism, with its myths of continuous rebellion,

and reworked the siren call of the rebel heart. They imposed the elemental categories of the old order on the chaotic demands of the civil rights protests and urban riots of 1969, and once again it was Rebels versus the Crown. Nothing the British could have done except leave would have appeased them.

The IRA leadership based in Dublin had split into two factions, the Officials and the Provisionals, over the supply of weapons to the North. The Provisionals were keen to fight but had no great plan or strategy to wage war. In Belfast, the riots caught the few men who considered themselves allies of the Provisional faction by surprise and it was months, years, before there was any systematic attempt to arm and train a Belfast Brigade.

When the Provisionals, the Catholics' self-declared defenders, went into action in that role, like everyone else they were party to, not the controllers of, the conflict, defending their homes, streets, schools and churches from marauding Protestants. The official obituaries of the Belfast Brigade's Volunteers in the republican publication *Belfast Graves* give an insight into the first few years of IRA activity. In 1969 the Brigade lost two Volunteers, one in a traffic accident and one in the sectarian rioting of August 1969. In 1970 four Volunteers were killed, two of them in a chance traffic accident with a British Army truck near the border as they returned from a training camp in the Republic. But by 1971 the IRA's military operation was gearing up and twelve Volunteers were to die; the details of their deaths in the obituaries highlight the IRA's increasingly aggressive campaign. 'Charles Hughes ... shot dead in a Worker's Party feud ... Billy Reid ... ambushed a Brit mobile patrol and was shot dead ... Tony Henderson ... died as a result of an accidental shooting at a training camp near Portlaoise ... Gerard Bell fell victim to an accidental explosion.' By 1972, Northern Ireland's most violent year, the death toll for the Brigade, still the IRA's largest and most significant unit, rose to thirty-four, the vast majority of the deaths being the result of premature explosions and gun battles with British troops.

The effective collapse of civil power in the August 1969 riots produced an anarchic vacuum in which competing military forces – Protestant paramilitaries, the British Army and the IRA – fought for strategic advantage. The IRA at first were defenders, but as the battle on the streets escalated into a sniping and bombing campaign, the Republicans increasingly took the initiative in their encounters with the British Army.

A reborn IRA bombed and rebombed Northern Ireland's towns and fought daily gun battles with the British Army and Protestant paramilitaries. In 1969 there were eight recorded explosions, in 1972 there were 1,382. In 1970 there were 213 recorded shooting incidents, in 1972 there were 10,628. The civilian government of the last Stormont regime lurched from one security crisis to another until its final dissolution with the introduction of Direct Rule from London in 1972.

'It was probably a gut feeling more than an articulation of any political ideology at that stage,' said Seamus, who was soon to join the ranks of the IRA's Volunteers.

The campaign was very destructive with little direction I would have understood at that time. I would not have been able to understand why the IRA were bombing Belfast city centre, killing Brits or killing policemen. But I knew that the IRA were our defenders, looking after our interests, fighting for our rights. There was a great sense of anger.

Percy Street was a turning point, it was our introduction into politics. We lived through fifty years of misrule by Stormont, all the bigotry, the gerrymandering and sectarian killings. I can remember my brother John going for jobs and once they heard where you lived or what school you were at, then they knew you were a Catholic: 'Ah don't call us, we'll call you.' We were always at the tail end of things. But after 1969 it was like: 'Out of the ashes arose the Provisionals' and 'The great only appear great because we are on our knees.' There was a sense that this was the time to change things and stop being pushed around, stop being downtrodden. 'Let's get off our knees and do something – start fighting back.' None of us were brought into the world to become involved in politics and fight wars. The politics of the struggle ended up taking over our lives, even the RUC man who arrested me said: 'You have never known anything else, how can anyone expect you to change.' It was something that we all felt we had to do when we were fifteen.

Not everyone in the Finucane family agreed. Over the ensuing years Pat Finucane consistently attempted to persuade his younger brothers to stay at school, get educated and avoid joining the IRA. Pat was on the cusp of the generation whose lives would soon be swallowed up by the Troubles. His degree from Trinity, the future career he planned as a lawyer and his maturity made it inevitable that he would be less euphoric about the IRA than Dermot or Seamus. 'He tried to talk to them all but was of course powerless to stop them doing what they wanted to do. They were determined. Pat respected them for their decisions but thought it foolish,' said Geraldine.

John Finucane, who became a member of the Brigade's 1st Battalion, was amongst the first wave of recruits to join the newly formed Provisional IRA soon after his nineteenth birthday in the spring of 1970. Belfast was at war and the IRA was for most Catholics a heroic organization, its Volunteers fêted as the people's defenders. '1969 was a new phenomenon for all of us but we were all proud of John. There was a sense of adventure about people taking up the gun and the bomb at that time. Yes, it was exciting at times. You got satisfaction out of it. If you are playing centre-forward for Manchester United then you get satisfaction out of that as well,' said Seamus, recalling the motivation that led his brother, himself and many others to join the Provisionals. 'We would have been delighted in all honesty to hear of Brits getting whacked, delighted in the sense of scoring goals. But when you bring it down to brass tacks, when you are talking about the grief of that person's family, the misery and the anguish that this death will cause to that family – no, it is not exciting and it is not funny, it is real.'

Dermot and Martin, who spent their spare hours with other neighbourhood kids on the streets, were the IRA's strongest admirers. Said Martin, who was thirteen in 1971:

These people were our defenders, although the whole concept of what they were fighting for and why the soldiers were shooting at them was a mystery. We had no idea at that stage why the IRA wanted the Brits out. Every day there were gun battles on the streets. You enjoyed it when you heard gunfire against the Brits, you did not understand that it also meant the taking of someone's life. You just thought it was fantastic to hear the roar of gunfire and there was also that hatred, that intense dislike of these people who came in and invaded your area in these big foreign metal vehicles. The only time you ever saw them was when they were invading or arresting someone.

I remember seeing the IRA ambush a foot patrol in Glenvale [an area of Belfast]. Six or seven IRA men cautiously crept up behind them, got into a position and were shooting down at the soldiers. There was a big mass of kids watching those IRA men just casually walking back from it – no one was running and dispersing, thinking the soldiers were coming back after them. You looked up to the IRA because they had fired at the soldiers.

I saw a British soldier, a black fusilier, being killed in the riots of '71–72. He crouched down in the middle of the street and he would have been too far away to have been hit by a stone or bottle but the IRA appeared from behind a hedge and shot him a number of times. He fell and you could see that the man was in agony. The IRA disappeared into the crowd and the soldier was retrieved by his comrades. Later on that night it was reported that the soldier had died. Being caught up in the euphoria you cheered – the enemy was shot, the people who we supported had gotten away. That is the way that I looked at it then. Obviously now I am sad that the soldier died. I do not wish for the death of any soldier or any IRA man. I am sure his relatives still grieve for him but I also think that it is pathetic that he was over here and died for such a pathetic cause.

Dermot, aged twelve in 1971, recalled the early Troubles as a time of excitement and fear mixed with a dawning realization of the relative weakness of the IRA.

The IRA would walk about openly armed. You knew them all – there is so-and-so – and they acted as if there was nothing to be afraid of. I remember the first time I heard the IRA were coming, I stood in a bombed-out park, near where we lived at the time. I stood and waited for them. I was waiting on tanks and armoured personnel carriers coming, the way the allied forces came into Paris. That is what I was expecting and then these three guys walked down the road with rifles and I felt so embarrassed . . . not embarrassed, but it was an anticlimax. I was expecting not our John but the likes of our John riding on the top of tanks. It was deflating because I knew what was against us.

The Troubles were soon beating their way through the Finucane front door as John's involvement in the IRA provoked British Army raids on the family home. The raids searching for John, now a fugitive and living on the run, only inspired his younger brothers to support and join the IRA. 'The Brits came to the house this night, raiding, looking for him and then they raided it every other week looking for him. The whole area was against them so I was against them, it was a community thing,' recalled Dermot.

When they came into the house it was exciting, it was something that you boasted to your mates: 'They did our house last night.' My Da was always good at defusing the situation. Once they came in he would have made them tea, if they wanted a fry he would have made them a fry. I have to say that my father was not a Republican in any shape or form and he did not like what the IRA did; my father was too soft on the soldiers. His logic was that if he was nice to them they would think we were a respectable family and they would not beat his sons. Our logic was: 'Da, do you not know that they are going to beat your sons anyway?' You knew that they were going to take your brothers away and there was a sense of anger that you should not make them tea. We thought that my father did not really understand and that we did, though we were kids. He was just a real family man. My Ma would have been more angry and militant. We would have wanted to see hostility being shown towards them but my Da would not have permitted it.

Recalled Martin:

I can only remember their voices. They were taking away your brothers but my memory is of the English voice in uniform just ordering you about. I believe they would have knocked on the door but they would have then come into the house in great numbers. I remember them telling my father what to do. It was my father's house, it was my mother's house. But they were telling them what to do and going about our house as if they owned it, searching it, and looking at personal things and private things.

I began to hate them. Yes, I had a great dislike for them not just because of what they were doing to my family but what they were doing to friends of mine. There was a woman across the street, Sheila McCree. At the time of internment they were taking her husband out and I could see her fighting and screaming. I was just a nipper and she would have been fighting and punching the soldiers' backs as her young kids stood behind her in their bare feet screaming their heads off.

The soldiers just ignored everything and walked away with her husband, their father.

I can remember soldiers in open-air Land-Rovers going to arrest people and local people were standing there with bin lids, showing their hatred by throwing sticks, bottles and spitting at them. You just got involved because you were caught up in it.

Dermot and Martin were soon taking part in the new boyhood games of the Troubles. 'When we were kids we played IRA men and British soldiers. The soldiers had sticks and sometimes they would beat the shit out of you if they organized snatch squads. We were the rioters and usually the IRA won. Everyone wants to be a cowboy.'

The game quickly progressed to stone-throwing at passing British Army patrols, and rioting. 'We lived in a cul-de-sac that overlooked a main road. If there was a riot in the area it was always in our cul-de-sac because you could safely throw stones at the soldiers and then run back into the cul-de-sac. If they drove in after you it was easy to escape up the entries [alleyways] and the Saracens [Army heavy personnel carriers] couldn't follow you. It was a safe place to throw and if you missed, the stone would land on a bit of waste ground on the other side of the road,' said Dermot.

One day there was a riot going on and one of the Saracens drove into the cul-de-sac. Our John grabbed a pole and was ready to throw it at the Saracen. I knew he was on the run but he just stood there waiting for it. He was really being a big eejit [idiot] – the pole was not going to do any damage to the armoured vehicle – but at the time I thought: 'That is my hero.' Just standing there waiting on them coming.

Internment, detention of suspected IRA members without trial, was introduced in Northern Ireland on 10 August 1971. Internment of suspected rebels was a traditional weapon and had been repeatedly used by both Unionist governments in Northern Ireland and anti-IRA Nationalist governments in the Irish Republic to quell the Troubles' periodic outbreaks. But in 1971 internment was a security disaster that brought Northern Ireland to the edge of civil war. The IRA's support-base in the Catholic community was already too wide to be jeopardized by the summary arrests of key individuals. The British Army bungled the initial arrest operation and later blamed the RUC for supplying faulty intelligence that resulted in hundreds of wrongful arrests. Far from isolating and containing the IRA, the partisan nature of the operation – only Catholic paramilitaries were targeted – intensified support for the Provisionals and their violent struggle to overthrow the Northern Irish state.

The war heated up and the Finucanes were again in the front-line. John was picked up and detained. Dermot related:

> I remember my Ma crying when he got arrested along with my sister's husband at the time. My sister's husband was an ex-British soldier who she met in an ice-cream shop in the Falls Road. That was the time when soldiers were still welcome. He left the Army, became republicanized and started to help the local Republicans to organize, which is why when he got arrested he was given a savage beating. My sister, Rosie, said that was it, and when he got out they left Ireland. John was also badly beaten but was then taken to Crumlin Road jail, interned, moved to the prison ship HMS *Maidstone* and then transferred to Long Kesh.

The annual death toll tripled following the introduction of internment and political pressure from constitutional Catholic politicians forced the British Government to release some of the internees in batches. John Finucane returned home to a hero's

welcome in June 1972. 'We were at the house and someone
came to the door and I remember my mother screaming and
then the whole house was up,' said Dermot, who was twelve in
1972. 'Everything was chaotic. John had been interned for
eight months. Martin and me headed down to John's flat to
celebrate and there was a bit of a party going on and I
remember my Ma saying: "Well son, is it worth it?" And John
said: "Yeh, I might not see the day but he will" and he pointed
at me. Those words have always stuck in my head.'

Not everyone in the family was pleased with his release.
'When I found out,' said Martin, 'I was really disappointed. I
had really wanted to go to Long Kesh to see the soldiers and
see what the inside of a prison was like. I was due to go up to
the prison with his wife on the next visit but before that he was
released.'

Two weeks later John Finucane was dead. Martin
remembered:

> I was thirteen. I had two days left at secondary school before
> the summer break and I remember waking up and Seamus
> was sitting on the edge of the bed crying and I said: 'What's
> wrong with you?'
>   'John's dead.'
>   'What?'
>   'John's dead.'
>   'Dead on, you must be joking.'
>   I did not take it fully in but it hit me when I went down
> the stairs and saw all the other people who were in the house.
> My mother and father had obviously known all about it since
> the early hours of the morning. I was really cut up about it. I
> think what I was really cut up about was that I had lost this
> brother at an early age and I did not really get to know him.

After his release John Finucane had reported back to his IRA
superiors. On the night of his death, 28 June 1972, he was
travelling in a car with another IRA Volunteer, Tony Jordan.

Both men, the IRA said, were on active service. The car crashed and both were killed. The exact circumstances of the accident are hazy but they were given heroes' funerals. John Finucane was the forty-fifth Belfast Brigade member to die and the twenty-seventh killed in 1972. Said Seamus:

> It was the first time death ever came to our own doorstep. It was my first experience of it. It was traumatic. John had just been married, his son was only six weeks old, and he was only out of prison two weeks when he was killed. If he'd known he was going to die he would probably have wanted to die operating against the Brits. But that was not to be. At that time I thought John was old, twenty-one. I was fifteen. When I reached that age myself I realized that he was just a kid and he had his whole life in front of him. His son has never known his father, his wife has remarried, and I regret all that loss. It was only when I got out of prison when I was twenty-nine that I was able to formulate the type of family relationship that Pat knew and John might have known if he had lived. A family helps put things in perspective and that is why there is such a strong bond between myself, Martin and Dermot. We really appreciate being with each other, the value of it.

Like his brother Pat, Seamus is a tall man not given to unnecessary chatter. He has spent many years in prison, many of them as a teenager, and his face is chipped and battered. Seamus looks hard, drawn in, as if expecting the very worst to happen. In common with many ex-prisoners, his movements are slow, purposeful and surprisingly graceful. Every gesture seemed to be measured and calculated, even in the simple act of making tea – his body was still keeping step with prison time in his own home.

Seamus was the last Finucane brother to live in Belfast and did so under constant threat of assassination. When you knocked on his West Belfast front door you could hear him answer but then had to wait for two minutes for the bars and bolts to be removed. When the RUC came with sledge-hammers to arrest Seamus, they failed to break this barrier and in frustration threw their heavy hammers through the front window. The week before we met, Seamus had been arrested under the Prevention of Terrorism Act for the umpteenth time, held for several days and questioned about IRA operations. 'They consider me as a very active Republican and as a result you are threatened day in and day out. Last week I was threatened with the UFF.'

The Troubles are Seamus's life. He was thirty-seven in 1994, unemployed and unable to work for security reasons. Prison and the loss of family and lovers made Seamus more cautious, more reflective and perhaps the wisest Finucane brother. But the years had not softened his militancy nor dissolved the strands of bitterness, only increased his determination to resist. He said, waving out beyond the repaired window:

Where else in Europe do you see this kind of military hardware, troops in combat gear with machine-guns on the streets? It has become part of the environment. They try to use the civilian population as shields, only patrolling when people are going to Mass or kids to school. Every day of my life is cat and mouse, every time I leave the house I am looking over my shoulder seeing who is following me, who is taking photographs. You can become paranoid, you can even go bonkers. You do not have to be a Republican or even a nationalist to be murdered. There is no such thing as impartiality of law and order in this area. In order to live here you have to adapt to it or bail out. Subconsciously we become immune to it, it becomes part of our culture.

In contrast to Seamus's self-possession, Martin was more fragile, vulnerable and dependent on his older brother. Even after a decade of grieving, Martin appeared emotionally broken by John's death.

John did not have an open coffin; he was badly mutilated in the crash and we never got to say our last farewells or touch

or hug him. That has really hurt. I know Pat is dead, I know
he died a horrible death and we never got to say our last
farewells to him either, but I spent as much time near the
coffin as if I could touch him and hug him and hug him. But
with John it was completely different, all you could grasp on
to was the last moments, the last talk you had with him, and
that was it. I was very proud of my brother because he had
given up so much of his life not only to protect me but to
protect his community. He spent many nights patrolling the
estate with a rifle in case anything happened say from a
Loyalist attack. He manned checkpoints and foot patrols in
his own community and I respected that. He was defending
the community against the British Army. I still reflect even
now on the few weeks I did have with him, the last talk, the
last smile. I still try and keep that image of his face within
my memory.

For Dermot, the bolder, more aggressive brother, the abiding
memory was not of John but his funeral:

The local IRA companies openly marched down the street,
sixty men all in formation, and they were called in Irish to
stop outside our door and then in single file they marched in
to pay their respects. It was very military looking and
organized. My older brothers told me that it was the biggest
funeral up until that time to leave Andersonstown. I remember being very proud that John was getting a military funeral.
I remember people on the sidelines were giving the coffin a
military salute; I was told that a few British soldiers saluted
it as a mark of respect. The crowds were massive. Some
people went there because he was an IRA man, others
because they knew our family and we were a respectable
family, and others came because at that time in the IRA you
had ranks and officers and our John was a lieutenant.

John's death on active service only intensified the family's
commitment to the IRA and the authorities' interest in the

remaining Finucane brothers. Seamus, already active in the IRA, was soon arrested and interned without trial; he was fifteen years old. 'They were very forceful about the manner in which they arrested you. They did not break the door down but I was taken to Fort Monagh, a Brit Army camp, and they told me: "You are going to the Kesh and that is it."

Seamus was one of four schoolboy internees imprisoned in the Second-World-War-style prison. The detainees, who at their peak numbered 924, were housed in Nissen huts set inside a barbed-wire compound, the 'cage'. The perimeter of the prison was patrolled by British troops. Under a special regime the prisoners were accorded de facto prisoner-of-war status: no one was forced to do prison work and the detainees, within the confines of the cages, were able to establish a military command structure and use their time as they wished. Later attempts by the British authorities to remove these concessions led to a bitter prison protest campaign that culminated in the 1981 Hunger Strikes.

> Being so young the older prisoners looked after us until we understood the daily routine. After three or four weeks you began to realize that internment was not a holiday camp. Life was confined to three or four huts and a small area of your cage and that was it. It was a maturing process. I can say that the two times I have been in jail I have had a better education in terms of life than I would have had in school. But internment was not a bed of roses. Every month, every six weeks, you had British Army raids in the cages. It was frightening, they had the dogs in and big batons and if you moved when you were not supposed to they just clipped you with them. There were escape attempts. I was there for the Kesh being burnt and all the subsequent rioting and Hugh Cooney being shot whilst trying to escape.[3]

Seamus was interned for over a year and then released. He rose in the ranks of the IRA and became head of his own active service unit in the Lenadoon area of Belfast. In October 1976 he planned an IRA operation with a fellow ex-internee who was later to become the most famous IRA Volunteer of the recent Troubles, Bobby Sands. Sands led the 1981 Hunger Strike and from his prison cell was elected as a Member of Parliament to the British House of Commons; his death-fast made headlines around the world.

The plan formulated by Seamus and Sands was simple: to use petrol-bomb incendiaries to destroy the Balmoral Furniture Company showroom near the staunchly Catholic Twinbrook Estate on the outskirts of Belfast. A nine-strong IRA unit drove to the showroom, held up the security guard at gunpoint and marched him into the store. All the staff and customers were then herded into the basement whilst four bombs were planted upstairs.

The showroom was destroyed but the IRA men were spotted by staff in an adjoining building and one staff member defiantly used his car to block their getaway. The police were called and by the time the IRA men emerged they were surrounded; a brief fire-fight ensued and two Volunteers were shot and wounded. Seamus and Sands and two others, including another hunger-striker, Joe McDonnell, attempted to bluff their way to freedom by hopping into a parked car and claiming to be visiting the area in search of work. The four remained silent in police custody and were thus able to evade explosive charges but were convicted of possession of a pistol found in the car and sentenced to fourteen years in September 1977.

The IRA were ready to make our [sic] exit and the RUC came upon us. They just got out of the jeep, shouted at us to halt and then we came under sustained fire. I was allowed to cross-examine one of the RUC men at the trial. One IRA man had been hit in the leg and would have bled to death but for emergency medical aid. This policeman said he saw a gunman and he fired at him and he saw the gunman fall. He also said no one went near the gunman between the time he was shot and them reaching him, and I asked him where did the gun go and he was just dumbfounded. He couldn't answer. The whole thing exposed the farcical nature of the Diplock court.

The official position of the IRA was that the Northern Irish courts were a tool of the Crown and therefore illegitimate and their judgements void. But Seamus felt he needed to score points against a system his ideology should have told him was inherently unjust. It sounded as if he was not entirely convinced by the IRA's own arguments.

The IRA's commercial bombing campaign hurt, and sometimes killed, members of their own community. Catholics, like Protestants, lost their jobs when the factories were burnt down and everyone suffered from the loss of services when shops disappeared. Many Republicans justified the campaign by claiming that 'no one in West Belfast has a job anyway' so blowing away a furniture salesgirl's position was not going to hurt their community. But the subject was an uneasy one. It was difficult to take seriously calls by Republican leaders like Gerry Adams, the former West Belfast MP, for greater British Government economic investment in Catholic areas when the military wing of his organization was investing its time in blowing businesses up. As part of Sinn Fein's propaganda efforts to justify the commercial bombing campaign, their publicity department once produced a 'Before and After' poster. The poster consisted of two pictures and a caption. The first picture was of a horribly burnt-out shop building; the interior had been gutted and the roof rafters were falling down into the street. The second picture was of two Scottish soldiers from the early Troubles searching a man in the street as his wife and child stared on. The soldiers are holding rifles but they look bored and the search appears as routine as that we have come to expect at airports – an everyday ritual without sense of threat. The insistent caption stretched above both pictures declared: 'THIS [the burnt-out shop] is necessary to prevent THIS [the street search].' The apparent disparity in the level of violence was lost on the poster's creators.

For Seamus, like the poster-makers, it seemed that bombing

factories and shops was a justifiable act of war and there was
no sense of remorse. 'It was part of the strategic overall
bombing campaign. The city centre during the day was very
heavily patrolled and fortified. By attacking other targets it
stretched the Crown forces and made it a lot harder for them
to patrol our areas and harass our people.'

Not all IRA propaganda was so unequivocal about the
economic bombing campaign. In Joe McDonnell's obituary
after his hunger strike, his role in blowing up the Balmoral
Furniture Company along with Seamus and Sands was justified
on the grounds that the store had been selected as a target only
after the IRA had noted the 'extravagantly priced furniture it
sold'.[4] Would the factory have been spared had there been a
sale on?

Irish Republicanism has sustained itself through centuries of
military defeats by reclassifying its failures as mythic victories.
Defeated in the Irish Civil War of 1922–23, the anti-Treaty
IRA faction simply adopted denial as a political philosophy.
The first great denial was that of the 1922 partition of Ireland
into Northern Ireland and the Irish Free State. Other denials
flowed from this; the IRA denied that the Dublin or Stormont
parliaments were legitimate; they denied that British laws and
British courts and certain Irish laws and certain Irish courts
were legitimate. IRA Volunteers on trial in the British courts
were expected to maintain this tradition and deny the legitimacy of the courts despite the personal costs to themselves.
Any IRA Volunteer who hired legal counsel, like Pat Finucane,
to right the charges – thereby implying recognition of the court
– ran the risk of being ignominiously expelled from the
movement and declared a traitor. In the late seventies the IRA
leadership, under pressure from individual Volunteers, dropped
this philosophical objection. IRA prisoners employed legal
counsel, paid for by the British taxpayer as part of a legal aid
scheme, who tenaciously fought every aspect of the prosecution
case.

In 1977 when Seamus was tried the old IRA policy was still in force and he refused to recognize the court. It seemed a doubly strange decision for the brother of a lawyer knowingly to deny himself the right to a legal defence when facing a possible twenty-year prison term. 'At the time that was the policy. Pat or anyone could offer me advice but I did not have to take it and at the end of the day that is what happened. Pat never made any decision for me or me for him.'

Seamus's answer shocked me and it seemed impossible to bridge the gap in our understanding. Like most outsiders, I found the thought of being in prison for a long time terrifying. I would feel my life would be destroyed, wasted. I would try hard to resist and would use any opportunity to fight the charges. But in Seamus's world it was normal to be stopped and arrested as you walked down the street by any passing policeman, it was normal to be in the IRA, it was normal to fear the assassin's bullet, and it was normal to get twenty-five years. Any analysis of Seamus's decisions based on life-values beyond the Troubles was doomed to failure; Seamus had already forsaken pragmatic self-interest when he defined himself as a rebel and joined the IRA. Refusing to recognize a British court of law and knowing you would therefore automatically receive a long sentence was no great step.

I asked Seamus what he felt like after he had been sentenced to fourteen years when he was twenty years old. 'Quite relieved because I was expecting to do twenty to twenty-five years,' he said flatly. 'Conviction was a virtual certainty with our arrest. We all refused to recognize the court and I was expecting to be convicted of the bombings. The thing that saved us was that none of us made statements.'

With Seamus back in prison the security forces began to focus on Martin.

I became the brunt of heavy security forces harassment and that was pretty scary for me. I was never involved with the IRA but that did not make any difference. I would have gone out with mates for a drink or knocked around street corners but that was all. It was the same for everyone whose brother or sister was directly involved, you were always being stopped. Once they found out who you were, they would introduce you to all the other soldiers. After that you were stopped all the time; I was kicked and threatened and beaten. I was also arrested three times. When I was arrested they did their damndest to force me into becoming an informer. On one particular occasion I was taken to Fort Monagh in Belfast and a soldier produced a wad of notes. It was a hell of a lot of money, there were twenty-pound notes and ten-pound notes. He asked me to look at my conscience and said I should work for them reporting anything of a suspicious nature. At one stage they said: 'Don't be worried, we will sort you out, if you need a plane ticket then we will get you a plane ticket.' They then actually produced a plane ticket and were about to hand it over when the door burst open and there was a photographic flash. This soldier had actually taken a photograph and they said: 'Well we have got you now so if you do not work for us we will do this and do that and tell people you are a tout.'

Martin was never jailed but he, more than Dermot or Seamus, seemed an emotional prisoner of the Troubles. His mind was overfilled with the rich remembrance of the past. I found it difficult to bear his raw pedantic recitation for long and I was always eager to turn the tape-recorder off. Perhaps it was this apparent streak of vulnerability that marked him out to British troops as potential informer material. 'At that time the paratroopers were in and I was frightened, especially being stopped by them at night because of their reputation in Derry and Bloody Sunday. I left the country and went to work in Holland in 1978. The brunt of the harassment immediately then fell on Dermot. They used to ask him: "Where is that fucker Martin?"'

Martin lived in the bleak Bogside district of Derry, a republican stronghold. Like Seamus, Martin was unemployed and

had been so for ten years. He had never been a member of the
IRA but was once active in Sinn Fein. He left for 'personal
reasons' and now campaigns for a small Derry pro-republican
political pressure group that wants to reopen the files on the
Bloody Sunday killings of thirteen civil rights demonstrators by
British paratroopers in 1972. Martin was also instrumental in
helping establish a civil rights office in Derry, the Patrick
Finucane Centre, in memory of his brother, to help investigate
potential miscarriages of justice. He shares his life with Julie
whose previous partner, Daniel Docherty, an IRA man, was
killed by the SAS in 1984.[5] They have a son.

Just before Martin fled overseas, Dermot was arrested under
the Prevention of Terrorism Act for the first time.

> The soldiers would raid the house for Martin to put pressure
> on him. It became a bit of a joke. I would get up and say:
> 'Here they come again'; I was too young to be arrested. And
> then one day as I was saying, 'They are here again for you',
> the soldiers turned to me and said: 'Put your shoes on
> Dermot.' 'What for?' I went into total shock. I was scared
> stiff. I was seventeen at the time and Mason was in charge.[6]
> Everyone knew that they were beating up wee kids in
> Castlereagh and getting them to sign confessions. I put on
> this tough guy act but inside I was shit scared. I was
> questioned by two old fellas who acted like they were father
> figures. It was a standard tactic, good fella, bad fella. I got a
> bit of a beating off one of them and after that I just collapsed.
> I would have told them anything, signed anything. But luckily
> I did not know anything.

The day after Dermot was released, Pat Finucane senior died
of a heart attack. The family believed his premature death was
brought on by the long strain of the Troubles, the raids, the
arrests, the prisons, the protests and the beating handed out to
Dermot in Castlereagh. Martin was always the emotional one
and the loss of his father amidst the strain of his brother's

imprisonment and his mother's involvement in the outside protests about Seamus's prison conditions hit him hard. 'It was just a room full of tears, we were all talking and hugging each other and he was away from all. I was angry that my father missed out on all my nieces and nephews growing up; John's son Patrick missed out on having his first pint with my father, the first adult human contact with my father. He was sixty-three when he died.' Seamus was given compassionate leave from prison to attend the funeral.

Dermot once estimated that his family home had been raided one hundred times. I asked Dermot if he could remember the names or faces of any of the soldiers who had raided his parents' house or arrested his brothers. He stopped, puzzled, and then after a long pause replied: 'You would think that if someone came into your house without your authority you would remember their faces but I can honestly say even thinking about it very strongly I cannot remember any of their faces.'

Unlike the soldiers, Dermot was not faceless and anonymous, and he was regularly stopped and questioned by Army patrols on the streets.

> The soldiers would stop me and ask 'What is your name?' and then 'Where is that brother of yours, Martin?' Martin was away but I would lie and tell them he was up in the house, and then they would go up and raid the house. Next time they saw me it would be: 'You lying wee shit! Where is he?'
>
> 'He must have just left. He is probably in the Suffolk Inn now.'
>
> I would never give them a straight answer. In the end they found out where he was so they started to harass me. I was not involved, it was just straight harassment. One night they stopped me in the street, gave me a hiding, and charged me with riotous behaviour. They trailed me into the Land-Rover and started beating me. I was found guilty.

Dermot seemed to be genuinely aggrieved at this old but minor charge. On paper both he and Seamus were the offspring of Attila the Hun; over the years they had been accused of murder, attempted murder, possession of firearms with intent, grievous bodily harm, wounding with intent, and causing explosions. But Dermot was always eager to stress that the Finucanes were a 'respectable family'; in the psychology of West Belfast his crimes were political offences rather than the product of lawlessness.

In contrast to Seamus, Dermot was more easygoing. The war, the years of defeat in prison or as a fugitive, had washed over him. His face retained its boyish charm even though the man within had inflicted mortal harm on others and had others attempt to inflict mortal harm on him. He was a wonderful raconteur and a brilliant mimic who would play every part in his account of police interrogations to perfection, including his own terrified self. He was boastful, a little vain, but never dogmatic or dull. Beneath the surface gaiety I sometimes glimpsed the man who hijacked cars, forced his way into other people's houses and attempted to kill British soldiers. Dermot never sought to justify those actions, he just stated the facts   if Dermot's IRA unit wanted your house, then they were going to take it. There was no hesitation, no doubt; personal emotions played no part in the equation. I was afraid of that Dermot.

Dermot joined the IRA when he was eighteen.

It was the time when the IRA was changing from companies to a cell structure in September/October 1978. I decided to join but I did not know who to approach. Seamus was in jail and so were the other guys who I knew were in the IRA. None of the rest of my brothers were involved. Seamus was also on the blanket protest and he only got one visit a month.[7] You did not necessarily get to be on that visit. I was with a guy one night when he made a sarcastic remark about doing more for the movement. I said: 'Well what the hell are you doing?'

'Well, what the hell are you doing?'

'I would if I knew who to approach.'

'Leave it to me.'

I never suspected he was in the IRA. It turned out that there was a waiting list at that time, a period when they had to check your background. I thought with me there would be no checking, it would be straightforward – after all I was a good upstanding member of the community. But it took a couple of weeks and I actually pestered him – going down to his house saying, 'What's happening, what's happening.' After three weeks I said to this guy: 'Am I in or out?' I was then sent for and there was this other guy who was apparently also a recruit. We were taken to a house and we swore an oath of allegiance to the republican movement. There were a couple of other men in the room and we held a piece of the tricolour in our left hand and we held our right hand up. We swore an oath but I do not remember the exact words, something like I so-and-so do solemnly swear to uphold and obey the constitution of the republican movement and obey my superior officers. I was nervous. I was thinking: 'This is IT! You are with the big boys now.' I had been a member of the Fianna but we had not really done anything apart from march.[8] But now with the oath you had joined the republican movement and I was joining an active service unit. If they had put me somewhere policing the area I would have said here: 'Come on, I did not join to do this – I joined to fight.' I was adamant, I was young. I thought: 'In three years time I will be dead so I am going to do my damnedest to hurt those who have hurt my family, my community.'

The next stage of Dermot's induction into the IRA was a basic weapons training course where new Volunteers learned to identify and field-strip weapons. The recruits were instructed to use false names even amongst themselves but it was inevitable in the narrow world of Belfast's Catholic communities that their identities would become known. One of Dermot's fellow recruits, James Kennedy, later turned informer and divulged the details of IRA activities including Dermot's membership. Kennedy was subsequently executed by the IRA.

I had to make excuses to my mother because I was away for three to four days. I also had to smuggle out a rough pair of clothes with me. I remember at the camp seeing the guns for the first time and feeling my breathing going heavy, I could feel the nerves in my stomach. We were way up a mountain miles away from anyone. It wasn't that we were afraid of being caught, it was just the adrenalin pumping away. You would describe a weapon from the muzzle to the butt and there was four recruits there and two training officers. We got a big buzz out of the arms training. I came back with my chest sticking our – 'Big man!' I should have had a sticker printed on my forehead – 'TOP MAN NOW!' It gave you a lift and a sense of achievement.

Dermot was soon waging war in his native city.

My first attack was a failure. We opened up on the Brits and missed. The Brits were walking through the area and we were attempting to take over a house. We failed because the people were not in. But the next thing we saw was a patrol crossing in front of the safe house, so we jumped in the car, got the weapon together and drove two blocks away and waited at a gap between the houses. When the foot patrol passed we opened up on them. It was quite spontaneous, the run-back [escape route] was not prepared properly. It was stupid. The most dangerous time was in the immediate aftermath of an attack because you have alerted them that you were there. You had fired on them and the Brits' response time was usually two minutes to seal the area. In those two or three minutes you had to be away. Most of us would be regarded as republican and that would be known to the Brits. It wasn't as if you could move freely once you were round the block.

You had to change your clothes, give them a wash, get rid of the forensics. You also had to dump your weapons away from where you were and then dump your car some place else and then get away from the two of them. Everything in the end went okay. We got away, we got the weapon away. A couple of weeks later I got arrested and was questioned but I gave an excuse and got away. Being on active service was exciting but afterwards it was also a bit of an anticlimax. There was a sort of a slow realization that you were now getting into much deeper things.

For this interview with Dermot we borrowed the boardroom of the ramshackle Sinn Fein Headquarters in Dublin. Old campaign posters, half-torn, hung from the walls, an aged upright piano stood in the corner. The room was strewn with old pamphlets, the natural disorder of campaigning politics. Dermot sat at the head of the table gently rocking back and forth on the chair. Behind him two windows framed a vivid Dublin evening sky. Somewhere over the rooftops, an unseen Crown agent was spying on the building. I wanted to know if Dermot had ever seen the faces of the soldiers he had shot at.

You are firing at their uniforms. You do not see faces, just uniforms, you just aim for the uniform. You know that when they are arresting you they are trying to do you harm, they are trying to put you away. This was another type of battle, only you were armed and they were armed. They were your enemy, they were trying to kill you, you were trying to kill them. It scared me, I was afraid to admit it even to myself. I did not want to get caught or go to jail and I did not want to die.

The first few attempts were failures. Success was when you attacked them and got away – the IRA did regard that as a success. I personally regarded them as failures because of the failure to inflict casualties. The more casualties we inflicted then the harder it would be for the Brits to maintain their grip on the North. We had to create instability, we had to destabilize the North, and you could do that by attacks on the British and their garrisons. But the unsuccessful operations did become successful operations; I was being drawn deeper into the movement.

I remember one occasion when I opened fire on a target and I wounded him. It was a Loyalist area and I don't know what happened but I was almost going to fire at civilians in the street, they were the enemy and available. I stopped myself but the feeling totally shocked me. When we went back to base, the person who was in charge, who was monitoring the radios, was jumping for joy because his 'wee team' had successfully engaged the enemy. We had wounded one and we had come back. But when I told him what I had felt he went ape-shit. 'Jesus Christ, do not ever get into that.' I told him I didn't but the feeling had frightened me. I was overcome with hitting the target, bang, bang. And then there was this other sensation of: 'What the hell am I doing here?' I am glad that I have never been involved in an incident where civilians have been injured or killed. I am lucky and glad.

West Belfast was one of the most intensely patrolled military sectors of the world. The air vibrated with the sound of British Army surveillance helicopters. A network of bases and observation posts, equipped with numerous electronic spying devices, bisected and ringed the boundaries of Catholic districts. Armoured Land-Rover patrols, capable of withstanding rocket attack, cruised housing estates. Sixteen-member squads of professional soldiers from one of the world's better armies, equipped with SA80 assault rifles, general purpose machine-guns and sophisticated radios, patrolled the streets. The soldiers were backed up by Western Europe's most powerful and heavily armed police force, equipped with the latest anti-terrorist weaponry. In addition, this police force had, over twenty-five years of secret intelligence-gathering, recruited and conscripted a network of informers within the Catholic community. Common sense dictated that fighting the Crown under such conditions was a near-suicidal activity. Listening to Dermot I could think of only one question: 'Did you think you would be killed?'

I used to have this recurring scene in my head that I would be killed running a road block. But I wanted to be fully committed and I wanted to inflict casualties. You are told when you join that in all likelihood you will end up in prison or shot. It's obvious then that the more active you are, the shorter the run unless you are lucky. I remember seeing Dominic McGlinchey and Ian Millen and Francis Hughes 'Wanted'[9] posters when they were on the run as the most wanted men in Ulster, and I remember mentally saying: 'That is what you want, you want to inflict so much damage on the enemy they want you badly.' There is no point in doing it Mickey Mouse style; I was always putting myself on the frontline. Looking back I now remember people holding back, shying away. I was maybe naive but I wanted the honour of doing it. I very quickly made contact with a small group of good fighters. We regarded ourselves as the best. I used to have a reputation at being good at my work, other units sent for me. I was an excellent driver even if it was a dodgy job. Militarily and politically, I have inflicted damage and I am glad. I am glad I have been a thorn in their side. I did set out to fight them and I fought them.

'How much damage?' I asked.
'Dunno.'
'Tens? Dozens?' I ventured.
Dermot paused. I was not sure if his memories blurred into one or if he was deciding on the right choice of words. 'Let's just say it is in double figures. I was involved in lots of firefights in 1979, 1980 and 1981. It was a very quiet period for us but our unit was very active. I have never fought as much as

I did during the hunger strike. I have done everything that needs to be done in the movement.'

'Shooting and bombing?'

The question created a long silence. I looked at Dermot and then out past him at the Dublin rooftops. Dermot looked back at me with his strong stare and nodded his assent.

'Shooting and bombing,' I repeated to fill the silence.

Compromised by information revealed by an informer and his own profile, Dermot was forced to go on the run, staying in safe houses, abandoning his job as a labourer and never leaving the IRA strongholds of West Belfast. There were close escapes.

One time the Brits came to the door. I dived out the back window and ran along the back entries. I knew if I hit the entry they would shoot me dead so I just jumped all the fences until the end and jumped into the entry for five seconds. All I heard was: 'Stop or I'll shoot.' I jumped out the way and burst into this house. The girl inside started screaming, thinking she was going to be raped. I calmed her down and told her not to open the door to anyone. She didn't but the soldiers knocked – one of them must have seen me go in. The soldiers started shouting, saying someone has run in here, and she said no and they threatened her with the RUC and she said 'Get them' and slammed the door. I climbed into the attic and hid behind the chimney-breast. I heard the door being kicked in and I thought to myself: 'Oh mother of God get me out of here. I'll never do it again. I'll go to Mass every Sunday. I'll give money to the plate.'

I could hear the soldiers tramping through the house and coming towards the attic. I heard the attic lid opening a tiny amount and the guy says, 'There's no one here.'

And then this other voice shouted: 'Have a proper look.'

'He's not here.'

And the man shouted: 'Get in and have a look.'

He came right in and was shining the torch all round and

I was thinking: 'What will I do if he ducks around. What will I say about being in here in the dark.' Just at that moment the man of the house came in drunk and started screaming: 'What the fuck are youse bastards doing in my house?' He started giving them all this abuse and the guy in the attic dropped down.

Dermot was a threat that the authorities wanted to neutralize.

At one stage their interest in me grew ridiculous. We would get a weapon, test it, and they would raid my house. It was incredible; they have not even been attacked and they are raiding my house. So then we thought of this idea that we would attack them and then attack them again when they raided my house. We set up two ambush positions; I kept saying to the other team: 'My mother lives in that house, be sure she is not standing in the door.' In the end the second part of the operation was unsuccessful.

Dermot's growing reputation as an IRA gunman placed great strain on his personal life and his relationship with his long-term girlfriend Ailish. She said:

It was an unsaid thing between us. I never asked him and he never said 'I am involved', but it just became known between us. When he went on the run he was eighteen. We had known each other since we were fourteen. My parents were very concerned, they did not want their daughter going out with someone who was going to end up in prison. My granny would have been very anti-IRA. She had seen Dermot's mother on parades about prison conditions when Seamus was on the blanket protest. Dermot's mother wore blankets as a symbol of what her son was going through and my granny did not like that. My friends thought I was totally mad once it became common knowledge that he was involved. They thought I needed my head examined. What future is there really? If our daughter came to me and said she was going out with an IRA man I would certainly attempt to get her away from him. I would point out the heartache that there is in it for a start, the loneliness, how hard it is. You have to stand up to everybody else in a lot of ways. When you work in a place that is mixed religiously, if there was anything in the news about Dermot I would have got a hard time. People stopped speaking to me or would slam doors in my face. Finucane is not a very common name so I got hassle all the time. It was two extremes; Protestants would not speak to me because of what he did and Catholics were afraid to speak to me because of the fear of being tainted.

Perversely, because Ailish and her family were not Republicans, Dermot was able to date her without risking arrest. Said Ailish:

We did not socialize in republican circles and that helped a lot. No informers could ever finger us. The Brits would be hunting for Dermot all over Belfast but they never came near our family. Republicans would say, 'They hit Charlie's house looking for you, they hit Joe's house, so-and-so has broken in the barracks and he has named you,' but Dermot could visit my aunt's or my granny's at will and the Brits would never ever go there.

We even arranged the wedding with Dermot on the run, it was amazing. Dermot got fitted for his suit the day before. It was very chaotic.

On the way to the reception the wedding party ran into a British Army roadblock. 'Pat was my best man and had just got to Andersonstown Barracks and the Brits stopped the car,' recalled Dermot. 'I said to our Martin: "You are Dermot." "Oh God, all right." They stopped the traffic near the hotel but all the limousines were let through. It was a bit scary.'

Dermot was promoted to leadership of his own active service

unit. 'When I was appointed I was still the child, everyone else was nine years older, but the man who appointed me trusted me because he knew I was level-headed and that I was learning far quicker. I was frightened of the responsibility but he was saying you will be okay. And things started going all right.'

The logistics behind even the simplest IRA ambush were complex and often dangerous. The weapon had to be retrieved from a dump or safe hiding place, transported to the ambush site and assembled. IRA Volunteers frequently commandeered a local house against the owner's will to secure a safe vantage point for the ambush. Cars were stolen or hijacked to transport weapons and Volunteers to and from the ambush position. To avoid leaving forensic tracks, hijacked cars were often deliberately burnt out. Civilians suffered regardless of whether or not the IRA unit abandoned their attack. Dermot did not flinch from that responsibility.

There was a case where I had to put local people through hardship. I had to commandeer their car and their house. You had to be forceful. Once you got into a house, that was it, you had it no matter how much screaming and fighting. Once they calmed down you could set about your business but you had the house and no amount of aggravation would change that.

I felt that we were putting them out and that this was a necessary wrong. I always tried to explain that to them. In ninety or ninety-nine per cent of the time people accepted it. I remember one occasion we went into this woman's house unmasked – you could not walk in the street masked – but as soon as we were in there we pulled the masks on. The woman thought she was going to be raped and started screaming. I calmed her down, told her we were the Irish Republican Army.

'Thank Christ for that!'

'We are taking over the house.'

'Oh Jesus, no, no, no.'

The house was in darkness so we told her that we were going to switch the lights on but put our masks on as well. She said, 'Those masks will terrify me', but she ended up sitting up all night talking to us because we were not planning to do the attack until the next day. I was going to be look-out all of the next day so I fell asleep and let the other fella do the talking. The husband came the next day, he had been on night shift, and he was angry, rightly so, that his privacy had been invaded. And his wife came in and said: 'Don't be listening to him, youse do what you have to do.' We were going to attack the Brits from her windows. She was going to get an awful lot of grief afterwards from the British and she was aware of that. She had no control of the situation, she just had to make the best of it.

'Did the attack go ahead?'
'No they did not turn up.'
'How often did they turn up?'
'It depends. You could plan three or four ops and every one was successful and you could plan three or four and they were all unsuccessful.'
'What happens in the aftermath of an operation like that?'
'The whole priority was getting away, getting cleaned up. In one instance I headed back home and the Brits had already been there and had already searched it. I went into the house and my mother nearly had a heart attack and she shouted: 'They are just away, get out of this house.' But I think I had this feeling of invulnerability so I just stayed.'
Dermot was gung-ho for action against the Brits.

I was once described as erratic. You can be too careful, sometimes people put obstacles up because they are afraid. Sometimes I would say: 'Fuck it, let's do it anyway.' The other members of the team were older, more cautious. I was saying: 'Give it to me, I'll do it.' At one stage we had this plan to drive right into an RUC barracks, shoot everybody

and leave bombs behind. I said okay. We trusted the leader.
He was going with us and we thought if he says it's okay
then we'll do it. We will lose men but hopefully it's not going
to be me. Now I was going to be the driver on this one. It
was a van. We were going to drive straight into the base's
gate area, jump out and when the cops came over to the van
it was going to be just whack, whack and then start shooting.
It was going to be chaos. The plan was that when I hit the
gates the other Volunteers would jump out and I would be
sitting there in the road. Everyone else had rifles and grenades
and I said: 'Here, come here a wee sec. I do not have a
weapon.'

The leader said: 'But you are not going in.'

'But do policemen not drive up and down the road?'

They gave me a wee handgun just to appease me. In the
end the operation was cancelled. One man said: 'We've got
the weapons, we've got the hand grenades, but what about
the Ned Kelly suits?'[10]

'Ned Kelly suits?'

'Yeh, because I'm not going in without one.'

We probably would have got away with it.

On other operations the risks of being shot did not all come
from the forces of the Crown.

We were setting up British soldiers at this spot. We were
setting a pattern and they were setting up roadblocks and we
were weaving in and out, whack, whack, whack. We were
the flea; we were biting and biting and it was sending them
crackers. We had done it a few times and were getting away
through this little lane, and then the car in front of us slowed
– a roadblock. 'Ah, merciful fuck.' And the guy sitting beside
me next to the driver's seat pulled out a Browning, jerked it
into my stomach and said: 'Drive on.'

'What?'

There was a car in front of me.

'Drive on!'

It was physically impossible. You couldn't do a U-turn, there was a car behind us in the road. The next thing was that we arrived at the roadblock and he dropped the gun down between his legs. I remember our attitude towards the Brits was: 'We are not being taken alive.' But I was shitting myself because I was driving and this guy had the gun at my waist threatening to shoot me. So the Brit turned round and said, 'Pull in.' I nodded, 'Thanks very much, officer', and drove on pretending that I thought he had just waved us on. The Brit went 'Hey!' But I just drove on casually and he shouted something like 'You stupid Paddy bastard'. But he let us go.

Round the corner there was another roadblock to stop the traffic coming down in the opposite direction and the soldiers had a machine-gun positioned to fire straight into any car coming round the bend. If we had broke through the first block the soldiers on the second one would have wiped us out. We would have been killed before we had a chance to fire a shot. We went back to base and the first thing your man said to me was, 'I'm sorry, I'm so sorry, you did everything right. If I had been driving I would have done the same as you, blah, blah, blah.' It is now a private joke between us but they were life and death situations and you really bonded to each other.

Every significant IRA operation was condemned by both the local and national media but nothing that was said in the press influenced Dermot and his comrades. 'I always took it that the media was part and parcel of the British establishment propaganda effort. And anyway I knew that a lot of people would be glad that the IRA were fighting back, hitting back and being successful. Of course some people in the community would be critical.'

Like any organization, the IRA makes mistakes; an active service unit goes to the wrong house, a bomb goes off prematurely, civilians get in the way. The IRA leadership, whilst attempting to shift the blame for its atrocities on to the actions of the security forces, usually issues an apology to the victims, but few are consoled. Unlike other organizations, the IRA's mistakes are almost always fatal; children are killed, Australian tourists are shot in the back of the head and a bride's legs are blown off. One of the worst atrocities was the November 1987 Enniskillen Remembrance Day bomb, which killed eleven civilians who had gathered close to the market town's war memorial to watch the proceedings commemorating the war dead. The bomb exploded without warning and brought a two-storey building down on the waiting spectators.

Dermot condemned the Enniskillen bombing but admitted that no single IRA operation, no matter how disastrous, would shake his belief in the justness of the IRA's cause and their methods.

I do not know who did the Enniskillen bombing, I know from my own experience that those people would have been devastated. I was once on an operation where the guy I was with believed he had shot a civilian. He was shattered, he was saying, 'Oh God, Oh God.' He hadn't killed a civilian but he was wrecked. I know that if I had such a thing on my conscience it wouldn't stop me being a Republican but I would be very, very sorry. I would be so full of remorse. After Enniskillen, when we were in jail, two comrades said we cannot criticize those on the outside. But I told them, 'Don't be so bloody ridiculous. Are you saying that we, the IRA, are infallible, that we cannot be criticized, because that's crap.' It was complete incompetence and I believe that it was not deliberate. I know that the people who did that must be completely devastated. I have seen suffering, I know families whose kids have been shot away with plastic bullets. My own family has suffered, I know other families who have suffered, I would dearly like to see it ended but not at any price because I know it would only start again. I am not so foolish to say that if we stop, everyone will stop and we will all live happily ever after. It won't work like that because it will start again until there is justice.

Whilst Dermot was fighting the Brits on the streets, in prison Seamus was on the front-line of the battle for political status for IRA prisoners. At the time of Seamus's arrest in 1976 the British Government had withdrawn the de facto prisoner-of-war status accorded to those interned or imprisoned in Long Kesh's cages. From March 1976 IRA prisoners were treated as common criminals, forced to wear prison uniform and forced to do prison work. To implement the criminal regime, the authorities built a new prison officially called HM Prison Maze (Cellular) next to the old cages of Long Kesh; Republicans continued to call the new prison Long Kesh to remind everyone of its origins as a makeshift internment camp housing illegally detained republican suspects. The new prison was also known as the 'H-blocks' because of the distinctive 'H' shape of the jail's eight units from the air.

The first IRA prisoners to be convicted after March 1976 refused to accept what they saw as an attempt to criminalize their political struggle and began a blanket protest, refusing to wear prison uniforms and instead clothing themselves in their prison blankets. The blanket protesters were punished under prison rules and locked in their cells for twenty-four hours a day. 'We knew that we were going to be banged away after our arrest,' said Seamus. 'We also knew that once we were convicted it was straight on to the blanket.'

In April 1978 the dispute escalated into the 'no-wash' protest over the authorities' alleged refusal to allow the prisoners a second towel to wash themselves when they went to the bathroom. The 'no-wash' then escalated into the 'dirty protest' where IRA prisoners refused to leave their cells, and urinated and defecated in them. Seamus was 'on the blanket' for four years. He recalled as we sat in his kitchen sipping tea:

> It was rough. I would not like to go through it again. On the blanket you had nothing; you had a blanket, a mattress, a piss pot, a gallon of water and a bible. You were alone in your cell, naked, for twenty-four hours a day. The smell was sickening. We used to put the excrement on the walls and the ceiling to dry it with the sponge from our mattress. I am not saying our hands did not get dirty but we washed them with the water. Sometimes we got sick, the food was horrible. The deprivation and the torture that went on in that place cannot be overestimated. There was physical torture, scalding hot water was thrown over prisoners, scalding hot tea.
>
> The hatred between us and the screws was unbelievable. They enforced a policy of brutalization to break our spirits and to break us up in the blanket blocks. A lot of the screws were there for the money but there was also a lot of them who enjoyed what they were doing; they would piss under our doors at night. The IRA executed numerous screws; in some cases they were killed as symbols of the uniform but some of them deserved it, like the Red Rat or the Horse as he was known, Brian Armour [killed on 4 October 1988].

'Did he get shot?' I asked.

Seamus's response was casual and matter of fact, as if we were discussing dry technicalities.

> No, an under-car bomb blew him up. He was head of the Prison Officers' Association and was involved. He was a Reinhard Heydrich sort of character or Doctor Mengele, an animal. He loved it, he really revelled in it. I am sure a lot of people were glad to see him getting his just deserts. We would get our tea on Sunday afternoon, just a salad at 4.30 pm. At 6.30 pm you would get a cup of tea or bun. If he was on he came round, gave you your salad, wet the arse of your cup with tea and was then back with your supper in five

minutes. They would put glass in your food or human excreta or give one prisoner a big dinner and the other prisoner a small dinner, hoping the two of you would fight over it. At one stage in 1978 I could never envisage myself walking round the yard. I thought I would have to do the whole fourteen years like that, but I was prepared to carry on.

Brian Armour might have been a sadistic British prison officer but he was not a Heydrich or a Mengele.[11] Language was another victim of the Troubles. The metaphors and vocabulary of global warfare and the Holocaust were conscripted in the service of Ulster's episodic affliction; sectarian riots were termed pogroms; the IRA were depicted as waging a campaign of genocide/ethnic cleansing against the Protestants along the border; poor working-class communities were described as ghettos. The choice of words was deliberate, designed to emphasize the political points of the speaker, but over time exaggeration falsified the reality of the Troubles. These descriptions, however real they may have appeared to the participants, were false. Maybe the hatred between the prisoners and their guards on the H-blocks made the Armour–Heydrich comparison real for Seamus.

If the prisoners hated their guards, the bonds of their mutual suffering and deprivation drew them together.

There were some happy days on the blanket in terms of unity and comradeship. We communicated with other comrades through holes in the wall or out the windows. I learnt my Irish. I don't move in Irish circles now so it's gone. The camaraderie was brilliant at times, we really improvised. We had classes going in French, mathematics, Irish history. Some people became quite acclaimed story-tellers from the books they had read, others from what they made up. There were sing-songs, some people memorized two hundred songs.

In October 1980 seven republican prisoners began a hunger strike to finally resolve the prisoners' demands for a return to the previous special category status. The fast ended in confused circumstances in December 1980 with the prisoners claiming they had been promised major concessions by the authorities. When the alleged concessions failed to materialize, Bobby Sands, the IRA prisoners' leader and the first of ten new hunger-strikers, began another hunger strike on 1 March 1981. Sands died sixty-six days later on 5 May; his death and that of the other nine hunger-strikers had a huge impact on the blanket men.

> The Hunger Strike period is very difficult to talk about. It was a very emotional period, very frustrating and very demoralizing. I met Bobby the week before he went on hunger strike and it was like talking to a dead man. He had personally decided that he was going to die, he at least was going to have to make that sacrifice. When Bobby was elected it was fantastic; being an MP we thought would probably save his life and when he died we were stunned. It taught us something about the Brits that the Free Staters [a term for the Dublin Government] always forget – the Brits don't give easy. They played brinkmanship with people's lives, they gave the illusion of movement but ten men died.

The British Government under Prime Minister Thatcher refused to give in to the hunger-strikers' demands and after the tenth man, Mickey Devine, died, the families of remaining fasting prisoners intervened as they lapsed into comas. The IRA leadership bowed to the inevitable and called off the protest. The IRA were defeated over the issue of prison conditions but the publicity and the street protests dramatically increased their political support in Northern Ireland's Catholic communities. Many of the prisoners' demands – the right to wear their own clothing, the right not to work – were conceded by the prison authorities on political or security grounds. Said Seamus:

> After it was over there was sadness and regret because of the people we lost during the Hunger Strike. But there was also

a sigh of relief that you were out in the fresh air and could
leave your cell to go on a normal family visit. The blanket
protest was a political tactic at the end of the day. I thought
I was fighting the system, passive resistance. It was a sign of
our determination not to be beaten by the Brits. Maggie
Thatcher said the Hunger Strike was our last card. Well, the
IRA is still here, the republican movement is still here.
Thatcher was wrong.

After the pressure to be recruited as an informer passed, Martin
returned from Holland. But there could be no return to an
ordinary everyday life. The family were now actors or victims
in the Troubles; the possibility of a nine-to-five existence was
gone for ever. In the course of the Troubles, many Catholics
have been intimidated out of their workplace by more numerous Protestant workmates. The threats have ranged from verbal
warnings to notes or bullets being placed in lunch-boxes. With
the exception of Pat, none of the Finucane brothers had ever
been in sustained employment. I never picked up any sense of
regret or dismay at that situation from any brother; a regular
job was something outside their world.
    Said Martin:

I left school in 1975 when I was sixteen. I had a job set up
for me but it only lasted for two years. From 1975 to 1977 I
worked in Lisburn, a Protestant area, and looking back I was
a fool. There were many Protestants working up there and
the name Finucane is very, very rare. I can count myself very
lucky that I was not harmed in any way. I had another job
around the time of the Hunger Strikes but there were
disruptions in transport and I ended up losing it. Even if we
had jobs now, none of us would work outside our own area
for our own security reasons – many Catholics were killed
because of their religion. It's the same with Seamus. He
worked for a time in Mackie's engineering factory but the

majority of workers were Protestant and he was forced to leave. Dermot worked as a labourer doing joinery but he was also forced to leave his job.

What was not alien to the Finucane family was protest. Their mother Kathleen Finucane was active in the wave of demonstrations that accompanied the blanket protest. Martin said:

The relationship that my mother had with her sons was so involved and so immense. She was involved in all the street protests, walking in the marches with just a blanket round her, going on a twenty-four-hour solidarity fast. My mother was a Republican; she was the rock of our support. She was the one who organized for us to slip out of the house and then slip back in without the knowledge of our father, who would have been saying the rosary or going up to bed praying or reading. She was fully supportive of what her sons were doing.

In February 1981 Dermot was arrested and charged with the murder of a policeman. The original incident was reported in the *Irish News* on 7 February 1981 under the headline 'Policeman Shot Dead in Ambush':

A 38-year-old police Reservist shot dead in Belfast yesterday regularly called at the newsagent's shop on Balmoral Avenue which was the scene of the attack.

Constable Charles Lewis, a married man with two children, who lived in the Finaghy area, died in a hail of bullets fired at close range by two gunmen as he and a colleague came out of the Classic newsagency.

The colleague, also a full-time Reservist, was still in a serious condition in hospital last night. The victims, who were travelling by car to work at the police playing fields of

Newforge Lane, stopped as usual at the newsagency shortly before 8 am to collect their papers.

The gunmen were lying in wait in a golden-beige Fiat Mirafiori parked opposite the newsagents. They opened fire as the policemen were returning to their privately owned Allegro parked in the forecourt of the shop before escaping into the morning rush-hour traffic.

The getaway car was later found burned out at the corner of Corrib Avenue and Lenadoon Avenue.

Police said yesterday that the attack was obviously a 'well-planned ambush'. They believe that at least two gunmen were involved, with possibly a third man to drive away the car. Both policemen were wearing sports jackets over their uniforms.

Children arriving for classes at the Malone Primary School adjacent to the newsagents narrowly missed the ambush and were escorted through a police barrier. Alliance security spokesman Alderman John Cousins last night condemned the shooting as 'disgraceful'.

He said: 'All law-abiding people from whatever section of the community must come together behind the police to stamp out this menace and not be fooled into supporting sectarian retaliation groups.'

The murdered policeman, who had a 10-year-old daughter and a nine-year-old son, joined the RUC Reserve as a part-time member in December 1977 and switched to the full-time Reserve force in January 1979. Following the shooting the President of the Methodist Church in Ireland visited Lisburn RUC station to which the two men were attached and later travelled to the men's homes.

Dermot related:

They had me for five months from February to May 1981 and during the time I was in prison four hunger-strikers died, Sands on the fifth of May, Francie Hughes, Raymond

McCreesh, then Patsy O'Hara. When I got out, West Belfast was like a scene from Beirut, every single street was barricaded and there were nightly riots, burning vehicles. The charges failed. I just went to court one day and the Crown lawyers said we are not pursuing it. An eyewitness was supposed to have seen me running away from the scene of the shooting and getting into the car, implying I was the person who shot the policeman. I was charged with murder. I don't know who the policemen were. Someone said they were the bodyguards of Reverend Bradford MP, who was assassinated by the IRA. But they must have been popular because the day I arrived in jail several prison guards threatened my life. In one incident twelve of us were being taken out for a bail hearing and we were standing in a group being handcuffed. The cops were pointing over. There were several senior Republicans there and I stopped beside one and told him they were pointing over at him, but he said it was me. We got handcuffed and we were just entering the building when one of the RUC men put his rifle right into the middle of my throat and said: 'I ought to blow your head off ye Fenian bastard ye.'

I just stood there and stared at him, and we walked on and the senior Republican said: 'Jesus Christ, I'm not going to get handcuffed to you.' I made a complaint to my solicitor, our Pat, but he said there is not really a lot you can do. I was really frightened because if someone did that in fun or seriously, as in this case, and the gun goes off, you are dead. Ailish had a bad time at work about it.

Dermot had been charged on the basis of eyewitness evidence but the Crown's case was weak.

They asked me to go on an identification parade and I said I would if I had my lawyer in. Pat advised me not to go on it but the cops can put you on an informal one, they can force you on. I was taken to a small room where everyone else in the room was thirty to forty years old and dressed in suits. I was twenty and I wasn't wearing a suit – they had taken my entire wardrobe away with them and left me in working clothes and jeans. Because they had been questioning me for several days my hair was dirty, unkempt. This detective sat beside me and crossed his arms when I crossed mine. I thought the whole thing was a set-up. A person, dressed in brown clothes and in a motorcycle helmet with no visor and red paint on their skin, came into the room – the cops were trying to disguise the identity and even the sex of the person, but I was sure I saw the outline of breasts. They asked her if the person she had seen was here and the helmet wobbled and she came over and tapped my shoulder. I knew it would not stand up in court but I knew I was going to be charged.

In May 1981 Dermot was released; three months later he was back in prison for good after being trapped in the aftermath of an IRA ambush on a security patrol in which a sergeant of the Royal Regiment of Fusiliers was hit four times in the legs. Dermot's run was over. He was twenty-one years old.

The *Irish News* of 21 August 1981 carried a report of the incident that led to his arrest:

Hijacking and burning of vehicles in West Belfast, Derry and Newry, as well as a series of suspect car bombs in Belfast city centre, followed yesterday morning's death of hunger-striker Michael Devine. Three men were arrested and two rifles were seized by the RUC in West Belfast following a sniper attack and a high-speed car chase through the area. The incident happened shortly after 11 am when gunmen on Rosnareen Flats in Shaw's Road fired at an Army patrol near a club on the Shaw's Road, injuring a soldier in both legs. The wounded man was later described by an RUC spokesman as 'not serious'. Following the shooting, an RUC patrol in the area spotted a car at Koran Ring and rammed into the rear of the vehicle. The car made off, chased by two Land-Rovers, and speeded into Kennedy Way, stopping in the forefront of a garage. Three men, one with a rifle, jumped out of the vehicle and tried to escape through the back of the garage, but they were quickly surrounded by police and taken away in the back of Land-Rovers. A second rifle was found when the car was searched. The three men were later being interviewed at Castlereagh interrogation centre, and forensic experts are carrying out ballistic tests on two Armalite rifles found at the scene.

Dermot commented:

The day I got caught they rammed the car and subbed [sub-machine-gunned] it but I still got away. We had planned to ambush a patrol on the Shaw's Road. The leader said, 'How are you getting away?', and he suggested a few changes, and comically on account of those few changes we came in contact with the RUC. If we had done it my way we probably would have been free for at least another day; we probably would have been killed or caught on the next one. That is the way it goes.

There was a patrol in the Shaw's Road that had been ambushed and we were driving away. We hit a roundabout half a mile away and we saw two RUC Land-Rovers coming towards us from the opposite direction. Just after the ambush there was a helicopter in the air so it could have said 'Stop that car' or it could have seen the car; the patrol that had been attacked would not physically have been able to see the car and we believed it was a reasonably clean car. I was concentrating on my gloves so that the cops could not see them. What I was not aware of was that the RUC took the roundabout the wrong way so that they were coming head on to us. Trying to keep calm I gave them the right of way but the guy with me realized that something was up. I shouted 'It's all right!' but he was shouting 'Move!' The first Land-Rover drove in behind me so there was no reverse and the second pulled in front. I just froze and the guy beside me screamed: 'Get me the fuck out of here!' The front passenger shocked me out of my frozen state and I mounted the pavement. The RUC Land-Rover then rammed us right into the wall. They jumped out and started firing into the car but I just put the boot to the board and managed to scrape through and drive on.

Being a good driver is knowing when to drive fast and knowing when not to drive fast, knowing how to park the car so that you can get away quickly, knowing how not to attract attention and knowing how to get the hell out of there – we were getting the hell out of there. When the cops were firing, the other people hunkered down and I kept screaming, 'I'm all right, I'm all right, I'm all right . . .' so as soon as I was hit they would know to steer the car. I wanted to let them know that I was okay. I was doing my job. It wasn't thought out but it was like telling them to leave me alone until I'm hit.

We got away but ran smack-bang into a line of Saracens coming at us. At roughly seventy miles an hour I did a hand-brake turn and shot off in another direction. More Land-Rovers came so we were caught between the two groups and we decided to ditch the car and run for it. Just off Kennedy Way there was a garage and behind it a nationalist housing estate. The guy in front said: 'Pull in.' I'm shouting: 'There's railings.' I was sure there was six-foot-high railings at the back.

'No, there's not.'

'You can't get out of the fucking garage!'

'No, you're wrong, there's no railings. Pull in.'

'There fucking better not be.'

I jammed on the brakes and jumped out and ran in round the back – there were these big ten-foot-high railings! As we ran we threw everything off, coats, rifles, there was no ammo left, the lot. That was it. They were on us and we were trapped.

'Stop or I'll fire.'

I was down on the ground and there was a cop with a gun to my head and I was saying: 'I don't know mister, I don't know what you are talking about.' I felt stupid calling him mister. I didn't want to call him 'sir' either. My thoughts were: 'I'm dead, I'm gone and that is it.' I just had my eyes closed waiting for the darkness to descend, the curtain to come down. I thought that was how I was going to die.

Someone started shouting. 'We have found the gun, found the gun.'

'Put the handcuffs on the bastards!'

They put our hands behind our backs, we were lying on the ground, and then the brave men that they were, as soon as they had the handcuffs on, they started beating us, kicking us round the courtyard. One cop, according to one of my comrades, went berserk and two other cops had to disarm him. There was a lot of feet kicking at us but we were so high on adrenalin that I could not feel the blows. They were punching each other to punch us and I was using my shoulders to protect my face. There were six or seven men but only one or two were really hitting you. When they eventually pulled us up there was a female cop there and she was saying: 'Is that the bastards? Kill them! Kill them!'

Their hatred towards us was phenomenal. A Brit soldier was shot four times. I thought we would all get life. We were charged with attempted murder and possession of two rifles and a quantity of ammunition with intent. We beat the attempted murder charge because they could not actually prove that we had pulled the trigger. Normally the Brits had a response time of two to three minutes. After that they hit an area with roadblocks, an influx of troops and helicopters. From the scene of the shooting to the first confrontation with the RUC there was a gap of a mile and half, two minutes. In that gap the actual gunmen could have got out of the way, we could have been transporters.

Like every major IRA suspect, Dermot was shipped to the RUC's main interrogation centre at Castlereagh where crack police interrogators worked on him for seven days and seven nights. In theory the procedures, albeit elongated, would be familiar to any ordinary British bank robber but in practice seven nights in Castlereagh is a world apart from a night in the cells with an English bobby. The IRA tell their Volunteers to say nothing whilst under interrogation, but seven days is a long time to stay silent in the intimate space of a police interrogation room. Dermot said nothing.

Your interrogators never introduce themselves. It's not like that. The first time I knew the name of the cop in charge of my case was when he appeared at an extradition hearing in Dublin seven years later. You have to give your name and address – that is compulsory – so you give it.

'What can you tell us about such and such?'

And you say: 'I am not answering any questions.' And you try to say it as friendly and as hospitable as possible because you do not want a slap across the face. I don't want a hiding, I don't want a beating. 'I'm just letting you know that I am not answering any questions. If you want to ask me questions, ask me in front of a solicitor.'

'None of that crack. You'll answer our questions.'

And then right away you can feel the atmosphere changing just like that. There is this right build-up of terror in the room. Being in Castlereagh is a bit like being in a warm comfortable room when suddenly the door is banged open. Lots of guys in uniforms appear and you're pulled out into the freezing cold and driven off. You're shivering with fear and cold – that's Castlereagh. Keeping silent is monotonous, tiresome, frightening. Sometimes you are sitting in Castlereagh listening to them and you are saying: 'Fuck you.' Other times you are in a dream world; you block them out or stare at the wall and then they slap you or bang something next to you. It's hard, it's all mind over matter.

My interrogators were shrewd. They were good at their job but they were stupid too. The cops destroyed a lot of potential evidence when they battered us around the garage floor. The dirt contaminated everything. They took every-thing away from me for forensic testing but they missed the top layer of clothing. I was later able to get rid of it. They were wee things but they all added up.

The interrogators named the wrong person as the driver. The person they named was a good friend of mine. During IRA briefings we used to slag each other off, swopping fatalistic jokes. We'd point to his balls and go 'Phewww!!!' and pretend they were the size of grapefruit. The joke was that his balls were going to be that swollen from the hammering he was going to get when the RUC caught up with him. He would laugh but he would also be very nervous. When they did catch him with the rest of us he did not get a beating but they mistakenly assumed he was the driver. They asked when he had picked up that 'wee murdering bastard Finucane to do the hit'. It was obvious that the cops didn't know anything.

The case went to trial eleven months later. The two other defendants – Bobby Storey, twenty-six, and twenty-year-old Bernard Shannon – and Dermot were all convicted.

We got eighteen years and we were glad. Afterwards we burst out laughing – 'Brilliant, brilliant, magic, magic.' A lot of that was to keep your own strength up, but it was also a sense of relief. Eighteen years meant you would do nine, but of course there was protest on, which meant you would lose remission.[12] I had a brother who had been on the blanket protest for four years. I was twenty-one, thirty to me was an old man. I might have been thirty-nine before I was released, if you add three years for bad behaviour. I met one guy who had been in since 1977 and he said to me: 'What do you think you will do?' I thought it was such a naive question. 'I hope to do nine but I expect to do twelve.' He said: 'I never thought we would be in this long.' He was mad. It wasn't 1972 when the IRA thought the Brits were on the verge of pulling out and everyone would be released in an amnesty.

An estimated sixteen thousand Republicans have passed through the Northern Ireland prison system since the Troubles were renewed. Over twenty-five years the IRA's active corps at any one time has never exceeded a thousand fighters, so statistics dictate that virtually every IRA member from the Chief of Staff to the lowliest Volunteer has spent some time behind bars. In 1994 there were just under seven hundred IRA prisoners, but previously the prisoner total has been well over the thousand mark. More IRA Volunteers are currently in prison in Northern Ireland, and scattered handfuls in prisons in England, on the Continent and in the United States, than were on active service prior to the 1994 ceasefire. Most Volunteers began their long sentences in their twenties, some serve decades. Prisons and prison conditions are always high on the IRA's political agenda.

The 1981 Hunger Strike escalated into an international propaganda battle but it began as a protest over prison conditions. The IRA's fight against criminalization was both a political and a pragmatic campaign. Had a criminal prison regime been successfully imposed, it would have broken their internal command structure and led to a worsening of conditions for individual prisoners. In prison, Republicans elected an officer commanding, an OC, to maintain discipline and to liaise with and pressurize the authorities for better treatment. The prisoners' sense of unity and comradeship softened but did not obliterate the loss of the most fruitful and potentially dynamic years of their young lives. Each individual Volunteer, man or woman, had to endure their own burden of imprisonment. Dermot said:

You can do jail well or you can do it badly. If you do it badly, then no one will help you. We can put our arms around each other but it does not take away the pain, the loneliness, the hardship. I think I did it well. The Hunger Strike had ended; we had to do prison work, mix with Loyalists, but it was okay, we got to wear our own clothes. We were determined to get segregation, so there were fights with Loyalists; there were fire-bombs, Catholics got battered with hammers, Loyalists got stabbed and scalded with hot water. In one instance a Loyalist attacked me and luckily I knocked him out. He made the noises 'Ya Fenian bastard' before he came at me so I had a bit of a warning.

The Republicans had the tactical advantage of a two-to-one majority and a clearer ideology. Dermot did not rate his paramilitary opponents highly.

We exploited the fears they had of the blanket men – the blanket men were sickos. They could not imagine how men could live like that for five and a half years, shit all over the place. In general I would say Republicans know what they are fighting for, Loyalists don't. They came across as street boys, thugs with tattoos, who would attack when they were drunk. They were not brave men, just uneducated, working-class yobs. None of them could articulate why they were in jail. They became more efficient at killing Catholics but that was because of collusion – someone was helping them to co-ordinate their attacks.

In the jail the Loyalists knew what you were in for and you knew what they were in for. On one of the wings there was a child molester who was in need of psychiatric care. Two Loyalists got themselves transferred to give him a hiding. They were in for raping three nurses because they believed the nurses were Catholic – that was their claim to political status in the Ulster Volunteer Force. We battered them before they battered the man. How can anyone turn round and say they were political prisoners? Unfortunately, when this war ends a lot of these prisoners who were involved in actions which you and I might find distasteful will have to be pardoned. They have been caught up in this extraordinary environment. I have never gone out to harm someone because of their religion but I also recognize that a lot of these people would never be in prison apart from the abnormal society that we were living in.

*

Irish Republicanism has a repetitious history of penal incarceration, transportation and execution. In Dublin, the city's old prison, Kilmainham Jail, has been turned into a national shrine in memory of the generations of rebels caged and executed within its walls. It was from the grey stone walls of Kilmainham that the United Irishman Robert Emmet – revered by the Provisionals as a republican forefather – was led to the gallows in 1803 for his part in the United Irishmen Rising. Within Kilmainham's walls the great Irish Parliamentarian Charles Parnell was imprisoned in 1881 as a result of his political agitation. In 1883 five Fenian political assassins were hanged in Kilmainham after being convicted of slashing to death the Chief Secretary of State for Ireland, Lord Frederick Cavendish. The prison work area known as Stonebreakers' Yard was chosen as the site for the execution by firing squad of the fourteen Easter Rising leaders in 1916.

Kilmainham's history of incarcerating Irishmen violently committed to overthrowing British rule rested uneasily with the Dublin Government's disavowal of the Provisional IRA and its methods. The prison's historical role was uncomfortably close to that of its contemporary equivalent – the Dublin Government's own high-security jail in Portlaoise and Long Kesh in Northern Ireland both full of Irish men violently committed to the exact same purpose. Funding of Kilmainham Jail Museum was never a high priority for the Irish Office of Public Works.

Republicans attempted to obliterate the defeat of imprisonment by creating a counter-history of glorious prison escapes. The founder of the mid-nineteenth-century Fenian movement, James Stephens, broke out of a Dublin prison in 1865. In 1867 Irish bombers first came to London in an abortive bid to rescue two Fenian leaders, Richard O'Sullivan Burke and Thomas Casey. A few die-hard IRA men escaped from the Free State's Curragh internment camp in the 1920s. In 1943 twenty-one IRA prisoners, who had been involved in a doomed Second

World War terrorist bombing campaign, tunnelled their way out of Derry Jail and fled across the border in a truck that was quickly captured by Irish Free State troops. The renewal of the Troubles added new episodes; in 1972 seven IRA prisoners broke out of the prison ship HMS *Maidstone* and swam ashore; in 1973 three IRA leaders were airlifted out of Dublin's Mountjoy Jail in a hijacked helicopter; in 1981 eight IRA men shot their way out of Belfast's Crumlin Road Prison; in 1991 two IRA men broke out of London's Brixton Prison using a gun that had been smuggled to them in the base of a training shoe.

Many of the IRA escapees, like those in the Derry Jail break in 1943 or the Brixton escapees, were recaptured in the immediate aftermath or within a few months. There was no safe home country for the Irish rebel to escape to. Ireland was too small a country, its paramilitary networks penetrated by too many informers, for high-profile fugitives to disappear. If an escapee returned to active service, recapture was only a matter of time. But to the rebels, the inevitability of recapture never diminished the glory of an escape attempt. A successful escape was another act of physical defiance, a rallying point for republican supporters, and concrete proof of the ingenuity and daring of IRA Volunteers. An escape attempt, even if it only made it to the front gate, was symbolic of the indomitable will of rebels to be free.

Dermot began his eighteen-year sentence in Long Kesh, unique amongst the world's maximum security prisons. Designed to end for ever the republican track record on escapes, it was constructed of eight separate blocks, known as H-blocks because of their 'H' shape. Each block housed 160 prisoners and was surrounded by its own thirty-foot barbed-wire-topped fence before a twenty-foot-high, anti-scale perimeter wall. Each block had its own electronic air-lock entrance and all movements between blocks were controlled by means of daily passwords, identity tags, double air-lock gates, guards and Alsatian dogs, and the usual electronic security camera hardware. The prison perimeter was surrounded by another thirty-foot-high fence and a twenty-foot-high perimeter wall, and was guarded by British troops in watchtowers armed with rifles and machine-guns. All staff and visitors were required to undergo searches before entering the prison.

On the blocks the prisoners were housed in the four wings that comprise the arms of the 'H'. Access to each wing was controlled through electronic air-lock gates; in order to pass from one wing to another a prisoner would have to pass through one electronic gate, which would close behind him, before the next electronic gate would open in front of him. The guard operating the gate was housed behind thick steel bars. An individual wing could be sealed off at the flick of a button. Each wing was a mini-prison in a block that was a separate prison in itself.

In the central bar of the 'H', an area known as 'the circle', were the block's administrative offices and an ultra-secure sealed communications room. The circle, like the rest of the block, was dotted with panic buttons designed to raise the alarm in the event of a riot or an attempted escape.

Long Kesh's walls are thick, the foundations deep, and everything was made of reinforced concrete packed with steel rods. The sheer distance of the individual blocks from the perimeter wall, between half a mile and a mile, made an escape tunnel an impossibility. But it was not the security procedures that made Long Kesh special; it was, according to a report by her Majesty's former Inspector of Prisons, Sir James Hennessy, the prisoners: 'They were quite unlike the population of any prison in England or Wales in their dangerousness, their allegiance to a paramilitary organization, their cohesiveness, their common determination to escape and their resistance to the efforts of the prison authorities to treat them as ordinary criminals.'

Long Kesh's architecture and the elaborate security systems did not diminish the constant prison chatter about breaking out. Dermot recalled:

It would really start off with a 'what-if' joke between ourselves.

'What if a helicopter landed just now, what would you do?'

'Landed where?'

'Just over there. Visualize it as being right there on the football pitch.'

'Right there?'

'Yeh. Now what if the OC said you can't go?'

'CAN'T GO!'

'Yeh . . .'

'I'M GOING. NO ONE'S STOPPING ME!'

One guy got so worked up he was ready to tear everyone else apart to get on that imaginary helicopter.

Most of the talk was just the gate fever of men with too much time on their hands and too little to entertain them. But the prison's IRA leadership concentrated in one block, H7, had not given up hope of a real escape attempt.

Dermot was in H1 when he got a communiqué, an illicit prison message written on cigarette paper, telling him to go back to H7, where Seamus was incarcerated.

The message was simple – 'Get back here!' I did not know why I should transfer but I went to the H1-block governor and told him there was a problem with my family and I wanted to sort it out with Seamus. He asked what it was. I said, 'It's personal!' He was the most unhelpful wee shite you could imagine and he turned and said: 'I do not care where you go just as long as you stay in jail.' At first there was a problem. They, the screws, did not want me in H7. I had not been involved in anything, I was just an ordinary prisoner, but the H7-block governor was against it on numbers. The H7 OC said we'll make the room and so the block governor capitulated; we controlled the block and I got transferred up.

In the block this person I trusted said: 'Would you be interested in an escape?'

'I dunno. I would need to know a bit about it first.'

'Look Dermot, you are nobody special. There is a move on here and that is all you are getting told for security reasons. You cannot be told until the move. I do not want your answer now but think about it.'

He got his answer a few months later.

Dermot had been picked out because of his skills, record and his personal connections – the leader of the escape attempt was Bobby Storey, his comrade-in-arms who had been convicted with Dermot for the Shaw's Road shooting.

Outside, I'd dealt with lots of stuff. I was a good driver. I used to be in the quarter-master's department. I used to fix guns, clean guns. I was a jack of all trades. One day we were walking in the prison yard and this prisoner turns round to me and says: 'Do you know them pistols point two-fives?'

'Yeh.'

'Do you know much about them?'

'A bit.'

'If they were broke would you know how to fix them?'

'I could have a good go at it.'

And he pulled one out and said, 'Try and fix that.'

'Jesus Fucking CHRISTS!!!!'

He burst out laughing. If a screw had walked by, you were doomed. There was nowhere to hide, no run-back. Because they needed my help with the guns they brought me more and more into the escape. I also practised for the role of driver of the escape lorry. We had a drawing of the cab and the gear stick – no one wanted to put the whole bus into reverse when you wanted to go forward. I was asked questions about that too.

'If you were stuck near Andytown Barracks in a bus and they were coming after you, could you handle it?'

'I would make it fly, I would drive it.'

The IRA prisoner leadership, led by the overall prison OC Brendan McFarlane and escape leader Bobby Storey, had concocted an elaborate and ingenious plan to overwhelm the physical security of Long Kesh and break out *en masse*. The initial groundwork for the escape had begun two years earlier in the aftermath of the 1981 Hunger Strike. The IRA leadership deliberately provoked fights with Loyalists to force the prison authorities to segregate prisoners and make H7 an all-republican block. The prisoners also exploited political divisions between the Northern Ireland Office and the prison administration. In a bid to defuse the prison issue, the Northern Ireland Office pressurized prison staff to find every prisoner work, thereby to recover remission lost through the years of the blanket protest. The IRA prisoner command happily volunteered its closest and most dangerous adherents for the menial jobs of block orderlies, thus allowing its men a wider range of movement around the block under the legitimate guise of cleaning duties. Once the prisoners had achieved physical domination of H7 through segregation, they began a long process of conditioning H7's prison warders to accept their presence as block orderlies close to or in each of the block's eleven electronic gate security segments. It was a tedious, incremental process but vital to the IRA escape plan. If the plan was to work the entire block and the twenty-six officers on duty had to be captured within seconds without the alarm being raised.

The take-over plan relied on total surprise. But there was one other key element – six small handguns. These had been smuggled into the prison in pieces in the vaginas of female visitors, then past metal detectors and anal mirror searches into H7 in the anuses of prisoners returning from visits. By 25 September 1983, the day after the prisoners had watched *Escape from Alcatraz* on television, the IRA were ready.

No one broke security, no one told their mate or ever discussed it with their cellmate. Some guys had spent years and years looking at escapes and it had never happened and so they were fed up with it. But you knew that when it happened they would be there helping to do whatever had to be done. Everyone's role was lettered and I remember reading the plans. I was shitting myself because they were so detailed and someone said, 'Are you looking for loopholes?', and I said, 'No, I am looking for me.'

The escape plan went into operation just after the normal 2 pm head-count on Sunday afternoon when the prison was expected to be quiet. The eighteen IRA prisoners on the initial escape team began to shadow their assigned prison officers waiting for the correct signal. Dermot was shadowing one of the officers on C-wing so his task was relatively easy, but other prisoners had to manoeuvre their way into the senior prison officers' office, stand close to the communications room to prevent any attempt to raise the alarm, whilst others waited to simultaneously enter the two electronic gates between the wings and the circle, and overpower the guards at the precise moment the escape operation began. At 2.35 pm an IRA block orderly began calling for a 'bumper', indicating he wanted the floor polisher from another wing. The message of 'bumper, bumper' was shouted down the wings and the Great IRA Escape of 1983 began.

On that signal IRA prisoners produced guns and stolen workshop chisels and overwhelmed their guards. There were brief fights; Senior Officer George Smylie managed to wrestle the gun out of the hand of his IRA opponent before being overpowered by Bobby Storey. In the confusion Communication Officer John Adams in the secure control room tried to raise the alarm. An infamous IRA prisoner, Gerard Kelly, part of a team that bombed London's Old Bailey Courthouse in 1973, shot him in the head. The officer was not seriously wounded but the sound of the gunshot marked the end of the officers' resistance and H7 was successfully taken by its

inmates. The prison OC Bik McFarlane used the Lobby Officer's keys to let himself out of the block and asked the Block's
Gate Lodge Officer if he could brush the double-gated searching
area that guarded the entrance to the H7. Against instructions,
the officer allowed McFarlane into the segment, from where the
IRA prisoner produced a gun and marched the hapless prison
guard into the block to join the rest of his trussed-up colleagues.
The entrance guard was replaced by a prisoner dressed in
prison officer's uniform.

Inside the block the escapees were already stripping prison
officers of their uniforms, demanding their car keys and the
registration numbers of cars parked in the officers' car park,
and blindfolding them with pillow-cases. Once blindfolded, the
prison warders were passed to the control of a rearguard – a
squad of selected prisoners who stayed behind to prevent a
premature alarm being raised. Stage one of the IRA operation
had been successful; stage two would begin with the arrival of
the high metal-sided prison food lorry which was due to deliver
the prisoners' Sunday meal.

The IRA operation was a combination of deadly seriousness
and schoolboy revolutionary farce, as prewritten IRA documents recovered on the cell-block floor by the authorities
revealed:

TO ALL PRISON STAFF WHO HAVE BEEN ARRESTED BY
REPUBLICAN POWS ON SUN 25TH SEPT

What has taken place here today was a carefully planned
exercise to cause the release of a substantial number of
POWs. The block is now under our control. If anyone has
been assaulted or injured it has been a result of his refusal to
co-operate with us. It is not our intention to settle old scores,
ill-treat nor degrade any of you regardless of your past.
Though should anyone try to underestimate us or wish to
challenge our position, he or they will be severely dealt with
. . . Should any member of the prison administration ill-treat,
victimize or commit any acts of perjury against Rep POWs in
any follow-up inquiries, judicial or otherwise, they will forfeit

their lives for what we will see as a further act of repression against the nationalist people. To conclude, we give you our word as Republicans that none of you will come to harm providing you co-operate fully with us. Anyone who refuses to do so will suffer the ultimate consequences – death! Allow common sense to prevail, do not be used as cannon fodder by the prison administration nor the faceless bureaucrats at Stormont or Whitehall.

— CAMP STAFF REP POWS[13]

I doubt if the helpless prison officers needed the additional emphasis of the exclamation mark to persuade them of the escapees' sense of purpose. McFarlane was serving five life sentences for a sectarian bomb attack on a bar which killed five Protestants; Storey and Dermot were just beginning their eighteen-year prison sentences. Like most IRA prisoners on the escape they had very little to lose.

The second document recovered showed that the IRA leadership's tone was no lighter or less obdurate when it came to its own men:

TO ALL POWS CHOSEN BY CAMP STAFF
TO GO ON ESCAPE

Very few of you are aware of what is now taking place. This is due to security and the possible refusal of some of you to go on this escape. Since it is the duty of all POWs to escape I now instruct you to go to this yard to board the food lorry. Regardless of your feelings we are taking you with us, we have no time for arguments. Just do as instructed. Any refusals will be met with force.

— OPERATIONAL OC

When the food lorry arrived it was let through the block's Gate Lodge and the driver was quickly overpowered. The frightened officer was informed of the IRA's plan to drive the food lorry to the prison's main front gate. To ensure his compliance with their instructions the prisoners tied the man's

foot to the clutch pedal of his lorry and told him he was sitting
on top of a bomb. For good measure, Kelly, dressed in prison
officer's uniform, crouched on the floor of the lorry and kept a
gun pressed against the driver's stomach. Kelly, the man was
told, was already serving a minimum of thirty years and had
nothing to lose by killing a prison guard. Thirty-seven IRA
men, half of them dressed in commandeered prison officers'
uniforms, piled into the back of the truck and pulled the back
door down.

The prisoners were still a long way from freedom. It was half
a mile from H7 to the prison gate, the Tally Lodge. The prison
food van had to pass through two separate security gates,
including the air-lock segment gate that divided the H-blocks
from the rest of the prison. In the event of discovery the IRA
escapees planned to overpower the guards in the control booths
of each security gate and sacrifice an individual prisoner,
leaving him behind to guard the prison officer and stop the
alarm being raised. But the closed van, in defiance of procedures, passed unchecked through the security barriers and
drove on to the Tally Lodge, the sole prison entrance, where
prison officers entered and left the prison for their daily
shifts.

Dermot related:

There were two stages to the escape, there was taking the
block and then taking the Tally Lodge. The prisoners taking
the Tally Lodge were a group that had been assigned to stay
behind to sacrifice themselves in order that the others could
get away. After everyone got away they were to commandeer
screws' cars and then try and get away themselves. But their
primary role was to let the others away. Now some of those
people were lifers, some of them had tens of years to do, but
they all said yes; that escape was something special.

Dermot had been chosen as the driver of the van but his role
would only begin after the van had made it through the last

barrier, the main hydraulic-operated prison gate which was controlled by the Tally Lodge guards. Along with the other prisoners, he hid inside the food lorry and played no part in the Tally Lodge take-over. But it was soon obvious to all of the escapees that something was very wrong.

Eight or ten prisoners dressed as screws had gone into the Tally Lodge and all you could hear was banging and shouting. Everyone was looking at me for reaction and I said to myself, 'Do not show any reaction', because I did not want to demoralize them. I also knew that if we were caught we were going to get the biggest hiding of our lives. I heard someone shout 'The balloon has burst' and 'Aw, come on to fuck!' There were too many screws. There were supposed to be four but we were late in getting out of the block and by the time we arrived at the Tally Lodge it was in the midst of the shift change; screws were coming on and coming off duty. As more of them arrived they started to act with more bravado. The screws were ratty, they were like Alsatians, teeth snarled, saliva coming down. They were riled and lashing out. Someone shouted 'Everybody out!' and we jumped out. No one wanted to be the last one out, somewhere in the middle would be safe enough, and I remember someone saying, 'It's only fucking screws! The Brits are not here yet.'

Someone said 'Advance', so we advanced, the screws backed off and when they did that we saw a fence chest-high and then fields, green fields. Freedom! One screw had blocked the lorry in so we abandoned it. Someone shouted 'Run' and we ran and there was sporadic fighting. I got straight to the barbed wire and then jumped over it. Other people like Skeet Hamilton [serving a twenty-five-year minimum recommended term on five murder counts] fell straight into it and other people ran across his back. Skeet was a bit nasty at the best of times. If you said 'Good morning' he would have said 'What the fuck is good about it!', but he was a nice fella and everyone was using him to climb the wire and he was shouting 'Get off my back ya fucking bastards!'

The IRA escape operation had come within seconds of failure. The delay in the arrival of the food lorry meant that instead of facing four guards in the Tally Lodge, the prisoner take-over squad were soon confronting fourteen. The prisoners were not able to coerce the prison officers into operating the gate, and the sheer number of captured prison officers meant the IRA guards were unable to prevent two officers pressing emergency alarm buttons – alerting the prison's Control Room to an escape attempt. The escape leader Bobby Storey, one of the Tally Lodge team, was in the process of surrendering when another prisoner, in an act of desperation, hit the right button and the main gate began to open. At almost the same moment the official alarm was raised, alerting the whole prison, the RUC, the Army and the Northern Ireland Office.

A massive security operation swung into action. Helicopters, Army and police units converged on the prison, throwing up ring after ring of concentric roadblocks to prevent the prisoners breaking through predetermined security cordons. The first helicopter reached the prison within ten minutes; within another ten minutes the British Army's General Officer Commanding in Northern Ireland and the RUC's Chief Constable, Sir Jack Hermon, were in their command bunkers. News of the escape was flashed through to Prime Minister Thatcher, then on an official tour in Canada. Every prisoner was now in a desperate race to get away from the prison before the area was sealed.

As the prisoners streamed through the gate they were still officially within the prison grounds; the public highway was half a mile away. Most of the prisoners jumped over the barbed-wire fence that marked the external boundary of the prison and ran over fields. There were running fights between the fleeing prisoners, dressed in prison officer uniforms, and real prison officers. A British Army sentry in a guard tower was forced to hold his fire because he could not distinguish between the two groups. Later, he was able to identify a clear target and shot one prisoner in the leg. In the chaos and confusion it was every man for himself.

When I was running, Gerry Kelly was in front of me. I was saying to myself: 'Kelly has tried to escape two or three times. He is more experienced. I am willing to let him take the lead here.' We hit this house, there was a Mercedes there, eight got into the Merc and drove away. Twelve or thirteen of us got into a Hillman Hunter, a saloon-type car. Someone wound down the back window and I dived in with my legs in the air as the car sped off. At the same time the others were screaming: 'What about the others?'

The driver did not want to go. He wanted to take as many as possible. He was screaming: 'What do I do!'

'Drive on! Drive on!'

'What about . . .'

'There's no room.'

One prisoner was hanging on to the driver's door and as I was pulling him in, me and Gerry Kelly looked at each other and we gave eye contact and it was 'me and you together'. We had never spoken to each other before but there was this gut feeling. He was mentally saying 'I'm going with him because he is a good driver' and I was saying 'I'm with him because he has tried to escape before.' We knew we needed to break up. We also knew that if the cops fired into the car they would kill everyone. We were driving along and we met a guy showing off his car to his girl. We stopped and said, 'Does that car work?' 'Of course.' We pushed him out of the way and drove away. We drove another half-mile and the car just collapsed on us. Me and Kelly then said: 'Let's go, everyone behind the hedge.'

Everyone did what they were told. We were not in charge but we just assumed control. The two of us backtracked down the road hoping to get to a farmhouse but as we were going down I was thinking to myself: 'Farmers, shotguns, farmers have shotguns, make sure they don't shoot. If we burst in – Bam, you're dead!' Just then I heard a car coming; I lay down on the road pretending to be dead. Kelly, again without speaking, knew exactly what I was doing. Kelly was in a prison officer's uniform and he flagged it down and he started crying: 'There has been an accident, etc . . .' I had one eye on the car but they were fifty yards away and I could see the driver, a big fat heavy woman, putting it into reverse and the male passenger, a heavy man, getting out. The male passenger was saying, 'Come on, come on, we will get an ambulance.' As Kelly was approaching him, Kelly was going 'My friend! My friend!' It was a two-door car. Kelly got into the car, they lifted the seat up and Kelly jumped the woman. I got up and ran like fuck down. The man had frozen and the woman had frozen and I grabbed the driver's door, trailed her out and that was it, we were away. We got to the hedge, beeped the horn and the whole hedge came alive and every- one jumped in.

But it was obvious that there was still too many of us and we'd have to break up. We drove into this garage, a couple of guys were still in uniform, and we said: 'Take that car, yer man has just filled it up with petrol.' They ran out and they said: 'We need your car.' And of course the man would not give it to them, he started fighting and struggling. A couple of the lads came back and said: 'What will we do, he won't give it to us?' I had never heard of this, no one says to you: 'You are not getting it.' Or if they do, you still get it. I was saying 'Use your batons' [requisitioned prison officer's batons]. And the next thing was that they had pulled the batons out and attacked yer man and started beating the hell out of him. But it was hopeless, the driver had thrown his keys over a hedge or something. I told them, 'We're wasting time here, get in the car', and we drove away.

Just ahead of us at a roundabout there were two pension- ers having a picnic by the side of the car and we went right up their arse so they couldn't reverse. The boys jumped out and took the car. The old man was shouting, 'My wife's sick, my wife's sick.' One of the boys shouted back, 'Not half as sick as we are.' We now had two cars and we headed away. Straight away we took the wrong road and started heading back to the Kesh. We turned round and then saw the other car behind us and we told them: 'Do not follow us, we do not know where we are going.' We headed off.

We knew they would be throwing up roadblocks – there was a five-mile circle that you had to be out of. I think we were about ten miles out but we were expecting a roadblock any second. At one stage we had stopped to ask directions and two UDR Land-Rovers came flashing towards us. I thought that was it but they were flashing – 'Get out of the road!' As we drove alone, Kieran Fleming, who was in the car with us and supposedly had good eyesight, kept shouting: 'Roadblock!' I would slam on the brakes and it would be nothing. Everyone shat themselves. Everyone wanted to go to their own area, their own wee niche. Padraig McKearney knew Tyrone, which was on the other side of Lough Neagh from the prison, and he said: 'Look, we should swim Lough Neagh.' Lough Neagh is the biggest lough in Britain, it must be fifteen miles wide! I can do two lengths of the local swimming pool. Fuck! But I did not want to be the one to hold us back and then Kieran Fleming, who did later drown on active service, said: 'I can't swim but I'll try.' And I turned round and said: 'It's all right Kieran, we are not going that way.' Eventually we decided to go to a nationalist area surrounded by Loyalist areas.

When we got to the area, we went into this shop. Padraig McKearney, who was later killed in the SAS ambush at Loughgall, went in and said in Irish: 'Do you speak Irish?' But in his nervousness he must have shouted out what sounded like gibberish to the girl: 'Ahmalcucal.' The girl probably thought he was a Loyalist so she did not respond. Padraig ran back into the car. We drove on and then saw these four or five kids and so we said to them: 'Do you know where Mr X lives?' Mr X was the name of the Republican in the area who had been interned, but the kid goes: 'No.' People are wary when there are shifty-looking men in a car. So I said: 'Tell them who we are.' And the rest of them just looked at me and Padraig turned to the nine-year-old kid and said: 'We've just escaped from the Maze, fucking help us 'cos we have got to see such-and-such a fella.' The kid jumped off his bike, hopped into the car and took us to the house.

When Gerry walks into the house the guy goes: 'Fuck Gerry, what are you doing here?'

'I have just escaped.'

'You are supposed to be in the Kesh.'

'Well, I'm not.'

This Republican brought us to a safe house. When we got there we found that the others, in the other car, were there too. They had gone to the exact same shop and their guy had said 'Do you speak Irish?' to the same girl and she said 'Yes' and had taken them straight to the house.

The eight IRA men were moved to another safe house and hidden under the floorboards, between the floor joists and the foundations.

Beyond the safe house, Northern Ireland turned into a prison camp as the largest manhunt in British history, code-named Operation Vesper, was mounted. All police leave was cancelled and every one of Ulster's thirty thousand policemen, soldiers and part-time reservists were deployed to man the roadblocks. Thousands of vehicles were searched, thousands of people were stopped and questioned, hundreds of acres and farmhouses and sheds were combed by troops. The Army's helicopters flew from dawn until dusk.

A number of prisoners never made it beyond the barbed-wire fence and were quickly recaptured. Five, including Bobby Storey, were seized hours later as they hid under water in the nearby Lagan river breathing through reeds. One was picked

up after the taxi he hired was stopped at a roadblock. Four
more were arrested the following day at roadblocks or after
commandeering houses. A total of nineteen prisoners were
returned to Long Kesh's punishment blocks but by the following Wednesday it was clear that the other nineteen, including
almost all the senior members of the IRA's planning team, had
made their escape.

On the day of the escape, the IRA rearguard squad, using
pillow-cases as masks, held H7 for an hour after the food lorry
left and then retreated to their cells, locking themselves in. The
disguises and the blindfolds were effective and none of the
prison officers was able to identify any of the rearguard from
amongst the remaining eighty-three H7 prisoners, most of
whom knew nothing about the escape. In addition to the
shooting of Officer Adams in the block's Communication
Room, six prison officers had been injured during running
fights at the main gate. One officer, James Ferris, had been
stabbed in the chest and collapsed and died. A post-mortem
later revealed that the knife wound was superficial and that
the cause of death was a heart attack, but on the day of the
escape every prison officer in the Maze believed the IRA had
murdered a brother officer after callously shooting another
guard in the head. Seamus could only wait in his cell for the
prison administration to retake H7 and the inevitable wrath of
the screws:

We all got a hammering. They moved us from H7 to H8. We
had to run a gauntlet of screws shouting at us and beating
us. They set dogs on us and denied us clothing, food and
medical attention. I thought they were going to kill someone.
You could hear the screams and squeals of someone in the
cells along the row as the screws opened the door, hauled
them out and beat them up. They strip-searched me, threw
back half of my clothing, put me in handcuffs, threw me
against walls, against gates. One screw grabbed me by the
handcuffs and tried to pull me into the dogs. They beat me

about the face. I'm six foot one but big blokes can be hurt too. I swerved and dodged to avoid being thrown in to the dogs.

All of the remaining eighty-three H7 prisoners were later awarded sums of between £1,500 and £3,000 compensation in the Northern Ireland High Court for the injuries they received as a result of the warders' rampage. In the course of the 1988 test case, brought by a H7 prisoner who was not involved in the escape, twenty prison officers denied that any assaults on prisoners had ever taken place or that prisoners were refused medical treatment. Documentary evidence from the prison's doctors directly contradicted the officers' testimony and at the last moment the Crown conceded the prisoners' case. But no prison officer was ever disciplined or reprimanded for the assaults. The beatings, and the failure to discipline prison officers, was, however, to have long-term implications for extradition proceedings involving the escapees.

In the safe house Dermot and seven other IRA men lay beneath the floorboards.

We were lying in the foundations of the house, it was like a coffin. We had to clear the rubble to get somewhere to stretch out. Gerard Kelly was number one and I was his second-in-command. We deliberately made the decision not to take solids so that the need to go for a crap would be kept to a minimum, and we had a coffee jar for piss; I have great bowel control and I did not go for a fortnight. All the negotiations were done through the trapdoor and people could only smoke when the food was being handed down to us. At first the local OC told us that we would be there for a couple of days but it stretched out to two weeks. We did not trust the IRA because of the supergrasses and we did not trust the local unit because all the experience in the world was under the floorboards. We kept saying: 'Give us a gun and we will look after ourselves.' And they kept saying, quite rightly: 'No way!'

Underneath the floorboards we were divided into two groups of four by the foundations. We found out that Kieran Fleming had broken his arm before the escape but he did not tell anyone in case he was taken off. Four of the boys, including Kieran and Padraig, were from the country and they shared one section. Kelly and I shared our section with the other two lads, including Goose Russell [Robert Russell, doing twenty years for the attempted murder of an RUC Superintendent] who annoyed everyone but who kept morale up. The woman we were staying with was pregnant and Goose kept saying: 'You tell her husband that when she goes into labour she is not to use any anaesthetic. She is to have that child without drugs. I do not want her talking.' It was funny, very comical. We even enjoyed laughing at ourselves on the wanted posters printed in the newspapers. I had finally got myself on a wanted poster even if there were thirty-seven other faces there as well.

It was depressing to see so many of our guys being picked and so we actually planned for our arrest. We swopped stories about the layout of Castlereagh and Gough barracks. We knew how many guards would be on; once we got one guard and stole his gun we were all dead anyway so it didn't matter. We were going to take Castlereagh, break out, and then we would live like a flying column, stay outside. We would get like hardened guerrillas, live off the fat of the land. We would be the team that would be sent in to hit a barracks, do or die. We said we would do it once we got into the South, but we were scared almost thinking about it.

The Maze break-out was a security catastrophe for the British authorities. One of the world's most secure prisons had failed to contain the IRA. Republican moral soared; Martin Finucane was ecstatic.

> When the news broke I just knew that Dermot was on it and then when it was confirmed I just felt great. I was really glad that he was out. I knew he had not escaped to full freedom because he was not over the border yet, but it was still great news. The security thrown up was unbelievable. The very next day our house was raided at five-thirty in the morning by the RUC and British soldiers. My Ma started to cry and I said: 'What are you crying for? He is away from these people. If you are crying, cry for joy.'
>
> At the same time I was worried for him. I understood why Dermot got involved. Dermot got his politics from the streets and even now I don't think that the Brits realize how much harm they did to people, whether it's through a house raid or being stopped in the street, and how that could coerce someone into joining the IRA.
>
> I was devastated for Dermot when he was sentenced to eighteen years. He was married and he had a young child. He was missing out on his freedom and what he had enjoyed outside. It was sad but you had to live with that. It was not going to grind us down. Being in prison is better than being dead. I could still go up and visit him, shake his hand and write letters. A lot of the families that got burnt out with us lived near us and a lot of their sons got involved in the IRA and their sons were caught as well. We understood that Dermot knew them risks and we knew them risks. It's inevitable that at some stage you may be caught, you may be shot dead. That has to be accepted. My brothers could have been shot dead. I know I would have been devastated. But you have to live your life, you have to go forward.

Dermot's wife Ailish's emotions about his escape were more complex; at first she was angry at him for disrupting her life.

News of the escape came on the 5.30 pm news and the cops came round the next morning looking for him, so I knew then that Dermot must be one of the escapees. Things got very hostile at work again and no one would speak to me, but people also found the whole thing exciting – they kept rushing out to buy the paper or listen to the next news. I had visions of him being drowned. When I got back to my own house that night I got under the table and started to cry. Our daughter came over to me and said: 'Don't worry Mummy, it'll be all right.' I spent my time worrying about how to get both of them over the depression that would occur if he was caught. After four weeks someone gave me a letter and I knew he was safe. I was upset that he had escaped because I had my life mapped out for me. 'Dermot's in prison now and he will be out in 1990.' You get yourself settled into that way of thinking and then something disrupts it and you think – 'Where do we go now?'

Being an IRA prisoner's widow had hardened Ailish and given her a strong sense of her own political identity, separate from Dermot. Ailish describes herself as a pacifist and it was clear she did not share Dermot's belief in the IRA's armed struggle. But she supported her husband's commitment.

I did not see Dermot as a Republican. I saw him as a person. He was dedicated to his family and obviously believed in the sacrifices that his family had to make. I would not want Dermot to stop. I feel he has given too much of his life to give up. If he did give up it would be a waste of all these years. Me saying 'Would you not give up now?' would be a purely selfish act. I did not want him to get hurt but that was the risks he had to take. The alternative was like wanting your own wee family to be fine but ignoring what was going on round the corner. At the end of the day our daughter has to go out into the outside world. What Dermot was doing was making it a better place for her to live in.

After two weeks Dermot and the other IRA men were driven south over the border into the Republic.

We came up from under the floorboards and washed and shaved. Gerard gave the woman a poem he had written. All I had was a Catholic cross and chain and I gave it to the woman. The man said: 'My wife would like you to name the baby.' And then we wrote a list of boys' names down and a list of girls' names and voted on them. We left soon after.

We wanted to be armed but the IRA refused. We said: 'Look, if the UDR were at the house now and we were armed, a Browning apiece, we would open the door to them and just whack, whack, and start coming at them, whacking them.' That was the mentality we were in – we thought we would escape in the panic. If two of them came to the door – that is two of them dead. It made sense to us because the kids who were looking after us did not have arms training. But the OC of the area said: 'Fuck off. Youse are going to keep our guns and you're not going to give them back.' It was true we would not have given them back.

The IRA fugitives had a clear run to the border and were soon in the South, but the Irish Republic was no sanctuary. The IRA had no country, apart from a few enclaves along the border, and held no territory. In the Republic, IRA men were grudgingly tolerated and periodically suppressed. Wanted IRA men might not have been sent back across the border to Northern Ireland but they would be imprisoned pending protracted extradition hearings. In the rural communities of Southern Ireland, strangers and strange accents were noticed and because republicanism was often a family tradition, IRA sympathizers were well known to the local police, the Gardai. None of the escapees could expect to live in the open. Dermot's run began again.

For the next four years Dermot's life was a bewildering round of short stays in republican safe houses all over Ireland.

He was continually on the move, hiding away in a top bedroom in case the neighbours visited, constantly in the company of someone's wife whilst the man of the house worked, endlessly bored in the lost hours of a rainy afternoon, and always waiting for the knock on the door from the Garda. He had no life beyond the run. After the triumph of the escape, it was a dispiriting anticlimax.

> You get really depressed being on the run. You say to yourself: 'Will I have to go through this for the rest of my life, will I be on the run for the rest of my life?' When I was caught it was: 'Phew, it's over.' I did everything not to get caught, I was very security conscious. I only ever saw my family every three months. One of the Crumlin Road boys was free for eight years and I thought as long as he was free I wanted to be one of the last of our lot.

Dermot was eventually captured along with fellow escapee Paul Kane in the attic of the home of a republican sympathizer in County Longford in late 1987. Both men were picked up in a nationwide security sweep in the Republic following the IRA's disastrous Enniskillen Remembrance Day bomb and the seizure of IRA weapons aboard the *Eksund* trawler.[14]

> There was a big nationwide sweep on, fifty thousand houses were searched, and we had just arrived the night before and moved to a house half a mile away. We were trying to get some sort of transport organized and the woman failed to notice the Branch [the Irish Special Branch, the intelligence arm of the Garda that monitors 'subversives'] car until it was upon us and she shouted: 'Oh my God, it's the Branch.' We went into the attic, there was nowhere else, and we thought hopefully that they would just check under the beds. There was no time to hide. We were sitting next to the trapdoor like kids with our eyes closed thinking he can't see me and your man climbed in but did not look around. We were three

feet away and he was saying to his mates, 'Pass me up the torch', and when he got it he just screamed 'Oh my Jesus!' He jumped down and we heard the cocking of rifles. We gave ourselves up.

Both Dermot and Kane initially refused to identify themselves to the Garda but relented after demanding and receiving a steak-and-potatoes meal from a local hotel. Both men were remanded in custody pending the inevitable extradition battle with the British authorities in the Irish courts over their return to Long Kesh. Dermot was back in a prison cell.

By the time Dermot was recaptured Seamus had completed his fourteen-year sentence and had been released. He served a total of ten years, spending every year of his twenties in jail. Soon after he was freed Seamus became romantically involved with a female volunteer, Mairead Farrell, who had in turn recently been released after serving ten years for a bombing offence.

Farrell was a rarity in the IRA. Her parents were shop-keepers, middle class by West Belfast standards, and she was a bright convent school-girl who joined the IRA at eighteen out of revolutionary zeal. Later, Farrell, who was just over five foot tall, became a republican star with the glamour of a sixties revolutionary. She was charismatic, articulate, and able to bridge the gap between the Provisionals' version of power politics and feminism. She was written up as a hero in the London-based women's liberation magazine *Spare Rib*, a journal not noted for sympathizing with the patriarchal politics of Irish republicanism.

Farrell had been jailed for bombing Belfast's Conway Hotel when she was nineteen. The hotel was partially destroyed but the operation had been a disaster for the IRA unit. One of the Volunteers on the bombing mission, twenty-year-old Sean McDermott, was shot in the stomach at point-blank range and killed after he attempted to commandeer the car of an armed off-duty policeman during the run-back. Farrell was captured and another Volunteer, Kieran Docherty, who later joined the 1981 Hunger Strike and died in the H-blocks, was arrested months later and convicted.

In prison, Farrell became OC of the twenty-odd female republican prisoners in Armagh Jail. She studied for an Open University degree and dominated her fellow prisoners and warders by the force of her will and intellect. Farrell was one of the leaders of the 1980 Armagh 'dirty protest' when women prisoners emulated their male counterparts on the blanket in the H-blocks and smeared their own excrement and menstrual blood on the cells' walls in a year-long protest over prison conditions. In December 1980 Farrell also led three Armagh women prisoners who joined their male IRA colleagues on a nineteen-day hunger strike. In interviews at that time Farrell appears full of passion for the cause. 'I am a Volunteer in the Irish Republican Army and I am a political prisoner in Armagh Jail. I am prepared to fight to the death if necessary to win recognition that I am a political prisoner and not a criminal.'[15] After her release she enrolled as a social science undergraduate at Belfast's Queen's University, stood for election as republican candidate in Cork in the Republic and toured Ireland giving talks on the necessity of the armed struggle in the North. Farrell also returned to the IRA as a Volunteer attached to one of its most secretive departments, GHQ, General Headquarters, which carries out all overseas IRA operations.

On Sunday afternoon, 6 March 1988, eighteen months after her release, Farrell and two other Volunteers, Daniel McCann and Sean Savage, were shot dead by British soldiers on the streets of Gibraltar. Farrell and the others had been planning to plant a powerful car bomb close to the Governor's residence in the British colony on the southern tip of Spain and blow up members of the Royal Anglian regiment, which had just finished a tour of duty in Northern Ireland. Had they succeeded, many soldiers, and possibly a number of civilians, would have died. But somewhere between Belfast and Spain, Farrell and McCann, who also had a high profile within the IRA, were spotted and the entire IRA operation compromised. The IRA Volunteers were put under intensive surveillance in Spain by both Spanish and British intelligence services and lured into a trap in Gibraltar.

All three were shot dead by SAS soldiers, who claimed they had no choice but to open fire after the terrorists made 'suspicious movements'. Farrell and McCann were shot in the face and back four or five times from a distance of three feet. Savage was hit sixteen times and finished off with bullets in the head as he lay on the ground. None of the IRA Volunteers was armed and no explosives or weapons were recovered in Gibraltar. It was, by the Troubles' standard, a great hit. Farrell and her comrades had planned to murder British soldiers but had instead been whacked in a precise pre-emptive ambush.

Farrell knew the risks of being an IRA Volunteer active overseas. 'You have to be realistic. You realize that ultimately you're either going to be dead or end up in jail. It's either one or the other. You're not going to run for ever,' she said in an interview shortly before her death.[16]

Seamus's life had moved on after the death of Mairead and he had a new partner, children, and the family relationships he had missed so much in prison. But a picture of Mairead Farrell had pride of place on top of the television set in his neat living room, whilst an elaborate photographic tribute to Mairead and the IRA Guard of Honour which fired shots at her commemoration ceremony adorned the mantelpiece wall. Following her violent death, Farrell achieved martyr status in the republican movement, but she was still Seamus's ex-girlfriend. It was not the sort of daily reminder I imagined Seamus's new partner would appreciate, but perhaps I failed to understand how deeply Mairead's killing and the distorted chronicle of her death at the subsequent Gibraltar inquest were burned into Seamus.

I was in love with her. We had been involved for eighteen months, living together for five. We set up together the first home for either of us — we'd both spent our twenties in prison. She was very, very special and we spent a lot of that time together. It was a very, very precious time. Mairead was very independent, very determined, a strong woman. She wanted children, she was like any other girl, she liked socializing, dancing, music, fashion, and loved meeting people. We talked about the possibility of both of us going to prison and the effect that would have on kids.

I knew she was away but I did not know where she was. She was murdered without a shadow of a doubt, irrespective of what she was there to do. There were no weapons or explosives in Gibraltar. Obviously they were under surveillance; if the Brits had wanted to arrest them it would have been easy — there is only one way in and one way out of Gibraltar. Instead they killed them and claimed it was because of 'suspicious movements'. By the same token the cops here could have shot me when they threw the sledgehammers through the front window — one false movement which they would call a 'suspicious movement' and you are dead. Who is there to argue on your behalf? I think it was done as a lesson for people operating on the Continent and in England, plus Dan McCann and Mairead were two high-up Republicans in Belfast and so they sent a message to Republicans.

Mairead and I talked about fatalism. If you work out the law of averages and if you were active, the odds were that sooner or later something was going to happen to you. The older you were, then the more you realized that next time it could be your turn to go to jail. You took precautions, you were always wary, but the risk was there. The risk was also there even if you were walking down the street and a soldier lined his sight on you. He could be a wanker, they have killed themselves in their barracks; he could have done the same to you.

At the Gibraltar inquest, the SAS gunmen appeared behind screens and were identified just by letter: Soldier A, Soldier B. The precision of the Crown's intelligence and the ruthlessness of the Gibraltar killings reinforced the SAS's Rambo-like image. As we sat in Seamus's front room, across from the picture of Mairead Farrell, I asked him how good, how competent an enemy, in his opinion, were the killers of Mairead.

'They were both good and bad. If you take me on a one-to-one basis, it's a fair cop. But if there are five of you and one of me, then you are going to overcome me. They have everything at their disposal and yet they can't beat us. We are still here, they cannot eradicate the republican struggle.'

Seamus had no regrets about the IRA bombing mission to Gibraltar and its potential for the taking of life.

Everything that happened abroad put the IRA on the agenda and the Irish struggle. If there were no civilians killed and if the IRA were selective and the targets were of high quality, then I think it was a good thing. If you cannot justify to yourself that it is right to bear arms to defend your country or your position, then you have no right to do so. You do not bear arms not to take life. It's the same for all the parties here whether it's the Brits or us. That morality must equally come to bear on the RUC, the British Army and the British Government. It's not just a one-way morality.

Seamus turned to Dermot for comfort in his grief over the death of his lover, but Dermot's prison walls came between them.

I remember being in Portlaoise Prison and Seamus came on a visit after she had been killed. He cried, that man my brother cried on a visit with me, and I could not put my arms round him. I physically could not. There was nothing to stop me but I did not know what to do. I felt so ashamed afterwards because I did not put my arms round my own brother. He cried saying: 'I will never get over her, never get over her.' I couldn't comfort him the way I wanted to. I remember when I got caught after being on the run and I was outside the courtroom and the cops said: 'You have got a big reception committee waiting, Dermot.' I was not sure if the crowd would be hostile or supportive, Longford was a sleepy town. As I was being brought in I spotted Seamus, there was a moment's silence and then he clapped his hands and there was a big shout. Seamus shouted 'Come on' and the whole crowd erupted. He was always there for me and he had done the right things. And then when his fiancée was killed I could not comfort him. There was a prison guard there and if I had put my arms around him I would have probably started crying too. I was trying to keep my strength up.

Gibraltar is not a country, just an enclave of thirty thousand people crammed into an area of two and a quarter square miles and dominated by its history as a military garrison of the British armed forces. Farrell, Savage and McCann came to plant a bomb that would have killed British soldiers and murdered Gibraltarian civilians. No reasonable person could expect any relative of these people to be treated with sympathy. And so it was with Seamus, when he went to Gibraltar with Mairead's brother and Sean Savage's sister and their lawyer Paddy McGiory to question the Crown soldiers on their actions at the inquest. It was a difficult experience exacerbated by the antics of the British tabloid and broadsheet press, competing to out-do each other in the patriotic fervour of their 'Why the Dogs Had to Die' headlines. 'We were followed everywhere we went by surveillance people. We even came close to assaulting some photographer over the things they were saying and photographs they were taking. They kept trying to imply we were on holiday.'

The harassment from MI5 and the British press was petty in comparison to the chilling drama of the courtroom as Seamus listened to the SAS men's voices from behind the screen describing how they shot Mairead.

They were so cold and clinical about it that it was strange. It was as if he was describing having a cup of tea. Of course you were angry. We inadvertently saw the photographs of the death they gave Mariead and Dan; they just peppered their bodies. If they were that close to be able to shoot them like that, then they were close enough to arrest them. The officers [who controlled the operation by radio from a command point] were cold, disciplined, cynical, but their evidence was full of apparent contradictions. If you saw the size of the place and the resources that these people had at their disposal it would not have mattered if there had been a dozen IRA Volunteers, they still should have been arrested. Had they been armed you could have said maybe there was a chance of 'suspicious movements' but the only people armed were the Brits. It was murder, pure and simple.

In the course of his last interrogation, just a week before we talked, Seamus had remained silent during five days detention. His frustrated RUC interlocutors, in a bid to entice him into conversation, had asked if Seamus thought that the twenty-five years of IRA violence had achieved anything. They asked what he had got out of it; what personal satisfaction had being an IRA Volunteer brought him? Seamus had kept his silence – but they were good questions. I wondered if Seamus ever questioned the value of his involvement in the IRA.

'Certainly, everyone has to reassess their position within the struggle at certain times, when grief comes to your own door or mistakes are being made or things are not going well. You have to sit back, think of things, and reassess your position. It's an individual decision to partake in an act of republicanism, military or political.'

But the prison years and the murder of Mairead had not shaken Seamus's faith. Like Pat before him Seamus was still viewed as a serious enough enemy of the British state to merit a personal mention of the House of Commons. In the spring of 1994 under the cloak of parliamentary immunity, Unionist

MP David Trimble, using information presumably provided by the British security forces for whatever reason, identified Seasmus as being the Intelligence Officer of the IRA's Belfast Brigade.

Five months after the Gibraltar inquest, Pat was killed. Lawyers had been indirectly threatened by police interrogators almost from the start of the Troubles but in the year prior to his murder the death threats intensified. Pat's republican clients were warned by their RUC interrogators in Castlereagh detention centre that 'Finucane is an IRA. He's a dead man'; 'Fucking Finucane's getting took out, tell his brother [Seamus] that he's nothing but scum and that he's going to be taken out too'; 'We'll give Pat Finucane the same as Mairead Farrell got, we'll just drop Pat's name to the UDA.'[17]

Pat Finucane should have been under no illusions about the hatred felt towards him by the RUC. In 1984 the Deputy Chief Constable of Manchester Police, John Stalker, was sent to Northern Ireland to investigate six disputed killings of suspected IRA men by an SAS-trained RUC unit. The men's families claimed their sons had been shot outright and that no attempt was made to arrest them. Stalker was tasked with examining whether or not the specialist RUC unit was operating an official but covert shoot-to-kill policy. He was removed from his own inquiry in 1986 in controversial circumstances and subsequently retired early. In 1988 he published an account of the investigation where he recalled a brief conversation with Pat Finucane in the main foyer of Crumlin Road Courthouse within sight of a group of uniformed RUC officers. Afterwards an RUC sergeant walked up to Stalker and denounced him for speaking to Finucane. 'The solicitor is an IRA man – any man who represents IRA men is worse than an IRA man. His brother is an IRA man and I have to say that I believe a senior policeman of your rank should not be seen speaking to the likes of either of them. My colleagues have asked me to tell you that you have embarrassed all of us in doing that. I will be reporting this conversation and what you have done to my superiors,' wrote Stalker, recalling the RUC man's words and noting that he had never encountered such open hatred between police and a lawyer in his twenty-six years as a British police officer.[18]

Seamus knew about the threats through his IRA contacts and had long been concerned about Pat's vulnerability in north Belfast, a predominantly Protestant area.

Long before they threatened Pat directly, Dermot and I had been on to him about moving out of north Belfast. There had been a lot of sectarian killings there, but Pat liked it and he would not move. We even discussed him getting a gun, carrying a licensed firearm, but Pat would not have a firearm in his house to protect himself. His refusal to do that explodes the whole myth that Pat was an IRA man. People on the outside may have seen us as one just because he represented IRA men and I was an IRA man but that would never have been the case.

Pat was thirty-nine when he was killed. He was a father figure to all of us, someone to look up to. He was probably too overbearing and domineering at times, although he was always like that even from schooldays. We would argue over things, he did not necessarily agree with what was happening. Pat had republican beliefs, nationalistic tendencies, but not enough for him to take up arms and kill people for it. Pat's full-time life was the law, he loved it so he did. He formed a good team, barristers and solicitors, that was winning cases, making inroads into oppressive laws that were designed to put Republicans and activists away. And that was why they killed him.

Douglas Hogg did not get up in the House of Commons and make that speech without it being cleared by senior officials. I have no love for him, I have no love for the people who planned, orchestrated and executed Pat.

The first call Seamus made after ordering the RUC off the phone on the night of Pat's death was to Martin.

I was in a neighbour's house when someone rang and said Seamus was looking for me and it was urgent. I knew something was wrong. I went into panic and I was just shaking. I couldn't put the phone down. I rang Pat's and Seamus answered the phone and he told me Pat was dead. I was crying, it just screamed out of me, and I thumped the wall. He tried to tell me to control myself and said: 'Where's Ma? Where's Ma?' I said she is down at Mrs Gillen. 'Get down there right away.' When I walked into the house she saw the look on my face and just started screaming. I had nightmares about the way I would have reacted in the house if I had been there, if I had been shot. What would I have done if I heard the doors being smashed in? Would I have jumped through the window or out the back door? Who gives them the goddamn right to do that? What gives them the right to make threats? Pat had to be shot dead because he was too successful in exposing their violations, their abuses.

Dermot heard the news on the radio in the Republic's high-security Portlaoise Prison where he was being held pending his extradition.

It was on the 9 pm news. I wasn't really listening and then I heard the words 'leading solicitor' and 'Finucane'. I had my own sad wee tears. When the comrades seen me do that they were all putting their arms around me. I know what it is like to cry and be really hurt and I also know that I have inflicted that pain on others. I do not want to go through that again. I also know that when I have talked about operations my eyes have lit up with excitement but that is because of the company, comrades talking of when we fought the enemy, like men talking of World War One or Two battles that they have been in. But I do not want any more death.

I met Geraldine Finucane in the Crown Bar in Belfast and over a few glasses of Guinness we discussed Pat. Geraldine, a handsome woman in her early forties, was still adjusting to her widowhood, still finding a place for herself in the world in the absence of her murdered husband, still coping with the awkwardness of lone dinner party invitations from reluctant hosts. It was clear that she still missed Pat, missed his energy, his anarchic obsession with the law, his clients and his soccer. Pat's work had given them both a place in the world and all of that was lost at his death. Geraldine had been very strong at Pat's funeral and she was no less strong now.

> At the time of the funeral it was very hard for me to get a sense of what was happening because of my injuries. But before I left the house I called the children together and told them not to cry in public. 'Outside there will be TV cameras, photographers, hundreds of people. I do not want those who did this to see how they have wrecked our lives. I don't want you crying.' Other people do cry on camera but I could not do that. It would seem wrong – maybe that is a weakness.

I asked Geraldine about the night she witnessed Pat's murder. She said something quite strange and wonderful about the love that can exist between two people. 'I was glad, not glad that it happened but glad that if it happened, it happened in front of me and not someone coming to my door saying Pat had been killed in some arsehole in the middle of nowhere. I was glad that I was with him.'

Dermot was denied compassionate leave to grieve with his family. For the following year he fought a lengthy extradition battle in the Irish Republic's courts to avoid being returned to Long Kesh. Dermot's defence team, originally led by Pat,

argued that he faced a real risk of being beaten or tortured by
prison guards for his part in the escape. The central pillar of his
defence rested on transcripts of the 1988 test case for compensation brought in the Northern Irish courts by his brother on
behalf of an H7 prisoner for injuries received as a result of
prison officer beatings during the transfer of prisoners from H7
to H8. The Irish Supreme Court concluded that they could not
accept the assurances of the Northern Irish prison system that
Dermot Finucane would not be similarly abused and his
fundamental human right not to be tortured violated. The
Northern Irish Prison Service's failure to discipline its own
officers for the H7 beatings ultimately destroyed the Crown's
extradition case. Dermot was freed in March 1991.

He lives openly in Dublin and is a full-time worker at Sinn
Fein's Headquarters and in his own words is 'an active member
of the republican movement'. He is still wanted by the British
authorities and cannot visit any British jurisdiction without
risking arrest and imprisonment.

Partition has created two Irelands, however much the IRA wish
to deny it, and two Irish souls. The southern soul is less
concerned with the certainties of time and place, or ambition.
It is harder to hold southerners to an appointment, or a deal,
or determine what they think. Ironically, the northern soul is
more British, harder, and seeks to classify the world in more
precise terms; the IRA are good or the IRA are bad. Dublin is a
world apart from the familiar streets of Belfast and Dermot
freely admits he is often homesick. He is an exile in the capital
city of the country he is fighting to unite. But Dermot is
unrepentant about his life as an IRA Volunteer.

> I did set out to fight them and I fought them. Even the
> political damage of the escape was tremendous; extradition
> had the two governments at loggerheads, militarily and
> politically, for months.
>
> My family never started this, we never wanted this. It was

the Brits who started harassing our John, put him in prison;
John got out, died. They started harassing our Seamus, put
him in prison, then they moved on to Martin. They wanted
our Martin to work for them as an informer; he was never
involved in anything so he fled to Europe. And then they
started on me, put me in prison; I got out. And then they
murdered our Pat.

But what was once the politics of family was now, in
Dermot's mind, the politics of nationalism.

It is unjust that someone else governs us. I think the Brits
have made a bit of a mess of it from their involvement. I
think our worst could only be as good as their best. I think
as intelligent people, Catholics and Protestants, we are
capable of doing it. I am just ordinary Joe Soap. But what I
said to myself about the people I was up against was, 'I am
as good as you.' That is how I approached it. And when I
was being interrogated I looked them over and said, 'I am
better than you and you won't bring me down.' And I have
no problem with our ability to partake in the rebuilding of
our country. I see a lot of competent people around me, I
also see a lot of incompetent people. Maybe we can do the
job a lot better than the Brits are doing.
     Britain is finished in Ireland. It's over. It's all a question of
when, when do they decide to pull out. Why not sit down
now and create the conditions where you can demilitarize the
situation and set about bringing their departure so that no
more people have to suffer and die? It is not as if we in Sinn
Fein are going to create a *coup d'état*, take over in the North
or take over in Ireland. That is a ridiculous idea. The British
can very easily create the conditions where they can hand
over power to the Free State Government in Ireland. In a new
Ireland there would be a realignment of political forces and
you would probably find Fine Gael and the Unionists finding
common cause, the SDLP and Fianna Fail would join up, and

you would probably find Sinn Fein on their own. It makes
sense to have good neighbourly relations. The Troubles cost
a billion a year. There is everything in it for the Brits to leave.
The last two big bombs in London cost them hundreds of
millions of pounds, the Baltic Exchange alone cost something
like £635 million.[19] That one bomb was the equivalent of
what they had paid out in compensation in Northern Ireland
for the last twenty years.

I do not recognize the Brit legitimacy in my country. I do
not give a sweet fuck what the Brits in a sense impose. If it is
against my will then I will rebel against it and so will an
awful lot of people. The Brits have no right to be in our
country. They have no more right to be there than they have
a right to be in Australia or America or anywhere else.

Pat Finucane's killers abandoned their hijacked taxi back on
the fringes of the Loyalist Shankill Road; their journey of
murder which began so long before in Percy Street had at last
been completed and the Fenian enemy extirpated. Nothing
remains of Number 78; the area has been redeveloped and the
old street pattern broken, although the site of the once temporary barricades is marked in concrete and steel by the Peace Line
that now severs the Falls from the Shankill like a prison wall.
The red, white and blue kerbstones and the murals of masked
UFF gunmen on every gable-end with their slogans – 'There is
no such thing as a nationalist area of Ulster, just areas of Ulster
temporarily occupied by nationalists' – proclaim Percy Street to
be once more safely within the domain of Protestant Ulster.

But the other journey, the greater journey of the Finucane
family from being on their knees in Percy Street to being at the
heart of the IRA's rebellion in the disputed province of Ulster,
is far from over. At the end of my final interview with Dermot
in the ramshackle room in Sinn Fein's Dublin Headquarters, I
stood up, made my goodbyes and walked towards the door of

the room. As I was leaving I turned and caught a glimpse of Dermot framed, still, against the evening sky. There was the slight trace of a smile on the lips and his eyes were open, bright and sparkling. The murders, the killings, the pain, the prisons and the loss had somehow not diminished him. This IRA soldier, this inflictor of harm, this gunman and brother, was quietly and confidently waiting for the next onslaught. He still stood the ground, a rebel heart, and a very dangerous enemy of the Crown in Ireland.

NOTES

1. *Legal Defence in Northern Ireland*, report of an International Delegation of Lawyers, National Council for Civil Liberties, London, 1989. *Report on the Assassination of Patrick Finucane*, Michael J. Graham, Hartford, Connecticut, 1989. *Human Rights and Legal Defense in Northern Ireland: The Intimidation of Defense Lawyers, The Murder of Patrick Finucane*, Lawyers Committee for Human Rights, New York, 1993.

2. The B-Specials were a part-time police reserve force that were viewed by the Catholic community as a state-licensed Protestant militia. The B-Specials were disbanded in 1970.

3. On 15 October 1974 the IRA prisoners burned down their huts as part of a protest over prison conditions.

4. *Belfast Graves*, National Graves Association, Dublin, 1985, p. 184.

5. See Chapter 3, p. 195.

6. Roy Mason was the Labour Government's Northern Ireland Secretary of State from 1976 to 1979. He took a hardline pro-military stance against the IRA. Evidence later emerged that IRA suspects were being systematically beaten in police custody.

7. The blanket protest was a campaign by IRA prisoners to resist being classified as common criminals and being forced to do prison work and wear prison clothes. It started in 1976 and finally ended with the 1981 Hunger Strike.

8. A republican version of the boy scouts.

9. In April 1977 the RUC took the unprecedented step of issuing 'Wanted' posters on three notorious IRA Volunteers in a bid to capture them.

10. Ned Kelly was a famous nineteenth-century Australian outlaw who wore an iron chest-plate as a primitive form of body armour.

11. Dr Mengele was the chief camp doctor at Auschwitz extermination camp. Heydrich was the SS head of the Nazi puppet state of Bohemia and Moravia.

12. Protesting IRA prisoners were denied the normal fifty per cent remission of sentence then accorded to all prisoners in the Northern Ireland prison service.

13. From court documents of the trial of the escapees.

14. In October 1987 a 150-ton Libyan arms shipment to the IRA aboard the *Eksund* trawler was intercepted off the coast of northern France.

15. Quoted in Eileen Fairweather et al, *Only the Rivers Run Free*, Pluto, London, 1984, p. 224.

16. Quoted in Ian Jack, 'Gibraltar', *Granta*, No. 25, London, 1988, p. 34.

17. Quoted in *Human Rights and Legal Defense in Northern Ireland*, p. 50.

18. John Stalker, *Stalker*, Harrap, London, 1988, p. 49.

19. The Baltic Exchange bomb in the City of London in April 1992 killed three passers-by and caused widespread destruction in the heart of London's financial district.

4

INFORMERS

A local woman out for an evening walk with her dog found him lying on the verge at the Coach Road junction, about a mile and a half from the village of Newtownhamilton in the IRA 'bandit country' of South Armagh. Patrick Flood's hands were tied behind his back with masking tape and a black garbage bag had been pulled over his head; the bag dripped blood. It was a still July night in 1990, a quiet night for the quiet death of an IRA informer.

The following day the Derry Brigade of the IRA announced that Patrick Gerard Flood had been an IRA Volunteer for five years – a bomb-maker. For the last three years, the IRA said, Flood had also been a police informer who had sabotaged bombs and given the RUC information about IRA operations. When the Brigade leadership found out, they killed him.

Paddy's body was found less than a mile from the border with the Irish Republic. All land movement in South Armagh was controlled by the IRA – the area is nicknamed the Provisional Republic of Crossmaglen – and Paddy's final journey had been safe for his killers. The IRA gunmen would have crossed the border on a nearby unmarked road, turned on to the Armagh road for 250 yards, and then stopped at the Coach Road junction where the two-lane Newtownhamilton—Armagh road widens as the carriageway splits. It's a lovely spot, surrounded by thick hedgerows and green rolling hills. The junction is a handy place to stop for a moment or two if you wanted to rummage around for something on the back seat or dump the dead body you had lying there – which is exactly what killers did that evening.

The RUC were afraid of South Armagh – it was a bad place for them, and for the British Army, which lost one third of their casualties in its green fields. The discovery of a man's body at the junction was first reported to the police at 21.07 pm on Thursday, 26 July, but the corpse had to lie all night by the side of the road until the safety of daylight allowed Her Majesty's Armed Forces to examine the body.

That night, the powerful microwave radio masts atop Newtownhamilton Police Station, RUC HQ in Belfast and the main RUC Strand Road Barracks in Londonderry streamed with police messages, but no one would have been surprised by the news from the border road. A week before, British Army squaddies on foot patrol in the Catholic Bogside district of Derry had stopped people and asked if they were going to be 'a tout like Paddy'. Flood's Special Branch handlers, Detective Sergeant L and Detective J, code-named Mark and Phil, had already written him off and were fully engaged in trying to find a replacement.

In Derry the IRA came to the home of Paddy's father, Seamus Flood, the same evening. 'The night I did get word a man came to the door. He must have been five foot ten because I am not that tall myself and there is a double step at our front door.

"Seamus Flood?"

I answered: "Aye, that's right."

"Your son is not coming back. We have got to go." '

The men walked away.

Paddy Flood was not the first IRA member to be shot as an informer by his one-time comrades. In the last twenty-five years of the Troubles nearly forty Republicans have been executed by their own side. They were casualties of the secret intelligence war between IRA and the British security forces; hundreds of others, loyalist and republican, were forcibly or willingly recruited, primarily by the RUC's intelligence division, the Special Branch.

The recruitment of informers has long been the primary British method of gaining intelligence on their republican enemies. Over the centuries informers have been used, with devastating effect, to disrupt and destroy republican rebellions, and despite the electronic hardware of the twentieth century, the Crown's most powerful weapon in the present-day Troubles remained the human informer.

In republican communities an atavistic hatred of informers runs back to the Dublin Castle spies who betrayed the 1798 United Irishmen Rising and were deemed responsible for sending the father of Irish Republicanism, Theobald Wolfe Tone, on the road to the gallows. On the bloody stage of Irish history, the informer is the villain, a cultural bogeyman who has played his part in the downfall of endless fine and noble patriots. The informer is the Judas within, the betrayer, the fountainhead of all Irish misery and a convenient scapegoat for centuries of glorious failure.

In 1882, almost a century after Tone's death, a Fenian conspirator, James Carey, betrayed his fellow Republicans after they had hacked to death Lord Frederick Cavendish, the newly appointed Chief Secretary for Ireland, and Under-Secretary Thomas Burke, with surgical knives in Dublin's Phoenix Park. Five of the assassins, members of an extremist faction known as the Invincibles, were hanged as a result of the informer's testimony, but the long arm of republican revenge reached out for Carey off the Cape of Good Hope as he fled Ireland for a new life in South Africa; bricklayer Pat O'Donnell shot him dead on board the *Melrose*. O'Donnell was in turn hanged for Carey's murder, but republican honour had been avenged.

For Republicans, 'touting' (informing), for whatever reason, remains the ultimate crime. Provisionals subconsciously use the term 'turn' in a unique way to signify the irrevocable stigma attached to informing. Someone 'turns' informer or they are simply 'turned'. The waters cleave and the life of the informer, and their kith and kin, diverges from the tribe. There is no language for, no possibility of, 'turning back'. In Ireland the same term has only one other usage – to describe the social betraying of turning one's religion and adhering to the other, Catholic or Protestant, faith.

Informers were a different breed of creature to the Cold War spy. It was not possible for the Protestant policemen of the RUC or English foreigners from MI5 intelligence to insert trained spies into tight-knit republican communities. IRA men grow up together in the same area, drink and socialize with each other from their teenage years, riot together, and inter-marry with other republican families. They are a unique product of their particular community; other IRA men from different areas in Northern Ireland would be viewed with suspicion and treated with caution. There is no place for outsiders to be slotted into this complex web of social and extended family relationships. Informers must come from within; they must be turned.

In their war against the Provisional IRA, the RUC did not hesitate to use every means available – money, coercion, blackmail and, perhaps, murder – to recruit informers. A member of the RUC told me:

> In dealing with a ruthless terrorist organization you are not going to get intelligence just by asking for it. Intelligence was crucial in the fight against the IRA and the major way of getting that information was getting informers. Of course there were pressures and there were financial inducements. If someone was giving information the credibility of that information would be tested and the payments adjusted depending on its value. It was a necessary step in saving lives.

Informers and the information they provided were the key battleground in Northern Ireland. Their recruitment and con-tinued co-operation were the most covert part of Britain's intelligence war. But the agents themselves soon ceased to be men. Their lives were cheap, their relationships with their handlers governed for the most part by fear, and their worth determined by the intelligence they brought in. No one loves an informer; no one, apart from their family, would mourn their death. To survive, the informer had to walk a lethal tightrope between his police handlers and the IRA. The more successful the agent was in foiling IRA operations, the greater the risk of his discovery. And there was no escape; after an informer like Paddy Flood had passed his first piece of information to the police, he was trapped, facing the certainty of death if the IRA found out and open to blackmail from the Special Branch. Once turned, an informer had to endure the paranoid lifestyle of the double-agent, with its code-names, unlisted telephone lines, secret rendezvous and clandestine meetings with handlers, in the suspicious and secretive world of Ulster's paramilitaries.

Informers, through their knowledge of impending paramilitary operations, provided their handlers in RUC Special Branch with the active power to take life, and the passive power to prevent the taking of life. The RUC used this active power to intercept and kill their IRA enemies in carefully prepared ambushes. The RUC used the passive powers of their intelligence system to thwart the IRA by warning potential victims of the imminent danger. But the secrecy of the informer world also allowed the Special Branch a third option: the power to do nothing if they believed it was necessary for some people, albeit British soldiers or civilians, to die in order to protect the source of their information.

The Provisionals hated but also feared informers. In the early morning winter darkness of 6 December 1984, two Derry Brigade Volunteers, Daniel Doherty and William Fleming, were shot dead by a five-man SAS assassination squad in the grounds of the city's Gransha Hospital as the IRA men rode a motorcycle to ambush and kill an off-duty Ulster Defence Regiment soldier. Doherty was hit nineteen times, twelve of them in the back. Fleming was shot on the ground, his right leg shattered, after an SAS soldier had rammed the IRA's motorcycle with his car. Fleming was hit by four bullets, numerous bullet fragments, and had fifty-six separate gunshot wounds. The IRA men's only weapon – a handgun – was recovered *inside* a holdall where it had been placed, SAS Soldier 'A' claimed, after he had removed 'the gun from the gunman's hand'.[1]

The Troubles were a civil conflict, governed by civil not military laws, and members of the British security forces were obliged to use the minimum force deemed necessary to carry out their lawful duties. The SAS soldiers claimed that they believed their own lives to be in danger and had no option but to open fire on Doherty and Fleming. The SAS soldiers' legal textbook answers ensured that, according to civil law, their use of lethal force in the grounds of Gransha Hospital was justified. But the legal chicanery of their well-rehearsed statements about 'engaging' the gunmen fooled no one in Derry. Doherty and Fleming may have been on a murder mission but once they had entered the SAS ambush zone no action on their part could have saved their lives. No attempt had been made to arrest them, no warning had been given and the IRA men had no chance to surrender. The SAS executed Doherty and Fleming as part of the Troubles' hidden war, acting on high-grade intelligence that could only have come from an informer within the IRA's ranks. Whether the informer realized it or not, the information he passed to the British security forces sent Doherty and Fleming to their deaths. A local RUC officer, off the record, described the SAS ambush as 'outright murder'.

Hard, accurate, informer intelligence was essential to the RUC if they were to stay one step ahead of the IRA. On 24 October 1990, three months after Patrick Flood's death, three IRA active service units in different parts of Northern Ireland carried out the IRA's most audacious military operation in Ulster for ten years. In co-ordinated attacks 150 miles apart, the IRA used three 'human proxy bombs' – men they regarded as collaborators – to deliver three thousand-pound car bombs to separate military installations within minutes of each other. Six soldiers and one civilian were killed.

The most successful attack was in Derry, where the IRA burst into the home of Patsy Gillespie, a canteen worker at a nearby British Army base, and took his family hostage before driving him across the border by a back road into the Irish Republic, four miles away. There, they forced him to drive a van, packed with explosives, towards the Coshquin border checkpoint which the British Army used to search traffic on the main road crossing between Buncrana in the Republic and Derry. An IRA squad, armed with rifles, followed Gillespie by car to ensure he obeyed their instructions. Four minutes out from the checkpoint, the IRA triggered a detonation device designed to evade the base's electronic counter-measures, which jammed the frequencies used by IRA radio-controlled bombs. In the final four minutes of his life Gillespie was driving a ticking bomb.

Gillespie drove into the checkpoint at 3.55 am. Eyewitnesses reported hearing shouting, screaming and then shots. Within tens of seconds the thousand-pound bomb exploded, killing five soldiers from the King's Regiment. The bomb devastated the Coshquin base; a huge crater was gouged into the earth where the operations room had once stood, pieces of human torso were found on rooftops; the body of Patsy Gillespie was never recovered. Armoured cars, their inch-thick plate buckled like melted plastic, littered the fringes of the blast crater. Windows and roofs of houses hundreds of yards away in the nearby Benview housing estate were smashed and ripped off by the force of the blast. The death toll would have been far higher if off-duty soldiers had not been sleeping in a recently built mortar-proof concrete bunker, whose walls absorbed the tremendous shock wave.

Eleven IRA men and the entire resources of the Derry Brigade had been committed to the Coshquin operation but Special Branch had only been able to obtain a vague outline of an impending assault against a security force base somewhere in their area. If Flood had been alive and employed as the bomb-maker, he might perhaps have been able to warn his RUC handlers; the dead soldiers and Gillespie might have been saved. The catastrophic loss of crucial intelligence allowed the IRA to deploy their most powerful weapon – surprise.

Paddy Flood's quiet death on the Irish border did not rate much news coverage. The world of the IRA informer has always been closed off, immune from outside scrutiny, and deliberately distorted by the men who recruit and the men who kill informers. The London *Guardian*, on Saturday, 28 July 1990, carried just two lines: 'The IRA in Londonderry yesterday claimed responsibility for the murder of one of its members, Patrick Flood, aged thirty, whose body was discovered on a border road late on Thursday night. It alleged he was a Royal Ulster Constabulary informer.'

That paragraph was the starting point for my own search for the real story of Paddy Flood's life. The *Guardian*'s terse paragraph concealed one of the most awful human stories of the Troubles. It was about the worst things in human nature, about profound betrayal, about a man who believed in one set of ideals but was blackmailed into denying them. It was about terrifying emotional pressure, physical terror and, surprisingly, it was also about love – of one man's desperate desire to save his wife. His story ran deep into the heart of Ulster's informer war. In that hidden world, men lived frightening double lives. The IRA had only one sentence for informers – execution. Everyone knew that. Paddy Flood knew it too; he could have thought of nothing else for the seven weeks he was held and interrogated by the IRA killer squad in their safe house, south of the Irish border.

Officially the RUC had a policy of neither confirming nor denying that someone was an informer. But the last trick RUC Headquarters in Belfast played on Paddy Flood was to feed the London *Sunday Times* a line on the day of his funeral emphatically denying that Flood was a police agent. It was difficult to disprove. Who could one check with? The IRA who murdered him? The RUC Special Branch who manipulated him? His family who loved him? The informer world was built on lies, betrayal and deceit, and even a dead tout had his users.

In Derry, as I was to learn, someone said the police were telling the truth. Paddy's wife Elizabeth vehemently denied Paddy was a tout. Elizabeth Flood said the IRA killed him as part of an internal feud. 'Those people really believe Paddy was an informer. But they are wrong. They do not want to admit they are wrong. They are covering up. Paddy hated touts.'

But Paddy's only brother, David Flood, still committed to the IRA's cause, did accept reluctantly that Paddy had become that despised thing – a tout. 'Me and Paddy were very close. I can understand it, accept it and still not believe it. You still love him no matter what he did. If I saw it happen to another family – their son to be shot as an informer – I would say "tough shit". So it would be hypocritical of me just to say it could never have been Paddy and blame the IRA.'

Officially the police denied that Flood was an informer; unofficially they admitted to me he was. I was able to establish from a wide variety of republican and nationalist sources in Derry that Paddy Flood was not the victim of an internal IRA feud.

There was also Paddy Flood's own testimony. His IRA interrogators taped his last confession. It was a horrifying document recorded by a man in mortal fear, knowing he was about to be shot. For the first time in twenty years an outsider was allowed to listen to an IRA informer's confession. I was able to hear the voice of Paddy Flood, sometimes calm, sometimes sobbing, on this secret tape. It was the voice of a frightened man but his message was unmistakable: 'The police were always reminding me about my wife. They could bring her in at any time. They would break her like a plate. She would fucking go down a long, long time. It was the really big hold they had over me. The fact that they would do her. It shattered me. If it had just been me it would have been all right.'

Irish Catholicism celebrates death, its funeral rituals are public, ostentatious. The doors of houses are thrown open, the neighbourhood descends on the bereaved to share their grief, acknowledge their loss, and wake the dead. But Paddy Flood's funeral was a hurried and secret affair, as closed from public view as the sealed coffin — the undertaker advised the family not to open the casket — that shielded his ruptured face, blown in half by the exiting high-velocity round.

The Requiem Mass was subsumed into the normal Sunday morning Mass at the local St Mary's Church, where Paddy had married two years earlier. The Sunday morning congregation, as was usual in the devoutly Catholic Bogside community, was large but by the time Flood's cortège left for the City Cemetery the numbers had dwindled away. In a town like Derry, in a community like the Bogside, four thousand people would have normally attended the funeral of a victim of the Troubles, an IRA Volunteer would have got a thousand, an ordinary heart attack victim could expect a couple of hundred. For Paddy Flood there were barely a hundred people; doors were closed, the streets were empty, his mourners shunned — Paddy had turned. 'It was the worst funeral I have ever been to in my life. It was sombre and very sad. There was this awful feeling of irony that this man had devoted his life to a cause and had been killed by his own organization. And then his wife started squealing at the graveside,' said one of the reluctant participants.

The shame of Flood's betrayal could not be expunged by death. In a grim attempt to soften the blow, the official IRA statement on his execution said his treachery was all 'the more regrettable because of the high esteem in which the Flood family was held by the Republican Movement in Derry'.[2] The statement was designed to protect Paddy's brother David, a one-time republican activist, from being ostracized by the community. But the trace of being the brother of a tout will linger with David Flood for the rest of his life.

The Derry Brigade were unrepentant about Paddy's murder. Flood had become an RUC military asset who had to die to protect the IRA and deter other would-be informers. 'Paddy Flood was a personal friend of mine. But Paddy Flood was also an IRA Volunteer who from the outset was guilty of treason and he more so than anyone knew the consequences of his actions. He was involved in active collaboration with the enemies of Ireland,' said Hugh Brady, a Derry Sinn Fein councillor.

After Flood's murder, the Derry Brigade offered other informers in the city a week-long amnesty to come forward. The IRA said no one would be harmed, but they warned: 'This opportunity may never arise again.'

Paddy Flood was a true child of the Troubles. Born in 1960, he was nine years old when British troops first came to Derry to save the Catholic population from the wrath of the Protestant-dominated RUC. Hailed as saviours, the British troops were initially welcomed with open arms and cups of tea in the streets. But the welcome quickly wore out and instead of tea the troops were met with stones. In 1972 British paratroopers shot dead thirteen unarmed civil rights protesters during a march in Derry. Bloody Sunday was a watershed; the war between the IRA's Derry Brigade and the British Army began in earnest.

Paddy Flood came from an ordinary working-class family in the Catholic Bogside ghetto. Derry City Corporation was notorious for the way that Unionist parties manipulated the electoral boundaries to ensure that the Catholic majority were always excluded from power. Paddy's family suffered from the usual forms of anti-Catholic discrimination endemic to the old Protestant-dominated Stormont regime; his father Seamus was frequently unemployed, their housing was poor, their economic prospects meagre.

The Troubles shattered any hope of normality. Every night for fifteen years there was rioting on the streets, and Paddy soon became the most notorious rioter in the city. 'The norm would have been riots, pitched battles in the street, petrol bombs, barricades and burning buses. You have a kid whose pals are doing that sort of thing. "Are you coming down to the riot?" they would ask. If you refused you would be taunted: "You are nothing but a coward,"' said a Bogside parish priest, describing the atmosphere of the early Troubles.

Peer pressure can be a terrible influence on a young lad who has nothing to look forward to in life, no job, no prospect of a job, who maybe has no self-esteem and feels the community does not esteem him because there is nothing for him except the prospect of standing around at the corner of a bookie shop or pub or heading off to England for work. If suddenly someone then whispers in your ear – 'We want you' – then it is obvious the prospect can appear very attractive. Added to that was the perception that the police were against them, the army against them. It was a simple our side, your side, thing that brought out all our history and feelings of discrimination and anger. Joining the IRA could seem a handy way out for a young lad.

Paddy first began rioting when he was twelve years old. It became a kind of sport in the city. As evening fell youngsters and children would gather close to the ancient medieval walls and throw stones at British Army vehicles. More soldiers would come, petrol bombs would be thrown, and plastic baton rounds, lethal at close range, would be fired in return. It was great 'crack' (exciting). A whole generation of Derry Catholics, some now doctors, teachers and lawyers, passed through the rioters' ranks; rioting was a teenage rite of passage.

Paddy's father Seamus tried to stop him. 'I told Paddy: "If you are going down there you are going to be arrested by the police and it's not going to do you any good. The people there, egging you on, are only using you for their own ends." But Paddy did not listen.'

Paddy founded a loose organization of hardened rioters, Bogside Republican Youth, which was active in the street demonstrations and riots that marked the deaths of ten IRA hunger-strikers in 1981. At six feet three inches, he was unusually tall for Northern Ireland and even masked he was easily identifiable amongst his fellow rioters. He was nicknamed 'Warhead' and soon began to amass a string of minor convictions, twenty-eight in total, for riotous behaviour, assaulting police, blocking traffic and hijacking vehicles. He won an awkward sort of fame in the nationalist community as both a daredevil and a fool, and was regularly stopped and harassed by British Army foot patrols. 'Everybody knew Paddy was a Republican. The weans [children] in the streets, even the dogs, knew he was a Republican,' said his brother-in-law Kevin Mooney.

The rioting was militarily ineffective, but Paddy went on throwing petrol bombs long after his contemporaries had moved on to more fruitful occupations and the IRA had become embarrassed at this nightly charade of the people's anger. Paddy was still trying to prove himself; he was desperate to join the IRA but had been rejected a number of times on the grounds of his notoriety.

Paddy had left school at sixteen with a basic education. Work is hard to find in Derry for anyone – male unemployment in certain areas is over fifty per cent – and if you had a bad security record like Paddy it was impossible to find a job. For most of his life he was unemployed or drifted from one menial job to another as a bricklayer or community youth worker. 'He was always going to be a foot soldier. He did not have any leadership qualities. But he was game for anything and would always do what he was asked,' commented an old schoolfriend.

Paddy wanted what we all probably want – respect from our peers. Ironically, his wife Elizabeth said Paddy told her that if they had been living at peace in a different country he would have wanted to be a policeman. 'He liked that type of thing. He was idealistic and he thought the uniform was sort of glamorous.' But in the republican Bogside ghetto there was only one organization that gave the close sense of camaraderie that Paddy longed for – the IRA.

In a small city like Derry, with a Catholic population of 55,000, the IRA was a close-knit organization of perhaps fifty active Volunteers, backed by a more numerous network of supporters. It was a small clan made up of leading republican families, figures from the IRA's political wing Sinn Fein, and individual IRA men. Blood and family ties were particularly important. At the time of Paddy's killing, according to RUC court testimony, the commanding officer of the IRA's Derry Brigade was William McGuinness, the brother of Martin McGuinness – a key Sinn Fein spokesman and effective leader of the Provisional IRA.

The Derry Brigade organization was structured into three distinct layers. At the top of the hierarchy was the Brigade's Officer Commanding, the IRA's overall leader in the city. Beneath him was the Derry Brigade Command, composed of around ten experienced IRA members, including one or two prominent Sinn Fein politicians. The Command Staff included the quarter-master department with responsibility for supplying weapons and explosives, the engineering department for making bombs, the finance department for raising funds and paying Volunteers' wages, and the internal security unit for hunting out informers. These departments were small, one or two people, and the divisions between them fluid. In reality the IRA structure was more like an extended family than a military hierarchy.

The Command Staff would include the Officers Commanding of the Brigade's four area active service units. Each republican stronghold in the city, the Bogside/Brandywell district, Shantallow, Creggan and the Waterside, had their own active service unit composed of five or six Volunteers working under the direction of their individual Officer Commanding.

The activity of an active service unit depended on the enthusiasm and overall standing of its particular Officer Commanding within the Derry Brigade. One of the men, Anthony Miller, who was caught and convicted on information that Paddy Flood passed to the RUC Special Branch, was the commander of the Bogside unit. But Miller would also have been regarded by the police as one of their most formidable and experienced IRA opponents in the city. At his subsequent trial Judge Anthony Harte described Miller as a 'dangerous and unrepentant man' and sentenced him to twenty-three years. Miller and his two co-defendants successfully appealed and were released in December 1994.

Theoretically the cell-like structure of the Derry Brigade was designed to limit penetration by security force informers. Ground-level Volunteers were not supposed to have access to the identities of their superiors. At Command level, information on arms dumps or operations was supposed to be rigidly compartmentalized. But in the small Derry neighbourhood communities, such security precautions were often meaningless. Ordinary IRA Volunteers were easily identifiable, both to the wider nationalist community and the security forces, by the company they kept and their regular attendance at republican commemorations. The Brigade's senior members, each with their long personal list of arrests and convictions for terrorist-style offences, were very well known indeed. A careful eye on court reports in the local newspaper, the *Derry Journal*, would have furnished an interested observer with a rough and ready inventory of the personalities of the Derry Brigade.

In 1985 the Provisionals at last accepted Paddy, then twenty-five, into the IRA. He worked as a general dogsbody at first, ferrying arms and taking part in a couple of punishment shootings against local criminals who fell foul of the Derry Command. Paddy was keen; he was a dedicated Republican who believed passionately in the removal of the British presence from Northern Ireland and the reunification of Ireland. The walls of his home in the Bogside were plastered with posters of republican icons – the 1981 Hunger Strikers, the 1916 Easter Rising Proclamation and portraits of the Irish socialist leader James Connolly. He developed an interest in Irish history and read republican literature voraciously. He believed in the IRA and defended their actions to Elizabeth's family – who were less sympathetic to the republican cause. His friends, his drinking companions, his wife's friends, were all Republicans. He lived, breathed and, in a bitter twist of fate, died in the company of Republicans.

Flood had no sympathy for policemen or soldiers killed by the IRA; he was a killer himself. He was directly responsible for the deaths of two British soldiers killed in a landmine explosion in March 1989 and took part in dozens of IRA operations aimed at killing the Crown forces who patrolled the Bogside's shabby streets. 'He hated the police because of the harassment we had. We were always getting raided. Paddy grew up in the Troubles, where he had seen Bloody Sunday and things like that. It made him very republican-minded,' said Elizabeth Flood.

Paddy Flood was also a physically courageous man. In March 1988 a deranged Loyalist gunman, Michael Stone, attacked mourners attending the funeral of Seamus Finucane's girlfriend Mairead Farrell and her two companions, known as the Gibraltar Three after the SAS killings in the British colony, at Belfast's Milltown Cemetery. Stone lobbed hand-grenades and fired at random into the crowd before attempting to flee. Three men were killed and scores wounded. Paddy, although unarmed, was at the head of a group that ran towards the gunman, attempting to trap Stone, and was wounded by shrapnel from one of the Loyalist's grenades.

But Paddy's intelligence and bravery masked a flaw: he hungered for a sense of self-worth. His life was anchored in the respect he received from the stronger personalities in the Derry Brigade leadership. Being in the IRA made Paddy feel good, it gave meaning to his life and it made him different from all the other defeated, unemployed and powerless Bogsiders who filled his world. This simple desire for social acceptance drew him inexorably into the mesh of the RUC's intelligence war. 'Paddy always seemed to be searching for status. If he had admitted to the Derry Brigade that he had confessed to the RUC it would have been all right, but he would have been kicked out of the IRA. Paddy could not have faced that,' said a close friend.

In the spring of 1987, two years after he became involved with his future wife Elizabeth, the couple were arrested and taken to Strand Road Barracks. Police had found arms in a communal drying shed attached to the apartment where Paddy and Elizabeth had set up their first home. Paddy had been storing the weaponry for the IRA; there were explosives, mercury tilt switches, a rifle and a rocket head of a shoulder-fired grenade launcher. The police had a strong but circumstantial case against both Paddy and Elizabeth.

According to the IRA, based on the confession they obtained from Flood during his final interrogation, Elizabeth broke down under police questioning. Liz, as she was known, had never been a mentally robust person. She had a fractured and unhappy life history; she came from a broken family background and her previous boyfriend had been killed in an IRA-related car crash – Liz had been traumatized by his death. Paddy had been her salvation, just as she had filled the gaping hole in his own life. Until he met Elizabeth, Paddy had always been awkward with women but together they blossomed into a loving couple. 'There was something about the two of them that just fitted. Paddy idolized her,' a close friend commented. Liz was a vulnerable woman. Paddy knew that and so did the Special Branch when they told Paddy they were going to charge Liz with possession of explosives.

Did Paddy Flood have any choice that night in Strand Road Barracks after he and Elizabeth were arrested? I tried to imagine what Paddy must have thought. In the interrogation room the two Special Branch men, L and J, both in their early thirties, came and went. Under the Prevention of Terrorism Act they had seven long days and seven long nights to work Paddy over, and if they wanted to, Elizabeth. The Special Branch men were deadly serious; they told Paddy all about what they were going to do to Liz, how they would break her like a fucking plate, how she would go to prison for a long, long time. And finally, the policemen asked Paddy what he was going to do to save her.

On the tape of his IRA confession I heard Paddy's final response to the cops. 'The girl really wasn't very well at the time. Her previous boyfriend had been killed. She had had a nervous breakdown and she suffered from anorexia. We planned to get married within the next year or so. I was worried sick about her. I knew she could not hack prison. She'd die there . . . I agreed to work for them if they agreed to release her.' Paddy turned.

To make sure Paddy kept his side of the bargain, the RUC made him sign forty undated statements admitting his personal involvement in numerous IRA offences.

It had taken months of patient negotiation with my republican contacts to listen to that tape. One day I flew to Belfast to meet a man who represented the IRA Army Council, whom I will call John. His arms were covered in the scrawl of tattoos and he was a powerful muscular man – the type of guy whose glance you would avoid in a bar. But that was where the resemblance to a street thug ended – John was clever, intelligent and had a host of funny and threatening stories about making big bombs in other people's front kitchens. He made me laugh, and he scared me.

We met in West Belfast and drove to an IRA safe house in one of the drab public sector housing estates that engulf that part of the city. We arrived at a block of flats that appeared to be abandoned; all the external and internal lights of the building were smashed and the block's stairwell was in pitch darkness. A key was hidden in a specific place, enabling visitors to come and go, and John used it to open the flat's door. After we entered the freezing flat, John manhandled an electric cooker across the living room floor and jammed it against the front door as casually as other people would flick the snip on their door lock. He then turned on a small lamp and pulled on a pair of woolly gloves; he did not take them off for the rest of the evening. He went into the adjoining bedroom and returned with a brown envelope and cut it open. Inside the package were two documents and an ordinary, unmarked cassette – it was Paddy Flood's confession.

John's security precautions were well founded. The tape was prima facie evidence of murder; anyone connected to it risked arrest. The two accompanying documents, a handwritten transcript of the tape and a signed confession in Paddy Flood's hand, were equally lethal. John passed the documents to me and I read both the confession and the tape transcript, taking notes whenever I wanted to. A lot of the tape transcript was technical; there were complex details about different IRA operations, the names of the IRA men who introduced Paddy into the Provos, his early career as an IRA runner and general dogsbody. The compelling human interest in his confession was his fear for Elizabeth. 'The cops were always on about my wife. I'd a wee wean (child). They said what would she do if I was shot by the IRA or put away for a long, long time because of the statements I had signed. They kept on reminding me about that at different times, about how deep I was in.'

John finally slipped the tape into a cassette-recorder and we sat back to listen. A burst of Donald Duck gibberish emerged from the speaker. After ten seconds the gibberish slowed to snatches of intelligible speech and then speeded up again – the tape-recorder was broken. John, in arranging to borrow the safe house, had forgotten to ask if the cassette-recorder worked. We rushed into the bedroom to try out a music centre that stood by the bed. We slipped the cassette in but something was wrong with the speakers, there was hardly any sound. I lay down on the floor with my ear pressed to the speaker picking out the faint sounds of Flood's confession. On a bedside table there was a walkman but when we tried it out, we found that it too was broken. I was in despair. Just then there was a knock on the door, the flat-dwellers had returned, and John, after heaving the electric cooker out of the way, dispatched one of them to obtain a working cassette-recorder. It arrived a few minutes later and we both sat down on the bedroom floor and played the tape of Paddy Flood's confession.

My feelings of self-congratulation at being the first journalist to hear an IRA informer tape quickly turned from elation to self-disgust. The voice on the tape had the same strong nasal twang as that of Paddy's brother David. Sometimes the voice was calm, and sometimes it broke into a near sob, holding back tears, desperately trying to please its interrogators. 'If the same thing should happen to anybody else, do not believe a word the cops say. They will not keep their promises. Sooner or later they will have reasons for arrests, for breaking their promises.' It was the voice of a man in mortal dread; whenever it sounded as if he was about to break down there was a muted click of the off-button. But whatever he said to please his interrogators, and whatever kind of amnesty they promised, they knew and Paddy knew that they were still going to kill him.

Halfway through the tape a feeling of obscenity akin to physical nausea gripped me; I felt as if I had been stained by something unclean. By listening to the tape of this man, so close to dying, I felt as if I was participating in his murder. The tape was dramatic but did not end with a director's shout of 'Cut'. It ended with a bullet being fired into the back of Paddy's brain at nine hundred miles an hour, blowing his nose and two front teeth out. It was revolting to listen to this, to be alive when the speaker was dead.

I listened to the whole tape and then played back some key passages: 'Break her like a plate.' At the end of the evening I watched John, still with his woolly gloves on, burn Paddy's handwritten confession and the tape transcript, both now covered with my incriminating fingerprints, on an open fire. It was around midnight by the time I left, walking out into the

Belfast night. I took a taxi into town; the driver tried to make the usual chit-chat but I didn't feel like talking. I had had enough of Northern Ireland for one night.

From the day of his turning until his death, Paddy was a full-time informer for the RUC. His recruitment was not a unique event; the RUC's strategy was to spread their net wide. Almost everyone from the nationalist community who could be a source of information was viewed as potential informer material. In August 1990 the New York-based paper, the *Irish Voice*, claimed a member of the RUC Special Branch, aided by two FBI men, had tried to recruit an undocumented Irish emigrant in Manhattan. In the same year the Belfast *Irish News* reported on eighteen separate attempts by the RUC to recruit informers. The true figures across Ulster must have run into hundreds of recruitment bids per year.

In Derry, local lawyers complained that the most casual contact with the police could result in a recruitment attempt. 'I had a lot of clients who have been questioned about serious terrorist-type offences, and also clients questioned about the most trivial motoring offence, who were approached by the RUC and asked to "keep an eye" on certain people. Arrangements were made to meet them at a later date or telephone them at a certain number,' said Paddy McDermott, a leading Derry solicitor, who represented Flood and others accused of IRA offences.

For the Catholic Church, the RUC's strategy was just a further turn of the screw for a community already racked by paramilitary violence. 'I know pressure was put on people. Very often the police got young people who are involved in petty crime and pressurized them. Most young people resisted. There were young people who were frightened and got caught in the situation,' said the former Bishop of Derry, Dr Edward Daly.

Most informers were turned through pressure. One low-level

Derry informer, David Doherty, told a Sinn Fein-organized press conference in March 1991 that he had turned RUC informer six years earlier after being arrested on petrol bomb and hijacking charges. After agreeing to work for the police, Doherty only had to serve eight months of an eighteen-month sentence. On his release he was instructed to join Sinn Fein and watch known Republicans in his neighbourhood. Like most informers, the police paid what can only be described as trivial sums, given the penalties Doherty faced if the IRA caught him. Initially he was paid three pounds per fortnightly meeting, but this was gradually increased to thirty pounds. Over the six years, he received a total of six thousand pounds.

At the press conference Sinn Fein officials and David Doherty told reporters he had voluntarily come forward as a result of reading a lengthy article on Paddy Flood that I had just written for the *New York Times Magazine*, but this was just another lie in the bewildering world of lies of the Irish informer. Doherty had been secretly unmasked by a senior member of the Derry Brigade, who was himself an RUC informer.

RUC Special Branch did not need to pay their agents large sums of money. Almost all of the nationalist men they targeted were likely to be long-term unemployed, living just above the poverty line. To such people thirty pounds a fortnight could seem like a comfortable supplement to their meagre social welfare benefits. There was also a limit to what these informers, like David Doherty, could safely spend in local shops and bars without raising embarrassing and potentially fatal questions.

But in other areas of Northern Ireland the RUC or MI5 have paid out substantial sums of money to certain individuals for high-grade information. Manchester Deputy Chief Constable John Stalker recorded that one informer, whose information led to the killing of two IRA men, was reportedly paid thirty thousand pounds. The logic behind such large payments remains a mystery.

The IRA were acutely aware of the RUC's informer strategy and their paranoia about informers within their ranks was ceaseless. In order to avoid that suspicion, Flood, even after he agreed to inform to save Elizabeth, was charged with possession of the explosives and remanded in custody in Belfast Jail for three months. In court, the police fought bail but the case eventually collapsed after Flood's solicitor was able to prove other people had access to the area where the arms were found. The IRA say that the court case was an elaborate ploy to neutralize any potential suspicion in the Brigade leadership over Flood's release. In their official statement, the IRA said that his two Special Branch handlers, Detective Sergeant L and Detective J, met Paddy in Crumlin Road Prison in Belfast on the day of his release and briefed him on what to say to the IRA and how he should contact them on a special unlisted number at the Strand Road Barracks. They also arranged a number of different meeting points away from prying republican eyes in safe Protestant areas of the city for the fortnightly meetings Flood was told he had to attend. Paddy was given the codename Finn and then he was freed.[3]

Paddy was not the first Volunteer from the Derry Brigade to be recruited as a tout. For nearly a decade the Brigade had been an embarrassment to the national IRA leadership. In August 1982 a long-time police agent and IRA Volunteer, Raymond Gilmour, had devastated the Derry Brigade by turning supergrass and testifying in open court against his former comrades. Nearly seventy people were arrested and 180 separate charges laid, including murder, attempted murder, possession of arms and explosives, hijacking and membership of the IRA, on the basis of his statements. The sheer volume of arrests in the city's tight-knit republican circles led to a memorable piece of graffiti on a Bogside wall – 'I knew Raymond Gilmour, thank fuck he did not know me!'

Forty-four people went on trial as Gilmour, like John Carey a century before, turned Queen's Evidence and took the stand against the Crown's republican enemies. Decimation of the Derry Brigade was only averted when the trial collapsed in December 1984 after the Northern Ireland Lord Chief Justice,

Lord Lowry, declared Gilmour a liar who was 'entirely unworthy of belief' and released the defendants.

Gilmour wreaked havoc amongst republican ranks, sowing a debilitating, albeit justified, paranoia about touts for the next decade. Most of the defendants, many of them active IRA men, had been behind bars for one and a half years and the Derry Brigade had come close to collapse as an operational force in the city. And whatever the judge might have said, much of Gilmour's information was accurate; the man Gilmour named as his unit commander, Eddie McSheffrey, blew himself up in a premature explosion three years later.

Within the IRA the Derry Brigade was tarnished with a reputation for lax security and police penetration. Even by the late eighties far too many IRA operations in the city were bungled or aborted. Bombs failed to go off, IRA Volunteers were arrested on their way to plant them; the British security forces seemed to know everything. A huge number of IRA arms dumps were seized – seventy-six in 1987, sixty-six in 1988 and more than sixty in 1989. The IRA found it increasingly difficult to kill any member of the security forces, and if they did it was by fluke.

Flood's Special Branch handlers broke him in gradually. According to his confession, Paddy's handlers reassured him that his information would be used to save lives. None of his comrades would be arrested and the police gave guarantees that the IRA would never be able to trace anything back to Paddy. Flood appears to have believed he had struck a bargain, but from the winter of 1987 through to the summer of 1988 his handlers were drawing in him, overcoming his ideological resistance. 'During some meetings he would offer me money, saying it was to cover expenses. I would not take it. I still had some sense of pride. I made it clear that although I would work for him I did not like him,' the tape recorded.

After his release from prison, Paddy Flood had volunteered

to become an IRA engineer, a bomb-maker. He would assemble bombs in IRA safe houses and other IRA Volunteers would transport them to the target. Paddy impressed his IRA superiors with his technical proficiency and was promoted to Brigade Engineer – the top bomb-maker in the city. It was a pivotal position in the organization; as the chief technical expert Paddy bypassed the IRA's internal cell security divisions and worked with all of the city's different active service units. He was involved in dozens of IRA operations and probably came into contact with every member of the Provisionals in Derry. In 1988 he made eighty to ninety per cent of all IRA bombs in the city.

Paddy's new skills had become a key asset to the Derry Command, and the RUC. The police were remorseless at their fortnightly clandestine meetings in driving home Paddy's vulnerability from the IRA, and Elizabeth's emotional inability to withstand imprisonment, to make sure he kept supplying them with information. 'The peelers [police] told me if I went to the Movement I would be shot right out of hand. There was no way back for me. They were always talking about my wife – she wouldn't be able to do the barracks. They could bring her in at any time, they would break her like a plate.'

Paddy was in a unique position to do the IRA a lot of damage, but the Derry Brigade was reluctant in their official statement on Flood's execution to describe the full extent of his collaboration. 'During his three years as an agent he met regularly with his handlers, passing on detailed information. He gave names and details of the IRA's structure; at least three arms dumps and five Volunteers were captured as a result,' they tersely stated.[4]

Later, in private, Republicans acknowledged that Paddy's dual role as Brigade Engineer and informer was far more damaging than they cared to admit in public, and that Paddy was in a position to compromise huge areas of the entire Derry Brigade structure. In his taped confession Paddy actually admitted that he had only become an engineer at the instigation of the police. 'He [his handler] made me look at books of photos [of IRA suspects]. He told me to try and get on an Explosives Officer course and find out where we were trained, who by, and who was the Explosives Officer Trainer.'

But there was another reason for the Provisionals' reluctance to discuss the full depths of Paddy's betrayal: Paddy had been involved in an infamous IRA operation in August 1988 that was so embarrassing that no one in the Derry Brigade wanted to speak of it even after they shot Paddy dead two years later. The operation became known as the Good Neighbours Bomb.

On Friday, 26 August 1988, an IRA active service unit went round to the Creggan home of Gerry Laird and kidnapped him at gunpoint, held him hostage at a secret location, and took over his flat. To the IRA, Laird was an anti-social, drug-taking alcoholic with a notorious reputation for petty thievery, who had already defied an order by the Derry Brigade to leave town.[5] The following night someone broke into the local Marlborough Street fish and chip shop, robbed the till and stole cigarettes. On the way out, the thief dropped his UB40, a social welfare document which lists the holder's name, giving the police a strong lead as to the identity of the thief – it was Laird's UB40. But the police did not go round to Laird's flat to arrest him.

After two fruitless days waiting for robbery detectives to appear, the IRA unit, observing the flat from a safe house in an adjacent block of flats, tried to entice the RUC into visiting Laird's apartment by other stratagems. They stole a car, used it in a shooting incident against a security base, dumped it outside the flat with the hand-grip from a rocket launcher on the passenger's seat, and splashed a blood trail from the vehicle to the door of the flat. In another manoeuvre through the social services, they alleged that Laird had been buggering a seventeen-year-old boy, who had gone missing and could have been being held against his will in Laird's flat. But still the police did not take the bait; someone had told them that the IRA had attached a booby-trap device, hidden inside a fisherman's wellington boot, to the handle of Laird's front door.

The Creggan district, like the Bogside, has a troubled political and economic history and is a particularly close community. Ties between neighbours, even if the neighbour is a man like Laird, can be strong. After six days Laird's neighbour, sixty-year-old Sheila Lewis, became so concerned about his unexplained disappearance that she persuaded two friends, Sean Dalton and Jed Curran, to help her break into Laird's first-floor balcony flat to make sure Laird was not lying in his bedroom in a coma. Outside Laird's door, Dalton spotted an open window and climbed in. Lewis and Curran stood outside the front door waiting to be let in.

In the block opposite, three IRA Volunteers were supposed to be standing guard, protecting local people from any accidental encounter with the booby-trap. But it had been boring sitting about all day for six days staring at an empty flat, so the Volunteers relieved the tedium by watching television. On the morning that the three neighbours broke in, two of the Volunteers had gone off to the local unemployment centre to sign on for their welfare benefits. Only one Volunteer was left to keep sentry over the bomb.

In an interview afterwards, Curran said he and Lewis could hear Dalton make his way towards the front door.[6] But as Dalton pulled on the inside door handle he detonated the two-pound booby-trap. The force of the explosion blew the flat apart and destroyed the building. Dalton took the full force of the powerful bomb and was killed instantly. Lewis, directly outside the door, was hurled into the garden twenty feet below as the walls blew out and was crushed by falling debris – she died at the scene. Curran was blown halfway across the garden and covered in rubble but survived, only to die two months later of his injuries.

The Good Neighbours Bomb provoked fury in the Bogside and brought the Derry Brigade to their political knees. No other IRA operation in twenty-five years of bombings and shootings had so alienated the entire nationalist host community. The Derry Brigade later admitted that the last Volunteer left guarding the flat had been watching television when the bomb was detonated. Paddy was shot dead two years later, but no one in the Derry Brigade was eager to revive memories of their greatest fiasco.

Although it is impossible to be certain, the IRA were not the only organization keeping the flat under surveillance. Both the Creggan and Bogside districts were continually spied upon from the huge British Army communications towers that dominate every high point in the district. The towers bristle with cameras, infra-red surveillance devices, microphones and various other gadgetry of the electronic spy. A police informer had indeed given Special Branch the power to save lives and the Branch had used that power to warn members of the security forces to stay away from the flat. But the Branch's protection did not extend to civilians from the Creggan; the police chose to use their power to do nothing, and allowed the Good Neighbours to climb in to their deaths.

The rationale behind the police's decision was brutally simple: if the Branch had intervened and stopped Dalton from climbing into the flat, it would have been obvious that the police had prior information of the booby-trap. The Derry Command would quickly have asked questions about how the police knew, and who was the tout. In the Branch's eyes, the lives of three innocent Catholics from the Creggan did not counter-balance the RUC's need to protect the identity of their informer in the IRA's ranks.

The Good Neighbours Bomb provoked a confrontation between Paddy and his mother-in-law, Mrs Margaret Mooney, who denounced the IRA for their recklessness. Mrs Mooney, a large woman, was the matriarchal head of her household and dominated her entire extended family, including her sons-in-law. Although it was never openly discussed, Mrs Mooney knew Paddy was involved with the IRA and she turned to him for an explanation for the IRA's actions. 'What a terrible atrocity. How could the IRA do this? How could innocent people be caught up in this?' said Mrs Mooney. Paddy sat in the corner of the room looking at her but he said nothing. What could he say? If he had said anything it would just be the usual easy lines about the armed struggle and inevitable civilian casualties. Paddy after all had made the bomb, informed his handlers, and along with others murdered the Good Neighbours.

Perhaps Paddy was thinking of his own troubles and his latest arrest. He had been a full-time Special Branch informer for a year when the Good Neighbours were killed but Derry's uniformed RUC men, denied access to Special Branch's secrets, were mistakenly convinced that he was a cop-killer and were determined to make his life hell. In March 1988 a small IRA unit were moving rifles from an arms dump when they spotted an RUC patrol in the distance. On the spur of the moment they opened fire and killed a popular RUC Constable, Clive Graham. It was a good stiff; RUC policemen on duty were not easy men to kill. Months later an IRA man, Damien Nicell, was arrested and confessed to being involved in the killing. Nicell, confused about the identities of his IRA comrades, wrongly named Flood as the trigger-man. The first Paddy knew of Nicell's claim was at Belfast airport in August 1988 as he was about to board a Greece-bound flight to celebrate his honeymoon – the first time he would have ever been outside Ireland. Paddy was arrested and held for five days under the Prevention of Terrorism Act; he lost the air tickets and the holiday. Police had already disrupted his wedding plans twice by arresting him before the planned ceremonies. His honeymoon was ruined.

It seems a strange way to treat a valuable agent, but the IRA insist that Flood was told he was not 'fireproofed' against the actions of other policemen. His handlers told him never to mention his Special Branch connection to other police interrogators. 'All they were interested in was the information I was providing them with. What happened to me on the streets was my problem. All they could guarantee was that I'd be able to walk the streets with my wife,' confessed Paddy on the tape.

Back in Derry, uniformed RUC men, enraged that the alleged murderer of their colleague had beaten the rap, tried to make Flood suffer. He was constantly stopped and questioned, and was even arrested for urinating in the street. The harassment got so bad that Paddy went down to the offices of the local *Derry Journal* to complain. The *Journal*'s photographer took a picture of Paddy standing beside Liz, towering over her. Paddy placed his hand around her shoulder as if to protect and comfort her for the loss of their honeymoon. Liz is looking down towards the ground and her expression is both bitter and defeated. Paddy is staring directly into the camera lens but his expression reveals nothing. The IRA say the uniformed RUC men's vindictive campaign was good cover. No one could have suspected that the most harassed man in Derry had turned.

Six months after the loss of his honeymoon, Paddy was involved in a major operation against the British Army which questioned how far the Special Branch were prepared to jeopardize British Army lives in order to protect their sources. In March 1989 Paddy was assigned as bomb-maker to a six-man IRA unit planning to attack a mobile Army patrol on the outskirts of Derry, as the patrol drove along the Buncrana Road to the Coshquin border checkpoint three miles away. According to the IRA, Flood made up the bomb the day before and was then called in again to increase the size of the device on the day of the explosion. He had ample time to warn his RUC handlers. Details of the impending IRA ambush also became known to one of the Brigade's quarter-masters, Patsy Moore, who within two months of the Buncrana Road bombing was unmasked as yet another informer within IRA ranks.

On the day of the ambush the Buncrana Road was saturated with army units and specially trained Close Observation Patrols, experts in undercover surveillance. In hindsight, it was obvious that the security forces were forewarned of an IRA landmine attack. Finding the bomb should have been easy for the British Army search teams; the device was the size of two big potato sacks stacked together and it was hidden on the fringes of open sports fields.

Just after 11 pm, a two-vehicle armoured army convoy drove down the Buncrana Road towards the checkpoint. As the second jeep passed the posts of an adjacent rugby pitch, a forty-five-kilo bomb detonated by command wire erupted beneath it. The explosion hurled the jeep into the air and the vehicle landed upside down on the roadway, crushing the roof and the soldiers inside. Two soldiers were killed and four injured, two of them seriously.

From the British Army's point of view the Buncrana Road operation was a costly mistake which raised difficult questions. How could the security forces have obtained precise information from two important informers, yet fail to have located the landmine and prevent the IRA ambush? Why had the soldiers entered an area where a known landmine had been planted? Had an Army undercover operation to ambush the IRA bomb-firers gone wrong, or were the soldiers just pawns to be sacrificed to protect Patsy Moore or Paddy Flood?

RUC Chief Constable Sir Hugh Annesley, stung by this criticism, denied that his force 'allowed people to die' at Buncrana Road. 'It is the primary duty of the RUC to protect life. The suggestion that a police force with such vast experience of informant handling betrays its principles . . . has no basis in fact.'[7] But police denials in Ulster do not convince everyone. What is certain is that an RUC inspector told the coroner at the soldiers' inquests that despite extensive enquiries no one responsible for the explosion had as yet been found.[8] Both Flood and Moore would have been able to furnish Special Branch with a list of all the IRA men involved in the operation. Republicans claim that Flood was involved in eighteen major operations, nine of which his handlers allowed to go ahead despite the injuries they inflicted on British Army soldiers.

The Derry Command were soon dealing with a full-scale

informer crisis unleashed by Patsy Moore. In April 1989 the Gardai arrested Moore in the Republic and charged him with taking part in the armed robbery of a County Donegal pub. Almost immediately Moore's wife and three children were taken into RUC protective custody. It was obvious that Moore was singing like a canary and telling the Gardai where the Derry Brigade was hiding its weaponry. Moore was seen in the company of Gardai detectives pointing out individual arms dumps in the isolated regions of County Donegal, which borders County Londonderry in Northern Ireland.

The Derry Brigade had blundered badly in appointing Moore to a key position in their quarter-master department. Moore was a weak character and a gambling-machine addict with a desperate need for cash to fuel his compulsion. He was an easy target for the Gardai and the RUC recruiters. The Derry Brigade were soon frantically trying to shift their precious weaponry on both sides of the border before their arms dumps were seized. The battle raged for a month across the lonely Atlantic strands, isolated moorlands and lakes of Donegal's peninsulas. It appears that the IRA were successful; Moore's collaboration led to the seizure of a number of rifles and ammunition, including a flame-thrower, but failed to uncover a major arms haul. Moore later pleaded guilty to the armed robbery charge and received seven years, but he only served four months after a pardon from the Republic's Justice Minister. He then fled into hiding in England with his wife and children.

Three years before Patrick Moore's defection, another Derry Brigade quarter-master, Frank Hegarty, fled into MI5's protective arms just before the Gardai raided a major arms dump in January 1986. One hundred and forty assault rifles were seized at three separate dumps in two southern counties bordering Northern Ireland. Hegarty, an informer for seven years, had found out about a major IRA arms shipment, part of their Libyan hoard from the *Eksund* arms shipments of the mid-eighties, and pointed out the locations on an ordnance survey map for his MI5 handler, who then informed the Gardai.

In his brief exile Hegarty stayed with his girlfriend at 77 Bell

Road, Sittingbourne, Kent, in an MI5 safe house. But he missed
Derry, and his familiar interlocking circle of family and friends,
badly. Hegarty's upbringing, and lack of employment skills, did
not instil the social attitudes and sense of independence required
to start life afresh in a foreign environment. He telephoned his
mother every day until he had persuaded himself that it was
safe to go back home. The IRA statement on his killing noted:

> After some months away from Derry he decided to return,
> convinced that if he firmly maintained that someone else, not
> he, was responsible for the weapons seizures then he could
> also convince the IRA that he had been kidnapped and
> compromised to made [sic] look the scapegoat for someone
> else within the IRA . . . Whilst we strongly suspected him and
> concede that his brazen return to Ireland baffled us, we were
> not prepared to take action until we had proof of his guilt.
> When confronted by the IRA he voluntarily admitted he had
> been lying.[9]

Irish Republicanism is imbued with the culture and imagery of
Catholicism. During the 1981 Hunger Strike, West Belfast was
covered in murals depicting the emaciated IRA hunger-strikers
as the martyred Christ figure. In the informer war, the powerful
Catholic sacrament of confession and its sub-elements of recantation, repentance, redemption and absolution, subconsciously
guided the IRA's own interrogation of informers, like Hegarty,
and its outcome. A confession from the informer was the
definitive and often the sole proof of their guilt. The IRA
interrogation was remorselessly driven by the need to obtain
this confession, for without it there was still doubt. The
conditions in which these confessions were obtained, whilst not
involving outright physical brutality, could hardly be called
voluntary. But to be of value, to be sincere, the confession must
be freely given; a valid confession could not be the product of

torture. Suspected informers might be slapped around and threatened as Hegarty was but they were not beaten into submission.

Whether IRA interrogators realize it or not, there was within their pursuit of a confession a latent drive, as in the Catholic sacrament, to obtain a recantation of the betrayer's work. The sinner's former masters must be denounced and their false ideology rejected. The informer must recant his turning in the same way the Inquisition sought a recantation of false belief from a heretic; the betrayer must show that he has been betrayed. 'Hegarty said he was extremely angry that contrary to his assurances his cover had been blown,' said the IRA statement.

The IRA Army Council amended their standing orders in the late eighties to make it at least verbally clear that any IRA man who had been recruited as an informer would not be executed if, but only if, they voluntarily gave themselves up to their IRA comrades. There were sound pragmatic reasons for the amended policy but the Provisionals were again being sub consciously guided by the psychological foundations of their own faith. No matter how great a sinner, no matter how vile the deed, the Catholic Church teaches its schoolchildren that salvation is always open to those who repent. The IRA told its Volunteers that no matter how long and extensive their collaboration with the British, their lives would be spared if they came forward.

The new policy was recognition of a blunder by the Derry Brigade in murdering twenty-four-year-old Kevin Coyle in February 1985 after he had appeared at a Sinn Fein news conference and told local journalists that he had been approached by the RUC and asked to turn informer. The day after the news conference the Brigade abducted Coyle, who was not an IRA member, obtained a confession and shot him twice in the back of the head. His family was given a tape which purported to say that he had been a police informer since 1981 and that his appearance at the news conference was a ploy to fool the IRA and disguise the depths of collaboration.[10] Coyle's killing was later viewed by the local IRA leadership as a serious error and counter-productive.

For those who do not repent in time, the IRA's version of confessional sacrament contains no possibility of redemption or absolution. Hegarty broke under hostile IRA interrogation and confessed to collaborating with MI5. The Provisionals then killed him, dumping his body just inside the border near the town of Castlederg in County Tyrone, on 25 May 1986. His hands were tied behind his back, his eyes covered with tape, and he was shot once in the back of the head. The Derry Brigade made it clear then and for ever that once caught there was no way of turning back.

In August 1989 in the aftermath of Moore's exposure, Paddy Flood's RUC handlers turned on the pressure. It was the twentieth anniversary of the arrival of British troops in Ulster and the Derry Command planned a major offensive. Flood was assigned to a two-man IRA unit planning to ambush soldiers with a booby-trap bomb hidden inside a sealed concrete block. The block was to be camouflaged as part of an ordinary wall and detonated by command wire in the path of a passing British Army foot patrol.

On the afternoon of 11 August Paddy was contacted by an IRA superior and told to go to a house in a back street of the Bogside to prepare the bomb. He went to the address and began assembling the device, then left to 'get something' between five and six that evening. He returned to finish the job but at 7 pm the house was raided by an RUC unit just as his two IRA colleagues, twenty-three-year-old Martin Molloy and nineteen-year-old David Doherty – unrelated to the IRA informer David Doherty – were driving away with the concrete-block bomb in the trunk of a car. Spotting the approaching RUC armoured jeeps, Flood hid in one of the surrounding houses. The police arrived seconds later, ramming the IRA car and sealing off the area for hours as bomb disposal units dealt with the unexploded device. Molloy and Doherty were arrested but Flood escaped.

To most outsiders this would seem proof that something was wrong. Paddy had acted strangely in the house; he had persuaded his two companions, for no apparent reason, that they should drop their original plan to transport the bomb across open fields at the back of the house and instead use a car from the front entrance – making it easier for the RUC to capture the IRA cell by ramming the car. The ambushing RUC unit did not have any of the normal police identification numbers on their uniforms and were, unusually, armed with high-powered Heckler and Koch machine-guns. The arresting officers were clearly members of a specialist RUC unit from outside Derry, suggesting that they had been drafted in for this particular operation. How could the police have had such precise information about a bomb being made in this ordinary street in the Creggan? And why was Paddy the only Volunteer to escape?

Paramilitaries lived on the edge in Ulster, constantly risking death or imprisonment. The danger bred a kind of protective fatalism amongst the IRA's Volunteers; sometimes an operation would run like clockwork and the Volunteers were back in their safe house before the security forces were on the alert; and sometimes the same operation with the same Volunteers was disastrous and everyone spent the next ten years in prison. Paddy told his IRA superiors that he had run into a nearby house and been sheltered by a local woman who allowed him to change out of his explosive-tainted clothes. The Derry Command, through incompetence or naivety, believed him.

Molloy and Doherty, locked away on remand in Belfast Prison seventy miles away, although not initially suspicious, soon became convinced that Paddy was lying. But even terrorist organizations have red tape and no one in the Derry Brigade paid much attention to their complaints until six months later when the men received police forensic reports as part of their defence trial documents. Hidden away in the dry forensic recitation of the bomb's components was one glaring omission:

the sealed concrete-block bomb had not contained any batteries. A bomb-maker is just as likely to forget to put batteries into a bomb as a car mechanic is likely to forget to put a battery in a car. Without batteries the bomb was an inert collection of chemicals and wire. Flood had specifically told Doherty that the bomb was primed and ready to go. To Molloy and Doherty, who received ten-year prison sentences, the forensic report was absolute proof that Flood was a traitor. Time was now running out for Flood the informer.

Why did Paddy's handlers allow such damning evidence to fall into the hands of his IRA comrades? It would have been easy to have had their own police forensic reports altered and the absent batteries inserted into the bomb's list of components. Was it incompetence or were the RUC playing a deeper game, sacrificing Paddy to protect someone else, another informer in the Derry Brigade?

Some Derry Republicans believe that Paddy was exposed simply as the result of a bureaucratic bungle: perhaps his handler was on holiday or simply forgot when the forensic reports were being prepared. But the IRA Army Council's view was that the forensic reports and the sacrifice of Flood were a stratagem. No other IRA informer had ever been exposed in such a detectable and documentable way. In the late eighties it was an open secret in Derry that the Derry Command believed their senior ranks had been penetrated. Even after Paddy's death their hunt in the shadows for this super-informer went on. And as it turned out, their suspicions were justified.

Flood was mortified by the arrests of Molloy and Doherty. The RUC had broken their promise about no arrests and Paddy contacted his handlers for an angry showdown. 'I challenged them about the arrests. L said it wasn't his problem. It had been taken out of his hands by headquarters in Belfast. There was nothing he could do. He was sorry about it. It might compromise me. He had tried to stop it. I asked him about the promise of no arrests. He said it would not happen again. He said the boys were lucky. They could have been shot. I was shattered,' his grim confession records.

Six months later, in January 1990, Paddy was involved in a copycat concrete-block booby-trap bomb that was again to prove disastrous for the Provisionals. Every year since the 1972 Bloody Sunday killings, Sinn Fein had organized a commemoration parade. The Bloody Sunday march was one of the highlights of the republican calender and groups of supporters from all over Ireland travelled to Derry. Republican leaders used the event as a propaganda platform to commemorate the dead, focus protest against British rule in Ireland, and re-enthuse their followers.

The proceedings were closely monitored by the British security forces, some of whom gathered each year at a certain point on Derry's medieval walls to observe the demonstrators parading through the Bogside two hundred feet below. The Derry Brigade decided to ambush the security forces during the January 1990 march by placing a concrete-block booby-trap, disguised as part of the ancient walls, close to where the soldiers would stand. It has since been claimed that Paddy Flood actually instigated the operation, but that is impossible to verify independently. What is clear is that the Derry Command okayed the operation despite the potential risks of detonating a bomb in the vicinity of thousands of their own supporters.

The IRA waited until both policemen and soldiers had gathered at their usual surveillance position on 28 January and then detonated the device. The bomb blasted huge chunks of masonry from the medieval wall but the security forces suffered only minor injuries. A piece of rock was hurled three hundred yards over the top of a block of flats and fatally struck seventeen-year-old Charles Love, a Sinn Fein supporter, in the head. The IRA had murdered one of their supporters at a rally organized by Republicans to commemorate republican suffering.

The killing of Charles Love was a freak event in the sense that no one, no matter how devious, could have predicted or engineered his death. But the killing of the seventeen-year-old was a public relations nightmare for the Provisionals. After Paddy Flood's exposure, the Derry Brigade were understandably keen to shift some of the blame for Charles Love's death on to the British security forces. After all, a police informer had made the bomb and the security forces had allowed the operation to go ahead. The Provisionals were also careful to trail the claim that the Semtex charge in the booby-trap had been altered to blast out from the wall rather than up towards the gathered soldiers, thus making it more dangerous for the marchers parading down below the city walls.

The British security forces were not under any moral obligation to save the IRA from the bloody results of their own recklessness. But they were, according to the RUC Chief Constable, duty-bound to save rather than endanger innocent lives. The RUC had foreknowledge of Paddy Flood's bomb, yet they did nothing to abort the device; the IRA were not the only organization playing with other people's lives for their own ends on Bloody Sunday 1990.

Around the time of the bombing, Elizabeth had given birth to a daughter, Aoibheann, and the family had moved into a small house in the heart of the Bogside. Although Paddy never earned a regular wage, life was good; the couple had a wide circle of friends in the close world of Derry republicanism and they were strongly in love. Money was never important to Paddy; he was not a gambler, not a drinker, and he lived moderately. If he was not out on IRA business attempting to murder British soldiers, his favourite relaxation was sitting in front of the video at home and sucking his way through packets of boiled sweets. After his marriage he developed a paunch. 'When he met Liz everything went well for him. The two of them never looked back,' said a relative.

Liz had always been vulnerable. She had been adopted by the Mooney family as a child but had neither the ability nor the desire to share the aspirations of her university-educated sisters. Liz, highly strung and nervous, had always been the weakest child in the family and emotionally dependent on those around her. She was not very articulate and never had much interest in the world beyond the Bogside's frontiers. Liz was what Derry people describe as a home-bird, someone who rarely ventured outside the small network of streets and relationships which she had known since childhood, and where she felt emotionally safe. Her friends described her as a 'giddy blonde' – a young woman who was only interested in fashion and boyfriends. With Paddy she finally found the protector and the emotional security she craved.

Liz always denied that Paddy was a tout or that he became an informer to save her. In the Bogside, being a tout's wife can be physically dangerous; families of imprisoned IRA men have taken out their retribution on informers' families. The social stigma attached to informers makes it difficult for anyone to accept that their closest relative has turned; being indirectly responsible for your husband's death must be even more difficult to live with.

Did Liz's fragility condemn Paddy to betray his friends to save her? I interviewed Liz by herself in her own home, in her mother's home with her parents present, in the streets of Derry and in Paddy's parents' home. She was a strange half-woman, half-child, who confusingly combined paramilitary street cunning with a child's naivety. She knew how to lie if she wanted to, but she was also a victim; Liz had been brought to the edge of a second nervous breakdown by the protracted ordeal of Paddy's interrogation, the long weeks of waiting, the unending string of promises about his imminent release from her one-time friends, and her own desperate desire to believe them. Only once did I come across a crack in her denial of Paddy's turning. In a sing-song girlie voice, Liz defended both the man who died for her love and herself:

Paddy always said to me if I was going to be lifted: 'Never say anything. Just sit there as I do and say nothing. At the end of the day, Liz, if you say anything it will not be me that is going down, it will be you.' It's hard-going in the barracks.

You are getting lifted and you have these three or four detectives giving you abuse, steadily asking you questions, especially being a girl. They are lowering you down to that level and you are sitting there and saying nothing. Not that I knew nothing but the police, you could get talking to them and they could put anything on you. But I did like Paddy told me.

The precise level of Liz's knowledge of Paddy's betrayal remains unknown.

Paddy's run as an informer came to an end in May 1990, three years after he had turned. On the last day of the month he was contacted by the Bogside's Officer Commanding, Anthony Miller, and told to help out with the building of an anti-personnel mine aimed at killing soldiers on foot patrol. Seven kilograms of powerful Czech-made Semtex explosive were to have been wrapped round four kilos of shrapnel and detonated by a hundred-metre-long command wire. The IRA say that Flood immediately contacted his handlers by telephone and told them about the bomb, named the IRA members involved in the operation, and gave details of where the device was being made at a house in Marlborough Terrace in the Bogside. Detective Sergeant L promised there would be no arrests to 'cover his back'.

Flood went to the house and worked on the device until the early hours of 1 June. Minutes after Flood left, a British Army covert surveillance squad arrested the remaining three IRA men, Anthony Miller, Gerard McFadden and Sean McMonagle, as they were leaving the safe house along a back alleyway. The plainclothes soldiers drew non-issue Magnum revolvers and shouted: 'British Army. Get up against the wall!' The soldiers' strong English accents were immediately identifiable but for Miller worse was to come. One of the soldiers turned to him and asked: 'Where is the bomb, Tony?' The IRA unit was shocked – how had the soldiers found out about the bomb and how did they know Miller would be there?' The presence of the undercover soldiers in the heartland of the republican Bogside stronghold could not have been a chance encounter. The bomb was soon discovered by a police search team. The IRA unit had been betrayed.

The arrests were a blunder; the soldiers, who were using sophisticated night-sights to track the IRA team, had only been tasked with watching the IRA unit. The original security force plan was to have allowed Miller, an IRA veteran who had already served eight years for possession of explosives, and his colleagues to reach the proposed IRA ambush site before killing them in an SAS ambush. The plan might have confused the Derry Command into believing the ambush was the result of a chance surveillance operation and not an informer. The Army operation was thwarted by a chance event; McFadden had unexpectedly turned round in the alleyway and spotted the soldiers in the midst of a radio transmission. The undercover soldiers believed they had no alternative but to arrest the three IRA men. Only one IRA Volunteer escaped, Paddy Flood, and his fate was now sealed.

Paddy disappeared a week later. 'He went out a message [sic] and said he would be back. I told him not to be long because we had to buy Aiobheann some shoes. I was afraid when he did not come home that night. Paddy had never been away from me for the whole night long,' said Elizabeth.

Liz, applying her own sense of paramilitary guile and still fearful of the Derry Brigade's reaction, at first told me an edited version of the events surrounding Paddy's disappearance. In this version some unknown men came to her door two weeks after Paddy's disappearance. The hall light was broken and it was dark and Liz was unable to see their faces. In a grim parody of police procedure, they asked for a change of clothing for Paddy and left warning her not to contact the police or her local Catholic clergy. The men's words still haunt her: 'They said: "Paddy's all right. He will be back. There is nothing to worry about. Just keep it to yourself. It will only make things worse for Paddy." ' They walked away down the street.

Liz was caught in a clash of social and personal loyalties. The historical taboo on informing within her own republican community prevented her from openly identifying her IRA interrogators. If Liz had publicly said she knew who the IRA men were, the police might have decided to question her and she might have told them, and then the IRA might have been forced to shoot her as an informer. The IRA would not have wanted to do that because it would be politically embarrassing to murder a young woman, even though the Derry leadership already believed that Liz knew Paddy was a tout. For her own safety and out of a sense of loyalty to her own community, Liz felt she needed to lie to protect the IRA killers of her husband.

In a later version of events, Liz gave a more accurate account of her own interrogation by the Derry Brigade's internal security unit.[11] The two IRA men, whom Liz knew because she had socially met every Republican in the city, arrived at her house within twenty-four hours of Paddy's disappearance and questioned her for hours, day after day, about Paddy's whereabouts on the evening of the August 1989 bomb-making incident when he left Molloy and Doherty to 'get something'. The IRA men were gathering evidence to confront Paddy and break the cover story he was using to explain his movements. But there were five days of interrogation before Liz was told Paddy was being held as a suspected informer.

> I just went off my head. They had a tape and they were asking me questions. I kept telling them they had the wrong man. I said to them: 'Look at what we have been through. Where is the money if it's for the money?' I know Paddy was innocent and I'll always say that to the day I die. They kept asking me questions but I couldn't answer I was crying so

much. I asked them why they were taping me and they said they wanted to compare my story with Paddy's.

Not everything in Liz's original story was untrue; the men did warn her that if she told anyone about her husband's disappearance, she would get Paddy into deeper trouble. For seven and a half long weeks Liz was silent as the Derry Command churned out a series of lies, excuses and false promises to keep her quiet until they had decided what to do with Paddy. On one occasion a Sinn Fein representative promised her a visit to the secret IRA prison where Paddy was held. 'They told me to get the bingo bus to Buncrana, where someone would put me in a car, blindfold me for security reasons, and take me to Paddy. The bus went at seven o'clock and at about five to seven somebody came up to me and told me it was all cancelled.'

The IRA were frightened that if Liz went to her priest the Catholic Church would intervene and denounce them from the pulpit. For a month she kept the secret from Paddy's father and mother, who lived less than a mile away.

I couldn't take it any more. I went to see a Sinn Fein representative. He was real nasty but when I told him I was going to the bishop he changed his tune and went over the usual: 'We all know that Paddy is innocent, he'll be home soon.' He told me there were ten men there [at the secret IRA prison] and they all agreed Paddy was no informer. There was just two wee slip-ups but that it would all be sorted out soon and then Paddy would be home. The worst that could happen was that Paddy would be kicked out of the IRA. So I waited again, every day going to their doors. This Sinn Fein representative told me Paddy was definitely coming home that Saturday. I was dancing for joy, but Saturday came and there was no sign of Paddy. I went to the priest then, more for comfort than anything else, for I was desperate.

The priest had a chilling message; he told Liz she would never see Paddy alive again.

From the location of his body, near Newtownhamilton in South Armagh, it is probable that Paddy was taken to a secret IRA interrogation centre just across the border in the Republic. South Armagh is a traditional dumping ground for the corpses of IRA informers and the area is home to an IRA counter-intelligence squad that specializes in informer interrogation. Very few men have ever returned alive from the hands of this deadly IRA unit. But there is one man who has: Martin O'Hagan, a professional journalist and former Official IRA activist, who worked for a Northern Ireland newspaper, the *Sunday World*.

After writing a series of articles in his newspaper about political splits between the IRA and Sinn Fein, O'Hagan was tricked into going to South Armagh by a republican contact. At a secret rendezvous a masked gunman carrying a rifle jumped out from behind a hedge, hooded O'Hagan and bundled him into a car. He was taken on a twenty-minute drive to some-where just south of the border, near the town of Castleblaney. 'When I got out of the van I said: "What do you want to talk about?" They started to laugh and said: "You are the one we want to talk about." I heard the click of guns. "We want to talk about some of the stories you have been running. Who are your informants?"'

It was the start of a fourteen-hour interrogation. Blindfolded and threatened at gunpoint, the helpless journalist had question after question fired at him by two IRA interrogators. 'At one stage I thought I was going to be shot. I was actually told I would be shot and my body dumped on the border and I would be branded as an informer. I was high on adrenalin all the time. Nothing so focuses the mind as the prospect of being shot dead in a few hours,' said O'Hagan.

The IRA prison had the facilities to cope with a lengthy series of interrogation sessions; there were showers, toilets and bed-rooms; O'Hagan was offered dinner. 'They could hold you there for as long as they wanted to, just as they held Flood for weeks. Every day would have been the same routine: the mask and the interrogation. Those boys [the interrogators] would be convinced that he was an informer. They are very dangerous people. The man said to me: "There is no room for doubt." Their job is to get a statement and they will continue the interrogation until they obtain one.'

As an IRA activist in the early years of the Troubles, O'Hagan had been frequently arrested and interrogated by RUC detectives and was familiar with the techniques used by the police to break or entrap a suspect. He was impressed by the skills of his IRA questioners. 'They were as good, if not better, than the cops. All their techniques were classic RUC techniques; they never hit me but they threatened to hit me. They had guns, they even had a tape-recorder.'

The IRA's interrogators were cunning but dogmatic.

They were intelligent in a narrow sense; they knew their own republican position but they could not see anyone else's point of view. At one particular stage they made a reference to the fact that 'there are no Protestants in the Provisional Republic of Crossmaglen and any that are there know how to keep their mouths shut'. They lived in a cocoon world, a rural world; I doubt if they knew what was happening thirty miles away, never mind Derry. One of the men was a very experienced bomber. He boasted about how he lured the British into traps and blew them up. He was in his late forties, which meant he had been involved for twenty years.

At the end, convinced he was about to be shot, O'Hagan was dragged out, still blindfolded, and bundled into a car.

I was told this was the official hearse, which they used to transport people before they blew their brains out. Their were no seats in the back and you are just lying there. I panicked and said: 'You bastards are going to kill me now.' They just laughed and said: 'Och, we are not going to shoot you. You are lucky, but there are a lot of others who lay where you are lying now who were shot.'

The IRA did not physically torture Paddy Flood; they did not need to. The IRA said that Paddy confessed to sabotaging bombs just sixteen hours after his interrogation began. His former comrades in the Derry Command played a key role in his interrogation. They went over every operation, maybe hundreds in number, that Flood had been involved in or knew about. They were worried that he had put electronic tracing devices into IRA timing switches and had jeopardized future IRA operations. Finally the IRA say that Paddy Flood admitted, after they had cross-checked his movements with his family, that he had lied about his whereabouts between 5.15 pm and 6 pm on the night Molloy and Doherty were arrested in August 1989. They say Paddy Flood met Detective Sergeant L at the City Cemetery, close to the Bogside, before returning to finish off the device. Paddy confessed he had deliberately left the batteries out of the bomb on the RUC officer's instructions. Paddy's interrogators also closely questioned him about his final operation with Miller. The Provisionals say his handlers promised Paddy there would be no arrests. After the arrests, in Paddy's last encounter with the RUC detectives, they told him police headquarters in Belfast had overruled local members of the Special Branch.

Paddy felt the police had betrayed him. He said on the tape:

J told me he did not give a fuck. He just told me to keep calm and everything would be all right. It wasn't up to me to decide who got arrested. That decision was up to them. I went mad. I wasn't too sure if the cops had done the rat on me again or if the lads had bad luck. As it turned out they had the whole fucking place staked out for hours beforehand.

The dirty fuckers fucked me over again. Three suspicious cars had been spotted in the neighbourhood. They had done the officer commanding.

Paddy appeared to be genuinely angry at the duplicity of the police, who had broken his version of their bargain with him. It seemed as if he had become convinced that he could juggle with Special Branch and the IRA and survive. The emotional pressures within this frightening isolated existence must have been intense. Other people caught in such a cruel trap would have fled and made a life for themselves far away from the RUC's informer war. But Paddy did not have that escape hatch; he was a small man in his small world and he knew no one and nothing apart from the Bogside. He was a prisoner of the Troubles long before the RUC or the IRA touched a hair on his head.

The IRA say that Flood's interrogation took a long time, but their explanation as to why it took seven weeks is puzzling; most other informers get the bullet within forty-eight hours. There is some evidence to suggest that Flood, because he had been blackmailed through his wife into becoming an informer, was treated as a special case and some members of the Derry Command argued that his life should be spared. But Flood's plea for clemency was rejected by the IRA leadership.[12]

The IRA interrogators taped Paddy's final confession. After his murder, the IRA came first to David Flood with the tape and their long tortuous justification for his execution. David and Paddy, nicknamed the Ugly Brothers because of their lack of looks, had always been very close, marching and rioting together from their early teens; they were not just brothers but comrades in the Derry Brigade.

The tape was a damning indictment but the clash of loyalties to his brother, to his family and to his comrades shattered David. At Paddy's wake he had shed no tears until Elizabeth's mother Mrs Mooney began to bitterly denounce the IRA. David went into the hallway and began to cry alone. 'I have family here who hate republicanism but I have friends,' he said, vainly trying to explain his dilemma after he had reluctantly agreed to an interview.

Paddy never shared his secret burden with his brother and Paddy's arrest by the IRA had come as a total shock. David's love for his brother made it impossible for him to say openly that Paddy had turned. 'How can I believe it when Paddy used to say: "No matter what you do, even if they have you by the balls, say nothing." I will never know until I talk to him.'

The IRA's rationalization for his brother's murder had become an obsession as David struggled to resolve his own conflicting emotions. He turned to me, an outsider, in the course of our interview and asked for the solution to his own, and Paddy's irresolvable dilemma. 'If someone was not working for an organization but being used by them, why did the IRA have to shoot him? The IRA say he could have gone to them and he would not have been harmed. But how was Paddy to know that? You still love him as your brother no matter what he did. He did it to save himself and his wife. They had him by the balls.' I did not have any answers.

Paddy's death did not stop David being a Republican even though he must have been able to guess the identities of his brother's killers. A month after his brother's death David was stopped in the street by a British Army foot patrol. When they found out who he was, they taunted him. One soldier said: 'I hear your brother Paddy got the OBE.' David shrugged and gave the soldier a quizzical look.

'Yeah, the One Behind the Ear,' the soldier laughed, jabbing his finger into the side of David's head. Like Paddy, David saw no purpose in life outside the Bogside republican world.

David's confused loyalties and Elizabeth's bitterness towards the IRA had riven the Flood family. Paddy's father Seamus, a quiet, ordinary man, was still frozen in grief when I interviewed him many months after Paddy's death. 'My son dying or anyone else's son dying is not going to change things. The British Government is not going to care how many soldiers are killed or policemen. It's just a mark in a book. It's just the same as some people in the North could not care how many young fellas is killed or blew up or put in prison, just as long as they are not put in prison.'

Unlike O'Hagan, Paddy Flood was not lucky and there was not much honour about his death. Paddy's murderers said they were going to move him and got him to change into a blue boiler-suit to avoid leaving any incriminating hairs or forensic traces. After that, they bound his hands with brown masking tape, stripped him of his shoes and shot him once in the back of the head with a high-velocity rifle, before pulling a black bag over his head to catch the blood. They threw his body into the back of the official hearse and dumped him at the Coach Road like a sack of potatoes.

The informer war between the Derry Brigade and the RUC did not end with Paddy's death. The Derry Brigade remained convinced that there was a super-informer in their senior ranks. They believed that Flood had been sacrificed to protect someone in the Brigade Command, and their hunt to catch this arch-betrayer continued.

At first the IRA's internal security unit was side-tracked by a separate informer case. After the October 1990 Coshquin attack in Derry, the RUC were keen to strike back at the Derry Brigade. The police turned to twenty-one-year-old Ruairi Finnis, who had been passing scraps of low-level information to his handlers for three years. According to the IRA statement issued after Finnis's execution, the RUC wanted dead IRA bodies.[13] Finnis supplied the Special Branch with information about a planned IRA attack on security forces in the nearby town of New Buildings. The RUC called in the SAS and planned to ambush the IRA unit. But the undercover soldiers were spotted by the IRA and the operation was aborted.

Finnis's active service unit immediately came under suspicion as the source of the leak. The IRA say every member of that unit was offered the chance to come forward and repent. 'The IRA is prepared to be lenient to those who have been working for the British but such people must come forward voluntarily,' its statement read. But no Volunteers did come forward and a bogus operation was initiated to flush out the tout. Each of the five men under suspicion was left alone at different times in a house in preparation for what the unit was told was an impending IRA operation. Only one man used the tapped telephone, Ruairi Finnis.

Finnis had not repented and no mercy was shown. He was abducted one night in June 1991, held for forty-eight hours until the vital confession was obtained, and then shot three times in the back of the head. His barefoot, hooded body was found dumped near shops in the middle of the Creggan district in Derry.

Finnis was an ordinary IRA Volunteer and never privy to the secrets of the Brigade Command, so the IRA's internal security unit's hunt for the super-informer went on. In hindsight, the first shards of suspicion should have crystallized around the Brigade's Shantallow active service unit led by twenty-seven-year-old Martin Hogan. At four in the morning on 14 October 1990, days before the Coshquin operation, the RUC phoned up a Shantallow priest, Father Eugene Boland from the local St Joseph's Church, to ask for his help as an intermediary. The police told the priest they had information about a house in his parish taken over by gunmen; they were worried about the hostages being killed in a shoot-out with the IRA.

The police information was accurate. Three masked men, led by the Shantallow Officer Commanding, had burst into a family home in Elaghmore Park just after midnight and taken the householder, his wife and three children hostage. The family's van had been hijacked and then returned to the family garage with a five-hundred-pound bomb tucked in the back; the IRA had been planning to blow up a police station.

Father Boland walked up to the house, knocked on the door, and informed the masked IRA men holding the family at gunpoint that the police knew they were there. The IRA men fled through the back garden and escaped through gaps in the patchy police cordon. The area was sealed off for the next eighteen hours as the authorities dealt with the explosives.

The RUC's unusual action in calling in Father Boland was hailed by the city's nationalist politicians as a first-class example of sensitive police work. Unionist politicians bitterly condemned the operations as the 'Shantallow shambles' for allowing the IRA to walk away. The RUC, one of the world's best equipped anti-terrorist police forces, tersely defended themselves by saying the priest's intervention 'saved lives'. Ten days later the IRA launched their human-bomb assault on the Coshquin checkpoint and the odd outcome of the Shantallow shambles was almost forgotten.

The Coshquin attack itself was also the subject of an IRA security analysis after six key Republicans were arrested in two County Donegal safe houses in the immediate aftermath of the bombing and a British officer was heard shouting at the Coshquin rescue teams: 'Where were my surveillance patrols?' The speed of the Gardai's arrest operation and the British Army officer's comments were disquieting signs for the IRA that security forces on both sides of the border had been warned of an impending IRA operation. The information could only have come from inside the Derry Brigade even though very strict security had been imposed. After a protracted legal battle in the Dublin courts, the six men successfully fought charges of IRA membership.

Another operation to trigger the Brigade's suspicions came eight months later with the assassination of a prominent Derry Loyalist in June 1991. A few months earlier a popular County Donegal Sinn Fein councillor, Eddie Fullerton, had been assassinated in a cross-border raid by Loyalists. The Derry Brigade retaliated by killing the thirty-two-year-old chairman of the Ulster Democratic Party, Cecil McKnight, the man they believed to be the Loyalists' Commanding Officer in Derry.

Hogan's unit, which included the shooter, were tasked with

carrying out the operation. At first the IRA had some difficulty locating their victim. McKnight proved elusive, but the IRA squad finally struck at 7.45 pm on 29 June at McKnight's home in the Protestant Waterside district of the city. The masked IRA shooter crept up to the front window and, seeing McKnight chatting away to what looked like two insurance salesmen, fired three times through the glass, fatally hitting McKnight in the back. The insurance salesmen dived for cover. Afterwards the shooter said he thought the face of one of the salesmen was familiar from somewhere; it quickly emerged that the salesmen were RUC detectives. The police press office lamely claimed that the two detectives were in the McKnight home by chance to advise on his personal security when the IRA assassin struck. The IRA were not fooled; the operation had been a set-up. McKnight had been warned and the RUC were there to ambush the IRA shooter.

But the final clue that betrayed the betrayer was something far more intangible, far more innocuous, a mere slip of the tongue, but enough in the world of the Irish informer to signal a man's death warrant. Martin Hogan related:

I just got called in by the Quarter-master who said: 'I want you to do a job over the border this weekend.'
  'I was going fishing.'
  'Cancel going fishing.'
  I knew then that they wanted to do [kill] me, so I called up the handlers. At the meeting my handler just said to me: 'You are being taken over the border this weekend and you are not coming back.' The handlers told me the 'RA had been planning to arrest me the previous weekend but they pulled out at the last minute because they couldn't get hold of some Belfast interrogator – their best man. It was obvious the cops had another tout in the 'RA's internal security. I had to make the decision there and then to rip my life up; I said yes. I knew that when I got out of that car my life was finished. We left Derry the same day, me, the wife and the kids with the clothes that we stood up in.

Hogan's last act just before he fled from Derry into RUC protective custody was to phone the men who now planned to kill him and admit he had betrayed them. 'The Quarter-master thought at first I was joking. He couldn't believe it. But I said: "No its the truth. I'm a tout."' The IRA's Derry Brigade are still not entirely sure who or what Martin Hogan betrayed but their latent hatred of informers meant they were likely to believe the worst; an arch traitor had again been in their midst. 'From the way they talk you would think Martin started the Second World War. He is being blamed for the rise of Hitler,' said his sister, Rose Hogan.

On the surface Hogan, the youngest of a family of ten, had impeccable republican credentials. His brother Willie, still in his early thirties, had spent a decade in prison for the attempted murder of a soldier. Hogan's mother ran a vegetable shop in premises that were rented from Sinn Fein. His exposure as a tout was utterly shaming for the Hogan family, as if their brother had been revealed to be a child sex abuser. 'Willie just came round to me and cried and cried. A big strong man crying in my sitting room. At first I was terribly angry. If I had had a gun I would have shot Martin,' said Rose Hogan. 'Now I feel sorry for him. He has lost everything, friends, family. No wonder he is depressed.'

The IRA, with the benefit of hindsight, now say the Elagh-more Park operation was an elaborate ruse to sabotage a major bombing operation and protect Hogan's cover. They say that Hogan acted suspiciously on the night the Brigade bombed Coshquin by twice trying to leave his position, and that Hogan tried to get a fellow Volunteer killed at the McKnight home. If the Derry Brigade ever got their hands on Hogan they would interrogate him until he revealed the full extent of his collaboration with the RUC, and then kill him.

Martin Hogan was living somewhere under a new identity provided by the RUC. It took a long time but I was finally able to meet him in a bar somewhere in England. He was a thin wiry man, unhealthy-looking, as if he had once suffered from acne and a poor diet. He was still unconsciously dressed in the uniform of the Provos – jeans, a leather jacket and trainers. His accent, soft and mumbly, was difficult to understand at first and he was a very troubled man. Hogan, or Hogie as he was known in Derry, was defeated; he was living in the wake of the catastrophe that had overtaken his life, waiting for the stasis in his life to end, waiting for today to become tomorrow because there was no hope in today and maybe something might happen tomorrow to make it less like today. He was a perceptive, clever man, full of remorse for having betrayed his brothers, his comrades in the IRA, for being duped by the RUC, for ruining his own life, his wife's life. The cross-loyalties that made him phone to apologize for his treachery still rocked his life and made him afraid. At our meeting his eyes continually flickered around the room searching out potential enemies and on the other side of the bar, unknown to me until later, there was a minder he had brought along to 'watch his back'.

Like the informer Hegarty, Hogie was finding his life of exile difficult. His Special Branch handlers had arranged the purchase of a seventy-thousand-pound house on a nice prosperous middle-class estate somewhere in England. They bought him a six-thousand-pound car and put thirty thousand pounds into a bank account. But he was still a prisoner of his own past. Like Hegarty, he missed Derry and had few life-skills to survive beyond the tight mesh of family and friends. He had no qualifications and no skills, so despite his middle-class house and big car the only employment he could find was as a barman paid at £2.50 an hour. Nothing in his previous life on social welfare in Derry had prepared him for money in the bank and like a working-class lottery winner, the money was burning its way through his fingers.

The day after the handlers left I went out and bought a Rottweiler for three hundred pounds. Three hundred pounds for a dog. Sometimes you're lucky in Ireland if you can get forty pounds a week on the dole – my mates in Derry would have laughed me out of Ireland if they knew about that. I found out a few days later that the dog wouldn't fit into the car so I went out and traded the car in for a ten-thousand-pound estate car. I was like a child spending it, playing with a new toy. I'd spend sixty pounds on a pair of shoes that I could have bought for twenty pounds. Most of the money is gone.

Unlike a lottery winner, Hogie was living under an irrevocable death sentence which isolated him from everything that was important to him, family, friends, a place in the world. He did not have any mates left in Derry, only deadly enemies. 'Willie, my brother, has talked to me on the phone but I doubt if he would be sorry to see me on some border road with a bullet in the back of my head.' Every encounter with his new English neighbours, workmates, acquaintances, raised awkward, sometimes dangerous, questions about his background. The need to live a lie, to be always on your guard, to explain to the kids about the need to lie, continually added to the sense of dislocation. There was no place for future plans in his life or purpose in saving for a rainy day. 'There is no way that the IRA, if they get the chance, can't shoot me. They have to do it for their own people and their supporters.' Martin Hogan was waiting for the IRA to come for him.

Hogan had joined the Derry Brigade in 1989 when he was twenty-four, after two years of unsuccessful attempts to join. The IRA is a rough meritocracy; Volunteers rise in the organization by carrying out successful operations and avoiding imprisonment. By day Hogan was just an ordinary Sinn Fein member. But at night he was an IRA Volunteer and a bomb planter. Hogan's operations, attacks on the security forces, were successful and he was marked for promotion. In 1990 Hogan, whilst still an ordinary Volunteer, was arrested for suspected involvement in a grenade attack on an RUC jeep in the Shantallow area of Derry. As he was being questioned by two Special Branch officers, two local uniformed policemen entered the interrogation room and after looking at Hogan, nodded to the interrogators, apparently identifying him. Convinced the RUC had eyewitness evidence placing him at the scene of the attack, Hogan 'made the biggest mistake of my life' and started talking. It was a ruse, but Hogan had cracked and on the basis of his admissions was now facing twenty years in prison for causing explosions and attempted murder of security force members.

Hogan was far more useful to the Special Branch on the streets than in prison and they immediately made a recruitment offer. 'They told me they did not want me to sign any statements, that they would let me go and that anything I ever told them was strictly between me and them. No one would ever be able to trace back anything I told them.'

Trapped by his own admissions Hogan agreed to work for the RUC, but the interrogations continued. In a bid to disguise Hogan's co-operation from fellow CID officers within the interrogation block at Strand Road Police Barracks in Derry, the two Special Branch officers continued to scream at Hogan and slap the table whilst in reality they were offering him cups of tea and cigarettes.

When Hogan told me this I found it hard to believe that any police officer could be so paranoid and would go to such lengths to disguise their own intelligence operations from other police officers within a police station. But as with Paddy Flood's statements in his confession, Hogan was adamant that throughout all his dealings with his handlers they were obsessed with disguising their state of knowledge from other policemen, including their own Special Branch superiors, and denying the informer any scrap of personal knowledge about their real identities.

At one stage later on I was arrested by a CID man who head-butted me because, as he later boasted to other cops, 'my eyes were pure evil'. My handlers laughed and thought it was great – and me a tout. But the real reason they were so paranoid is that some of the things they were doing were illegal and they did not want anything like that traced back to them. They were also really afraid of me finding out things about them. One of them was mortified when at a car hire firm, after we left Derry, I caught a glimpse of his real name on his driver's licence. He went crazy and tore up the form. Another time my wife inadvertently took a picture of him when we were going round Belfast Zoo. He took the film off us to 'get it developed' but surprise, surprise, his picture never turned out.

Released from police custody and with the sanctuary of the Irish border just a few miles away, Hogan initially refused to phone the unlisted number to set up his first meeting with his handlers. 'I didn't phone but I didn't have the balls either to come out to the 'RA and say I'd cracked.'

The Special Branch were not about to give up their prize so easily and cleverly organized a raid on a whole row of houses in Hogan's street ostensibly searching for arms. 'It looked like a normal raid, all the cops and soldiers were in uniform and so was my handler. He hauled me out and questioned me next to his car. He must have borrowed a uniformed cop's jacket because the sleeves were too short for him. He gave me a simple message – "Be there at the meeting place." ' Hogan capitulated.

Hogan's meetings with his handlers were governed by his fear and their paranoia. Fearful of a double-cross, his handlers arranged for Hogan to walk along a desolate stretch of road near his home district. Although his handlers never acknowledged it to be the case, three cars would cruise the road checking to see that Hogan was alone. If the coast was clear the handlers would stop and Hogan would immediately dive into the back of the car and lie on the floor. For six months the first sight that greeted him as he entered the car was the cocked pistol of one of his handlers, ready to fire if Hogan made the slightest wrong move. As they drove off, the RUC men would immediately radio to their unseen colleagues that 'the package had been picked up' and clear the round from the chamber. From the moment of the very first rendezvous Hogan was doubly incriminated. 'There was no way back for me after I left that car.'

As with Paddy, they broke him in gradually. After the first couple of meetings they threw a bundle of notes into the back of the car, rewards for his information.

At first I just left it there but then I thought I might as well have it. If I hadn't I am sure they would have. Later on, when they were with me in Belfast and England, I saw them cheating on their expenses all the time. One of them bought a second-hand Porsche and the other, a three-hundred-pound motorcycle helmet. They even got me to sign a blank receipt for all the money I supposedly got, but I bet for every three hundred pounds they gave me they had been given five hundred. Who was going to check up on them? The only thing they did tell me about the money was that the chit [authorization] for the seventy thousand for the house had had to be signed by someone in the Cabinet Office. They had a right laugh at that.

Hogan still hated himself for his betrayal. In our conversation he often referred back to the period prior to his recruitment as when 'he was a real IRA man'. His wife had known nothing about his touting and although she fled to England with her husband, knowledge of his turning made her, for a period of time, more pro-IRA. 'In England we would talk about how I had turned and how I hid things and she would say to me almost unconsciously, "That's the time you were a tout." It was true but I found it really hard. The first time she said it I burst out crying,' said Hogan, visibly wincing as he recalled the conversation.

In 1990 Hogan was promoted within the IRA and became

leader of his own Shantallow active service unit, with six Volunteers under his command. As the Shantallow OC he was expected to instigate or authorize all attacks in his area, control and stockpile the unit's limited small arms and liaise with other OCs on bigger IRA operations. More importantly, he was now, as a unit commander, on the Brigade Command and had access to details of almost every significant IRA operation undertaken in Derry. Hogan was now one of the top IRA men in the city, seventh or eighth in the hierarchy, and one of the main reasons for the RUC's success in foiling IRA operations in Derry. Hogan passed back information to his RUC handlers but, according to his own testimony, also tried to undertake IRA operations without their knowledge.

> I was living a double, double life as an IRA man. I was, I am still, a Republican. But trying to get away with anything was dangerous. At meetings the cops would tell me things about operations and about who was involved. It was obvious they had other touts at a high level in the organization. One time they accused me of not telling them about an operation but I was able to get away with saying I did not know the attack was going to take place, even though I picked up the rocket launcher.

Spinning his own web of deceit within the informer world, Hogan decided to remove one source of threat, the low-level informer David Doherty, who Hogan had become convinced was relating back details of Hogan's freelance IRA activities to the RUC. 'The funny thing was I could recognize the signs through my own touting, although they were quite subtle. You got your dole on Saturdays, sometimes Doherty would have had four tins of lager and then other nights he would have had a full bag. And then I saw him get out of a car – I recognized it as a Branch car. I could just tell, so I told the internal security officer and they interrogated him and he confessed. I never told my handlers of course.' Far from coming forward voluntarily as he and Sinn Fein claimed at his press conference, David Doherty had been betrayed to the IRA by the real Judas within their ranks.

Hogan's position on the Brigade Command made him a valuable RUC asset whose cover, like Paddy Flood's initially, could not be jeopardized just to thwart a simple terrorist operation. A number of operations had to be allowed to go ahead to divert suspicion and allow their agent to remain in place. Like Hogan, the handlers must in some sense have also had to walk a tightrope, constantly juggling disaster and suspicion and constantly lying to their superiors and brother officers. From the way that Hogan talked about this relationship it was obvious that handlers and informers, although by no means equal, shared a peculiar intimacy – as if their brief points of contact were the only honest relationship in lives given over to deception. They shared a kind of camaraderie based on mutual gossip about those they targeted for betrayal. But even this relationship had its own sub-set of lies. 'He [the handler] told me that Paddy Flood was not a tout. But then he would, wouldn't he? Paddy wasn't exactly an advert for the RUC.'

Being an informer was frightening. Even in the anonymous pub where we met, hundreds of miles away from Derry, and many months after his flight, Martin Hogan was still afraid of the IRA. As a Brigade Command member he was all too aware of the fate that befell touts like Ruairi Finnis. Hogie did not believe that the IRA offer of an amnesty for coming foward would have applied to his betrayal, he did not believe he would ever return alive from an IRA interrogation.

Hogan's run began to falter with the Elaghmore Park operation three months after Flood's execution. Hogan had been ordered by the Brigade Quarter-master to take over a house in the Shantallow area and hijack the family's van in preparation for what could only have been a large attack on a checkpoint that needed a vehicle like a van to deliver the explosives. Hogan was not told the target but he duly informed his handlers. The RUC clearly decided that the size of the bomb and the risk of casualties were too great for the operation to be allowed to go ahead and so came up with the device of calling the priest in to 'avoid the risk of bloodshed', but really to allow Hogan to escape. 'They thought I was in the house, which I wasn't, so they decided to deal with the priest.' The operation was a success, the bomb plot was foiled and their agent escaped undetected, but the unusual tactics of allowing cornered IRA terrorists to escape was bound to raise suspicions.

A week later, using much the same plan, the Brigade leadership carried out the Coshquin attack, except this time the Brigade OC imposed the tightest security on an IRA operation in the city for decades. Every one of the eleven IRA Volunteers directly involved in the Coshquin bombing was called to an IRA safe house in the afternoon, prior to the attack, and assigned their roles: ferrying the explosives, taking over Patsy Gillespie's house, holding his family hostage and accompanying Gillespie on the next stage of the operation. Only the Brigade OC and his lieutenant knew the identity of the target and they did not share this information with anyone else. Once everyone had been assembled and been assigned their roles, they were also assigned a partner, a shadow, who was to be with them at all times until the operation was completed – a move clearly designed to prevent any potential informers from phoning their handlers.

Despite the IRA's precautions Hogan was able to get away from his partner and telephone his handler. 'My pair was a right eejit and it was easy to get away from him, so I phoned them. They said: "We know about that, watch yourself."' But at that time neither Hogan nor his Special Branch handlers knew what the target was. A general alert was issued to every one of the dozen Army and police installations in the area and to the Gardai across the border, but the information was too vague to save the five soldiers from the Coshquin checkpoint bombing. Special Branch failed and the IRA won.

Later, during Hogie's flight, a senior RUC Special Branch officer in the Derry Division held a panicky meeting with him, urging Hogan to promise never to reveal details of the Coshquin attack and the extent of the Branch's prior knowledge of the operations to anyone. 'He was shitting it,' recalled Hogan. Hogan insisted that a week after the checkpoint bombing his RUC handler was able to reel off the entire list of the eleven IRA men, from both sides of the border, involved in the operation.

Hogan's cover was finally blown in the aftermath of the June 1991 Cecil McKnight killing. Hogan had given the gunman's name, twenty-nine-year-old Tony Doherty from the Shantallow district, to his handlers but to cover his tracks the RUC rounded up a handful of suspects, including Hogan, soon after the killing in June 1991. In the interrogation block Hogan could hear Doherty being interrogated. Doherty broke and confessed to a host of IRA offences. 'I could hear him crying for his mammie,' recalled Hogan. On 7 October 1993 Tony Doherty [not related to any of the other Dohertys] was given two life sentences and 750 years in concurrent terms for the murder of McKnight and other IRA operations in Belfast's Crown Court.

But Doherty's confession to involvement in twenty-six IRA operations and what the trial judge described as 'a relentless campaign of terrorist activity' was to have near fatal consequences for the man who betrayed him. Twelve other IRA members and supporters were arrested and interrogated principally about information obtained in Doherty's confession. In the course of one of those interrogations Hogan's identity was inadvertently betrayed to an IRA suspect. It was a simple error but the RUC ended up breaking the first promise they had ever made to Hogan – that nothing he told them would ever be directly traceable back to him.

The error arose through Hogan's innocent habit of confusing

the name, in a slip of the tongue, of a particular Derry Brigade IRA member. By way of an example, I shall call this man John Murphy; Hogie would continually and mistakenly call him *James* Murphy. Hogan's confusion was a trivial matter but he was the only Brigade member who ever made this mistake, so the use of the wrong name was a unique clue to the origin of the information. In briefing his handlers about IRA operations, Hogan told them about a two-man job that one of the Doherty suspects had undertaken with '*James* Murphy'. Whilst questioning this particular Doherty suspect the RUC interrogator, perhaps trying to frighten the IRA man into confessing, continually referred to the suspect's role in the job he did with *James* Murphy. As a ruse it never worked. The IRA man kept his mouth shut, was released uncharged and immediately reported his suspicions to the IRA's internal security unit. Hogan's days as a tout were over. He was forced to flee from Derry a few days later.

Was Paddy sacrificed for Martin Hogan? Probably. Paddy betrayed his friends and betrayed himself to save Elizabeth, but nothing could save him once he was trapped in the informer war. Paddy, with his fatal desire to be accepted, was always just a corporal, a front-line pawn that could be endangered and then sacrificed. The RUC risked his cover when they rammed Molloy and David Doherty's car in August 1989; they risked his life, perhaps deliberately, in the defence depositions showing the absence of the batteries from the bomb and finally they abandoned Paddy to get Miller. His handlers must have thought Paddy's usefulness was at an end. The RUC knew that if they lost Paddy, Hogan was still in place; and they had almost certainly turned others in the Derry Brigade.

It all makes a sort of sense but who can really tell what is the truth in a world filled with double deceptions, handlers, confused loyalties, liars, self-loathing, professional deceivers, disinformation, black propaganda and betrayers. At the end of this journey I began to doubt the motivation of almost everyone I talked to. Were they telling me lies, and if so, why? As my understanding grew, so did my doubts. The only hard certainty was the bullet that killed Paddy Flood.

Paddy Flood now lies in the City Cemetery where he once had his fateful encounter with his RUC handler. The black, grey and white headstones look down across the Bogside towards the medieval walls of Derry. His grave, squeezed between two concrete paths, is lost amidst the maze of Derry's coronary fatalities. One hundred yards away lies the republican plot with its elaborate panegyrics to Oglaigh na hEireann and the noble dead of the Provisionals' cause. Forty names are etched into the grey slate monument.

The strange thing about Paddy was that he remained a true believer in the republican cause even as he betrayed his best friends. Even when Paddy was an informer he chased after Michael Stone, the crazed Loyalist gunman who attacked the IRA funeral crowd, and was injured by shrapnel from the assassin's grenade.

In his heart Paddy had not turned. His life was warped by the Troubles and he built himself around its distortions; one day he was a betrayer and then the next day a hero. He went on with his double life the way we might all go on, hoping and praying something would turn up. The best he could have hoped for in life was an honourable death – killed in a premature explosion one day or shot dead by the SAS whilst on active service for mother Ireland. The IRA would have given him a nice funeral, a guard of honour and a black beret on the coffin. Paddy would have got what he always wanted – the status of a hero.

Poor Paddy, who longed all his life to be accepted, will never now be inscribed on the IRA's roll of honour; those who turn are cast out for ever. His grave is adorned with a simple wooden cross erected by his brother. Scattered across the brown earth mound are the fading plastic wreaths from his funeral. The soft Derry rain has washed his name off the few condolence cards, just as history will obliterate all trace of Patrick Gerard Flood, husband, father, Republican and informer.

NOTES

1. Raymond Murray, *The SAS in Ireland*, Mercier Press, Dublin, 1990, pp. 330–31. British Army soldiers cannot be compelled to attend Northern Ireland inquests and are only identified by a letter, as in Soldier 'A', in the written statements they supply to the coroner via the RUC.

2. *Republican News*, 4 August 1990.

3. *Republican News*, 4 August 1990.

4. *Republican News*, 4 August 1990.

5. Laird committed suicide in September 1992.

6. *Derry Journal*, 8 September 1988.

7. *Irish News*, 9 May 1992.

8. *Irish News*, 1 June 1990.

9. IRA statement, 25 May 1986.

10. *Irish News*, 25 February 1985.

11. Statement by Elizabeth Flood issued by the Northern Ireland pressure group, Families Against Intimidation and Terror, in August 1991.

12. Interviews with republican sources in Derry.

13. *Derry Journal*, 7 June 1991.

5

VOLUNTEERS

It was not difficult finding Frankie Ryan. Black flags lined the funeral route from the church to the house where the last embers of his protracted wake were dwindling away in the Poleglass district of West Belfast. At the entrance to the newly built Woodside Park council house estate, the RUC night watch, with their dull-grey armoured Land-Rover, were just handing over to the day shift and a friendly flak-jacketed, carbine-carrying policeman greeted me 'Good Morning'. I carried on walking, following the trail of black flags until they petered out close to the door of one of the otherwise anonymous brick houses. The streets and lanes of Frankie's penultimate home were deserted.

Woodside Park showed little signs of being a sanctuary for one of the most hunted enemies of the Crown; there were no murals glorifying the republican dead, no slogans denouncing the British presence. The architect's plans had been perfectly set down in one contiguous brick and wooden wave; the houses, shrubs and front gardens interweaved as neatly as the slabs in the parking bays. The same plan, with its same anonymous jigsaw of brick terrace houses, wooden gates, satellite dishes, thigh-high brick walls and cylindrical metal lamp posts, could be found in Liverpool, Glasgow, St Albans and Harlow. Woodside Park just happened to be planted on Irish soil on the outskirts of a city occasionally rumbled by the sounds of war. It was part of a sea of public housing built at great cost in West

Belfast by the British Government to appease their rebellious subjects. Over the previous twenty years seventeen thousand new homes had been erected at a cost of eight hundred million pounds and the city's public housing stock is the best in the British Isles.

The lavish bribe failed; anger over the old Protestant Stormont regime's discrimination against Catholic housing transferred itself to hatred of the Crown and the new houses in Woodside Park were slowly turning into slums. Tiny fragments of glass and waste paper were embedded in the surface of every piece of public ground; broken toys and broken tree stumps, their limbs garlanded in wind-blown plastic, testified to the abundance of local children and their vandalistic urges.

The narrow passageway outside the Ryan household slowly began to fill with mourners awaiting the removal of Frankie's remains to the nearby Church of the Nativity for eleven o'clock Mass. More police Land-Rovers arrived, blocking the estate entrance and lining the road outside. The police threw a cordon round the family home and began to stop and question. Inside the cordon, mourners bunched outside the Ryans' front gate as Sinn Fein officials, including Sinn Fein President Gerry Adams, argued with senior police officers. The police riot squads moved back to what was considered an acceptable distance and the coffin, topped with black beret and glove regalia and covered in an Irish tricolour, finally emerged from the front door.

Frankie Ryan had died two weeks before, on 15 November 1991, hundreds of miles away on the 'alien soil' of St Albans in England as he crouched in the darkened doorway of a disused Barclay's Bank, priming a seven-pound Semtex bomb designed to kill members of the military Blues and Royals band playing before a civilian audience in the town's Civic Centre. The bomb exploded prematurely, killing Frankie and an eighteen-year-old female Volunteer, Patricia Black; both bodies were badly dismembered by the explosion, rendering police attempts to identify the bombers impossible. Frankie and Patricia had been 'taking the war to England'.

It was a task for which Frankie was unusually suited; he could pass for an Englishman by speaking with an English working-class accent when he chose. In St Albans, Frankie, with Patricia at his side, would have been just another young working-class couple amidst the Friday night drinking crowd, making their way from pub to pub around the Civic Centre or cuddling in a shop doorway. Frankie was invisible because most of Frankie was English; he had spent the first twenty years of his life thirty miles away in Harlow, Essex.

The IRA revealed Frankie's identity three days after his death, and his involvement came as a shock to the British security forces. The RUC's network of informers, MI5's huge computer databanks, Special Branch's surveillance operations on ports and airports, and Scotland Yard's Anti-Terrorist Branch had all failed to identify Frankie as a republican suspect and a potential IRA bomber. Somewhat belatedly, British intelligence were taking no chances with his funeral. As senior IRA men mingled amidst the mourners and marshalled a phalanx of supporters to guard the tricolour-covered coffin, a pretty blonde security force camerawoman positioned herself on one of the estate's brick walls and filmed the entire proceedings.

It was the beginning of a ponderous six-hour tramp through West Belfast to Frankie's last resting place in the republican plot of Milltown Cemetery. Lines of grey RUC Land-Rovers preceded the cortège and guarded its flanks; mourners took turns in carrying the coffin; the priest prayed vainly for 'peace and goodwill, reconciliation and new hearts, for forgiveness and mercy', and he urged God to wash away whatever sins Frankie may have committed; a lone female piper with a ring through her nose wailed a plaintive air, then tired and lapsed into silence – filled with the low growl of police Land-Rovers and the thudded shuffle of the mourners' feet. At the Church of the Nativity the priest had said it was the beginning of the season of Advent, but it felt like the stub of the year, lost between the end of autumn and the beginning of Christmas.

The grey roadside shrubbery was stripped of its leaves, the sky and city seemed drained of colour, and the funeral as flat as day-old beer. Frankie's mother Margaret and his sister Jacqueline took a turn in carrying the coffin, but their faces were a mirror of the blasted vegetation and drained of emotion; they had already been in mourning for two weeks awaiting the release and return of Frankie's body.

The RUC's cordon had the effect of isolating the funeral, sealing us within a procession of death and blocking those without from approaching. Canvas screens were erected at a local flashpoint to prevent loyalists from a neighbouring district gaining sight of the cortège. We were a column of silence moving through a largely indifferent city, past St Kieran's School where the primary schoolchildren gawked at the procession through the schoolyard wire, past old men who blessed themselves, past Budget DIY, past Woodbourne RUC Barracks, past the Upper Falls Post Office and on towards the city centre as a few workmen on lunch break stared at the coffin as it passed. The mourners within the column came in all shapes and sizes; there were women with buggies and children; thickset young men in the unofficial uniform of the Provisionals – stone-washed jeans and leather jackets; old men and young women grown old too quickly by childbirth, cigarettes and poverty.

Milltown Cemetery has been burying Belfast's Catholic dead for generations and as the cortège approached its gates, as if encouraged by the familiarity of the last few yards, the numbers of mourners suddenly swelled to around a thousand. The cemetery had opened in 1869 as new industries attracted workers to the factories and shipyards of Protestant industrial Belfast and the old Catholic graveyard at Prior's Bush ran out of graves. But with its thousand upon thousand of decaying black, white and grey headstones, Milltown is a forbidding, depressing place. In the shabby office just inside its walls a simple notice lists the charges for the cemetery's services; a grave costs £467.50, the burial of a stillborn child, £45. In the distance, on the far side of the rows of endless graves, motor-way traffic from the more recently built M1, oblivious to the ritual of Frankie's internment, buzzed past as we made our way towards the markers of the IRA's war in a section of the graveyard devoted to the communal graves of religious orders. The republican plot, marked by a simple green metal surround, runs tight against the cemetery's perimeter fence, close to an industrial refuse depot. From an overlooking slag heap, soldiers and policemen looked down on the funeral party, partly to spy and partly to prevent a repetition of the loyalist assault on a funeral in which Paddy Flood was injured. Hemmed in by the mud and the adjoining graves of the Redemptorist Community, we waited under the shadow of the hovering surveillance helicopter for Frankie's last rites.

The elaborate rituals finally began with the stiff movements of the pall-bearers, who folded the tricolour flag and handed the gloves and beret to Frankie's mother. Wreaths were laid on behalf of the different divisions of the secret organization for which Frankie was a soldier; the first wreath was from the staff of the IRA's General Headquarters, who organize the bombing offensive abroad; the second from the Northern Command, who control all IRA operations in Northern Ireland; the third from the IRA's Belfast Brigade; the fourth from the National Graves Association, who would tend his grave in the decades to come. The piper played 'A Lament for the Dead' and decades of the rosary were said in Gaelic, and then there was a speaker, Jim Gibney, a smart Belfast Sinn Fein politician.

> We have visited this graveyard and many others too often in the last twenty years of conflict and no matter how often we walk behind the coffins of dead IRA Volunteers, and no matter how often we bury or we watch people being buried in this war, it does not make it any easier for us. Our community is haemorrhaging and we have a pain buried deep in our chests because of it . . . I know that the Ryan family won't mind if the tribute I pay here today is both to their son

and Patricia Black, who died alongside him. The first thing I want to tell them is that their son and daughter were not criminals, were not evil people . . . your children do not just belong to your family, they belong to our family, they belonged to the republican family. To us, the nationalist community of the North, IRA Volunteers Frankie Ryan and Patricia Black are two very special people.

The speech was polished and the delivery smooth, but as Gibney was speaking I remembered I had seen him once before in the dock of a supergrass trial in the early eighties. He had been accused by the Crown witness of wounding an alleged informer down some Belfast back alley in the seventies. In court, Gibney had looked serious, hollow-cheeked, withdrawn and afraid. Everyone in the court knew he was going down, innocent or guilty. He was convicted and sentenced to twelve years. Beside Gibney, the open grave was deep and ugly; the freshly dug earth spilled over from the tarpaulin-covered mound, got tramped on, and clung to your shoes so that you felt contaminated by the buried dead all around you.

Frankie and Patricia should not have died on a cold November night hundreds of miles away from their families, from those who loved them and cared for them. They should not have had to huddle in a darkened doorway handling explosives in alien and hostile territory to them. They should not have had to live secret lives, live away from their families and their friends; they should not have had to be introduced to weapons of death and destruction, have had to bend their minds to that end, to steel their will against the call of ordinary life for the difficult life of an IRA Volunteer on active service. But they did all of these things and that is what makes them special, because it is hard to leave the comfort of a loving family, to forgo the happiness that comes with being part of a happy family, to embrace an organization and a struggle that places intolerable, sometimes impossible, demands upon the human spirit. Few will overcome all of this and live life, as Frankie and Patricia did . . . they saw oppression and took a great step for liberty.

But Frankie and Patricia are not alone, they are representative of a generation of our youth that have acquired the skills to remain hidden, who come forward when called upon to do so. Even by their own admission the British intelligence apparatus could not detect them. How does the British government hope to overcome such dedication, how will they defeat this invisible force? . . .

Even as Gibney was speaking, the edge of a thin film of mud was already drying on my shoes. It would be clinging there for days after, the mud from Frankie's grave and all the bodies who shared this wet and marshy ground with him.

The long years of struggle have hardened us against insult. We do not hear it any more. Is that not obvious to those who hold this country against the will of its people? Don't they realize that after such a long and bitter struggle harsh words are meaningless and have no effect on the situation? Is it not time for them to stand outside their poisoned rhetoric and ask themselves what is it that motivates such young people as Frankie Ryan and Patricia Black, a teenager not even born when this struggle began?

Ten years ago we left the Twinbrook Estate and travelled the same route as we did today to bury Bobby Sands. In those intervening years many homes of both these islands have felt the tragedy of this war. It could have been different, it should have been different. How many British Governments, how many British ministers, must we go through before we come across one bold enough to face the reality of the situation? As the world continues to change we are entitled to ask, indeed, entitled to demand, when will the Irish people receive justice, when will the wrongs of history be righted? At this graveside, amongst much suffering, we are entitled to ask – when will we meet the British equivalent of a De Klerk or a

Gorbachev? Until we do, we can be sure that young patriots, like Frankie and Patricia, will continue to play their part in the freedom struggle. Until we do, we can be sure that the hurt we feel here today as a community will be felt elsewhere. Tomorrow it will be somebody else's turn to feel the pain and to mourn at a graveside. The pendulum of sorrow has swung long enough; let the British Government face the only sensible path and sue for peace by leaving us.

Gibney finished, and the mourners quickly broke away to visit their own special family graves or flee the chill of the impending evening. The Ryans and close mourners retreated to a funeral meal and drinks at a republican social club. In the fading light, the grave-diggers began to shovel the reddy-brown clay down on Frankie; the policemen departed for their warm barracks. It was finally all over for Frankie.

There was something disturbing about Frankie's funeral. The goal, the drive to war, the cause for which Frankie died, seemed on that day, and as part of that black pageant, as far from reach as ever. We were standing in a field of the IRA's fallen; directly opposite the funeral mound, Seamus's girlfriend Mairead Farrell shared her grave with Sean Savage and Danny McCann, all three killed by the SAS in Gibraltar. A few graves along, Seamus's colleague Bobby Sands shared his grave with the other hunger-strikers. Through the jungle of gravestones a hundred yards away lay John Finucane, and beyond him the memorial to all the dead republican Volunteers beginning with United Irishman William Orr, hanged in Carrickfergus on 14 October 1797. There were hundreds of names here. On the other side of Frankie's grave, the granite and white-stone chips stretched vacantly forward to the green metal marker round the plot; there was room for another twenty years' worth of dead Volunteers. There seemed no end to this infinity of sorrow, suffering and sacrifice.

Frankie's remains had been accorded a hero's funeral but the stiff gait of the pall-bearers, the elaborate folding of the tricolour, could not disguise the mood of defeat. After twenty-two years of conflict neither the dead Volunteers around us, nor the republican leadership before us, had brought a United Ireland into being. The war and the very means to prosecute it had become as cloudy and as compromised as Frankie's last actions; Frankie's had not been a heroic death but a fatal fumble in a darkened doorway. Frankie's target, the IRA insisted, was military, but the rest of the world saw only a group of army bandsmen at a public concert; the risks of killing a random number of St Albans' music-lovers would have been high. The family of his fellow Volunteer Patricia Black had refused to participate in a republican funeral, in effect publicly disowning the organization and the cause for which their daughter had died. Frankie's parents were messily divorced, his mother still living at home in Belfast but his father with a new wife in Dorset, and Frankie was in bits inside the coffin, blown to pieces by his own bomb. As the cortège had left the church I had asked one of the prematurely old women in the procession, wheeling a buggy and with a three-year-old child by her side, about Frankie.

'He died for what he believed in.'

'Did you know him?'

'You do not have to know them.'

'So . . .'

'He was a hero, an Irishman.'

But the ritual answers could not conceal a bitter truth. Frankie, like the IRA at this moment, had failed.

Frankie was an unlikely IRA Volunteer. He was born into a working-class family in the new town of Harlow in Essex, north of London. Harlow, with its planned estates, integrated services, shopping centres, multi-storey car parks and purpose-built sports grounds, is stamped with the optimistic vision of Britain's state planners of the 1950s. Life under the masterplan of the principal architect Sir Frederick Gibberd should have been a bright utopia of workers' neighbourhoods, decent homes, cycle tracks, schools, hospitals, and modern industry. It was the first new town to be built in post-war Britain and the names of the major roads – Southern Way, First Avenue, Second Avenue, Third Avenue – reflect the break from the past and its horrors. But by the 1990s the sheen of Harlow's naissance had been tempered by recession, the flight and decay of the once new technologies and the weathering of its own concrete structures. Forty per cent of the town's workforce commuted daily to London and Harlow's bright and shining future had been converted into the reinforced concrete and brick of another dormitory town, somewhere in the M25 corridor, servicing the capital. But if Harlow has settled down into a more mundane suburban existence, it remains a place of new beginnings, not a place for memorials to men who died violently for a two-hundred-year-old cause, and not a place for young men to pledge their lives to fight a historic, implacable enemy.

Like many Irish emigrants, Frankie's parents, Margaret and Christopher Ryan, had come to England in their late teens in search of work. They met in north London, married and moved to Harlow. Christopher Ryan first worked in one of the town's electrical plants but then found employment as a nurse in a local hospital; Margaret worked part-time in a bookie shop. Margaret and Christopher were just another working-class couple, with few aspirations to change their station in life, bumping along near the bottom of Harlow's economic miracle when Frankie was born in 1966. Frankie was quickly followed by Jacqueline and then their youngest child, Darren. Although Margaret was from Belfast, her husband Christopher was from Limerick and the family had few interests in republican politics beyond belting out Irish rebel songs on tipsy Saturday nights.

The Ryans were not an entirely happy or settled household. In 1969, at Margaret's urging, the family moved to Belfast to be closer to her mother, but the move was an economic failure and they returned to Harlow further impoverished by Darren's birth in 1971. Even in Harlow, life was an economic struggle;

neighbours complained that they often found the children on the doorstep after school, locked out, cold and hungry, and awaiting the return of their mother. In 1981 Frankie, aged fourteen, ran away from home for a week. The local paper, the *Harlow Gazette*, recorded a tearful Mrs Ryan in August 1981 saying: 'He stayed out one night before now, but this time we're really worried that something terrible has happened to him.' The family organized mass searches of the local neighbourhood with friends and relatives, all to no avail. Frankie returned home of his own accord and the following week under the headline 'Frankie's Safe and Sound' the same paper recorded Frankie's joyous reunion with his family after an adventurous week of living rough on the outskirts of Harlow and his thin confession that 'things had got on top of me'.

Like his parents, Frankie was a typical product of his class and economic circumstance. He attended the local St Mark's Comprehensive but failed or did not care enough to get any O-levels and at one point was expelled. He wanted what many other young men in his situation wanted – a bit of an adventure – but had no means or skills to achieve such a goal himself. He drifted from one menial factory job to another, never settling, never applying himself, never really wanting to. He started weightlifting, became a bit of a fitness fanatic, got very picky about his health foods, and abhorred cigarettes. He ran with a local pack of ex-schoolmates, being 'wild' in a small-town sort of way, and joined in the latest craze of playing 'war-games' in the woods of Essex with paint-balls. He supported Spurs football team. He could be lippy and challenging towards authority after a few pints of cider and got into minor trouble with the Essex police when he was seventeen – pulling his pants down and showing his bottom to a mobile patrol after a heavy drinking session in a local club. He was arrested but it was all petty misdemeanour stuff and part of a pattern shared by thousands of British working-class teenagers struggling to secure an identity for themselves. Frankie, in his brother's words, was a rebel without a clue. Like those others, Frankie was attracted to the notion of joining the British Army, leaving his muddled life in Harlow for the promised thrills of being a soldier. But he did not, because he was worried he would be sent to his mother's home city, to patrol her community's home streets. 'Frankie would have really suited the Army, he was that type, but the thing that threw him off was being sent here to Belfast. He did not want to know,' said Frankie's brother Darren.

Frankie, through his mother, had another identity; an exiled son of the nationalist community of West Belfast. Although money was tight the family returned every three years for summer holidays in Belfast. Once there, they like everyone else were exposed to what, in certain Catholic districts, could only be described as military occupation. The reality of the troops' presence and the community's justification of hostility towards them diverged sharply with the view of the conflict disseminated through the television screens of Harlow. For Frankie, the contrast between the seductive recruitment images of abseiling with the Royal Marines and the grim-faced pedestrian aggressors on the streets of West Belfast was too strong.

When he was nineteen his parents' marriage broke up. Christopher Ryan had an affair with a fellow nurse and left his wife. Frankie and Jacqueline returned with their mother to Belfast and Frankie started to carve out another life for himself in the Catholic district of Poleglass, a rapidly expanding new housing district in West Belfast. Within a month of arriving Frankie was selling the IRA paper *Republican News*. He approached neighbour Richard McAuley, later appointed Sinn Fein's northern Director of Publicity, to help sell the paper door-to-door around the three-hundred-home Woodside Estate.

He was quite persistent about it. The English accent made us wonder what we were dealing with but we let him get on with it. We'd split the round between us, maybe selling about 120 papers every Friday night. At the time Poleglass was filling up with families from different parts of Belfast, Short Strand, Ballymurphy, so the place was unsettled; there was no Sinn Fein office in the district. Selling the papers was a good chance to make contact with republican families or receive complaints and Frankie was good on the doorstep. It was a bit disconcerting to have a man at the door with an English accent selling *Republican News* but Frankie was a nice lad and was well liked. Looking back it seemed to me that even then Frankie had that position worked out in his head. He knew what he wanted.

What Frankie wanted was to join another army – the Irish Republican Army – and selling the paper was a means to that end and a test of his future loyalty. The test lasted one and a half years by which time, according to his sister Jacqueline, Frankie was fed up doing it and wanted to get involved. 'He wanted to be in more, doing more.'

I met Jacqueline nearly two years after Frankie's death. We talked in her new home close to the house where the family had held Frankie's wake. Like in many homes I have visited in Northern Ireland, a huge television screen blared in the corner of the room for all hours of the day. A sick toddler wailed in Jacqueline's arms and upstairs a man was snoring in the middle of the afternoon. A picture of Frankie holding a small white dog, expensively framed, held pride of place above the mantel-piece; he was dressed in casual clothes and leaning against a wall, not really looking at the camera. Strangely there was no past and not much future in Jacqueline's life, just the constant directionless present of bringing up her children, being unem-ployed, and living in West Belfast. She was vague about dates, times, exact motivations, and found my questions disorientat-ing and difficult to answer. Jacqueline and Frankie, because of their ages, had been close and she had known about Frankie's involvement in the IRA's most secret units, but she was unclear about why her brother had got involved. 'It was living here, hearing stories about friends. He did get angry, it upset him.'

Frankie, she said, did not like the soldiers on the streets, the paramilitary police presence in West Belfast, the checkpoints through which every nationalist had to pass on their way to the city centre. One day Jacqueline said he even spotted one of his old mates from Harlow in the uniform of the British Army. But there was no dramatic incident or event that changed Frankie. He was never in a fight with the soldiers and he never complained that he had been picked out as an individual target for harassment. He was only arrested once by the police for interfering in a raid on a local Republican's house. The arrest was viewed as a misdemeanour and Frankie's name must have been passed over by RUC Special Branch. 'He went looking to get involved. He believed in freedom, in Brits out. I always knew, I was worried and proud of him. It was something he had to do. This is Ireland for the Irish and he was dedicated.'

As would-be Irish republican activists inevitably do, Frankie started to read republican versions of history. 'Frank sat down and explained to me what a lot of people don't know, but what I know for a fact, that this has been going on for hundreds of years. It goes back so far and so many people have died,' said his brother Darren. 'The 'RA have gone back for loads of years and before that it was the Republican Brotherhood. There was always resistance, the Easter Rising of 1916 and there was a treaty signed in 1921 for the North. There used to be nine counties here but they say it's six. It was all rigged from the start. Frank was well into it as well. He read a few books, especially Irish history.'

Frankie's official biography in the paper he once sold declared both him and Patricia Black to be 'Courageous Soldiers of Freedom' and told its readers that:

Volunteer Frankie Ryan was a young man who came into the republican struggle because of his deeply held political convictions, convictions that led him to Ireland to see for himself the struggle for Irish freedom and to play his part fully in that struggle. Unlike his comrade who died alongside him he

did not grow up in a country which has its streets patrolled
by foreign soldiers. . . . Nevertheless, he developed an understanding of Ireland and the struggle of the Irish people to
achieve freedom from British rule.

In the official republican roll of honour Frankie is listed as
being a member of the First Battalion of the IRA's Belfast
Brigade, and it therefore must be assumed that this was the unit
he first joined. According to Jacqueline, he was active in the
IRA in Belfast for one and a half years prior to his mission in
England. 'He started to become very secretive – hiding things. I
used to laugh and he would tell me it was none of my business.
He was trusted, I am sure of that.' In his *Republican News*
obituary Frankie's IRA comrades allegedly 'found him to be
eager and enthusiastic about his involvement. He always listened to advice. For example, when advised that his own
personal security would be enhanced if he refrained from
socializing in known clubs and pubs, he immediately stopped
drinking altogether.'

Frankie certainly had a low ranking with the RUC Special
Branch, but their failure to identify a known IRA newspaper-
seller/sympathizer, once arrested in a fracas with the security
forces, as a potential IRA member remains puzzling. Far from
ceasing drinking on the advice of his comrades, Frankie,
according to Jacqueline, regularly drank in the most notorious
republican drinking club in West Belfast, the Felon's Club,
whose membership automatically includes all convicted republicans, as well as the inevitable scattering of police informers
within their ranks.

Of all the family members Darren, despite the six-year gap,
had the most insight into Frankie. Perhaps it was because
Darren's own life in Belfast was a mirror image of Frankie's.
Darren had failed to settle in Belfast when his mother had first
gone back after the marriage break-up and had returned to
Harlow to live with his father. Darren, aged nineteen, was still
living in Harlow when Frankie killed himself in St Albans and

only fled to Belfast on the advice of his sister hours before Frankie's identity was released to the media. Like Frankie, Darren knew what it was like to be unemployed in a strange community. 'Unemployment here is pretty sad. Frankie went through stages of finding work and it was great. He lost work and he was down, as we all would be; you get your ups and downs. I was out of work for a year myself. There is nothing worse than being stuck in a flat with no money, no prospects, nothing to do. You lose all your self-confidence.'

Fitting in to the tight world of Belfast's republican communities was not an easy task even for Darren, despite the community's knowledge of Frankie's heroic death. It must have been harder still for Frankie. 'It takes all sorts and there are some Republicans who are very bitter-minded. I have had a few fights actually that were not my own fault after someone started talking about my accent and accusing me of being a spy. All they have seen of the English is guys with guns so they are very hostile. I always think it's quite funny.'

Like Frankie just before his death, Darren was living alone in a small flat but eating meals regularly at his mother's home. When we met he was still dressed in his work overalls from the temporary ACE employment scheme that had kept him off the dole for a year. High on the wall of the poorly furnished flat was the same picture of Frankie holding the same white dog; in the corner lay Frankie's dumb-bells. And like Frankie, Darren was already involved in the fringes of republican activity, selling *Republican News*. Through Frankie, Darren had become a member of the republican family.

Darren had also known about Frankie's involvement. Frankie had even visited his brother in Harlow whilst on active service during his first undercover mission in the summer of 1991.

I knew he was over on an active service unit but I didn't really give a shit. He was my brother and at the end of the day a brother is always a brother and if he comes to my front

door then that door is open. I suppose he was a bit more
nervous than usual. He didn't speak about why he was there
or who he was meeting, what he was doing, but I knew he
was on a mission. I knew already that he was in the 'RA. I
had asked him about it and he just laughed and talked about
how he had gone down south to practise his shooting. There
was no way anyone would suspect Frank. Before Frank died
it was unheard of for an IRA man to be in England with an
English accent. The cops hadn't got a fucking clue.

Frankie was searching for a kind of glory but he also knew
what he was getting into. Before he left Belfast he bought the
tricolour that was used to wrap his coffin. 'Frankie knew the
only two things you get are imprisonment or death. The only
things they promise you is them two. I was afraid of him being
caught or killed,' said Darren.

Frankie was last seen by his family in Belfast in September
1991. He lied to his mother to protect her and told her he was
going to Cork in the Republic for work. She knew it was a
'whopper' but chose to believe him. Jacqueline knew more;
Frankie had even sent her a christening card from England for
her new baby during his previous operation. She understood
how Frankie was very useful to the IRA. 'I knew he was in
England. I was very worried for him but he was perfect to go –
the accent was perfect. He knew the place. No one was going
to suspect him.'

On 13 December 1867 three Fenian bombers, forerunners of
the IRA, wheeled a barrow containing explosives against the
wall of Clerkenwell Prison in London in a bid to free two
republican prisoners. The explosion tore a hole in the prison
wall but also destroyed dozens of the surrounding slum dwell-
ings. Six people were killed, including a seven-year-old girl, and
hundreds injured. Neither of the Fenian prisoners, locked in
cells on the opposite side of the prison yard, escaped. The

Clerkenwell explosion was the first 'Fenian outrage' ever perpetrated in London and induced, temporarily, a state of
national panic. Over 160,000 special constables were enlisted
and all police and army leave cancelled. Tanks of special
chemicals were prepared at the Home Office to extinguish the
phosphorous incendiaries expected to be fired at the building.
Fenian bombers, it was rumoured, were dynamiting gasworks,
sabotaging the railways, poisoning the water supply and plot-
ting the assassination of the Government and the Royal
Family.[1]

The threat never materialized and the bombing of a radical
artisan district of London proved to be a political disaster for
the Fenian movement, turning the vast majority of the English
working class against their cause. Clerkenwell Prison has since
been demolished and the area redeveloped, but a memorial in
St James' Church on Clerkenwell Green still commemorates the
'Memory Of The Victims of the Terrible Outrage Occurred in
this Parish, Perpetrated by Certain Misguided and Wicked
Persons, who, being Members of the So-Called FENIAN
CONSPIRACY, Placed a Barrel of Powder, Against the North
Wall of the Prison, and, Firing the Same, Suddenly Rendered
the Immediate Locality a Mass of Ruins . . .' Nothing changes.

The first Provisional IRA attack on London took place one
hundred years later in March 1973. Car bombs were planted
outside Scotland Yard, the Old Bailey and in Whitehall by a
six-strong IRA bombing team, which included Gerry Kelly, the
man who escaped from the Maze with Dermot Finucane. Two
of the four bombs were defused but the Old Bailey device
exploded, killing one man, injuring hundreds and causing
widespread damage. The IRA active service unit involved in the
operation were all arrested as they fled back to Ireland through
Heathrow Airport on consecutively numbered tickets, but their
capture did not deter the IRA Army Council from recruiting
more Volunteers for the war in England.

Over the course of the following twenty-one years, the IRA
sustained a sporadic guerrilla war of great cunning and stealth

that combined startling technical proficiency, bungling inepti-
tude and callous brutality. Twice, the IRA came within feet of
decapitating the democratically elected government of the most
powerful military state in Western Europe. At Brighton in
1984, a long-delay-timer bomb blew up the Grand Hotel and
narrowly failed to kill Prime Minister Margaret Thatcher and
her Cabinet colleagues. In February 1991, at the height of the
Gulf War security alert, an IRA unit precision-mortar-bombed
Downing Street and came within feet of killing Prime Minister
John Major's War Cabinet as they met to discuss the threat
from Iraqi dictator Saddam Hussein. IRA bombers twice devastated large areas of the City of London, causing hundreds of
millions of pounds worth of damage in each attack.

But these operations were the highlights of the IRA's campaign. The vast majority of incidents in Frankie's war, as in
Northern Ireland, were small-scale attacks on relatively vulnerable targets. Fire-bombs were planted on London Underground
trains, disrupting services and entailing a massive security
operation to fit special security tags on every seat on every
train. Regional shopping centres were the target of an incendiary campaign. Army recruiting offices were attacked and Army
recruiters blown up with under-car bombs. Army barracks were
repeatedly bombed before the Ministry of Defence announced
a £150 million scheme to strengthen perimeter defences around
every one of Britain's thousands of military establishments.
Small bombs were planted in London at the homes of established figures. There was a wave of litter-bin bombs that spread
terror across England, killing a London commuter at Victoria
Station in February 1991, two children in Warrington in 1993
and injuring hundreds. Londoners grew used to all or some of
the capital's train stations being closed through a genuine or
bogus 'security alert'. There were small bombs on railway lines
that blew out signal boxes and threatened the lives of com-
muters. The list could go on and on.

When Frankie slipped across the Irish Sea in the summer of
1991 to join the IRA's 'invisible force' on English soil, he was

taking part in the most protracted and sustained mainland and continental bombing offensive ever mounted by the IRA leadership. Learning from the mistakes of the seventies that had cost them personnel, IRA cells deliberately varied their targets and their *modus operandi*. They killed eleven Royal Marine bandsmen in November 1989 by planting a bomb in their barracks practice rooms in Deal in Kent. They assassinated Conservative MP Ian Gow with an under-car bomb in July 1990 and followed it up with a wave of incendiary devices in stores in regional cities. Ten days later bombs exploded in the early morning rush hour at the crowded Paddington and Victoria London commuter railway stations. A month later fire-bombs exploded in stores in Manchester.

The logic of the campaign was to 'sap the will of the British Government in regard to remaining in Ireland' by hitting the British economy and killing those deemed to be 'members of the coalition of interests that sustain the conflict in Ireland'. Knowing the capabilities of the British to record and intercept all electronic traffic between Britain and Ireland, the planners at the IRA's General Headquarters outlined a range of legitimate targets and left the details to their active service units. Behind the shield of their leadership's rhetoric, individual IRA units were free to attack just about any target they chose on the grounds that any IRA action was certain to further stretch the resources of their enemies. A bomb in a toilet in a crowded London West End pub in October 1992 killed one man and injured dozens. The IRA seemed to be operating on two levels, using some Volunteers to hit soft, easy targets, whilst separate, more determined active service units planned spectacular and complex operations like the bombing of Downing Street.

Apart from his IRA superiors no one knows the full extent of Frankie's clandestine activities in England or even where he was living. IRA Volunteers in England have used extended family relatives to store explosives or provide accommodation. Other units operated in three- or four-person cells and hired

English fixers to rent accommodation and pay for tools and equipment. But with Frankie's Essex accent it seems unlikely that he would have needed to revert to such subterfuge. Like other Volunteers, he would have used several false identities and paid for everything in untraceable cash. He probably avoided detection by any Special Branch informers within the Irish immigrant community by keeping his distance from any Irish-related activity. Establishing a secret life in England would not have been difficult; Britain remains one of the most open societies within the European community and the anonymity of its large cities and its social norms of indifference to strangers make it an ideal hiding ground. And Frankie, after all, was English.

He would have been aware that the British security services devoted huge hidden resources to capturing IRA personnel on the mainland. Every day of active service in England carried the risk of chance betrayal or detection. The psychological strains of the IRA's war must have been considerable. Like every other IRA Volunteer Frankie would have known that arrest entailed a life sentence behind the bars of an English prison.

Frankie's visit to Darren in Harlow took place in the summer of 1991 as a mini-break in an operation Frankie later described as having gone wrong. On 28 June 1991 a twenty-pound Semtex bomb was defused outside a theatre in west London where the Blues and Royals had been playing the night before. The circumstantial evidence points towards Frankie and a potential mission to track and kill the Blues and Royals as they performed at public concerts across England; the November St Albans bomb was probably his second attempt to kill the military band and the second time he would have endangered the lives of a large number of civilians for the goal of a United Ireland. 'He would have got the soldiers from the band, Blues and Royals. He was fighting for a United Ireland. You fight for who you live with,' said Darren.

Frankie did not set out to kill civilians but the possibility of their deaths did not deter him. 'Frank would have been pleased that the band was stiffed, but the civilian side he would not have liked at all. I do not think that any IRA man goes out with the intention to kill innocent blokes. If it went wrong and innocent people died, then I am sure Frank would have felt sorry for them and for their families. They would have been people like me, out to earn a living and make their way in life,' said Darren.

Frankie failed and killed himself, but other IRA Volunteers have succeeded and murdered the wrong people in the wrong place at the wrong time. On 17 December 1983 an IRA unit led by Thomas Quigley and Paul Kavanagh pushed a second-hand car into a pre-secured parking bay at Hans Crescent outside the prestigious Harrods department store. The streets were filled with Christmas shoppers. Half an hour before the device exploded, a caller phoned the Press Association and gave a confusing bomb warning designed to throw police off the track. At 1.23 pm the bomb exploded as an ordinary Metropolitan Police unit, the first on the scene, was examining the suspect car. Three officers, an American tourist, a young mother and a reporter, Philip Geddes, were killed.

On the first anniversary of the Harrods bombing a plaque was erected on the site where the police officers and the other victims had died. Geddes' parents had been invited to attend the unveiling of the memorial and had travelled down from their home town of Barrow-in-Furness. I was working as a reporter for the Dublin *Sunday Tribune* and contacted them, not expecting them to talk, but they readily agreed. Looking back, I think his parents' attendance at the memorial ceremony and their agreement to the interview had been part of a desperate attempt to understand the act of fate that had robbed them of their only son and destroyed their lives. We met in their hotel suite around six in the evening for what turned out to be a tense, sad and awful interview.

Geddes had been fresh out of university and been working a familiar route into national newspaper journalism via the William Hickey social diary column of the *Daily Express*, trading off his alleged glamorous contacts from his Oxford University days. In the hot hotel room Philip's father frenetically paced the floor and unpacked his own and his son's life story. He had come to Britain as a refugee from Poland during the Second World War and eventually settled on a tailoring business in Barrow-in-Furness. 'They call me Mike the Tailor,' he repeated endlessly in a thick Polish accent. He met and married Philip's mother but they failed to have a child until she was thirty-seven. Philip was not just a son but their gift from God, the vindication of his exile and the passion of both their lives.

Mike had never been to Ireland or paid attention to its problems. He was a small man, a maker of suits, a former refugee, whose life was fulfilled through his son's social transformation at Oxford where the once humble schoolboy had danced with Princess Margaret. Philip's life, it seemed to his father, was almost a fairy tale come true – their son, the son of a tailor, could indeed dance with the Queen of England's sister. He pulled out a picture to show me, as if he still could not really believe it had happened. It was a formal black-and-white photograph of an older woman in an elaborate ball gown and her younger consort dancing. It could have been taken in the 1950s.

Mike the Tailor's love for his son spilled over into his own working life. In December 1983 he had been working on two suits for his boy. He always made his suits. Philip was always a well-dressed young man and good clothes hung well on him. Hot tears began to spill from the father's eyes and he began to sob. 'You are making suits and then they come round and tell you your son is dead and it's over, your life is over . . .' His wife took him in her arms but there was no rest for his inconsolable grief, no answer to the blind unfathomable why, no means to undo the death of their slaughtered son. 'If they had killed me it would have been okay, I've lived my life, but my Philip had his future ahead of him.'

It was not easy to be in the room with them. They were convinced I was an ambassador from the same accursed race of people who had killed their beloved son, not a journalist with an open notebook. They wanted Philip to be alive, they wanted to understand how and for what purpose he had been picked out, they wanted a reason from me for his murder. I did not have any reasons or any answers but I took from that room an impression of the great weight of their tragedy. Philip's death had practically killed them too. Mike's interest in the tailoring business, in the world beyond his grief, had collapsed. There was nothing to live for, only a span of time between the present and their future death to be negotiated and endured. Across the room Philip's girlfriend Jane, a nice English rose, sat in silence. Philip had been shopping with Jane in Harrods minutes before the evacuation order came over the tannoy. Like a good reporter he moved towards not away from danger and was standing next to the policemen, close to the suspect car, when it exploded. Jane was still young and her life had moved on a year after Philip's death; there could now be no grandchildren either. It was already dark outside and this day of empty memorials was drawing to a close. The Geddes' invitation had been fruitless; I had been unable to bring them any nearer to a reason. Tomorrow they would have to go back to Barrow-in-Furness and their unremitting sorrow.

Geddes was just a random victim; he was not supposed to be a target. The IRA's Army Council's aim had been to hit British economic targets by bombing Harrods, not kill civilians. It was a mistake. Like the Clerkenwell explosion, the Harrods Christmas shopping bomb was a political disaster for the Provisionals, destroying their newly acquired alliance with the British radical Left led by Ken Livingstone in the wake of the 1983 General Election, when Sinn Fein President Gerry Adams won the West Belfast parliamentary seat. Later the IRA Chief of Staff set up an enquiry to find out what had gone wrong, but no amount of IRA internal investigations could ever restore Philip to life.

Darren, because of his very Englishness, could, unlike most

of his republican contemporaries, understand both the rage and incomprehension of the relatives of those randomly killed by the IRA.

> Obviously if it happened to me, then I would feel the same way. No one would understand why it happened. All they would see in the papers is that there was a bomb planted where there were lots of people to kill, lots of people. It's not their fault they think like that. You can't really blame them either. They are just living their own lives. No one cares until it comes to their own life and they suffer a grievance. It always seems to be the innocent ones in life that seem to get hurt. I must admit there has been too many killed by bombs and too many stiffed by loyalists and the IRA. I think it's about time it all stopped but this place is so complicated. It's so bitter, there is so much blood underneath the bridge, loved ones that have died, that I think it will go on for years to come.

News of an explosion in St Albans was carried on the late Friday evening television reports but it was Sunday before Sinn Fein officials came to Jacqueline's door. 'They said your brother has been on active service in England and he has been accidentally killed. We were advised to remove anything belonging to Frankie and we did. When them fuckers [the RUC] came the next night after his identity had been released, they could not even find his picture.'

Darren was summoned home from Harlow to the safety of West Belfast and the mourning for Frankie began. The Irish death ritual requires the physical presence of the corpse but the British authorities did not release Frankie's body, or what was left of it, for two weeks. Both Jacqueline and Frankie's mother were embittered. Night and day were subsumed within an endless wake and they became convinced the delay was an act of deliberate revenge and thus a further point of grievance to hold against their oppressor and vindicate Frankie's mission. 'It was just a military target as far as I am concerned. They were soldiers in the Army. He was a soldier taking the war to them,' said Margaret Ryan. 'It's a war, isn't it? It is for me. They shouldn't have treated Catholics like second-class citizens. It was a military target, he was at war,' said Jacqueline.

It was not easy to sympathize. Frankie had gone to a country with the intention of killing bandsmen and civilians but had inadvertently blown himself up. To complain that the authorities were being deliberately cruel in delaying the return of the dismembered cadaver seemed hypocritical. If you wage war, what else do you expect?

But Jacqueline had a strange intensity when she spoke about this issue, an emotional blindness that bordered on religious fervour.

> For two weeks we had a wake without a body. The peelers kept on coming to us with questions and demands for his dental records or asking about the tattoo, a swift, that Frankie had. He finally came home on the Saturday, two weeks after he was killed, and we buried him on the Tuesday. We needed to keep him that long, we needed to. We had him back out of the hands of England and the authorities; this was his home.

In death Frankie was the subject of one of the most intensive man-hunts in recent British history. His name, his identity, his associates and his potential whereabouts were the focus of a huge security operation code-named Operation Oregon. Both Frankie and Patricia were condemned by the British Home Secretary Kenneth Baker as 'vile and wicked people . . . who aimed to kill, to maim, to injure and to destroy'. The police ransacked what had remained of the family home in Essex, as well as Frankie's flat and his sister's home in Poleglass. A poor-quality picture of Frankie was eventually obtained and plastered across every British newspaper, but the operation failed to uncover the rest of Frankie's unit.

The England campaign did not stop because of two dead Volunteers. In April 1992 at the Baltic Exchange, an IRA unit perpetrated a devastating strike against the financial heart of the City of London by exploding a thousand-pound lorry bomb. The explosion blew out windows and destroyed offices within a quarter of a mile of the blast and caused hundreds of millions of pounds worth of damage. Windows on the thirty-fifth floor of Britain's second tallest building, the Nat West Tower, were blown out.

A year later IRA bombers returned to Bishopsgate, a few streets away, with another thousand-pound bomb that destroyed the twenty-six-storey European headquarters of the Hong Kong and Shanghai Bank and blew out every window in every office block within range of the huge blast.

Nor was Frankie the only IRA casualty. There are roughly forty IRA prisoners in British jails, almost all of them serving record life sentences for explosives or murder offences in England. Most had been captured by chance or their own stupidity, a few as the result of patient surveillance and informers. The IRA's England campaign was ultimately a war of attrition fought in the shadows, far from the public gaze. To sustain such a campaign, the IRA planners had to feed an adequate stream of guns, Volunteers and explosives into England under the intense scrutiny of the combined intelligence forces of MI5, Scotland Yard and RUC Special Branch. There had to be an adequate supply of men and women prepared to risk their lives and their future liberty to carry out the IRA leadership's command. Both the IRA leadership and the Volunteers it sent accepted that some of their number would be captured or possibly killed.

In May 1992, in the wake of the Baltic Exchange bomb, the British Home Office announced that MI5 was assuming control of the battle against IRA terrorism. In July 1993 MI5 revealed that the greatest part of its budget, forty-four per cent of an undeclared total of many hundreds of millions of pounds, was targeted against a small, impoverished, working-class guerrilla organization of around six hundred fighters with an estimated annual budget of five million pounds. The agency that once matched itself against the subversion threat from a world superpower with a population of 240 million and the most powerful and feared intelligence service this world has ever known, the KGB, now saw the IRA as the main enemy. Despite the change-over MI5 failed to stop the IRA plant the second devastating City of London bomb in Bishopsgate in April 1993, on the first anniversary of the British Government's decision to cede operational control to the security service. It was clear that by the beginning of the nineties the IRA's Volunteers had overwhelmed the security forces of the British State and had won its clandestine war in England.

Five months after Frankie's death his mother was stopped in a P-check – personal identity check   on the Falls Road by soldiers. Everyone in the black taxi was ordered out and asked for identification. On seeing Margaret Ryan's name, one soldier asked her: 'How's Frankie?' Spontaneously Margaret Ryan replied, 'Do you know my son?' before realizing it was just another little trick of the Troubles. The IRA's distant success in England did not ease Frankie's loss for his mother. The pendulum of sorrow over her dead son never moved. 'I go to the graveyard every week. At the start I was very bitter,' said Margaret Ryan.

> Walking that road on the day of his funeral seemed to be an eternity, though all I can remember is the silence and the stillness of the day. I still hate Christmas because of that empty, terrible feeling. I could not believe it, that Frankie, the apple of my eye, was gone. A light had gone out in my life. He was a terrible kidder, always laughing. I couldn't eat. Why should I be eating when Frankie is dead? I was bitter

for the loss of Frankie, bitter, blaming myself, for having
come back here. But it's what he believed in, he was twenty-
five.

Afterwards I did not want to get involved but then I felt I
had to do something. Frankie was one of their family. So last
Easter I carried a wreath commemorating one of the hunger-
strikers during one of the republican parades. I felt if I didn't
I was betraying him. My son dead for what? But I would not
wish this sorrow and heartache on anyone, be it the Shankill
or the Falls. Nobody knows how you feel until it happens to
them – it's the emptiest feeling in the world.

I had been wrong about Frankie's funeral. Frankie's loss had
been a low point in the unsteady rhythm of the IRA's struggle,
not a crisis or a significant defeat. I came to Frankie's life
believing he was one of the IRA's elite, trained for their most
dangerous missions, a key personality. But such a view was
erroneous both about Frankie and the IRA's campaign. Frankie
was a mirror image of the young green-uniformed men on the
streets of Belfast whom he loathed and hated. He was the
typical product of a working-class home, poorly educated,
unskilled and generally rebellious. The pathway of his life could
have resolved itself in a thousand conventional ways. He could
have joined the British Army, he could have settled down in
Harlow, married, had children. Instead he went to Belfast and
became a squaddie in the IRA. He was in a very real sense an
IRA Volunteer; he did not have to fight, he did not need to
fight, he was not born into conflict. Something drove him on to
embrace the IRA's war and gladly return to bomb the country
that had once been home; Frankie wanted to belong. He needed
to be involved in something beyond himself, something that
made him a somebody, and the IRA gave him that something. I
had been looking for a moment of epiphany in Frankie's life
that would explain his transformation from an Essex lout into
an IRA bomber, but there was no such moment, no such event.
Nor was there any great secret to uncover in his life, or in the
manner of his death.

The IRA's war in England was based on the same principles, technologies, understandings, as the conflict in their home territory. Waging war in civilian streets was always an inherently dangerous risk-filled enterprise. The margin of error between a devastating strike against the Crown and disaster was always tight. The IRA's operators overseas were probably no better and no worse or more experienced than their compatriots in the streets of Belfast. The England campaign was just more of the same. Frankie did not need to be very bright, very skilled or highly trained. He really just needed to be himself, a willing Volunteer with an English accent ready to plant bombs in English cities. Frankie's strength lay in his very ordinariness as Oglaigh na hEireann's foot soldier. His blundering sacrifice was a sustainable loss, his dedication by no means unique. As long as the British Army are on the streets of Northern Ireland there will always be enough Volunteers, like Frankie, to fight them.

NOTE

1. Patrick Quinlivan and Paul Rose, *The Fenians in England*, John Calder, London, 1982, p. 95.

6

CHIEFTAINS

'Fuckers.'

Martin McGuinness had his eye up against the peephole in the door of Sinn Fein's shabby office in the Bogside and was staring out at a squad of British Army soldiers milling around in the street outside. 'Bastards. Cunts.'

I was standing in the narrow hallway behind the man the army in Northern Ireland believes to be the leader of the Provisional IRA and wondering if the flimsy wooden door was just about to crash in on us. We had just finished a lengthy newspaper interview but as we left the building we had walked straight into the path of a British Army patrol cruising the streets of Derry's republican stronghold. At the sight of McGuinness, the soldiers immediately jumped out of their armoured Land-Rovers and ordered him to open the boot of his car, parked on the opposite side of the street. The patrol's intelligence officer, a corporal, at last rubbing shoulders with the enemy's chief general, struck up a false bonhomie.

'How's it going, Martin?'

'Open the boot of the car, Martin.'

'Nice day, Martin, eh?'

McGuinness turned defiantly away. 'Open it your fucking self,' he said as he walked back into the Sinn Fein office. I scuttled back inside as he closed the door. Outside, the patrol swaggered along the narrow pavement stopping and detaining everyone they encountered, waiting for us to re-emerge.

'What happens now?'

'We wait. If you're in a hurry there's a back route but you'd need to shin up a few walls,' said McGuinness in a tone that implied he had over the years shinned up a good few walls in similar circumstances.

'Don't these guys ever knock on the door?'

'Sure.'

'And what happens then?'

'We don't let them in.'

It was another confusion of the Troubles – the Crown's warriors, armed for combat and killing, did not have the authority to break down the door.

Outside, the soldiers' personal radios squawked, the static interrupted by their English voices feeding car registration numbers into their communications network. I decided to take my chances on the street and McGuinness threw open the door. Two seconds after my feet hit the pavement I was stopped by the soldiers under the Troubles' emergency powers.

'Got any identification, sir?' said the helmeted intelligence officer. A small group of Sinn Fein supporters gathered to watch my interrogation and McGuinness stood in the open doorway. I handed over my driving licence and the details were duly fed over the radio to the distant computer as the soldiers searched my bag.

'What are you doing here?'

'I'm a journalist.'

'What kind of journalist?'

The Troubles' legal constraints limited British Army soldiers' powers of interrogation but it was Army practice to exceed those powers to gain as much low-level intelligence as possible. Every detail, either casually or illegally gleaned, was entered into some sort of file somewhere.

'What are you writing about?'

'Pro-them or pro-us?'

'I'm a reporter.'

'Is that an Irish name, Toolis?'

I politely stopped speaking and waited for clearance to come back over the net. I briefly and inconsequentially defied the Crown in Ireland but it was more from calculation than bravery. I was indeed a reporter from a national London newspaper – my arrest would not go unnoticed. Unlike Martin McGuinness or Joan Doris, I was relatively immune from the power of the soldiers and their guns. After a couple of minutes the clearance came, the patrol released me and I went on my way.

McGuinness's simple but absolute denial of Crown authority had shocked me. There were fifteen British soldiers, armed with at least one general-purpose machine-gun and fourteen SA80 combat assault rifles, in the patrol. They had flak jackets, helmets, two armour-plated Land-Rovers and sophisticated personal communications equipment. They were not the type of people you tell to 'fuck off'. McGuinness had been alone, unarmed and wearing a tweed jacket; his only weapon of defiance was the Chubb lock on the door. He had been irritated but not, I felt, frightened or intimidated by the presence of these enemies. Despite their numbers and their weaponry, McGuinness had just denied their authority. But I was also struck by the crudity of McGuinness's response; this street-fighter turned guerrilla statesman had not moved far from his roots. His disdain for the Crown was still couched in the language of the rioter.

I had visited Derry to interview McGuinness in May 1990 about another set of IRA ceasefire rumours. For two hours in one of the upstairs rooms of Sinn Fein's Derry office we had verbally danced around a pin-head as the blonde-haired blue-eyed republican leader outlined an offer of an 'unofficial IRA ceasefire' in return for talks with the British Government. Similar peace offers had been made by other republican leaders, notably Sinn Fein President Gerry Adams, but the significance of this possible peace venture had been enhanced by the fact that McGuinness, privately believed by the Ulster security forces to be a military hawk on the IRA Army Council, was now saying it too. As usual, in all the numerous interviews I have had with him, McGuinness stayed close to a certain brief, almost robotically repeating the same narrow verbal formula. He would not, for internal political reasons, publicly endorse the offer of an unofficial ceasefire that his responses clearly implied. Whenever I attempted to make him affirm his private offer by reworking the question in a different form, he would stop momentarily, keenly fix me with the hard quizzical stare of his bright blue eyes and then repeat his previous reply. 'We are prepared to respond to any serious attempt to bring about a peaceful settlement in Ireland. We are prepared to be part of a peace process. We are prepared to help create a mood for peace in Ireland but it has to be done honourably,' was all he would cryptically offer.

All the subtle everyday expressive nuances that guide us to the mental state of our fellow humans, the arch of an eye to express puzzlement, the crease of a brow indicating concentration, were absent in McGuinness. His intelligence was confusing, his mind detached from his unlined face; no trace of emotion showed. You asked a question, his face stared out at you like a blank canvas, indicating no reaction whatsoever, and then he patiently and calmly responded. Disconcertingly, there was no way to anticipate his response.

Journalists have often described him as 'boyish' or as having an uncomplicated 'direct military bearing'. The adjectives partially capture the sense of a man in his mid-forties who seems remarkably self-contained, immune to despair. His self-assurance seems invulnerable to the thousands of setbacks, defeats, or even victories, of twenty-five years of militant Irish republicanism.

His equanimity is all the more surprising when you consider his position. For a generation he has been one of the top daily targets for the British security services. Every aspect of his life must have been spied upon and minutely analysed for some chink that would have allowed the Crown to trap, imprison or kill him; the intelligence files on him at RUC Special Branch

Headquarters must run into volumes. Outside his family, every relationship, every encounter, in his life must be tainted with the prospect of potential betrayal from an informer working for the Crown. Every knock on his door, every drive to the shops, carries the threat of assassination. After the loyalist killer Michael Stone, who attacked Mairead Farrell's funeral, was imprisoned, Stone revealed that he had made a determined bid to kill McGuinness as the republican leader bought his daily newspaper at a local shop. On the appointed day McGuinness failed to turn up and Stone got cold feet, but many other assassination attempts have gone unreported. McGuinness once gave me a lift in his car and even within the relative safety of the Bogside I started sweating, silently praying that the inevitable loyalist hit would not happen during my few minutes as a front passenger. The constancy of this threat did not seem to unduly worry McGuinness. 'I am careful about my security but I don't get up in the morning and say, "I could be shot at the end of the day." But I am aware that it could happen. It does not stop me from doing things that I want to do.'

In person McGuinness is charming, straightforward and without a trace of affectation. In a later meeting with him he arrived alone in a three-year-old family car and we sat in his mother's small terraced house in the Bogside surrounded by Holy Communion pictures of his brothers and sisters, and plaster-cast statues of Catholic saints, and drank and ate the tea and sandwiches he made as we talked. He is not a devious or slippery conversationalist and comes across as being sincere and honest.

He can be blunt and he has a temper. We have argued over the content of articles I have written on Northern Ireland. 'I'm not one of these people who lie about you behind your back. What you wrote, Kevin, was crap, total and absolute crap,' he once told me, his voice registering his disgust.

His RUC enemies say he is one of the most powerful men in Ireland, but McGuinness looks, dresses and talks like the articulate Catholic working-class man from the Bogside that he is. I have never seen him in a suit; he wears tweeds, polo-neck jumpers, corduroys, the workaday casual clothing of someone oblivious to their impression on the world. He appears to be devoid of vanity and, peculiarly, personal ambition. He waits in line in the queue at the doctor's surgery, he loves his four children and sends them to a local school. He rarely socializes in public, preferring the solitary pleasures of trout fishing.

McGuinness is not a theoretician or a deep political strategist. When he articulates the latest republican political nuance on the 1994 ceasefire and the peace talks process, one senses that he is delivering the ideas of other, lesser figures in the IRA/Sinn Fein northern republican 'think-tank', like Derry councillor Mitchell McLaughlin or the Belfast-based Tom Hartley. It is hard to imagine McGuinness at work in the small hours on the ninth draft of a report, and his views on the economic future of a United Ireland are primitive. This apparent lack of sophistication, his cold demeanour and blank mannerisms have given rise to the suspicion that McGuinness is nothing more than a gunman. But like McGuinness's countenance, such a judgement would be deceptive. McGuinness, unlike most of us, and I felt rather dangerously, did not seek the approval of other human beings. He had no need for surface chatter. Martin McGuinness is quite content at being Martin McGuinness.

McGuinness defines an Irish Republican as 'a person who wants the freedom of Ireland, a person who wants to see the end of British Government rule in Ireland'. The two things are synonymous in his mind. 'The British Government has no right to rule in Ireland. The IRA will deny them the right to rule us and it will do everything in its power to make sure they do not rule us easily,' said McGuinness, simply stating the fundamental republican position. His life is single-mindedly centred on two absolute ideological certainties – that Her Majesty's Ministers of the Crown will sit down at the negotiating table with the rebels if the IRA keep the pressure on and that the Troubles will only cease when there is a united Ireland. No other living person is a greater threat to the British State.

To his admirers and supporters, McGuinness has a heroic, exalted status that is unique within the Republican Movement. 'Martin personifies the armed struggle. Martin is the armed struggle. There are other people who have been around as long but Martin is a man who has come to epitomize the indomitable spirit of armed struggle republicanism and does so with great charm and amicability,' said Eamonn McCann, the chronicler of the Troubles in Derry, McGuinness's home town.

'Martin is a too-good-to-be-true IRA man,' said a former IRA Volunteer, who fought under him during the seventies. 'If you thought about the idealized IRA man that you would like to have, doesn't drink, doesn't smoke, completely principled, man of integrity, respected by republicans and non-republicans, a good Catholic, you are in fact thinking about Martin. A lot of people would disagree with Martin one hundred per cent but as a person they will say Martin lives by his word.'

In Derry, it is a mark of McGuinness's distinction that both IRA Volunteers and British Army squaddies stationed in the city refer to him by his first name. His identity can be conjured up in any conversation, distinguished from the mass of ordinary everyday Martins who fill the Catholic city, with a tiny shift in tone – 'Did *Martin* say that?'

Only one other republican leader, Gerry Adams, Sinn Fein President and ex-West Belfast MP, approaches McGuinness's stature within the republican leadership. But Adams' role as the first Sinn Fein MP for West Belfast, his tours of England and the United States as the public face of republicanism, his appearances on CNN, and the *Larry King Show*, and a decade of politicking and manoeuvring on Ulster's narrow ground have tarnished his reputation amongst militant IRA Volunteers. In a movement that disdains the ballot box and glorifies the gun,

Adams' image is dangerously linked with political slickness, equivocation and compromise.

McGuinness is a passionate and active enemy of the British State and proud to be so. He denies being a member of the IRA but as Officer Commanding the IRA's Derry Brigade in the early seventies he personally fought in countless gun battles with British soldiers and organized the destruction of the commercial centre of his native city. As Director of Operations of the IRA's Northern Command in the seventies he had a pivotal role in reorganizing and strengthening the IRA's structures and capabilities. He was, security sources insist, the IRA's Chief of Staff in the late seventies when the IRA Army Council authorized the killing of Lord Mountbatten and a host of other spectacular operations.

Twice, the IRA have come extremely close to decapitating the Conservative Government, at Brighton in 1984 and in Downing Street in 1991. IRA bombers have twice devastated large areas of the City of London.

Since his 1982 entry into electoral politics, McGuinness, it is believed, no longer has an official title on the Army Council, but then he does not need one. His stature within Irish republicanism is so high that everyone accepts that he is, as the Derry informer Martin Hogan describes him, 'the OC for Ireland'.

McGuinness does appear to genuinely believe that the British Government's presence in Ireland is wrong and the world would be a better place if they and their troops left. 'He believes he is fighting for Irish freedom. He is like Michael Collins, Patrick Pearse, James Connolly, they just seem to feel more intensely about these things than the rest of us,' said Pat McArt, the editor of the local *Derry Journal*, who has closely followed McGuinness's career.

In Belfast Gerry Adams, a former IRA Belfast Brigade Commander and fellow IRA Army Council member, wears a bullet-proof vest and lives on the run for fear of assassination by loyalist paramilitaries. But in the relative safety of Derry, where Catholics outnumber Protestants two to one,

McGuinness lives with his wife and five children in a modest private house in the Bogside. 'Martin lives a working-class life in a very ordinary house. His wife works in a local shop. Their kids go to school with other kids, every detail of their car, their clothing, is known to the community. Any time people heard talk of the Provos being racketeers or being sleazy, Republicans pointed to Martin. People knew it was not true,' said Shane Paul O'Doherty, a former IRA Derry Brigade member and one-time associate, who was released from prison early after denouncing IRA violence.

McGuinness's apparent incorruptibility has been a major political asset to the Provisionals. 'In many ways Martin McGuinness is an exemplary man. He is a good father, a good husband, a strong church-goer. I believe him to be honest and upright in his personal conduct,' commented the former Catholic Bishop of Derry, Dr Edward Daly, who has clashed with McGuinness countless times over the issue of IRA violence within the nationalist community. 'I fundamentally disagree with him on the issue of violence. I believe it to be immoral and wrong, he believes it to be morally justified. But no one should underestimate Martin McGuinness. He is a man of great capabilities, very able, and of considerable political ability.'

McGuinness's political opponents in the Protestant community hold, understandably, a diametrically opposed view. 'McGuinness is cold-blooded and ruthless. In the early seventies he single-handedly masterminded the partial destruction of an entire city, the city of Londonderry. Whole streets were reduced to rubble because he directed the operations. But he is also a rational being. He marks the percentages. He sits down and assesses the benefit to the republican movement of any individual action. The effects on wives or children would only come into the equation if he thought that operation would backfire on the Provo public relations machine,' says Gregory Campbell, the local Democratic Unionist Party councillor.

My newspaper, the *Sunday Correspondent*, printed my May 1990 interview with McGuinness under the headline 'IRA hints at deal on ceasefire', but privately I was sceptical that the British Government would abandon its long-stated policy of not talking to terrorists when McGuinness's commitment to a United Ireland was as obdurate as ever. I was wrong. The interview had been a message in a bottle from McGuinness to secret negotiators within the highest echelons of the British State. In November 1990 the head of the Crown Secret Service, MI6, in Western Europe began a series of protracted negotiations with McGuinness. In November 1993, despite many denials to the contrary, details of these negotiations leaked out and the contents of secret memos published. McGuinness had been right – the British Government can be forced to the negotiating table. Like every other commentator in Ireland, he ascribes the genesis of the 1993 secret talks directly to the 'cutting edge' of the IRA's campaign and the two city-blaster bombs in London. 'I am not a member of the IRA,' he explained somewhat half-heartedly, 'but at the same time people knowledgeable about these events can clearly see that the IRA believed the British Government could be put under more pressure on the streets of London. Most people in Ireland would accept that the large bomb explosions have inflicted grievous blows against the British Establishment.'

McGuinness's role as chief negotiator on the republican side was further proof to his opponents of his pre-eminent stature within the IRA leadership, despite his denials of involvement. 'McGuinness is the IRA. That is why the British Government were dealing with him. They knew that if he could be brought along, so could the IRA,' claimed a scornful Gregory Campbell.

Officially Martin McGuinness is just a member of Sinn Fein's National Executive, the Ard Chomhairle, and if asked he will as a matter of policy deny membership of the IRA – a sensible response given that membership of the IRA, an illegal organization, carries a six-month jail term in Northern Ireland. But this view of his role within the Republican Movement is not shared by the United States Government, which named him in a 1988 report, *Terrorist Group Profiles*, as leader of the

Provisionals. Nor are his denials accepted by RUC policemen and British Army officers, who, in private, simply state that he is head of the IRA. Nor is it the view of the British Government, which has twice negotiated directly with McGuinness in a bid to bring the IRA campaign to an end. Nor do the people of Northern Ireland, and certainly no one with what McGuinness would describe as a 'titter of wit' within Derry's nationalist population, believe his formal denials.

Martin McGuinness was born in 1950, ten years before Paddy Flood, in the Bogside district of Derry, into a society condemned by its Unionist rulers to failure and economic stagnation. The minority Protestant population ruthlessly excluded Catholics from all positions of power. Catholic families were corralled into the slums of the Bogside in order to prevent a shift in the narrow voting balances in the city's gerrymandered electoral wards and a subsequent threat to Unionist domination of Derry Corporation.

In general, the Catholic population, conditioned by its Church and its own political leaders, resentfully but apathetically accepted their inferior status. 'Expectations were little higher than the reality. As long as the state existed there would be discrimination, and as long as there was discrimination we would suffer unemployment and slum housing. Everyone knew that. Demands were made, of course, that discrimination be stopped, but more for the record than in real hope of a result,' wrote Eamonn McCann, in his definitive account of the outbreak of the Troubles, *War and an Irish Town*.

McGuinness came from a typical working-class Bogside family. His mother Peggy was a housewife, his father William worked in a foundry. Martin was the second oldest boy in a family of seven children. As with their neighbours, life held little promise of economic betterment for the McGuinnesses, nor was any expected. The family voted for the local nationalist MP Eddie McAteer and had no contact with the dangerous 'communistic' agitators like Eamonn McCann, who from March 1968 onwards had begun a series of protests against the local council over housing.

The year 1968 was that of student revolution, Vietnam War protests and the Paris uprising. In Northern Ireland streams of middle-class students took to the streets singing 'We Shall Overcome' and protesting against the Unionist monopoly of power. But the struggle in Ulster was far older than the fashionable battle between hippies and the riot police of the Western democracies. The reactionary Stormont Government had no means of coping with dissent, seeing the civil rights demonstrators merely as the ancient historic enemy in another guise. A major showdown with the protesters took place on 5 October 1968 in the Protestant Waterside district of Derry after four hundred demonstrators defied a ban on a protest march and assembled in the city's Duke Street. Pointedly, McGuinness, like the vast majority of the Bogside community, did not attend. The mainly Catholic marchers, in hostile territory, found themselves trapped between two police cordons with no exit route. The RUC, the Protestant police arm of a Protestant state, began batoning their way into the panicking crowd. The West Belfast MP Gerry Fitt attended the rally as a speaker but like everyone else received a severe beating. The film images of Gerry Fitt's bloodied head were broadcast to living rooms around the world. The latest eruption of Northern Ireland's Troubles had begun.

At the time, McGuinness was employed as a butcher's assistant in a shop in the city centre, having left school three years before at fifteen. 'Word spread back to the Bogside that Fitt had been assaulted by the RUC and other people had been beaten,' said McGuinness, recalling the reaction in the nationalist community.

> It was an absolutely shocking experience. It was the event that totally changed things in this city and made people extremely angry. The RUC had attacked the nationalist

people of this city, who were the majority. I found it
incredible that the RUC denied their right to march and then
they beat them. There was a lot of anger and tension. I was
eighteen at the time and like ninety-five per cent of my
acquaintances would have been very angry and distraught.

Prior to Duke Street McGuinness had had only one encounter
with the Unionist state. 'I had left school and there was a local
garage advertising for a mechanic. I went for the interview and
the first question was, what school did I go to? When I
answered "Christian Brothers" [a local Catholic school] the
interview immediately ended. I walked almost shell-shocked
from the building. I thought they did not like the look of me. I
went home and told my parents but there was no big discussion
about it.'

Three years later the mood of resigned acceptance was over.
There was an explosion of rage and an escalating series of
confrontations as the city's youth began to hurl stones, bricks
and petrol bombs at the now detested RUC. McGuinness kept
his day job but devoted his energies to rioting.

I threw stones, petrol bombs, whatever else I could lay my
hands on. I would be rioting in my lunch hour, going home,
changing my clothes and walking back through the same
RUC men in full battle-rig, some of whom were lying
exhausted on the floor because of what the likes of me and
other people were doing in their spare time. After work I
would go home, get my dinner, and go back down and throw
stones and whatever else was to hand until twelve o'clock at
night. It was unreal.

The riots, as these things go, were relatively straightforward
and soon established their own rules of engagement; no man's
land was an area on the outskirts of the city centre at the
entrance to the Bogside and the Saturday afternoon fixture was
known as the 'matinee'. But events across Northern Ireland

were spiralling out of control and in Derry the ill-disciplined police force made a series of midnight incursions into the Bogside district that amounted to police riots. In April 1969 they invaded the home of forty-two-year-old Sammy Devenney and savagely bludgeoned him in front of his wife and children. Devenney died of his injuries a few months later but no officer was prosecuted and relations between rioters and police deteriorated to a dangerous pitch. 'Suddenly people were not prepared to turn the other cheek any more. The RUC became the enemy, the Unionist Government was the enemy. I cannot say at that stage that I had worked out that the people who were responsible for all this were in Downing Street. That came later,' said McGuinness.

The final confrontation came on 12 August 1969 when Orangemen from all over Northern Ireland descended on Derry for the annual Apprentice Boys' March to commemorate the lifting of the siege of Derry in 1689. As the marchers skirted the edge of the Catholic district they were stoned by Bogsiders entrenched behind makeshift barricades. The police and Orangemen charged into the nationalist area after the fleeing rioters, indisputably violating the Bogsiders' self-declared defence threshold – the infamous Battle of the Bogside began. Pitched street battles broke out as rioters used everything to hand, stones, scaffolding rods, bricks and bottles, to fight the police to a standstill. The roof of a local tower block was used as a strongpoint to launch a withering deluge of missiles down on police heads; it rained petrol bombs. After forty-eight hours the police conceded defeat and the British Home Secretary, James Callaghan, ordered British troops in to restore order, thus effectively ending fifty years of Protestant autonomy and domination. The Bogsiders had won but not before the communal conflagration had spread to Belfast, where the Finucane family and hundreds of others were soon to be expelled from their homes by vengeful Protestant mobs.

The first British troops were hailed as saviours and protectors by the Bogsiders and local girls queued to offer them tea. The rioters were more suspicious. 'I could not work out what was going on. The RUC were beaten to defeat in the city and then the soldiers arrived. Some people said they were here to control the RUC and others said they were here to shoulder up the state. Before long those words turned out to be prophetically true,' recalled McGuinness.

In December 1969 a moribund IRA, based in Dublin, had split into two wings, the Officials and the Provisionals, primarily over the issue of recognizing the Dublin and Westminster Parliaments but more importantly over tactics on the erupting civil disorder in 'the occupied area'. The Officials, influenced by Marxism, wanted to see a cross-community, class-based workers' revolution and were reluctant to supply weapons for fear of alienating the Protestant working class. The Provisionals, led by a triumvirate of Daithi O'Connaill, Ruairi O'Bradaigh and Chief of Staff Sean MacStiofain, were more direct – get guns into the hands of Catholics so they could shoot dead the Protestant mobs attacking nationalist homes.

McGuinness, like many of the enthusiastic rioters, joined the more numerous Officials in October 1970 but soon left in disgust, bored by the tedious lectures on class warfare and the pitiful state of an organization that aimed to blow up electricity pylons with four ounces of gelignite. 'My own feelings were that the only way that this force that was being used against the community could be repelled was through resistance. The only people who were capable of doing that were Republicans, who were prepared to resist, whilst others were prepared to sit back and hope for change.' McGuinness went searching for the right sponsors and at a hastily arranged meeting with Mac-Stiofain and O'Connaill in late 1970 found the men he was looking for.

McGuinness's tone in interviews from the early years of the Troubles reveals a young man aggressively eager to take the war to the British Army. He told *Irish Times* writer Nell McCafferty in 1972:

The Officials would not give us any action. All this time there was fighting in the streets and things getting worse in Belfast. You could see the soldiers just settling in in Derry, not being too worried about stone-throwing. Occasionally the Officials gave out Molotov cocktails which wouldn't even go off and I knew that after fifty years we were more of an occupied country than we ever were. It seemed to me as plain as daylight that there was an army in our town, in our country, and that they weren't there to give out flowers. Armies should be fought by armies.

Derry, whilst remaining psychologically isolated from the sectarian conflict of Belfast, was gripped by revolutionary ferment, chaotic riots and a confusing struggle between the rioters and the Crown's soldiers. Said McCann:

Martin, at the age of eighteen, very quickly became convinced that the gun was the only thing the British understood. Throwing stones was not enough, there was going to have to be a war, a war of the nationalist people against the oppressive British presence. As a socialist it was not until Bloody Sunday in 1972 that I realized there was going to be a war and the Left had missed the boat. Martin was saying things that a couple of years earlier had only been said by people over fifty. He was young, fresh-faced, articulate, very self-confident. He was obviously held in high regard by his peers.

In the Bogside the British Army quickly became the target of the rioters' stones. In reply, rubber bullets were fired, snatch squads deployed, local youths beaten and harassed. The conflict escalated; the first lead bullets were fired in July 1971, killing two local youths whom the Army claimed were armed with a rifle and a nail bomb. 'I was there the day Desmond Beattie was killed, his body was brought round the corner near my home. It was obvious the fella was dead or close to death. At that stage there was blood everywhere. I found it shocking.

I was very scared and couldn't understand it. It was the first time I had seen anybody killed by a bullet,' said McGuinness. A few days later the Provisionals made their first determined bid to kill British soldiers, with a sub-machine-gun attack on a patrol manning a checkpoint. 'The Duke Street beatings, the attack on Sammy Devenney and the killing of Casey and Beattie were the four incidents why I became a Republican,' said McGuinness, as we sat at his mother's table, overlooked by black and white pictures of his father Tom, now dead, and a Catholic family blessing depicting the sacred heart of Jesus Christ.

McGuinness's power base within the IRA was built on his reputation as Officer Commanding of the Derry Brigade from 1971 to 1973. He emerged as a natural leader from within the rioters who flocked to the Provisionals' cause to channel their anger down the barrel of a gun. Until his leadership the Derry Provisionals had been poorly equipped and poorly led. The first attempt to manufacture explosives in June 1970 had been disastrous – the entire middle-echelon leadership blew themselves up, as well as killing two of the house-owner's children, in the house where the three Provisional IRA men were making bombs.

In August 1971 the Stormont Government introduced internment, the traditional weapon for suppressing the IRA. The wave of arrests removed the top echelon of the Provisional leadership but left the street fighters like McGuinness untouched.

> The day before internment I was a nobody, the day after internment I still regarded myself as a nobody. I did not know what to do. People credit you with this great military mind but it was a débâcle, a mish-mash. A large number of young people who had joined the movement wanted to be organized. I wanted to be as organized as they did. Unfortunately for me many of them felt I could do a good job. So that is what I did.

The job twenty-one-year-old McGuinness set about organizing was the systematic destruction of what was then considered to be the alien Protestant-dominated city centre. In a devastating onslaught McGuinness's volunteers blasted and re-blasted their own city until it looked, in Eamonn McCann's words, 'as if it had been bombed from the air'. Of the city's 150 shops only twenty were left trading. In interviews at the time, McGuinness justified the campaign as a means of putting pressure on the British Government and the Northern Ireland Secretary, William Whitelaw. 'We are prepared to bomb any building that will cause economic devastation and put more pressure on the Government. The aim of our campaign is to cripple the city economically. It is to let people like Whitelaw see we cannot be walked over any longer,' he told the *Daily Telegraph*'s reporter. McGuinness was careful to instruct IRA Volunteers to avoid civilian casualties and it is accepted that his soldiers were extraordinarily successful at avoiding killing the wrong type of people. 'Sometimes mistakes are made,' he admitted to the *Irish Times* in 1972. 'There was an explosion in Derry some time ago and I read afterwards that a man had been trapped in the basement. He lost part of his leg. Then you read that he's a cyclist and you feel sad,' confessed a naive sounding McGuinness.

Destroying your home town is a strange form of behaviour but one, at the time, that appeared perfectly natural to the teenagers who swelled the IRA's ranks. 'The city centre was near enough flat because of the way we had bombed it,' said a former Derry Brigade Volunteer.

Once the security forces decided to put security barriers around the town our strategy was then to break through them. It was – how many bombs can you get inside their net? Every bomb we got inside was looked upon as a victory for us. It was not so much the physical damage you were doing as the sheer number of attacks. But it was still nice to get a car bomb and then 'boom', a whole row of shops would be gone.'

There was no shortage of Volunteers but the risks of arrest or getting shot were high. The Provisionals might have viewed themselves as freedom fighters but in reality they were just a bunch of local kids with a few old rifles, led by McGuinness, up against one of the world's most professional armies. The first Volunteer to be killed was Eamonn Lafferty, an eighteen-year-old who died in a gun battle with troops eight days after internment was introduced. In republican eyes, Lafferty is a hero.

Lafferty, who was very poorly equipped, stood his ground against the might of the British Army and lost his life. A substantial number of soldiers had attempted to go into the Creggan and Lafferty and two or three other IRA Volunteers tried to stop them. There was a gun battle and he was shot dead. Lafferty had been an acquaintance of mine and his death had a tremendous impact on young people in Derry because he was seen as someone who was prepared to take on the might of the British Army.

We were recalling names and dates of events twenty years old but the details slipped from McGuinness's mouth with a weary, steely precision. I was unable to distinguish in his blank face whether his recall was the by-product of frequent repetition or a mind that still held the remembrance of these things bright. It was impossible not to wonder if McGuinness was one of those 'two or three' other IRA Volunteers. There were no secrets to be read on his smooth face in his mother's sitting room.

On 30 January 1972 British Army paratroopers shot dead thirteen civil rights protesters at a peaceful march on the fringes of the Bogside. 'Bloody Sunday' hurled Northern Ireland to the edge of civil war and in Dublin a mob burned down the British

Embassy. But on the day of the march, McGuinness, like the rest of the Provisionals, was unarmed.

> The decision was taken that Republicans would attend the march and that there would be no aggro whatsoever. It was more important to have thousands of people marching in the streets against internment as opposed to us trying to take advantage. We all went to the march and we ended up in the Bogside with the paratroopers shooting people dead. I saw people being killed all around me but there was nothing I could do. I was absolutely raging.

McGuinness and his companions quickly determined that it would be counter-productive to attack the paratroopers and instead the Provisional leader proposed a national strike until after the funerals. But his rage was not only reserved for the Crown.

> We were in a car driving through the Bogside that night when I saw men and women getting on the bingo bus to Buncrana. I got on the bus and castigated them. 'You should be ashamed of yourselves. There are thirteen people dead. You know some of their families.' They walked off the bus and we went home. I think now I was wrong to do that because at that stage everyone was in shock, but I was in a terrible rage. No one knew how to handle this event.

The shaming of the bingo bus reveals the degree of zealotry, social conservatism and self-confidence to order other individuals within the nationalist community around, that made McGuinness a natural leader. He was a rebel, not a revolutionary, and his respect for priests, the Church and the social mores of Catholic Ireland bolstered his position within the community as a true son of the Bogside. 'Martin was a celibate priest of Irish republicanism, a virtuous guy,' said Shane Paul O'Doherty. 'Whereas other people would go out for a jar with a girl, Martin was not into that. He had one girlfriend prior to his wife.'

McGuinness's leadership style is reputed to be oblique. He does not directly order people around but suggests they act in accordance with his predetermined wishes. His standing in republican eyes is so formidable that few IRA Volunteers have ever dissented from his judgement.

Despite his lack of formal education McGuinness was soon considered to be an astute strategist by his IRA comrades in the Derry Brigade. Said an ex-Volunteer:

> Martin was a relatively rare phenomenon in the IRA, he was a thinker at a time when there was a lot of blind faith: 'We are right, we might not be able to tell you how we are right but we are.' If someone with a bit of education came along they could tie you up in knots. A common response was: 'We know we are right and if you don't lay off we'll shoot ye.' But Martin was deeper than that, he could sit down and win the argument. He was articulate and could explain publicly where we were at. That was also unusual in the IRA and it secured his place very early on and kept him there because he is still able to think.

After internment the Bogside and Creggan areas were sealed off to the British Army by barricades and the mini-republican statelet of 'Free Derry' was established. McGuinness, with his good looks and coy boyish charm, came into his own as an IRA propagandist, giving tours behind the barricades to the world's media and holding daily press conferences where on one occasion he introduced journalists to the sniper who had just shot and killed a British soldier on the city's walls. In later years he found the semi-glamorous image of the 'Boy General' hard to shake off and to his acute embarrassment in 1976 he endured a visit from Hollywood film star Jane Fonda, dubbed 'Hanoi Jane' by American right-wingers for her well-publicized tour to Communist North Vietnam.

Behind Free Derry's barricades McGuinness gave his first brief but seminal speech to a crowd of cheering supporters. Grabbing a microphone at a rally in the Bogside, he succinctly encapsulated his political philosophy in two lines: 'Gerry Fitt and John Hume [Catholic constitutional politicians] can say what they like. We're not stopping until there's a United Ireland and that is that.'

McGuinness's elevated status did not find favour with his mother Peggy. In an April 1972 *Irish Times* article she was recorded as being worried about her son's future job prospects. 'His trade's been interrupted. His father is a welder, his brothers are at the bricklaying and carpentering, but what will become of Martin? That's why they'll have to get an amnesty, so's he can get back to work, and not always be on the run.'

The article also reported that both his parents had been panic-stricken after Peggy McGuinness had found her son's gloves and IRA beret in his bedroom. 'There was a big row. She and my father told me to get out of it, and for the sake of peace I said I would and they calmed down. But now they have to accept it. They've seen the British Army in action and they know I've no choice ... I used to worry about being killed before Bloody Sunday but now I don't think about death at all,' said a chilling twenty-one-year-old McGuinness.

Amongst the new seventeen-year-old recruits flooding into the Provisionals after Bloody Sunday there was no question about his pre-eminence in the IRA. 'Martin would always have been looked upon as a Volunteer's man. He was looked upon as being on our side,' commented an ex-Derry Brigade Volunteer.

He was very considerate and you felt he would never ask you to do anything that he had not done himself. If you were going out on a job that involved an attack on a shop or pub, Martin was the one to say: 'Have you got any money for a drink if you are in there?' Sometimes when you planned things you would forget things like that – sixteen-year-olds did not have money. Martin would be the one to say: 'Here, here's your money.' He was not detached, not way up there. It made all the difference to how he was viewed. We thought of him as one of us.

McGuinness's rapid promotion to command of the nascent Derry Brigade and the bloody events of the early seventies have been the shaping force of his life. One third of the 320 people killed in Derry because of the Troubles died in the street clashes and gun battles of 1971 to 1973; fifty-four of them were members of the British security forces. Over the last twenty-five years, forty IRA Volunteers have been killed. Derry city is a small close-knit community and McGuinness would have known all of the dead IRA men and been a personal friend to many. Inevitably that bloodshed must have inured McGuinness, and those like him, to violent death and the taking of human life. 'Obviously it does have an effect on you. Many of my friends have lost their lives. And on many occasions, through chance or whatever, I could have lost my life as well.'

I asked him what was his strongest personal memory of that violent life.

I was with Eugene McGillan [an eighteen-year-old IRA Volunteer who the Army claimed had fired on troops] the night he was shot by the British Army, fifty yards from here. I lifted him into the ambulance. There was only he and I in that ambulance. He looked at me, his eyes were wide open, and I looked at him. He had just been shot but he knew he was going to die and I knew he was going to die. It was deathly quiet and then when I left the ambulance Colm Keenan [who the British Army said was also involved in the gun battle] was lying down the street, shot in the head. They were two unarmed Republicans who had been murdered by the British Army and both of them were exceptionally close friends of mine.

Regardless of the exact circumstances of the men's deaths, it was clearly not an experience likely to induce empathy for the anguish of his enemies within the British political and military establishments when the IRA killed soldiers or politicians.

After Bloody Sunday the British State in Northern Ireland was under siege. The nationalist community, wrote Eamonn McCann, 'made a holiday in their hearts at news of dead soldiers'. Bombing and shooting incidents soared to record levels; nearly five hundred people were killed in 1972, including 150 members of the security forces. In defiance of his public rhetoric, Secretary of State William Whitelaw invited the Provisional leadership for peace talks on the future of Ireland in the splendour of Guinness family millionaire Paul Channon's house in Cheyne Walk in London. Although only twenty-two, McGuinness, as leader of the Provos in the North's second largest city, was included in the seven-man delegation, along with Gerry Adams. The former butcher's assistant had come a long way in eight months. McGuinness recalled:

> The whole experience was unreal. The house was a mansion. I came from a working-class area of the Bogside. But it wasn't just the house, it was the way the whole thing was done. First we were taken in a blacked-out van to Shantallow. An RAF helicopter descended and we took off and were flown to the military part of Belfast's airport where a private RAF plane was waiting to fly us to England. An officer was waiting for us at the bottom of the steps and as we walked past he saluted us. It was incredible.

In Cheyne Walk the Provisionals listed their demands in the form of an ultimatum calling for the British Government to recognize the right of Irish self-determination, to issue a declaration of intent to withdraw by 1 January 1975 and to promulgate an amnesty for IRA prisoners. Whitelaw prevaricated; the gap between the two sides was too great and the IRA ceasefire that accompanied the talks soon collapsed. But the venue afforded McGuinness the opportunity to put pressure on Whitelaw personally over the Bloody Sunday killings.

> I tackled Whitelaw when he said British soldiers did not kill civilians in Ireland. I said it was untrue and the city that I had come from had seen thirteen of its civilians shot dead. I said it was disgraceful that he could sit there and say that British soldiers were not killing Irish civilians in Ireland. But like everything else it was just glossed over, move on, to the next item.

The talks were a failure but the episode bolstered and sustained the Provisionals in their belief that sufficient military pressure would bring the British Government to the conference table and that ministers' protestations about 'never talking to terrorists' were just lies. Apart from showing greater flexibility about the date of withdrawal and the nature of the transitional political structures, the IRA's fundamental negotiating position remains unchanged despite a generation of conflict. 'The position of the Republican Movement is that the objective we wish to achieve is one where the British Government are politically and militarily no longer in Ireland. That is our goal and that has not changed and it is not going to change,' states McGuinness.

In January 1973 McGuinness was arrested in Donegal, across the border from Derry, close to a car filled with 250 pounds of explosives and five thousand rounds of ammunition. He was tried in the Special Criminal Court in Dublin but refused to recognize the court and was convicted of IRA membership and sentenced to six months. He struck a defiant note. 'I am a member of the Derry Brigade of Oglaigh na hEireann and am very, very proud of it. We fought against the killers of my people. Many of my comrades were arrested, tortured or killed. Some of them were shot, while unarmed, by the British Army. We firmly and honestly believed we were doing our duty as Irishmen.'

A year later McGuinness was again jailed in the Republic on membership charges and spent most of 1974 in prison. He has never been convicted of a terrorist offence in Northern Ireland, though he did spend several months in Belfast's Crumlin Road Jail in 1976 before membership charges against him were dropped. He was excluded from Britain under the Prevention of Terrorism Act for most of the eighties and the ban was only finally lifted in October 1994. His imprisonment in 1974 absolved him from blame within the IRA leadership for the disastrous year-long 1975 truce with the British Government.

On paper the IRA's structure has remained unchanged from the 1920s. The supreme IRA authority is the Army Convention, which acts as a delegate IRA Parliament with representatives from each active IRA unit in Ireland. In theory the Convention meets to elect a twelve-person Army Executive, which then elects from within its members a seven-man Army Council. The Army Council then appoints one of its members as Chief of Staff, the operational head of the IRA. One of the key functions of the Chief of Staff is to recruit the active service units, like Frankie Ryan's, that bomb British cities.

But the Provisional IRA's Army Convention has only met twice in the last twenty-five years and only at times of great revolutionary change in IRA doctrine. The first occasion was the split from the Official IRA in 1969 that founded the Provisionals and the second was in 1986 over the thorny controversy of dropping the traditional ban on taking seats in the Dublin Parliament. In reality changes within the IRA leadership occur infrequently and only at the behest of the existing tiny hermetic republican elite, termed 'the leadership', who already dominate the IRA Army Council. It is not a coincidence that the two youngest members of the 1972 IRA delegation to London, Adams and McGuinness, are the two most prominent republican leaders today. Co-option on to the IRA Army Council does confer considerable power. The IRA purports to be an army with military not political command structures; in theory refusal to obey an order from a superior is an act of treason and can be punishable by death.

In February 1975 Sinn Fein President Ruairi O'Bradaigh, backed by Daithi O'Connaill, both senior Army Council members, declared an open-ended cessation of 'hostilities against Crown forces'. The IRA leaders mistakenly believed that they had induced the British Government to leave Ireland and that the protracted negotiations, at arm's length, between themselves and British officials were the preamble to a public declaration of intent to withdraw. In fact the Labour Secretary of State for Northern Ireland, Merlyn Rees, was reforming the judicial system to try IRA suspects like Seamus Finucane as common criminals – the British Army was digging in for a long war.

The ceasefire had a mixed reaction amongst IRA Volunteers. The former Derry Brigade Volunteer commented:

> Amongst certain sections of republicans there was a feeling of 'All right, we gave it our best shot, another glorious defeat. Let's put away the weapons and get the best deal we can.' That feeling became more and more obvious as the ceasefire lasted. But there was another strand in the movement saying, 'We are not into glorious defeats. This time we will settle it for once and for all.' Martin would have been on that side but at that stage you accepted blindly what the leadership did.

The protracted and apparently aimless ceasefire sapped republican morale and confused IRA Volunteers. Without a clear offensive target like the British Army, republican anger turned in on itself in a series of debilitating internecine feuds and outright sectarian attacks on Protestant targets. By late 1975, as the truce petered out in ignominy on the ground, the Provos were falling apart.

The recriminations over the ceasefire brought out into the open the latent power struggle between the old guard Southern leadership of O'Bradaigh, a pious, bloodthirsty, priest-like fanatic, and his ally O'Connaill, a chain-smoking former gunman who favoured white gabardine trench-coats, and the Northerners, like Adams and McGuinness, who were doing the actual fighting but had little executive power on the Army Council.

Both O'Bradaigh and O'Connaill were veterans of the abortive IRA fifties campaign when self-styled heroic IRA Volunteers turned up in stolen tipper trucks at rural border RUC police stations on New Year's Day and machine-gunned the inhabitants to strike a blow for 'old Ireland's cause' – and usually did so by being killed themselves. Theirs was an intensely narrow, parochial vision which stressed Catholic piety, absolute ideological intransigence and near-religious veneration of the IRA martyrs of the 1923 Civil War – remorselessly crushed by the 'Free Staters' who had accepted the 1922 Treaty with England, and partition. It was a commonplace amongst O'Bradaigh's contemporaries to take Holy Communion from a sympathetic Catholic priest before going on a mission to murder RUC policemen.

Both O'Connaill's and O'Bradaigh's republicanism was founded on maintaining a purity of doctrine within the greater nationalist ethos of the Irish Republic; true Republicans differentiated themselves from sell-outs and traitors by refusing to join in the corrupt politics of the illegitimate 'usurping legislature' of the Dublin Parliament in Leinster House.

According to this purist IRA doctrine, the real Irish Republic, a thirty-two-county all-Ireland state, was proclaimed at the Easter Rising in 1916 by the republican leader Padraig Pearse. The Easter 1916 Proclamation was then ratified by the first all-Ireland elected parliament, Dail Eireann, established in defiance of the British authorities after Sinn Fein MPs won the majority of seats in the December 1918 General Election. The unity and indivisibility of this Irish Republic was again affirmed by the Sinn Fein majority of the Second Dail, elected in May 1921 in the last all-Ireland elections to be held this century.

The Second Dail soon narrowly split into pro- and anti-

Treaty factions and a civil war commenced in which the anti-Treaty IRA were defeated by their one-time comrades and the twenty-six-county Free State was successfully established as an independent state. It was the first of many schisms within republican ranks over the following decades as successive factions broke away to pursue pragmatic electoral politics. But the Civil War left the republican leadership with a bitter historical legacy; in the IRA, political compromise was for ever afterwards synonymous with betrayal.

Although the IRA were beaten, they and their lineage descendants, like O'Bradaigh, the Provisionals' official theoretician, denied their defeat by declaring the decision of the majority of the Second Dail's members to vote for the Treaty as invalid. In IRA terms they had broken their oath of allegiance to the real republic and turned themselves into a 'usurping legislature' that accepted partition. By use of an arcane legal argument, O'Bradaigh and his fellow unelected gunmen on the IRA Army Council actually claimed to be the legitimate government of Ireland, the true inheritors of Pearse's invisible republic.

The IRA logic ran as follows. In December 1938 the rump of republican members of the Second Dail transferred their authority to the IRA Army Council. In effect the membership of the last 'legitimate' Parliament of Ireland conferred upon the IRA the right to act for the Republic. The IRA Army Council was therefore the *de jure* government of Ireland. IRA Volunteers were informed that Oglaigh na hEireann was the 'legal and lawful government' of the Irish Republic and all other parliaments were 'illegal assemblies, the willing tools of an occupying force'. Sinn Fein candidates could fight elections but they had to pledge themselves that 'if elected I will not sit in, nor take part in the proceedings of any Parliament, legislating or purporting to legislate, for the people of Ireland other than the Parliament of the Irish Republic representative of the entire thirty-two counties of Ireland . . . any breach thereof will be regarded as an act of treachery, to be dealt with as such'. Non-recognition of the twenty-six county State Parliament at Leinster House became the fundamental bulwark of IRA political philosophy and the doctrine of abstentionism was written into the Sinn Fein/IRA Constitutions. The will of the Irish people and the political parties they endorsed in fifty years of democratic elections were arrogantly dismissed.

This self-denying ordinance ensured that a vote for Sinn Fein was always a futile protest. The IRA remained true to its ideals but from the 1920s onwards the movement, riven by factionalism, dwindled away to a fanatical core of believers, irrelevant to the electoral politics of the Irish Free State – whose chronic economic failures forced generations to emigrate.

In hindsight it seems shocking that legions of gunmen could be so confused about the nature of the campaign of political violence they pursued. IRA leaders affected to despise the corruption of electoral politics and stressed their own doctrines of militarism – fighting the Crown by shooting policemen dead. They were consumed by their own 'doctrine of the gun' but failed to see that their own bullets and their own killings were just another form of political symbolism. Political violence in Ireland has always been inextricably linked to the public electoral process and the pursuit of power. The IRA never have been and never will be a significant open military threat to the Crown's Armed Forces – in the period of O'Bradaigh's early guerrilla days in Ireland from 1956 to 1962, only six RUC policemen were killed.

The old IRA's self-willed refusal to confront political reality had one overwhelming tactical advantage – their very fanaticism sustained the movement through five decades in the political wilderness until the Battle of the Bogside and the rioters' leader Martin McGuinness rekindled their political fortunes.

From the renewal of the Troubles in 1969, O'Bradaigh's Civil War republican theology was irrelevant to street fighters like McGuinness, engaged in an open insurrection against the Crown in a hostile Protestant state. But that initially did not matter. The Northerners were after weapons and explosives, and the Southern old guard, firm advocates of the gun, were eager to supply them. Decrepit IRA fund-raising structures and arms-smuggling routes creaked back into action and a supply line of guns and gelignite was opened up to the war in the North.

But in the aftermath of the disastrous 1975 ceasefire the Northerners began increasingly to question the validity of abstentionism and the authority of O'Bradaigh and O'Connaill. From his prison cell in the Maze, Gerry Adams saw the need to broaden and politicize the IRA's campaign and break free of the 'rule from the grave'. A convoluted power struggle, led by Adams, his personable lieutenant, Danny Morrison, and McGuinness, ensued against the Southern leadership. The first indications of dissent clustered around control of the Belfast IRA propaganda sheet *Republican News*, which carried 'war news' of the IRA's operations. 'It was shitty,' said Morrison, who became editor in 1977. 'Just before we took it over there was a tirade against contraception on the front page. It was completely inappropriate and reflected the views of those who were out of the heat of battle. Republicans get drunk, chase skirt, don't go to Mass. So what? You cannot expect this pure emblem in the real world.' Morrison, a natural propagandist, dropped the Catholic piety and replaced it with a more forceful class-orientated journalism that increasingly questioned both moral and political republican orthodoxies. But Morrison's freedom to do so was ultimately founded on the support of leading figures, like McGuinness, who retained their emblematic position within the IRA through their unquestionable support for the IRA's military campaign.

To appease his internal critics, O'Bradaigh in November 1976 acceded to a new IRA structure that weakened the power of the Army Council and formally transferred control over much of the IRA's military campaign to the Northerners. A Northern Command, a mini-Army Council to oversee all offensive operations in the North, was created; its first Director of Operations was Martin McGuinness. The Northerners would soon come to dominate all areas of the IRA leadership but the rancour over the truce and the feeling that the older leaders allowed themselves to be duped persist to the present day. 'This generation of Republicans is not going to be fooled by the Brits' fancy diplomatic language,' states McGuinness.

From 1976 onwards McGuinness kept a low public profile, his energies devoted to his roles within the IRA leadership, first as Director of Operations, then as the organization's Chief of Staff from 1978 to 1982. He oversaw the reforms of the IRA's internal structures away from the old companies and battalions, where internal security was easily compromised by informers, to a tighter cell-like organization.

Although the IRA purports to be a national army, its command structure is fragmented. The actual fighting in Northern Ireland is undertaken by individual units reporting to a brigade like that of East Tyrone or Derry, whose membership figures would range from thirty to sixty IRA men. The rate of IRA activity is almost totally dependent on the leading IRA figures within that specific geographic power structure. British security sources allege that McGuinness, despite his Army Council position, still maintains an oversight role on all IRA operations by the Derry Brigade, including attacks like the Coshquin bombing which the informer Martin Hogan failed to abort. The role of the Army Council is really just to supply those brigades with weapons, explosives and training facilities. If a particular brigade or local IRA commander disagrees with certain aspects of Army Council policy, the leadership's power to enforce its will on him is limited. Membership of the IRA is voluntary and power flows from the bottom upwards. The potential for a split between the geographical factions is ever present and the IRA Army Council goes to great lengths to seek consensus rather than dangerous division. The Irish writer Brendan Behan, a one-time IRA activist, perfectly satirized the incestuous, sometimes murderous, factionalism within republican ranks in a mocking joke. 'What's the first thing on the agenda when three IRA men enter a room?' 'The split.'

Far from being revolutionary, the IRA leadership is extremely conservative when reforming republican doctrine. It took Gerry

Adams ten years before he felt ready to provoke the split with
O'Bradaigh over abstentionism. In 1986 Sinn Fein at its annual
conference finally dropped the traditional republican doctrine
of refusing to recognize or to take seats in the Dublin Parliament. The decision was the result of years of careful lobbying,
back-room alliances and consensus-building between the leadership and the different factions and IRA units. The most
important element in the whole process had been the calling of
an Army Convention, a couple of months prior to the Sinn Fein
conference, to endorse the Northern leadership's position. Once
that Convention had done so, it was axiomatic that Sinn Fein
would concur with the views of the IRA; in Irish republicanism
the IRA fire and call the shots. But the IRA leadership, of
course, would not have called such an Army Convention unless
they could have predicted and predetermined the result.

When the results of the Sinn Fein vote were finally announced
in Dublin's Mansion House, O'Bradaigh and a group of
supporters in a pre-arranged manoeuvre stood up and walked
out of the hall. A preceding piper struck up a republican refrain
whose lyrics run: 'Take it [the Irish tricolour] down from the
mast Irish traitor/Its the flag we Republicans claim/It cannot
belong to Free Staters/For you have brought on it nothing but
shame.'

Later that same evening O'Bradaigh, with O'Connaill in a
white trench-coat beside him, and a motley collection of aged
southern Republicans gathered in a pre-booked hotel on the
western outskirts of Dublin and founded a new party, Republican Sinn Fein, to maintain the true faith in an ever tighter
vessel. A hastily mimeographed statement with the name of the
new party handwritten on to the original typed text was handed
round to journalists. There was a mad theatrical air to the
proceedings. I was expecting Daithi O'Connaill, the archetypal
fifties IRA gunman, to produce a Webley revolver from each
pocket of his voluminous trench-coat, call the meeting to order
and urge his followers to attack a border post that night.

The new party was a tiny, geriatric minority destined to be

defeated by natural wastage rather than British Intelligence; O'Connaill, reputed to be the strategist behind the IRA car bomb, was to die peacefully in his bed a couple of years later. But O'Bradaigh, in an act akin to the papal laying-on of hands, had already been to the Mayo home of the last surviving member of the Second Dail, Commandant Tom Maguire, in his nineties, and had obtained a suitable ringing denunciation of the dropping of abstentionism. 'I recognize no Army Council or any such body that advocates participation in the usurping legislature of Leinster House,' Maguire was quoted as saying. But Maguire, the long-dead members of the second Dail and O'Bradaigh were ignored by the triumphant Northern IRA leadership. The killer-blow had in reality already been delivered by O'Bradaigh's one-time protégé McGuinness in his speech earlier in the day:

> We must accept the reality that sixty-five years of republican struggle, republican sacrifice and rhetoric have signally failed to convince the majority of people in the twenty-six counties that the Republican Movement has any relevance to them. By ignoring that reality we remain alone and isolated on the high altar of abstentionism, divorced from the people . . . The former leadership . . . has never been able to come to terms with this leadership's criticisms of the disgraceful attitude adopted by them during the eighteen-month ceasefire of the seventies . . . If you allow yourselves to be led out of this hall today, the only place you will be going is home. Don't go, my friends, we will lead you to the Republic.

In his keynote speech McGuinness was repudiating what had been sacred republican doctrine. He was rejecting the Civil War theology, the sacrifice of generations, and the ideology of denial which just years before had obliged both himself and Volunteers like Seamus Finucane to refuse to recognize courts, to refuse legal counsel, and voluntarily to consign themselves to decades of imprisonment. His speech was significant not just for its content but also for its place in the proceedings. He was the last speaker before the vote on the abstentionist motion was called – McGuinness was the Northern leadership's trump card.

It is significant too that the Army Council played the same card to dispel rumours within their own ranks of a sell-out when details of their secret negotiations with the British Cabinet were leaked to the press in November 1993. Sinn Fein press officers were anxious to leak McGuinness's name to journalists as the IRA's chief negotiator in order to stem potential splits. In republican terms, McGuinness could not be the source of potential betrayal. As the epitome of the armed struggle, McGuinness's commitment to the IRA and the politics of the gun was unchallengeable. He has remained distant from and immune to the criticism levelled at Adams' coterie of Belfast Sinn Fein advisers that they were politicians masquerading as Republicans and hence potential sell-outs. The IRA's rural defenders, like Fergus of the East Tyrone Brigade, could be reassured. 'If Adams or his allies came up with a deal with the Brits you could never really trust it. But if Martin endorses it, then there must be something in it. The Army (IRA) trust Martin. If anyone can sell them a deal, then he can,' explained a republican observer.

McGuinness's apparent integrity is respected by many non-Republicans in Derry and with one notable exception, McGuinness, in his home town, has remained immune from personal responsibility for the cruelties of the IRA's war. 'There has not been a sectarian war in Derry. The IRA in Derry and therefore the leader of the IRA in Derry would not be associated with a whole series of terrible things, deaths of innocents and so on, things that smell strongly of naked sectarianism as in Belfast and other places,' explains McCann.

Eamonn McCann may be accurate in assessing the way the nationalist community view their most famous Republican but McGuinness has implicitly endorsed what can only be considered needless cruelties. At the very beginning of his leadership of the Derry Brigade in November 1971, a group of local women seized Marta Doherty, the fiancée of a British soldier, and ritually sheared her hair, tarred and feathered her – the traditional punishment for female collaborators. No one intervened.

A decade later, in April 1981, a Derry Brigade Volunteer, now dead, cold-bloodedly murdered a twenty-seven-year-old Protestant housewife, Joanna Mathers, as she collected completed census forms from homes in the Waterside district of the city. Sinn Fein, as part of the agitation around the H-Block protest, Bobby Sands' hunger strike and impending election, had been campaigning for a boycott of the census. The IRA gunman attacked Joanna Mathers, who was working part-time for 'pin-money', seizing the forms, then shooting her in the neck at point-blank range. After the killing the Derry Brigade lied, denying being involved. The republican National H-block Committee publicly condemned the murder and the frenetic but unrelated efforts of other IRA Volunteers, like Dermot Finucane in Belfast, meant Mathers' murder was soon subsumed within a catalogue of more 'legitimate targets'. But that does not absolve McGuinness as leader of the Derry Brigade of his moral responsibility, any more than private republican regret could restore Joanna Mathers to her husband and infant son. Her murderer continued to live openly in Derry and went unpunished for his crime.

The IRA and McGuinness did not escape the political consequences of what was accepted to be the greatest blunder in twenty-five years: the Good Neighbours bomb, planted by Paddy Flood and betrayed to his handlers. Sean Dalton, Sheila Lewis and Jed Curran had families and were well known in the Creggan community. Unlike the death of Joanna Mathers, a Protestant, their deaths could not be marked down as number two thousand and something. The Derry Brigade issued a statement of apology, claiming that the Good Neighbours operation had 'gone tragically wrong'. 'The Derry Brigade has conducted thousands of operations over the past twenty years. We have always taken great care to ensure that civilians are not put at risk and even our enemies acknowledge that fact. This time we failed and we accept the consequences and the criticism of that failure.'

But the shock-wave of anger was not so easily dismissed and McGuinness badly misjudged the mood when he attended the crowded funeral. 'McGuinness might be head of the IRA but he was lucky he wasn't kicked to death,' said Sean Dalton's son Martin. 'Some cousins of mine, who were once members of another republican organization [the Official IRA], were prepared to take him at the back of the chapel and kick his head in. And if it had not been for some cooler heads that is what would have happened.' At the funeral McGuinness and other Sinn Fein councillors were jostled and kicked, and one mourner repeatedly swore at the republican leader and publicly denounced his presence in the church. 'This is all your responsibility,' McGuinness was told.[1]

'Sinn Fein came to us and offered us money for the funeral but they were told in no uncertain terms where to go. The IRA said they were sorry it happened but at the end of the day them people do not have any souls. They didn't feel any remorse – to them it was just another bomb,' said Martin Dalton. 'I challenged them on television to defend what they did there – put a bomb not only in a nationalist area but in a built-up area. And they are supposed to be fighting for the people?'

The hostile mourners at St Mary's in Creggan shared, however briefly, the outside world's condemnation of the IRA as terrorists who plant bombs in bars and railway stations and murder indiscriminately.

Since 1973 the IRA have 'brought the war home to England' through an episodic but sustained bombing offensive in London and the provinces and on the Continent. During

McGuinness's alleged personal tenure as Chief of Staff from 1978 to 1982, there were a number of IRA spectaculars, including the Chelsea Barracks, Hyde Park and Harrods Christmas bombs. Inevitably there were civilian casualties; Christmas shoppers were killed, members of an Irish emigrant family were blown up waiting at a bus stop near Chelsea Barracks. The pattern of attacks, and the resultant deaths of innocents, continued up until the declaration of the 1994 ceasefire under his authorization.

It is difficult for an ordinary English person to fathom the mentality of people who send young men like Frankie Ryan to England to plant bombs in streets. In his mother's house I asked McGuinness how he could justify IRA actions like the March 1993 Warrington bomb which was placed in a litter-bin in a regional shopping centre and exploded, killing two children and injuring dozens. 'I felt badly about the Warrington bomb, badly about those children and badly about the effect. I believe that the republican struggle was damaged as a result. I do not believe that the people involved in that intended for that to happen.'

I felt McGuinness was being disingenuous. The Warrington deaths were not intentional but they were foreseeable – a copy-cat litter-bin attack in Camden in north London on a crowded high street weeks before had injured fifty-six people. The IRA's intention to terrorize in Warrington contained within its insep-arable sub-clauses an intention to kill.

The Warrington bombing instantly provoked peace marches by middle-class housewives in Dublin and intense political pressure on the IRA. In a statement the IRA apologized, but saying you are sorry after murdering someone is not an acceptable defence under the criminal law.

Of course I totally understand that people in England would feel that statement was inadequate, but at the same time do they understand how we feel when our children are killed by the British Army by plastic bullets? I know that when you

say that, you get into the business of what-aboutery, which
goes on for ever and resolves nothing. But at the same time
do people even begin to imagine the hurt of the nationalist
community in the North whenever they look at the outflow
of sympathy, sorrow and grief from people in Dublin over
the Warrington deaths, people who look at the North as if it
was three thousand miles away? That has a tremendous effect
on the community here because they end up working out that
the lives of our children and our lives come way down the
list in importance.

McGuinness's enemies believe he is a lying hypocrite. 'You
cannot regret something that you have sanctioned. It's as if I
put a gun to your head, or got someone else to do so, and blew
your brains out and then said I regretted it. He is lying through
his teeth,' commented Gregory Campbell.

The Troubles has inured its participants to violent death and
it is difficult for any outsider to comprehend the numbing
emotional impact of twenty-five years of military occupation,
constant house raids, arrests, security force killings and loyalist
attacks. Eamonn McCann said:

For Martin and other Republicans this is war and in a war
people suffer. As a supporter of the Republican Movement
he is surrounded by people who have inflicted grief. But I
have no doubt that Martin McGuinness would be distressed,
at least as distressed by the deaths of civilians at the hands of
the IRA as would British Army officers be distressed by the
death of civilians killed by their troops. The evidence would
suggest to me that Martin McGuinness is rather softer and a
more sensitive, considerate man. The Brits have never said
sorry for Bloody Sunday.

As with Dermot Finucane, no single IRA blunder could ever,
nor would ever, I thought, shake McGuinness's obdurate belief
in the justness of the IRA's cause. Said McGuinness:

The reality is that the IRA fought a military campaign, which had an element in it of economic targets of some description. The natural conclusion you come to of those people who criticized the IRA was that their starting point was that the IRA should not do anything at all. They are people who are not prepared to address the issue of why there was an IRA in the first place or the circumstances under which the nationalist community were forced to live in the six counties.

McGuinness's measured tone and facial blankness made it impossible to ascertain how sincere, how deeply felt, his regret for the dead children of Warrington was. But in another sense his personal feelings were irrelevant. The campaign in England was the collective result of the efforts of dozens of individuals within the organization; the IRA's war was the summation of the actions of hundreds of families, thousands of individuals. McGuinness was a representative of their violent disaffection towards the Crown. It was pointless to attempt to over-individualize the republican struggle; McGuinness's assassination, or an even more unlikely personal repudiation of the Provisionals' deeds, would not stop violent republicanism. Nor would there be any shortage of like-minded substitutes to replace him on the IRA Army Council.

From 1982 onwards McGuinness ceased to be Chief of Staff and adopted a more political role, standing and being elected on an abstentionist platform to a reformed Stormont Assembly, before it too was wound up and consigned to the political dustbin as another failed political initiative. He stands against SDLP leader John Hume at parliamentary elections and consistently garners seventeen per cent of the poll or around nine thousand votes in the Foyle constituency.

In 1985 he was involved in the controversial BBC television programme *At the Edge of the Union*, which portrayed both McGuinness's and Campbell's family and political lives. An attempt by the Home Secretary Leon Brittan to force the BBC Board of Governors to ban the programme led to the first ever worldwide BBC news blackout.

Although he is no longer involved in the IRA's administration on a day-to-day basis and holds no formal title on the Army Council, McGuinness remains the most important republican leader.

Since the late eighties the IRA have been involved in a complex political process to align the Dublin Government and their electoral rivals, the SDLP, in a pan-nationalist front to negotiate a British withdrawal. By politically dissolving the border so that the mass of nationalists in Ireland can be consolidated into one powerful negotiating bloc, Republicans hope to reorder the political stalemate that has marooned them as a minority within the Catholic minority inside the boundaries of a hostile Protestant-majority-dominated state. Says McGuinness:

> Everyone is responsible for this conflict in Ireland. The British Government, the Dublin Government, the SDLP, the Unionists, the IRA, everybody, we are all responsible, and it is only by getting together and sorting it all out that there will be a resolution. I haven't got any grand plan or solution but what we are saying is, let's get together in a room, let everyone express their fears and their difficulties, and let the people of Ireland discuss what sort of political structures they want.

Such an all-Ireland political forum would be anathema to the current generation of Unionist leaders but a guaranteed victory from the republican perspective. If the Provisionals can immerse the blatant desire of the Protestants of Ulster to remain separate from a United Ireland within the greater Catholic majority of Ireland's desire to be united, then the IRA will have dissolved partition.

To create space for such a political reordering of present boundaries, the IRA leadership will trade a ceasefire for negotiations with the Crown. In return for such a prolonged IRA ceasefire and the prospect of peace, the IRA hope, the Crown will, however discreetly, signal its intention to leave its Irish province and gradually force a historic accommodation with the people of Ireland on the Unionists.

> Our position has not changed. We would like to see a unitary state, we would like to see a thirty-two-county Republic, but we recognize that we are only a small percentage of the total people of this island. The people of this island might decide on some other type of structure. I am not going to oppose it. I might oppose it politically but there is no way I would defend anybody's right to use armed force to go against the democratic wish of the people of this island.

The aim of the current republican leadership's pan-nationalist strategy is to achieve a 'historic handshake' with the Crown, like that between South African President De Klerk and Nelson Mandela before his release from prison in 1989, which indicated an intention to negotiate political change. The ANC did not overthrow the apartheid regime overnight or map out an exact plan for the transfer of authority but from that moment on power flowed steadily from De Klerk to the future President Mandela. Similarly in Ireland, power would at first trickle, then flow, from the Crown into nationalist Ireland until the balance of power was so weighted in the nationalist/republican's favour that a section of the Unionist community would break away and strike a political deal with the ancient enemy. Many parts of the republican plan are as yet unproven and after twenty-five years of conflict such a peace is likely to be gained slowly, only in piecemeal stages, and at the cost of considerable further bloodshed. But it seems certain that the long horror of Ulster's Troubles is dwindling away to a whimpering conclusion.

I questioned McGuinness again and again on the point about what was acceptable to the IRA as 'some other type of structure', trying to tease out the exact nature of the potential

IRA compromise implied by his words. And again he returned somewhat robotically to the same narrow formula. He found it easire to state what was not acceptable – there could be no return to the old-style Stormont regime.

> The Unionists want power, power they have abused in the past, power they have used to humiliate me, humiliate my father, my forefathers before. The British Government allowed them to behave like spoiled brats for years and now the British are reaping the harvest they have sown. That has got to change. The British have got to face up to Ian Paisley and the UVF. Britain has got to take its responsibilities seriously.

I asked the question again in another form: 'If I was to come back to Derry in five years would I find one of your nephews wearing a policeman's uniform?'

'If it's a situation where those security forces were subject to the laws of the Irish people and the Irish people alone, then there is every likelihood you would.'

'Could that be in the uniform of a modified RUC?'

'Certainly not. There has to be dramatic changes. I am not saying that the British Army must disappear overnight and that all the changes we require have to be brought about next week or next month or even in two years time. Republicans recognize this process is going to take time. There are no quick fixes in this problem.'

The IRA Army Council and McGuinness are prepared to be patient with the Crown but it is a patience that only stretches to the date, the period of transition, and the nature of interim political structures before the Union Jack flag is finally removed from Irish soil. The ultimate uncompromising aim of a United Ireland is never far from the surface. Says Eamonn McCann:

> Republicans like Martin are fixated on the idea of a United Ireland. The Republican Movement exists to get the British out of Ireland. They move to the left and they move to the

right, whatever seems tactically and strategically proper at a particular time. For the last four years the plan has been to form an alliance with the SDLP and the Dublin Government, a pan-nationalist front, but all these things are dedicated to the one object – to get the British out.

If the Provisionals' peace plan is to succeed, then the Army Council must maintain the IRA ceasefire against internal opposition and finally call an IRA Army Convention to declare the ceasefire permanent. Delegates from every IRA active service unit will gather to thrash out the final republican response towards the peace process in Ireland; their answer through a simple show of hands will mean war or peace. It is a certainty that the last speaker before the final vote on such a ceasefire motion will be Martin McGuinness. If McGuinness was convinced that the Provisionals' plan is right, his voice, *primus inter pares* within the republican leadership, would appeal to the delegates for their support for a permanent end to the savage butchery of Ulster's Troubles. If McGuinness believes the British Government is duping the republican leadership and is not convinced that the rhetoric of the Crown's emissaries is sincere, then there will be no such Army Convention, no more peace plan, and the IRA's answer will be heard, loudly, on the streets of the City of London.

Irish Republicanism is deeply embedded in the whole Irish national psyche. It is the founding philosophy of the Irish Republic. It is the cause to which the state's first leaders gave their lives in the 1916 Easter Rising, and are now revered for their sacrifice. Its ideals, of a United Ireland, would be affirmed by every living Irish man, woman and child. 'For generations our people have been reared on a notion of patriotism as fighting and dying for Ireland,' acknowledges John Hume MP, McGuinness's electoral Derry opponent. 'The Provisional IRA are just a product of our history.'

McGuinness is exemplary of the great Irish republican

passion. To reject him is to reject part of the ideological core of the Irish Republic. McGuinness cannot be dismissed, as the British press would usually put it, as an 'isolated or mindless terrorist'. It does not matter that he still calls British soldiers 'cunts' or that he lacks the political acumen or the manipulative negotiating skills of some of his Crown enemies. McGuinness's greatness within the Republican Movement and in the wider nationalist community across Ireland rests on his irreproachable, unwavering commitment to a United Ireland. Twenty-five years of bloodshed, the destroyed cities, the murdered enemies, the lost Laffertys, Bloody Sunday, the negotiations with his one-time masters and the IRA's attempts to kill them at Brighton and Downing Street have strengthened, never weakened, his commitment. His very existence is a denial of the will of his Crown enemies, their materialism and their machinations. McGuinness is a leader because his faith in a United Ireland is profound, complete, unshaken and unshakeable; he is not stopping before a United Ireland. His belief cannot be subverted this side of his assassination.

NOTE

1. *Derry Journal*, 8 September 1988.

7

MARTYRS

By an enemy's gun he was shot down
Far from home in another town
A freedom fighter he lived to be
And we'll not rest 'till his country's free
He'll be remembered for his proud deed
For his country's war another seed
And his memory will live and grow
Children now in years will know
Of Joe MacManus, his life he gave
Of how he died and was so brave
A country torn by war and hate
Decided Joseph's early fate
Now every year as spring time starts
Joe's proud memory will be in our hearts
And as I think and shed a tear
I'm proud to have him
In our child-hood years

Corina, 1992

On 6 February 1992 a forty-nine-year-old Fermanagh District
Council dog warden, Eric Glass, was called to a remote farm
on the border, near the town of Belleek, to remove and destroy
a black labrador bitch that had bitten the farm owner Pat
Loughran's niece. Glass arrived at the farm in the townland of

Scardans Upper, at 11.30 am. He had just stopped his van at the farm gate when two masked men armed with a Kalashnikov assault rifle and a handgun ran towards the side of the van and began to scream. The report was bogus; Glass had been enticed into an IRA ambush.

Glass, a veteran part-time UDR man, ducked down in the van's cab to retrieve his personal firearm which he had concealed beneath a coat on the passenger seat.

The first thing I heard was a man roaring: 'IRA, get out of that fucking van!' He was screaming blue murder. It was terrifying. I think instinct took over, I think training took over. My first thing was to get out, get out of the van. The weapon was on the passenger seat covered by my coat. It would have been sitting with a magazine on it but none up the spout. I say he [the gunman] seen me going for the gun. He seemed to stand back a step. I just whipped up the gun and he fired a shot in. There was this bang as the shot came through the passenger window and out through the front window. I just aimed through the window, three quick shots, bang, bang, bang. He must have fell, I did not see where he went.

I swung round quick. The other boy was opening the driver's door but luckily he had a rifle slung round his chest, so I pushed the door into him so he could not get at me. I jumped out, he run straight across the street and got into cover there. I ran round and lay down at the front wheel of the van. It seemed like minutes but I say it was a minute or less.

They were firing odd shots. Someone fired a shot and hit the front wheel of the van and burst the tyre above my head. It got me thinking, what am I going to do, what is going to happen? I decided to take an aimed shot when the fella put his head round the corner so I took a nice aimed shot, pressed the trigger and nothing happened. The magazine was empty.

Glass had been hiding by the front tyre of the van and using the open driver's door as cover as he fired back towards the rear of the van at his attackers. Forensic experts later found the van had been hit by thirteen Kalashnikov rounds. But Glass had to break cover.

I knew I had another magazine in my coat. I jumped up and run round the van. I had to run round the doors – the doors were open. It must have took them seconds to realize what I was doing. I must have had the coat nearly out when the next thing I saw was a guy jumping over a wall and a boy came from the corner running down the street with the guns on automatic. They definitely panicked. All they had to do was step out, go down on one knee and take one aimed shot. Luckily enough they came at me on automatic. All I can remember is them coming, running, smoke coming out of the barrels. The rounds seemed to be hitting the ground in front of me but I got hit in the leg by a ricochet. I whipped on a magazine, the empty one fell out. The two of them were coming down the road and another boy running across. I returned fire and then this other guy run round and said: 'Two, three, and four, run for it.' They disappeared.

The bone was out through the leg, and the other leg had seven bullet holes in it, but there were no bone injuries. I thought with a broken leg you could walk but you can't. You are all off-balance. Just at that moment an old man [the farmer] came out of the house. He said: 'How are you?'

'I'm all right.'

'You are an awful sight. There is blood coming out of your boots.'

I was still standing. I had a radio in the van and I said to them that I have been badly shot in the legs – 'Get me help.' They did not know where I was but there was a place near where I was, called Leggs Post Office. Someone said he is shot in the legs and someone else said that he's near Leggs Post Office. There was a good deal of confusion.

I said to the man: 'Have you a phone?'

'I have.'

'Will you go in and dial 999.'

'Sorry, I won't. They said they would come back and shoot me if I used the phone but if you make it in, it's just through the doors.'

'I can't walk. Can you get me a stick?'

So he brought me out a short stick.

'Give it to me.'

But I wasn't making any headway. I went up to the side of the van and I could look in the house. It was an old-time house, it had a pantry and I saw a sweeping brush.

'Can you give me out that sweeping brush?'

So he gave me the sweeping brush. Once I had the brush I got in. It's funny, your mind goes kind of blank. I couldn't remember where I was, the address. The only thing I could remember was the Belleek police number. I knew it was Belleek 212. In my work I have been in a lot of police stations.

'Is this Belleek?'

'Yes.'

I phoned, the sergeant picked up the phone and said: 'Eric, how are you? There is a helicopter in the air but they do not know where you are.'

With him being local I could tell him, so he directed the helicopter. The helicopter pilot had men in the helicopter and they heard there was an incident. The helicopter came in over the house. I thought they were coming in for me but as he came in he turned sharp right and the next thing I knew the van was moving. It ran about three yards down into a wall. I could see then. The man in the house said: 'You've shot one of them.'

He had a woollen mask on with holes for the eyes and mouth, a green army jacket, blue jeans and boots. I later found out he had surgical gloves and woollen mittens on top. He was just lying there by the side of the van.

His name was Joe MacManus and in death he was now an IRA martyr.

It is hard to think of a less glorious act. Four young men, two of them armed with automatic rifles, the others with hand-guns, lying in wait for a forty-nine-year-old dog warden who had been tricked into visiting a remote farm one and a half miles from the border; waiting with the intention of shooting him in the head, killing him in the cause of Irish Freedom. But Joe MacManus was accorded a hero's funeral imbued with the symbolism of martyrdom. Hundreds visited the family home across the border in the town of Sligo where he lay 'in state'; thousands turned out for his funeral, orations and eulogies were declaimed at the graveside; a few months later a memorial committee raised five thousand pounds for a gigantic headstone, a priest blessed the stone at the unveiling ceremony in July 1992, poems by his old classmates, like the one heading this chapter, were recited; twenty-one local schoolchildren, each carrying a rose for every year of his life, marched in step; more wreaths were laid, more speeches made, songs sung and tributes paid to 'Joe's sacrifice in the cause of Irish Freedom'.

A twenty-six-page leaflet was printed commemorating the dead Volunteer. The title-page shows a red-haired young man with John Lennon glasses, an ear-ring in each ear, wearing a white shirt and tie and smiling into the camera. Above the photograph an inscription reads – 'His name was Joe Mac-Manus' – and below it his full name, 'Joseph MacManus' and the dates 'May 1970–February 1992'. There is one final inscription on the page – 'A Sligo Tribute'.

Inside, the leaflet is full of pictures of the funeral, the unveiling ceremony, detailed accounts of the work of the memorial committee's efforts to raise the money for an 'unbe-lievably beautiful headstone', a short biography of the fallen Volunteer, the speeches by Joe's father Sean MacManus, an important figure within the Republican Movement, and the former MP Bernadette McAliskey, plus poems, songs and the inscriptions on the gravestone. The inscription on the main stone reads:

I Gcuimne,
Oglas Seosaim MacMagnais
Oglaigh na hEireann
A fuair bas ar saoirse na hEireann
[He died in the cause of Irish Freedom]
In proud and loving memory of
Volunteer Joseph MacManus
Irish Republican Army
Maugheraboy, Sligo
Killed in Action 5th Feb 1992 Aged 21 years
RIP
Erected by family, friends and comrades
'The fools, the fools, they think that they have pacified
Ireland. But they have left us our Fenian dead. And while
Ireland holds these graves, Ireland unfree shall never be at
peace.' – Padraig Pearse

There is also a small stone on the grave from MacManus's family inscribed with a short poem:

I lived my short life to the full
But also heard my nation's cry
With my comrades I answered her call
Prepared to fight, prepared to die
So loving, so brave, so sadly missed
With love and pride
Our precious son and brother

There was no shame, no shying away from Joseph's IRA role. Indeed the ceremonies were designed to affirm Joseph's politics, the belief in the gun, the efficacy of piecemeal murder to bring about political change. The phrase 'The fools, the fools ...' on his headstone had been coined by the Republican leader Padraig Pearse at the 1915 Dublin funeral of the old exiled Fenian O'Donovan Rossa to inspire a new generation to arms and complete the struggle of the past dead heroes. 'Life,' Pearse claimed falsely, 'springs from death: and from the graves of patriot men and women spring living nations.' Pearse's oration had become a republican mantra; the same slogan adorned Francie McNally's twelve-year-old son's chest.

Joseph MacManus's funeral rites were similarly designed to inspire another generation to arms and to deny the definitions the outside world used – 'terrorist', 'gunman' – to describe the men who tried and so pathetically failed to kill a lone member of the Ulster Defence Regiment, and replace them with 'hero', 'martyr'.

In the Shorter Oxford English Dictionary a 'martyr' is defined in one usage as 'one who undergoes death (or great suffering) on behalf of any belief or cause'. And this is the way that Joseph MacManus was certainly viewed by his father and mother and the mourners at his funeral. In dying for Ireland MacManus had, regardless of the circumstances of his death, become a secular saint in republican eyes.

As in the psychology of informing, this republican tenet of martyrdom is heavily influenced by the rites and liturgy of Irish Catholicism. Catholic schoolchildren are daily taught that 'Christ died for our sins' and thus saved the human race. Christ's followers, his apostles and saints, are venerated for upholding and dying for, being martyred for, the true faith. For republicans, dying for Ireland is a sacrificial act akin to those religious acts of Christian witness. Patriotism and self-sacrifice are synonymous and rooted deeply in the very fountainhead of modern republicanism, the 'men of Easter Week', the spiritual fathers of the current Irish Republic.

On Easter Sunday 1916 a disparate coalition of Republican groups seized Dublin General Post Office and a number of other prominent buildings, staged a rebellion against the Crown and flamboyantly declared an Irish Republic. The precise military and political aims of the rebels were never clear but the Rising, doomed to failure from its inception, is glorified as the founding event of the current Irish State. If the rebels' overall aims were murky, the intentions of the man who nominally led the Rising, schoolteacher and minor poet Padraig Pearse, are clearer. Two days after the week-long insurrection, which cost 450 lives and 2,614 wounded, and reduced the centre of Dublin to ruins, Pearse wrote from his prison cell to his mother:

> We are ready to die and shall die cheerfully and proudly. Personally I do not hope or even desire to live . . . You must not grieve for all this. We have preserved Ireland's honour and our own. Our deeds of last week are the most splendid in Ireland's history. People will say hard things of us now, but we shall be remembered by posterity and blessed by unborn generations. You too will be blessed because you were my mother.[1]

Pearse seemed to believe the Rising was a necessary blood sacrifice to sting the conscience of the vast, indifferent Irish majority. On the same day, 1 May 1916, two days before his execution, Pearse wrote a poem, 'A Mother Speaks', in which he made the comparison between himself and the martyred Jesus Christ explicit.

> Dear Mary, that didst see thy first-born Son
> Go forth to die amid the scorn of men
> For whom He died,
> Receive my first-born son into thy arms,
> Who also hath gone out to die for men,
> And keep him by thee till I come to him.
> Dear Mary, I have shared thy sorrow,
> And soon shall share thy joy.[2]

Pearse ran towards his own death in a drama of his own making. The Easter Rising was a political crucifixion with Pearse as Christ and Dublin as a modern-day Calvary. The British unconsciously, and predictably, fulfilled their role as the ignorant Romans and in the aftermath duly lined Pearse up against a wall in Kilmainham Jail, shot him, and completed the cycle. Pearse was a dangerous fanatic, a romantic with a callous disregard for the human consequences of his idealism. But he was right about his own martyrdom and the decisive symbolic power of the Easter Rising. Pearse's blood sacrifice transmogrified republican political fortunes and created the state of the Irish Republic. His martyrdom was both a blind denial of the existing political reality of Crown rule in Ireland and an affirmation of the mythic republic to be. The manner of his death would inspire a select handful, scattered across the succeeding unborn generations, to take arms, kill and die gloriously in, and for, Ireland.

For Irish Republicans, martyrdom is also a means of psychologically reordering the chain of defeat, the never ending stream of rebel failures, the dead volunteers, the blunders, the apathy of the vast Irish majority and the betrayals from within, inflicted upon them. It is a way of abstracting the war away from its grim, atavistic, pedestrian necessity and recasting it in the mould of Pearse's glorious Republic to be. Officially, as his headstone proclaims, Joseph MacManus was 'Killed in Action' fighting for Irish Freedom, rather than dying by the side of a Fermanagh District Council van after being caught off-guard by a dog warden who was quicker on the draw.

I first saw Joe MacManus's memorial leaflet in the Sinn Fein bookshop on Belfast's Falls Road amongst the pile of pamphlets, IRA T-shirts, history books and the enamel badges venerating Seamus Finucane's comrade-in arms Bobby Sands, the great H-Block martyr. I knew then that it was the beginning of my last journey into republicanism. In one afternoon I was to travel between two worlds, from the neat sitting room of the

Protestant grandfather, with pictures of his grandchildren smiling from the walls, who had killed MacManus to the home of
this grandfather's would-be killer just forty miles away across
the border.

The journey took two hours; the most direct route had been
blown up by the British Army, the road cratered, and boulders
and concrete emplacements buried into the earth to prevent the
IRA enemy, and local people, from using what had now been
declared an unapproved road. About five miles from the border
I drove into one of the newly built remote-controlled checkpoints erected all over the border after the Coshquin attack.
Cameras and traffic lights operating from a hidden bunker
photographed me and my hired car before, deciding I represented no threat, eerily raising the barriers allowing me to pass.
Like this unseen hand, the landscape of trees, silver lakes and
meandering roads was devoid of human life. It seemed as if the
border was badlands where human activity appeared sus-
pended. You travelled towards a dead-end, some invisible
barrier between earth and sky, and then by a miracle passed
through it to the other side where life at some safe distance
began again.

In Sligo, on the other side of this barrier, I sat in the small
sitting room of the MacManuses' terraced house surrounded
by pictures of the smiling dead Joseph. His parents were still in
pain, still grieving. It was a long, difficult interview and my
mind was crowded with the impressions of the still-living Eric
Glass hobbling around his sitting room on crutches. Joseph's
father Sean laboured over the vowels in his son's name,
J-O-s-E-p-h, as if the act of rolling them around in his mouth
could somehow return the boy to life. His soft voice caressed
the word, evoking in every sound the pain of losing his first-
born child. Joseph's mother Helen nervously lit cigarette after
cigarette and broke down in tears as she recalled the last living
sight of her son. Her one remaining son, Chris, a bright, boyish
nineteen-year-old, sitting just across the coffee table, wept at
the sight of his mother's tears. In the still and silent room Sean

touchingly held Helen's hands and vainly tried to comfort his wife over her irretrievable loss. I found the MacManuses to be honourable people; they were brave and straightforward. They did not hide what they stood for; they were Republicans, supporters of the IRA. That did not make them right but they were not afraid to share the burden of their pain with me, a reporter and a stranger.

It was in that sitting room, with its pictures of the 1981 Hunger-Strikers, the H-Block martyrs, on the wall, that Joe's parents handed me the original of the cropped picture which appeared on the front of his memorial leaflet. The original showed Joe sitting in a row of friends along a pub bench, laughing. One of the friends is pulling on Joe's tie as the group pose for the picture. They are all young men, swaggering teenagers, on the cusp of adulthood, free to pretend that life holds a ream of possibilities but still likely to get in trouble for staying out all night. Later in the evening one of them would almost certainly be sick in the toilets. It's hard to imagine any one of their number as a man in a balaclava shouting· 'IRA, get out of the fucking van!'

There was another picture that his father did not want to give me because he said 'it looks too military', even though it too appeared in the memorial leaflet. Joe is standing before a microphone dressed in a white shirt, black beret and gloves, and reading a script in front of a wall. The script, I was told, was the 1916 Easter Proclamation and Joe was reciting it at the annual Easter Rising Commemoration in Sligo Cemetery's republican plot ten months before his death.

> In the name of God and of the dead generations from which she receives her old tradition of nationhood, Ireland, through us, summons her children to her flag and strikes for her freedom. . . . In this supreme hour the Irish nation must, by its valour and discipline, and by the readiness of its children to sacrifice themselves for the common good, prove itself worthy of the august destiny to which it is called.

Joe looks tense and earnest as he intones the words of Pearse, who wrote the Proclamation. A wire trails up from the microphone to a wobbly speaker and a makeshift public address system. Beside him stand two old men, church-going farmers in their sixties, looking out at the invisible crowd beyond the picture's frame. The whole scene could be from the annual meeting of the local parish football team with Joe as a reluctant team captain called upon to give a speech welcoming the opposition. But it is not. On the right of the picture you can just see the memorial stone to Sligo's past republican martyrs, killed in the Tan War of the 1920s. And on the very top right edge you can just make out three stone letters on the top of the memorial wall – I-R-A. Joe's beret is an advertisement of his poorly guarded secret membership of Oglaig na hEireann; the republican dream of reuniting Ireland by force was in the hands of another generation.

Like Frankie Ryan, Joseph Edward MacManus was born in the country he came to view as his oppressor and for the first six years of his life grew up in Willesden in north-west London. Sean MacManus came from the poor rural farming community of Black Lion, just south of the Fermanagh border and its cratered roads, and the journey to London in 1966 when he was sixteen in search of work was a familiar route for many young men.

In London, Sean MacManus worked the building sites as a carpenter, his world circumscribed by the common round of Irish emigrant life: living in private rented accommodation, moving from site to site in search of work, socializing in the hermetic, exiled world of the Irish-dominated districts of Kilburn and Cricklewood with their pubs, folk singers and Saturday nights out at the National Ballroom on Kilburn High Road. He met and married Helen McGovern, another Irish emigrant from Sligo working in London as a bank clerk, and their first child, Joseph, was born in May 1970. Joseph was followed three years later by Chris and in 1976, when Joseph was six, the MacManuses moved back to Ireland to Helen's home town.

In returning to Ireland in the mid-seventies the MacManuses were again beating a familiar path. In 1973 Ireland joined the EEC and with the aid of European agricultural subsidies the once frail economy began to prosper. For a short period it seemed as if Ireland could sustain its major production industry – people. Members of my own extended family, like many others, joined the exodus from London to home. They, like many others, were disheartened by their relative failure in England, its alienness, the subtle and not so subtle cultural prejudice they encountered. Many Irish were also motivated to leave by their own racial prejudice – they did not like living in close proximity to the expanding black and Asian communities which competed for jobs, accommodation and houses in the heterogeneous world of north London.

In Ireland, the dream of prosperity at home was for many to prove a mirage but most of the returned emigrants continued to justify their decision, in defiance of objective evidence, saying that the Irish school system was superior, society more law-abiding and rural Ireland an altogether better place to rear children. And so too it was with the MacManuses, who told me that they found Joseph's six-year-old contemporaries in Sligo to be at a higher academic level than their London-educated son. They also said they would have been afraid for Joseph and Chris if they had been brought up in London.

But moving back to Sligo, population twenty thousand, after the urban millions of London was both an economic and cultural shock. 'It was definitely a narrower society. There was a real pressure about getting work. The wages were a lot less and it took a while to settle down. Irish people in London were far less afraid to speak out about the North. Here people were afraid to voice an opinion for fear of their dole being stopped,' said Sean MacManus.

In London Sean MacManus had been on the fringes of republican activity, attending 'Troops Out' marches, selling

Republican News in Kilburn's Irish bars. The outbreak of the Troubles and the reaction to it within Kilburn's exiled Irish community had a powerful impact. In 1972 an Irish exile from County Mayo, twenty-one-year-old Michael Gaughan, was convicted of taking part in a bank robbery in Hornsey in north London, which netted a meagre £530, to raise funds for the Official IRA. Gaughan went on hunger strike on 31 March 1974 in an abortive protest to secure political status within the British prison system. He died of pneumonia on 2 June and in death received a heroic funeral. His coffin was flown to Dublin from Parkhurst Prison on the Isle of Wight, via a funeral procession that solemnly paraded its way through the streets of Kilburn. The coffin lay in state in a local church overnight and crowds of sympathizers paid homage to another young man who was perceived to have given his life for mother Ireland. 'My heart would have gone out to him. Gaughan died, a young Irishman who found himself in a situation in England to do something about the Troubles and the British presence. He took action against it. I remember the crowds, huge crowds, dark and very sombre. I would have been very supportive towards him and angry, personally very angry,' said Sean MacManus.

Back in Sligo, Sean MacManus voted for Sinn Fein, always a hopeless fringe party in southern politics, but did not get politically involved until 1978 when IRA prisoners in the distant H-blocks in the North began their dirty protest. Sean became secretary of the Sligo H-block Committee, which agitated in support of the prisoners, and a hectic life as a full-time impoverished Sinn Fein activist and political rebel began.

The thing that got me were the conditions in which the men were living. The protest in the H-blocks led rapidly to the first Hunger Strike and there would have been a spontaneous coming together of support. It was the real beginning of my political activism. I regret that I did not come into it sooner but looking back over the last fifteen years there were times when our lives were totally dedicated to politics. My selfishness would have meant that everyone else's life in the house would have revolved around politics. I would not have been money-orientated and I do not regret not having spent more time making money.

Republican politics in the Irish Republic were unquestionably a minority interest. Sinn Fein was a legal party but its members were, often justifiably, viewed with suspicion by the Gardai as being little more than daytime politicians and night-time gunmen. In the Dublin media, Republicans were described as 'subversives', which accurately portrayed the Irish Establishment's view of Sinn Fein/IRA as a force attempting to subvert the political status quo. In Sligo the active cadre of Sinn Fein activists, even at the height of the 1981 hunger-strike crisis, was two hundred. In less traumatic periods the pool of members was around fifty. Sean was made a member of Sinn Fein's National Executive, later becoming the party's national chairman – a very prominent position in the small world of Irish republicanism. The MacManuses were soon identified as the pre-eminent republican family in Sligo and Joseph MacManus the elder son of the local republican leader.

You would have had people calling to the house, staying the night. I would not have liked to openly influence either of the boys, they were both entitled to make up their own minds, but I suppose the fact that people came here and meeting members of the republican movement would have influenced Joe. Living in an ordinary terrace house everything would have revolved around politics. Even if you took the decision not to talk about politics, that decision would only last a few minutes and then you would be talking about something else, giving out about some other aspect.

Inevitably in Sligo's small world his father's frequent contact with infamously glamorous republican leaders like Gerry

Adams, banned from appearing on Irish radio or television, gave Joseph and his young brother Chris notoriety amongst their schoolboy peers. As I interviewed all three of the Mac-Manuses in their sitting room, Chris said:

> Most of the other pupils did not have a clue what was going on in the North. We had better insight but it wasn't something I held over other people – I know Gerry Adams and you don't. Sure, we knew he was head of Sinn Fein but to me it was a normal thing after I got over the fact that Gerry Adams was in the house. He was just a bloke. You could sit down with him and have a chat over a non-political event.

'There were also a lot of books in the house but we were never forced to go to any of the meetings. You volunteered. "Sure, I will give you a hand at that as I have read the books and made up my own mind." At times I thought of myself as having a more left-wing persuasion than a lot of other members of Sinn Fein,' added Chris.

Although Sean stood as a candidate in subsequent elections, he viewed his chief political role as being an organizer, a political fixer. During the second Hunger Strike, when Bobby Sands and nine others starved themselves to death, Sean organized a continual stream of candle-lit vigils and street protests which at their height brought eight thousand people out on the streets of the twenty-thousand-strong town.

> On a personal level I found the death of Bobby Sands and the other men after him, very, very upsetting. You would be upset at these people dying and awed by their courage. I think they were fantastic heroes. I think Irish history will look back on them as heroes. In time they will gather the same respect, if not more so, than the people of Easter Week. But on another level at the time you are wrapped up in what you are doing. It was a very draining time.

Joseph's and Chris's upbringing was in some ways probably
no different in nature from that of any other intensely political
household anywhere else in the British Isles. Their father's life
was a constant round of meetings, placard-making sessions,
election runs, campaigning drives and more and more meetings
to generate enthusiasm within a largely indifferent electorate.
Like many political children, they grew up adept at licking
envelopes and manhandling ladders, wallpaper paste and election posters. Together, they sold their father's party's newspaper, *Republican News*. But there was one vital difference:
Sinn Fein was subordinate to the IRA, a self-declared army
engaged in war, not democratic debate. The attempted murder
of political enemies was in the IRA's lexicon a legitimate tactic.
Said Sean MacManus:

I was heartbroken when Thatcher wasn't killed in the Brighton bomb. I would have no moral crisis over that at all. Of
all the people representing the British Establishment she had
no redeeming aspect or facet. During the Hunger Strike she
played games with people's lives. There was no human side.
Also the way she treated the miners. Bringing her into society
was a waste of time.

In the room I asked Sean if he had ever had any reservations
about the IRA's campaign.
'No, not really. I would be very supportive. There might be
a few individual jobs that I might have reservations about but
they would be very few and far between.'
'Like the Remembrance Day bombing at Enniskillen?'
There was a long pause.

Well, yes, something like that. The fact is I would not like to
see civilians dying. But having said that, I recognize that the
IRA had a right to wage war for freedom, for self-determination. This is not meant to sound callous but there may well
be casualties. I do not condone casualties but they are a fact

of war. The bottom line for me would be that there would be
no war and no IRA if the British were not in Ireland.

At school Joe MacManus was a popular student with an easygoing personality. He attended two local schools run by Catholic religious orders and, whilst not being academically gifted,
did sufficiently well to attend the local regional technical
college, a kind of polytechnic, to study business. He felt no
contradiction in being an ardent supporter of the London-based
English football team Arsenal and a Sinn Fein party member;
his childhood dream had been to play for Arsenal and Ireland.
He was a keen amateur football player. 'He was an ordinary
bloke – he liked going out, having the crack with his mates. He
liked female company and was a very laid-back kind of guy.
Joe did not go around with his chest sticking out,' said Chris.
    'Joe would have made friends from the North. He would
have got to know a lot of people. He was a fellow that liked
people,' said his mother Helen. 'People got on well with him.
He would go up and stay in their houses, he liked the crack and
then I think he felt he had to help in some way to alleviate the
suffering. As he got older he would have gone to republican
funerals and meeting people from the North, hearing their
stories, and becoming aware of their suffering.'
    Strangely, for a family dedicated to reversing the partition of
Ireland, the MacManuses talked of 'the North' as if describing
some distant foreign country like China to which they had
never been, although Sligo was just thirty miles from the border,
an hour's drive. 'The North' was a land wracked by the
powerful forces of the grim faceless Brits. It seemed as if the
despised border, an arbitrary line drawn on a political map,
exerted a huge, insurmountable psychological force. And of all
the many Republicans I had met they were the most cagey and
security-obsessed, constantly downplaying any association with
the IRA as if still protecting Joseph's secret identity as an IRA
Volunteer. Throughout our long interview Sean mulled over

the right choice of words – 'Sinn Fein', 'IRA' – and tried hard to stick close to the politically correct propaganda brief; a UDR man was always a 'British soldier' and a 'legitimate target'. The MacManuses' relative remoteness from the struggle seemed to make them more determined to apply the correct, if clichéd, republican vocabulary.

Joe MacManus may have been a rebel against the Crown, but he was not a rebel against his father's political vision. At the unveiling ceremony of his dead son's headstone, Sean MacManus gave his explanation of his son's decision.

> Our Republican vision was Joe's vision. I know because we often talked about aspects of it. . . . He saw the denial of democracy . . . that is why, after much thought, he became a Volunteer of the Irish Republican Army, to push this struggle forward until Britain has no option but to leave this country. I know some people will not understand or agree. I do not expect everyone to fully support his decision. What I do ask is that you agree with his right to reach that decision, and more importantly, that you recognize that it was not a decision that Joe reached easily or lightly. It was a hard choice to make and he thought long and hard about it.

Joseph was twenty when he joined the IRA, leaving his course at Sligo Regional College to take up arms for Ireland. In his obituary in *Republican News* readers were told that Joseph decided he wanted to join when he was seventeen after attending the republican funeral of another IRA Volunteer – Jim Lynagh – killed by the SAS in an ambush at Loughgall in County Armagh in 1987. Lynagh, a veteran IRA member responsible for many attacks on the British secrurity forces, was buried in County Monaghan away from the cordons of riot-geared RUC men, and was accorded a full republican funeral with balaclavaed guards of honour. Subsequently, Republicans often describe the SAS ambush in which Lynagh and six other IRA men, including Eugene Kelly of the cracked gravestone,

were killed as the 'Loughgall Massacre' and the dead Volunteers as the 'Loughgall Martyrs'. Lynagh's 'sacrifice', Joseph's
obituary noted, had a 'deep and enduring effect on the young
Joe MacManus'. In the summer before his death Joseph, in a
chance encounter on a bus, apparently told an older family
friend, Sinn Fein Vice President Pat Doherty, that the struggle
against the British could not just be left to nationalists in
Northern Ireland. Southerners like himself also had to play
their part.

County Sligo borders County Donegal, the main storehouse
for IRA weapons and explosives. Initially, Joseph ran errands,
moved arms between dumps and carried out the commonplace
tasks needed to supply a steady drip of *matériel* for the IRA's
war in the North. Although not risk-free, his activities would
have been low-level and entailed little personal danger. As with
Dermot Finucane, he would have received some form of
rudimentary weapons training somewhere in the Republic –
IRA weapons training camps are discovered, from time to time,
in the Sligo area. But he was not an experienced IRA Volunteer
when he was killed. Chris MacManus believes his brother
would have been aware of the risks of active service. 'Joe would
have known that if he was going out on an operation where he
would be armed, then it was very likely that he would come
across someone else who was armed and their aim would be to
kill him. To go back to that old axiom – those that live by the
sword shall die by the sword.'

Joe's membership of the IRA was known to some members
of his family. 'Before I suspected he became involved in the
Army, he was always one hundred per cent committed. I
think he decided he could take that commitment a stage
further. "Jesus, I can do a wee bit more. Maybe that little
bit extra I could do would make that little bit of difference,"'
said Chris, describing his view of Joseph's decision to join the
IRA.

Joseph MacManus was not the only young man from Sligo
to join the IRA, nor was he the first Provisional to join the

ranks of the IRA's fallen martyrs. Kevin Coen, also from Sligo, killed in 1975, is commemorated too at the City Cemetery. But the most striking thing about both Coen and MacManus is the very singularity of their deaths, just one for every decade of the recent Troubles. The injustices inflicted upon the Northern nationalist community which Joseph so keenly felt failed to move the vast majority of his peers. Without the shaping force of the British Army, Ireland's Troubles were a matter of indifference to all but a handful of Sligo's townspeople.

Helen MacManus last saw her son alive on the Sunday before his death. Although his parents did not want to identify the town, Joseph had been living in an IRA safe house in Ballyshannon, a few miles across the border from Belleek, in County Donegal. 'He came home that weekend to go to his best mate's twenty-first birthday and to play a football match on the Sunday morning. I had been away for the weekend and got back at five o'clock in the afternoon and Joe . . .,' said his mother, her voice breaking. 'He was here on the sofa. He was catching the seven o'clock bus. Sometimes I sent food with him so I had some boxty [a form of potato bread]. "Do you want a feed now?" "Yes." So I made up a feed. He ate a few bits and pieces and I gave him a kettle because he did not have one where he was living. Sean took him down to the bus, said "cheerio" and said we would see him next week.'

Fermanagh is famous for having the highest electoral turn-out of any political constituency in the British Isles. Returning officers consistently record polls of eighty-six per cent compared to an average of seventy per cent or less in English constituencies. The high polls are not a reflection of an avid belief in parliamentary democracy but of a near tribal rivalry between the two antagonistic Catholic and Protestant communities along the long border with the neighbouring Irish Republic. Both communities are evenly matched in population and a handful of votes either way can determine the election of absolute political opposites, a Unionist or Nationalist Member of Parliament – votes count in Fermanagh. In 1981 following the death of the sitting nationalist MP Frank Maguire, Republicans nominated Bobby Sands, in the midst of his death fast, to stand for election in the Fermanagh–South Tyrone constituency in a straight fight against a hardline Unionist; Sands was elected with 30,429 votes, a majority of 1,446 over his rival. In the border country each community cleaved to its own side and its own customs. For years Protestants joined the British Army militia, the UDR, to defend their communities against the Irish enemy. And for years the IRA have tried to kill UDR men to remove the Crown from the land.

Fermanagh's meandering border with the Republic and the ease of sanctuary in the South have shaped the IRA campaign in the county. IRA active service units fought a guerrilla-style campaign, bombing army and police posts and assassinating off-duty members of the UDR militia in small-scale, often incompetent attacks, launched from the safe haven of County Monaghan or County Donegal in the Irish Republic. Around 250 people have died in the area since the Troubles began, most killed by the IRA. The majority of deaths have come in a steady drip-drip of assassinations of off-duty UDR men. The assassination campaign, the ease of escape and the low conviction rate have distorted the IRA's Roll of Honour for the county, a crude but usually accurate tabulator of IRA activity. There are just two attributed deaths of IRA Volunteers from Fermanagh; in neighbouring Tyrone the IRA casualty list runs to fifty-two.

In the late eighties IRA killings in the area were carried out by a notorious seven-strong unit known as the West Fermanagh Brigade, based in Ballyshannon in Donegal, who were responsible for a number of brutal killings. Members of the unit, referred to by nicknames like the 'Banshee', the 'Cuban', could have been pointed out in the street by most local people and lived just minutes away from their victims. In April 1987 they shot dead a UDR man, Jim Oldman, in front of his twelve-year-old nephew in the village of Ederney. In March 1988 they killed twenty-one-year-old chemist shop assiststant Gillian Johnston and seriously injured her boyfriend in the mistaken belief that he was a member of the security forces. In September 1988 they killed two elderly workmen, William Hassard and Fred Love, as they drove away from Belleek RUC station, as part of the IRA campaign against contractors. The same gang then murdered a former RUC Reservist, Harry Keys, shooting him twenty-three times at close range in front of his girlfriend at her home in County Donegal in the Republic in January 1989. Eyewitnesses alleged that the gang leader's trademark was to whoop in triumph at the scene of each killing.

The killings of Gillian Johnston, perceived to be an innocent young Protestant woman, and Keys, a former RUC member killed on the Republic's territory, were deeply unpopular and lost the IRA political support. In the same month as the Keys killing, Martin McGuinness informed Sinn Fein's annual conference that the IRA Army Council had disbanded the West Fermanagh unit because the 'killing of civilians is wrong, full stop'. For two years, aside from the bombing attacks against RUC border stations, the Fermanagh border was relatively quiet. And then some time in 1991 Joseph MacManus joined a replacement unit centred on former West Fermanagh Brigade member Noel Magee, a native of the village of Leggs, close to Belleek on the border.

On Monday, 4 February 1992 Joe MacManus and his three companions – James Hughes, twenty-seven, Conor O'Neil, twenty-nine, and Noel Magee – crossed the border and took over by force the home of local farmer Pat Loughran. On Tuesday they telephoned Fermanagh District Council dog warden depot and asked for Eric Glass.

Fermanagh is sheep-farming country and the county had in the past been plagued with sheep-worrying before council dog wardens dealt with strays and disposed of unwanted dogs for free. Eric Glass had worked with the council for twenty years and his work had taken him into farms, Catholic and Protestant, across the wild, lush Irish countryside; he was well known. Glass was also a part-time UDR man and a one-time member of their precursor, the hated and sectarian B-Specials. His service record stretched right back to the beginning of the Troubles. He had previously been injured in an IRA ambush in 1978, when he was wounded in the upper arm. It was inevitable that his military identity would be well known in the villages and small towns of Fermanagh; his job as a dog warden made him a soft target.

On the day of the IRA gang's first call to the dog compound, Glass was off work so the IRA men left a message and continued holding their hostage. On the following day, Wednesday, at around ten in the morning they called the dog compound again and this time they were successful.

On the Wednesday morning I went out to the dogs first and then into work and the girl told me I had a dog to lift in Belleek. Then the phone rang and the call was put through to me.

The man said, 'Did you hear about my black labrador?'

'No.'

'The black labrador I thought the world of . . . it bit the wee niece . . . what should I do?'

The fella was practically crying down the phone about the dog. I said, 'If it was my dog I would put it down. I wouldn't keep a dog that bit a child.'

'The niece only comes once a fornight.'

He asked me to come and get the dog, and then he said, 'What do you do with the dog?'

'We put it down.'

'Would I see it being put down?'

'I could put the dog down at the house or take it away.'

'I would not like to see the dog put down. If you took it away, then I need not know what had happened. What time will you be out?'

'I have to go for diesel but I'll be with you in an hour and a half.'

'Thanks, great. There's cows milking and I have a few wee things to do around the house.'

The 'few wee things' were arranging the ambush that went so disastrously wrong. To avoid the fiasco of another 'mistake' like Gillian Johnston, the IRA men planned to get Glass out of the van, ensure he was the right man, and then kill him. Their plan probably cost Joseph MacManus his life. In the Mac-Manuses' sitting room I asked Sean and Helen what happened. There was an uncomfortable pause and then Sean broke in.

'I suppose we do know to a large degree what happened on the operation ... He was shot dead ... I don't know ... I would not feel at liberty to talk about the operation, about what I know about it.'

'I think it's best to leave it,' said Helen.

In the memorial leaflet Sean was recorded at his son's graveside as saying he had no personal animosity towards the man who killed his son. 'As a family we do not hold any bitterness towards the British soldier who killed our son.' Throughout our interview Sean constantly talked about the 'British soldier' his son had planned to kill, not the man, the Northern Irish-born dog warden, Eric Glass. It was hard to reconcile this abstraction, this 'British soldier', with the man I had left hours earlier. It was all I could do to remain silent. I could not really believe that they had not analysed the events surrounding their son's death down to the minutest detail, including the age and identity of the man who pulled the trigger. What did they think of the man Joe tried to kill?

'A faceless form, to me that is what he is,' said Sean.

'He was a member of the British Army, an enemy,' said Chris.

'Joe would not have been shooting him as a person. He

would not have been attacking him as a person. He would have seen him as a member of an occupying force, which he is,' said Sean.

'Your man who shot Joe was not shooting Joe because he was Joe MacManus. He was shooting him because he saw Joe as the enemy. It was a war situation,' said Chris.

I wanted to know if they hated this killer of their son and brother?

'I take Joe's death in two ways. Obviously I would be grieving, deeply saddened, because I think of my brother Joe. But then I have to take Joe as Joe the Volunteer – that is a source of pride and you recognize Joe the soldier. Joe my brother is separate. Obviously, I am sad but if you let the two things collide then you become bitter and twisted and just show hatred towards people and the war becomes very personalized.'

All of the MacManuses denied that Glass had been targeted because he was a Protestant. Sean said:

> The basic fact is that they [the UDR] are a militia that is drawn up and that is there to be a part of the British war machine. The fact that they are predominantly drawn from the Protestant population does not impinge upon it. In the eyes of Irish Republicans, they are part of the British Army. He could have been any one of the forty thousand British soldiers, armed personnel, that is in the North of Ireland.

'He is a representation of the British occupation,' added Chris.

The room grew very quiet and I desperately wanted to ask more questions. I wanted to find out exactly what they thought had happened but it was not possible. They did not want to speak. Perhaps it was easier to remember Joe's actions in outline, to reduce the details of his death into clichés, 'Killed in Action'. Three hours before, I had been in the presence of this 'enemy', this 'faceless form'. Glass had been enticed into an ambush by an IRA Volunteer who was deeply familiar with Glass's job, his identity and his working methods; intimate enough and reassuring enough to fool the dog warden into driving to a remote farm so that the IRA could then kill him as a faceless 'British soldier'. It was not war between soldiers but a very personalized assassination.

Joseph might have been preparing to kill a representation of the Crown in Ireland but he was also going to kill Eric Glass, a grandfather, a husband, a father and a workmate. Did Eric Glass, the other soldier, have the right to kill Joe MacManus in a legitimate act of war? Sean replied:

> No, yes. It's not a simple question. How could his actions be legitimate when he is part of an illegitimate force in our country? In the eyes of Republicans he is part of the British presence, which is trying to coerce and maintain the union and keep part of our country sundered from the rest of it. So by that degree it was totally illegitimate. But do you mean — did he have the right to respond and shoot Joseph? He did have the right. If two soldiers are meeting in armed combat then he is entitled to shoot back.

'He is probably an Irishman to the extent that he was born, reared and living on the island of Ireland but he is upholding the British occupation. He has no right to be there armed as a British soldier but given the set of circumstances — he had the right to return fire,' said Helen.

Word of Joe's death had come a few hours after the fatal shoot-out. IRA men called at the MacManuses' home as news of a shooting on the border spread on the airwaves. It was a time of great pain in the MacManus family. Said Sean MacManus:

> Two comrades told us. At half six that evening the body was still lying in the field where he had been shot. We contacted the Gardai to verify he was dead. All these things are hazy in

my mind. They said they could not verify it but to the best of their knowledge they believed it was Joseph who was dead. The whole situation was very hectic. The house was filled with neighbours. I rang a priest in that parish and the priest told me he was dead. He described him to me and told me the body was still lying in a field. It was the winter season in February and it would have been dark at four o'clock. They did not take the body away until ten o'clock at night. They took him to the morgue at Enniskillen. I rang the RUC and they then wanted me to go and identify the body. This was at 11.30 at night; they wanted me to go down at that stage. I would not have got there until 1.00 am. I was advised not to go as I was likely to receive a lot of harassment from them. I asked, even though I thought it very unfair, my brother-in-law to go in my stead.

On the following evening the MacManuses and their friends drove in blinding rain through the badlands of the border to Enniskillen to bring Joseph home. Sean related:

It was a fairly big cortège and we knew the Brits would put on a show of strength. There were arguments with the RUC about putting the tricolour on the coffin. Basically we wanted to get Joseph back across the border out of the hands of the RUC. Little did we know, given all the dealings that we have had with the forces of this state, that the Gardai would be as bad, if not worse, than the RUC. When we started moving out, the RUC gave the undertaking that they would not move in behind the hearse.

'They had given a guarantee to my brother that if we put no flag on the coffin they would give us a free run to the border,' said Helen.

'Just as we were leaving the hospital they cut in behind the hearse and cut off all the family cars; it was two or three Land-Rovers. They slowed us down and slowed us down. Every crossroads was lined with RUC Land-Rovers and then when they got to the border they stopped and just looked at us.'

The RUC's jurisdiction ended at the border village of Belcoo, the same crossing my father used for our journeys to Achill, but there was no relief that night in the rain for the MacManuses.

> When we came round the bend from the border the whole village was lined with Gardai in riot gear. We just saw bus-load after bus-load of guards. We were actually stopped and asked where we were going. Later on we found out that they had besieged the house, two hundred guards had been positioned outside our home in Sligo. They were stopping women in the street, women who were in a bad way, and all for one dead Volunteer.

Sean, waving at a small shrine of pictures in the corner of the room marking the spot where the coffin had lain, said:

> When we got him home he lay here for one night. There was a guard of honour of his comrades. It was obviously going to be a republican funeral. Some senior Gardai came to the door and asked me, 'Were you aware that he was involved in the IRA?' They wanted to know if we would be firing shots and if he would have a republican funeral. I told them that was for them to find out and that I was not answering any silly questions at this time.

That night Sean MacManus issued a short press statement affirming the family's pride in Joe:

> Our son and brother, IRA Volunteer Joe MacManus, was Killed in Action in Fermanagh on Wednesday February 5th. We respect his decision to join Oglaigh na hEireann. He did not take that step lightly. Joseph believed as we do, that our country will never have peace until Britain leaves Ireland and

its people are free to decide their own future. We are deeply proud of him. In our own personal grief we are also thinking of all those other families who have suffered and are suffering as we are today.

At Scardans Upper the helicopter had lifted off within minutes and rushed the wounded Eric Glass to Erne hospital in Enniskillen at the same time as a huge security operation began, combing the remote border area for his attackers. Glass would spend months on his back recuperating from his wounds and would be disabled from the injuries to his legs from the Kalashnikov rounds. One of his visitors showed him a cutting of Sean MacManus's statement.

At first I felt very, very sorry for his people. The way the mind worked was that I had a son near that fella's age. Now if he joined some illegal organization that I did not know about and the army shot him, the police shot him, or anybody shot him and brought him home to me shot, what would I think? The more I thought about it, the more it went round and round in my head that I had murdered someone's son. The mental strain of that was desperate. The only thing that helped me was his father and mother put a notice in the paper, some paper, in Sligo saying they were proud of him and that he died for Ireland. He joined the juniors and then he joined the seniors. I read that over and over and over. They knew exactly what he was and it helped me mentally because even though he is an IRA man he is still somebody. It was easier to know that his people knew exactly what he was.

Joseph's three companions, James Hughes, Conor O'Neill and Noel Magee, fled across the border but were immediately captured. Hughes and O'Neill were found in a ditch by a Garda. The two men had tried to wash off forensic traces of firearms in a stream but, according to Gardai testimony at their subsequent trial, were shocked and trembling when arrested.

Two Kalashnikov rifles and a handgun were found nearby. Both men were tried in Dublin under the special legislation of the 1976 Criminal Law Jurisdiction Act, which allows offences committed in Northern Ireland to be judged in the southern courts, and received twelve years for attempted murder. Glass spent three days in the witness box testifying against them, with defence counsel attacking discrepancies in his statements. Even the RUC's forensic scientists cast doubt on his version of events. Cartridges and bloodstains near the door of the house indicated that Joseph, acting as back-up, was killed when he naively moved into the line of fire thinking Glass was already dead. But no testimony from the SOCO men could change the final outcome of the fire-fight at Scardans Upper.

> I don't forgive them. I think the blood would boil again if I seen them, particularly the ones that tried to kill me. I was as happy as anything going up that lane. I loved my job. In three minutes they took it away from me, I can never work again because of my injuries. You just wonder how people say they forgive them or how you can sit down with them or talk to Gerry Adams – the man who carried the coffin of the Shankill bomber.

In a strange fulfilment of the IRA's interpretation of its war against the Crown, Glass was later invited to Buckingham Palace for a rare one-to-one audience with the Queen of England and was given a tour of her son Prince Andrew's private apartments by the Prince, the Colonel-in-Chief of the UDR. Glass was awarded the Distinguished Service Order and the Queen's Gallantry Medal for, in effect, killing one of the Crown's enemies in Ireland, an Irish rebel, Joseph Edward MacManus.

The authorities of the Republic's state did not accord the new IRA of the Provisionals with the same honours as the 'old' IRA of the Tan War. When Kevin Coen had been buried, armed Gardai had patrolled the memorial site to prevent the seventies

Volunteer being interned on the hallowed ground of his predecessors. Sean MacManus would not ask for a permission that
would have been refused. The remains of Joseph MacManus
were interred amongst the common graves of the City Cemetery and not in the official monument from where Joseph had
given his rendition of Pearse's Easter Proclamation.

At his funeral, Republican leader Gerry Adams paid tribute
to the boy he knew from visits to the MacManus home and to
the young man who had become the latest Volunteer in a long
line to die in the 'cause of Ireland'. 'If Sean and Helen,' Adams
told the crowd, 'think for one moment that it's their fault that
their son was killed in Fermanagh, they're thinking wrong. Joe
made up his own mind.'

The tributes could not recover the dead Joseph from the
grave and his 'Troubles' suit – a pine box – nor banish the
MacManuses' grief, but the manner of his death in some ways
comforted them. Sean said:

> Trying to sum up Joe's life is difficult because it brings up all
> the questions that Joe might have done if he hadn't died. I do
> not regret his involvement. I am very proud of Joe. We have
> been sustained through the fact that although Joe was killed,
> he died as a Republican fighting for what he saw as a great
> injustice to his country.
>
> In his death he achieved something, something that he
> awakened within the people of Sligo, particularly young
> people – the awareness that there is a war going on in the
> North and that it does impinge on our lives to some degree.
> And that there are people down here who are prepared to do
> something about it. I think that is indicated by the number of
> people who came forward to join the Movement when Joe
> died. There were a number of factors involved but one of
> those factors would be Joe's death.

'It made people redefine the boundaries,' added Chris.
'Before, the war in the North was on the far side of the moon.
Suddenly the war was here. It was real. There was somebody

they knew, someone from the town who had been part of it — "My God, it's here. Jesus, it's not just something you read about in the *Irish Times*." It made people think — "Why does a young fella do something like that?"'

We had finally come to the end of Joseph's life story. Helen offered to make me a feed. But I was longing to be gone, to be alone with my own thoughts and away from the death rites of IRA Volunteers, blood, martyrdom and the dead Joseph, who hovered like a shade in the sitting room. At the end of that long day I was really glad it was not my war; glad to escape into the wet night air and the anonymous lanes of the Irish countryside and feel the breeze from the car window wash all of it from my mind. I had finished this part of my journey. I could not see how a dead Eric Glass, another dead UDR man, would have pushed 'the struggle forward', made Ireland a better place. But I left the MacManuses convinced of one thing: Irish Republicanism cannot be, nor will it ever be, militarily defeated. Every dead Volunteer is and always will be raised up in death by the Movement, venerated, and heralded as the latest true son of Pearse's mythic Republic and source of future inspiration for further bloodshed. That invisible Republic was founded in blood and is sustained by the death of its adherents. Like Pearse, it is oblivious to the substance of the future Irish state it would bring into being or the suffering inflicted on those who fight for and those who fight against its fulfilment. Joseph MacManus, a twenty-one-year-old who never knew the world beyond the narrow folds of his family's republicanism and who became an IRA Volunteer and would-be killer, was just another victim, just another martyr, of Pearse's savage bloody dream.

NOTES

1. Piaras F. MacLochlainn, *Last Words*, Stationery Office, Dublin, 1990, p. 19.

2. Ibid., p. 22.

8

REBEL HEARTS

In the summer of 1994 I was back home for a commemoration service at the *sagart a run*'s monument. The Dookinella Memorial bagpipe band, a cultural legacy of those Scottish potato harvests, led a small procession down the narrow road through the village of my ancestors towards the sea. Behind the band marched Sean and Brendan, schoolchildren, local Republicans, villagers and their wives, and the local priest, whose first designated task was to re-bless the stone pillar.

At the monument, framed by the natural amphitheatre of the mountains and ocean, prayers were said, flags unfurled, the National Anthem played, and speaker after speaker rose to proclaim the greatness of this fallen son. The last speaker was a man in his mid-thirties.

Much of the history of Father Manus Sweeney is lost to us. We know he was born here and that he was hanged by the British in Newport on 8 June 1799. We know that he spent many years in France in exile and that he returned as a parish priest to Newport. And we know he was a rebel . . . In late August 1798, just after the landing of the French at Killala, Newport rose in rebellion. Peter Gibbons, a yeoman in the local Crown militia, planted a Tree of Liberty in the central market square. The Tree of Liberty, a simple pine festooned with green ribbons, was a symbol of the rebels' desire to be free of their Crown masters . . . Rebel control of Newport

was short-lived ... The first thing local landowner Sir Neal
O'Donel did after recapturing Newport and seizing the *sagart
a run* was to burn the Tree of Liberty ... Sweeney was
hanged ... the rebellion defeated.

The speaker's voice carried above the sound of the waves of
the great ocean crashing indifferently on the empty strand a
few yards from the small crowd, much as those waves must
have crashed indifferently in the same place at the birth and
fate of Manus Sweeney two hundred years before.

But we know this also — the Tree of Liberty was not destroyed
by Sir Neal, it was not burnt, it could not be destroyed. The
physical tree might burn but the idea had planted itself in the
hearts of Irish men and women and could never be removed.
The flames, and Father Sweeney's execution, merely scattered
the seeds of resistance. ... Our very presence here today
vindicates Father Sweeney's judgement and his sacrifice. His
ideals, his purpose lives on in our minds and in our hearts
and in every rebel heart.

The words slipped so easily from the mouth of the speaker
that it was hard not to be swallowed up in the rhetoric. I, after
all, was that speaker, invited by the republican organizers to
render a historical account of the dead priest's life. I believed in
my speech and yet I was still troubled. The memories of long,
painful interviews, the dead sons' pictures on the wall, the visits
to gravestones and prisons, and the weight of these journeys
within the Republican soul kept flooding back to me. But it
was impossible to describe such a complex chain of memory to
the ruddy, fresh faces of the crowd. It was easier to slip into the
certainties of a neatly reordered past, reclaiming the dead
Sweeney as another patriot in an unbroken noble chain of
resistance and forgetting the very real men who were still being
selected out by their neighbours to be killed in their kitchens,
or shot in their driveways, 150 miles away, to fulfil the destiny

of a United Ireland. It was the final bitter contradiction of the Troubles; the justness of the political cause was invalidated by the cruelty of the murders carried out in its name.

When I was nine I went to my first theatrical performance on the Sandy Banks, a patch of dunes close to the village of Keel just across the bay from Dookinella. A tiny cast of travelling players, probably Ireland's last, visited televisionless Achill and on alternate nights staged plays or set up their projector and ran flickering Westerns. Their cinema and playhouse was a billowing tent, the seats, rough boards, and the nightly take derisory. But I never noticed, it was all magic to me. Like the black-hatted villain films, the company's dramas were easy farces or melodramatic potboilers, with every member of the company playing three or four parts. Each night I and my cousins would stroll through the long Western evening's light towards the players' tent for what seemed fabulous entertainment. Through the distance of the past, I can now only remember the name of one play, a Victorian gothic drama entitled *Murder in the Red Barn*.[1] The plot details escape me but it revolved around the usual woeful Irish tale of a servant girl, a lewd master, an illicit affair and the murder of a newly born bastard child, whose body was then buried somewhere near the Red Barn. It was a tale of betrayal, cold indifference and murderous revenge.

Irish history is an endless nightly rerun of *Murder in the Red Barn*. The exact plot details will always escape us and the locations may change – one popular variation is 'Murder in Your Living Room in Front of Your Wife and Kids' – but the core elements – betrayal, cold indifference and murderous revenge – like the final act remain an inevitable part of the script. The players only leave the stage after firing a number of bullets into another human body. The red blood is pumping out on to the carpet. The children are screaming. The curtain descends. As spectators we cannot be exactly sure if tonight's victim is already dead or just mortally wounded, or of the precise reason why this particular person was selected out at this particular time.

My speech had been rhetoric. In parts but not everywhere in Northern Ireland the Tree of Liberty had withered away, like the wishing tree of Arboe in Tyrone, into a naked contest for sectarian dominance. The rebels' cause had become immersed in murder and the flow of blood under the bridge had renewed rather than relieved loyalist and republican desire to go on killing. There was no moral foothold in such a landscape.

But I was saved from such savagery. The Troubles, as I discovered, were not my war. Many years before I was born, my parents had left their homeland and moved to Edinburgh, a city of cold winds, enlightenment and peace. No one threatened to burn my family's home and I never felt the need, as Seamus Finucane did, to take up the gun. My brothers fought for better exam results, not Irish freedom. Instead of prison I went to Edinburgh University to study Philosophy and English. I became a journalist, a writer, not a gunman, a Volunteer, or a terrorist. I was brought up in a settled country not a troubled one and I never felt the need to murder a judge. My life, and the lives of those close to me, are utterly different from the lives of those depicted in this book. But that was an accident of geography not of history. I could so easily have been in the IRA.

It would be simple here to hedge and qualify the issue of the morality of the IRA's struggle, but I won't. A great historic injustice was perpetrated in Ireland in the seventeenth century – the blueprint for all future campaigns of conquest, dispossession and colonization by the Crown. Ireland was the first English colony and it will be the last. The natives always resisted their subjugation violently, savagely; the land was always troubled. Ireland remains troubled today, not just through the burden of this history but by the failure of the Crown to relinquish its final hold on the provinces of Ireland.

It is not the fault of any living person that the system of government in Northern Ireland is unjust. The forces that drove the Protestants of Ulster in the 1910s to demand their own separate state and threaten civil war if they failed were too deeply ingrained in their history, psyche and politics. Nor is it any individual's fault that Protestants founded and maintained a Protestant state based on religious hatred and the politics of exclusion; everything in their history taught them that to compromise, to surrender, to accommodate the native Irish enemy, was destruction. When the natives again rebelled in 1969 the security forces of the state and its Protestant mobs could only react the way they had always reacted, with brutality, in a furious attempt to beat back down the rebel enemies who sought to overwhelm their citadel.

But equally it is not the rebels' fault that the Protestants of Ulster refused and still refuse to learn the simple lesson of history: that all colonizers will one day be overthrown by those natives they hold in bondage. For there to be peace in Ireland the Protestants must make the great historical accommodation that another Protestant people, the Afrikaners, made with their historic enemy.

In 1652 Van Riebeck landed at the Cape on the southern tip of the African continent and began centuries of conquest and domination that only ended in 1994. The first Planters of Ulster landed thirty-two years earlier and their chapter in human history is not yet finished. But the lessons are no different. There can be no ifs or buts or appeals to artificially created majorities and demographically tailored boundaries. The Protestants of Ulster, born Irish for three centuries, must come to terms with their fellow Catholic Irishmen.

Since the Rebellion of 1969 the Northern Irish State has ceased, in the eyes of a third of its citizens, to be a legitmate state. It exists solely and absolutely by force of arms of the Crown and its authority would fall tomorrow if the supply of troops and monies from the British Exchequer ended.

Unlike the Afrikaners, the indigenous Protestant leadership were deprived of power when the Stormont Parliament was overthrown in 1972 and the Crown itself took over direct administration of its Irish province. There is currently no value or necessity in compromise from within the Protestant community or its leadership. It is therefore the duty of the Crown, by persuasion, guile and ultimatum, to force that historic accommodation on the Protestants.

The rebels have waged a brutal, prolonged campaign of resistance. They have inflicted considerable losses on the Crown's soldiery and great suffering on both their own and the enemy community. Many innocent people have died for no good reason but none of that futile human misery will alter the inevitable political outcome.

There will be peace in Ireland and it will be a republican peace. It will be a peace that will accommodate both Catholics and Protestants and hence it will be hedged by safeguards, elaborate constitutions, dual symbols and the paraphernalia of laborious bureaucracy. But it will also be a peace, absolutely, that will entail, perhaps after a decent interval, the removal of the Crown from Ireland. And then and only then can the wounds of history heal and the Crown lay to rest the ghost of an old Empire which began in the provinces of Ireland hundreds of years ago and on which the sun will have finally set.

My journey in the rebel heart of Ireland has ended here. I cannot say I am truly an Irish Republican; I lack the intensity for it, I would not kill for it. I could never be the young man with the gun rushing towards the murder of Judge Doyle outside St Brigid's. Ten years of journeys within the Irish Republican Soul have made me weary of such political passion and the sacrifice of lives for ideals. But I remain a Republican, albeit a constitutional Republican, both for Ireland and for my adopted country, England. I am a product of my people, I too remain possessed of a rebel heart.

NOTE

1. Two decades later I found out that it was based on Bury St Edmunds murderer William Corder, who was hanged in 1829 for killing his mistress.

Index